P9-ASN-300

COLOUR
IN YOUR GARDEN

COLOUR
IN YOUR GARDEN

PENELOPE HOBHOUSE

COLLINS

8 Grafton Street, London W1

1985

Fortunately no author is alone in the task of writing, assembling and
presenting a book. The twin subjects of gardening and colour are so complex that without help and guidance
it would have been difficult to put this book together.
My inspiration came from colour experts such as Enid Verity and painters such as Budwin Conn and Derek Hill,
as well as from books, paintings and landscape itself. Dr Heino Heino of the Jardin des Plants in Paris long ago
introduced me to the works of Chevreul, and more recently helped me to understand how Monet made garden colour as
much an art as painting itself. To my own contemporary gardeners, among them Gwen Beaumont, Peter Healing and
Rosemary Verey, as well as to those such as Gertrude Jekyll who made gardens in the past,
I owe a great debt, and to photographers such as Pat Hunt and Tania Midgley
who have captured the nuances of garden colour with their cameras.
Although the book expresses only my own tastes and prejudices, and the choice of colour sequences and plants is mine,
I am very grateful to the editorial staff at Frances Lincoln for helping me to realize the full scope of my ideas and by their
own absorption in the subject making my task lighter. Frances herself invited me to approach the subject in this way,
and I am grateful for her continued enthusiasm. To Penny David, who helped me organize the text and frequently
guided me towards just the right emphasis I owe the greatest debt,
and the design skills of Roger Walton and Caroline Hill have made the conception visually satisfying.
Above all, I would like to thank my husband John Malins for his unending patience and support.

Tintinhull December 1984

William Collins Sons and Co Ltd
London · Glasgow · Sydney · Auckland · Johannesburg

Colour in Your Garden
was conceived, edited and designed by
Frances Lincoln Limited
Apollo Works, 5 Charlton Kings Road, London NW5 2SB

First published in 1985
© Frances Lincoln Limited 1985
Text © Penelope Hobhouse 1985
Reprinted 1987, 1988

British Library Cataloguing in Publication Data
Hobhouse, Penelope
 Colour in your Garden.
 1. Color in gardening—Great Britain
 I. Title
 712'.6'9041   SB454.3.C64

ISBN 0 00 217142 2

Printed and bound in Hong Kong by
Kwong Fat Offset Printing Co., Ltd.

Typesetting by
SX Composing Ltd, Rayleigh, Essex

CONTENTS

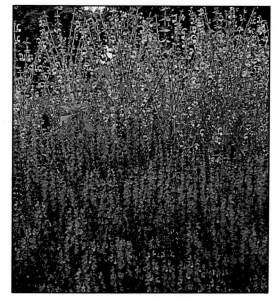

My fellow-gardener at the dinner table was dismissive when I told him the name of this book: 'Oh, I dislike any colour in gardens: I never have it in mine.' Obviously he meant *flower* colour, perhaps the bright confusion of a traditional herbaceous border, or even the gaudy mixture of annuals in a public park. I imagined his garden (he was a Frenchman) full of low-toned greens, textured foliage in clipped hedges or topiary, elegant limes and chestnuts reflected in still water: no place for intrusive or vivid eye-catching flowers.

I should have answered that *green* is a colour. That I had spent months observing the multiplicity of shades and tones in 'plain' green foliage, and searching for ways to describe the subtleties of what I saw: even the simplest specimen tree shading a green lawn conveys a constantly changing pattern of colour as the light alters from minute to minute, and as the seasons modulate the tones of the leaves.

Of course, it did not occur to the Frenchman that I might be concerned with these fine distinctions of green. Perhaps he thought I was writing for that other gardening school, for our modest neighbour who says, 'Please don't come and see my garden now, there's no colour in it.' To this gardener, also, 'colour' is synonymous with *flower* colour; or at least bright seasonal flowers, leaves and fruit. But this book is about *all* garden colours, how they alter and modify one another, and how to use them. Many garden visitors notice only the eye-catching hues: I believe that, stimulating as these are, the more subdued effects and the background greens and greys are also worth studying.

I might once have said much the same thing as my fellow dinner-guest. At Hadspen House I was a 'good-taste gardener', planning plant associations based on leaf colour, texture and form, with seasonal flowers just as a bonus. As I started to read Gertrude Jekyll, and through her began to study the theories of the French Impressionists, I began to see the infinite possibilities of weaving colour pictures with plants. The more I learnt about colour behaviour, the more I wished to practise and experiment with harmonies and contrasts, using the 'hottest' colours as well as the pale pastel tints, not only in pleasing compositions, but also to manipulate perspective and to evoke definite moods.

At Tintinhull House our task has been to restore a garden created before the war by Phyllis Reiss. Working here while thinking of the themes of this book has been a useful way to test out both theories and actual colour combinations. Looking around me as I weed, tidy and replant, I find some of Mrs Reiss's themes too strong – for instance, her gold and purple foliage border, but I now understand how it can be modified and improved. I love her use of dark violet-blue flowers weaving among dusky purple leaves, with neighbouring crimson flowers extending a scheme based on the shared bluish pigment in each of the colours. I find the white garden restful, the 'hot' border exciting and intense. In one shrubbery, blues undercarpet taller plants: bluebells, brunnera and lithospermum in different tones blend together and make the area seem larger than it is. There is plenty to learn at Tintinhull about how colours behave, and I use ideas from associations I find here, as well as from colour theory, to create new schemes for the people who ask me to design their gardens. Yet in a way my early interest in foliage remains, its basic importance in any cohesive design reflected here in the 'Foliage framework'.

The first two chapters of this book are a sort of extended introduction. Chapter I explains the design principles that I

think important in any garden, whatever the colour philosophy of the planting. In Chapter II, I share with the reader some of my exploration of more general colour theory, a process of defining terms and studying optical effects which heightened my own appreciation of colour as an observer, as well as increasing my confidence as a practical gardener.

However, by far the greater part of this book consists of the 'colour chapters' and their plant catalogues, and these merit some detailed introduction. Rather than using the conventional seven rainbow divisions, each chapter covers a colour range that makes sense in gardening terms. Some work as monochrome schemes: you can make a white garden from the plants in Chapter III, or a pool of yellow flowers and foliage from Chapter IV. However, there are suggestions throughout for combining plants effectively in multicoloured associations. Like the rainbow colours, our chapters merge and overlap. Not only is colour nomenclature vague, but growing conditions affect pigmentation and light alters appearance, so a plant in the pink-mauve-crimson range might qualify for Chapters V, VI or VII, depending on any of these factors. I have put the plants in the chapters I think suit them best; another writer might do this differently, just as he or she might choose different plants in the first place. The reader is referred to the index when in doubt.

The chapters' seasonal subdivisions show the palette of plants available at any given time of the year. Plants occur in the season when 'in average conditions' they *begin* to bloom. Thus 'early summer' roses may flower off and on all summer. This, too, is why my last season is 'late summer': plants linger in the garden until the first frosts, but few actually begin to flower in autumn. Variations of a season from the 'average' – and variations of the microclimate and aspect of a garden –

are discussed in an appendix. My own gardens have been in inland Somerset, but zoning information will help readers elsewhere to generalize from my own experience.

The plants themselves are those I know and love and have, in most cases, grown myself. On the whole I like simple, 'unimproved' flowers; so often the hybridizer increasing the size of bloom loses some essential quality of proportion, and modern colour ranges can extend to almost synthetic hues which look unsympathetic in a garden. But this is a very broad generalization, and I am the first to use some 'new' colour if it is exactly right for the planned theme.

A degree of idiosyncrasy applies also to plant nomenclature: the most up-to-date and technically accurate botanical name changes may take years to reach seed catalogues and nurseries, who anyway often prefer to use the names familiar to their gardening clients. Gardeners themselves often resent and resist change. In this book I have included synonyms and alternatives as well as common plant names. Here, again, the reader is referred to the index for cross references when in doubt.

The same plant recurs in different chapters when it exists in different flower colours, and also perhaps for its foliage. Cultivation notes may recommend full sun to encourage flowering, although the plant will tolerate shade when grown for its foliage alone. To avoid constant repetition, many plant entries have cross references to a fuller description.

Throughout the book we assume that the reader will use a popular gardening dictionary such as those cited in the bibliography for additional information and for detailed notes on cultivation, propagation and pruning – as well as for information on plants which do not rank among my chosen favourites.

CHAPTER I

DESIGN FOR COLOUR

The plants available to gardeners are nowadays so numerous, and the quality of their colour is so fundamental to the effect they produce, that they deserve careful choosing and arranging to give of their best. This is not just an aesthetic exercise which, in spite of theories of colour harmony, must be mainly subjective. It calls for some consideration of the needs and behaviour of plants, and their suitability as companions, so that they grow together to produce a healthy and flourishing picture throughout the gardening seasons.

The success of any particular plant colour association or border colour scheme will also depend essentially on the basic structure and design of the garden, which is the soberer background to brighter and more fleeting seasonal colour effects. What we see depends not only on the hue or brightness of the colour, but on the texture and form of the plants themselves and the nature of the daylight at the time: above all, colours are never perceived in isolation, but are always influenced by others that are present in the picture. Whatever the style of the garden, the framework planting, often in tones of green and grey, and the colours of building materials used for the house, paving, walls, paths and steps must first be considered. It becomes the textured tapestry frame on which incidents or whole themes of flower and foliage colour are then embroidered.

Before considering colour in detail, take the garden as a whole. Whether the picture is formal or informal, manicured or casual, instinctive or self-concious, even monochrome or multicoloured, all its elements must come together to make a coherent composition. Buildings, walls, perimeter fence or hedge, and flat surfaces of lawn and paving should give architectural balance and unity of design. Colour is everywhere, but look first at the relative darkness and lightness of the picture, the factors that a black and white photograph might reveal: these give architectural weight and define strong shapes, whether in hard man-made materials or in the softer textures of plant forms. Solid dark green yew gives strength, paler foliage of light green or feathery grey is more fragile, and mown lawns are pools of light. A balanced composition of these elements satisfies without the distraction of colour. A garden in winter often reveals the strength and unity of the design; in summer, this coherence is obscured by billowing foliage and bright seasonal colour.

Over and above its good structural framework, I feel every garden should have some element of mystery in its design: whatever the size, it is best if not all visible at once. The largest garden looks smaller if you can see it in one glance. Even in the smallest area it must be possible to plant so that there is some element of surprise: peer behind a shrub or over a low wall to discover some pleasant composition of textured leaves or a plant flowering secretly; turn a corner to be 'surprised' by some new colour; have your mood changed by stepping out of shadow into sunshine. Gardens should invite exploration with a path that curves out of sight: it may lead nowhere, but has the effect of making you feel that more is to come. Steps may link levels and invite you to ascend or descend to get a new view. Clumps of bushes screen and formal hedges frame tantalizing glimpses of colour at the far end of a lawn and draw you farther into the garden to discover what is there.

The 'mystery' of colour is the theme of this whole book. Perhaps it is synonymous with mood or atmosphere in a garden. Colour remains subjective; we can base our choice on a personal taste for pale 'peaceful' tints, a desire to see something bright and cheerful from the windows of the house, a preference for the stimulation of colour changes in different areas of the garden; changes which need a positive act of refocusing the eye and induce shifts in mood. One garden may have no bright colours at all, interest and stimulation given by subtle textural differences and dark or pale colours stressing shape and form; in another garden 'colour'

PREVIOUS PAGE This garden in the grand style deploys colour compartments as incidents in a strong architectural frame. High hornbeam hedges pierced with lancets combine with obelisks of yew and a soaring poplar to give contrasting vertical height, while a blue cedar in the distance gives a glimpse of a more romantic style of gardening beyond. Within the visible garden, cushions and hedges of clipped box make contained areas for separate garden schemes. In the foreground corner, blue spherical heads of agapanthus and darker aconitum are linked with mauve-pink phlox, while grey hairy-leaved *Phlomis fruticosa* fills the centre, with feathery *Artemisia lactiflora* to the right keeping the design from being too heavy. Across the garden, warm oranges and yellows combine to make a separate impact.

A garden's invitation to explore may be formal or casual. Whether paths are straight or meandering, glimpses of a favourite colour or half-hidden plant will lure the visitor deeper into the picture. ABOVE Informal shapes weave a tapestry of soft tints and yellowed blending colours, dominated by orange-yellow kniphofias, day lilies and golden marjoram. Pastel colours fade and lead into the distance, increasing dimensions.

Plants also blend and weave in the twin borders RIGHT where clumps of blue veronica, pale salvias, mauve catmint and white valerian make solid groups in front of scattered delphiniums and foxgloves. However, the mown grass path establishes a clear underlying structure of smooth lines and an atmosphere of orderly calm rather than drama and mystery.

effects dictate the style and the more minute differences of foliage surface become like the woven background to embroidered colours. Plant colour becomes a tool to extend and reduce dimensions, to give sensations of warmth or coolness, to provoke stimulation or induce moods of restfulness.

I once had a small paved town garden, less than 14 square metres in total area. Fortunately it was L-shaped rather than strictly rectangular, and it was possible to divide it into two strong individual themes, each one stressing the existing contrasts. In the corner of deepest shade I used only green foliage plants, strong in leaf form and textural interest, many of them evergreen but complemented in season with white flowers. Ferns, hellebores, sarcococcas and ivies were able to thrive happily under fatsia, elaeagnus and camellia. An arched trellis covered in climbers framed the area where there was relatively more sun. I stressed this different mood by growing shrubs with glowing golden leaves and flowers of pale yellow to give at least the illusion of sunlight. Beds raised

against the walls increased the feeling of space, and plants tumbled and trailed out over the edges.

If I had this garden again, I would keep the rich green 'jungle' area, but might use annuals to make a different colour impact each season. Containers of flowers both in the yard and indoors increase the colour possibilities. With a framework of silvery-grey foliage plants for winter interest, one year the 'colour' garden might be blue and silver, another season bright hot oranges and scarlets would glow, intensified, against the greys. Violet flowers with crimson and purple leaves linked by the deep blue pigment in each of the hues would make a stunning mysterious rich scheme. Colour contrast (red flowers against green – at the point of transition between the two compartments) would be confined to the area where the two schemes met; otherwise, each separate area would be of harmoniously related colours.

The size and type of garden limits the number of design features which can be used, and may restrict the number of seasonal or definite colour schemes which will 'work'. A rectangular garden seen from the road or from the windows of the house often shows a jumble of conflicting themes; a lawn, a pond, a rockery, some topiary, paths and paving, shrubs and trees with coloured foliage, geometric beds bright with flowers from seed packets in mixed colours. Each feature is individually excellent, perhaps, but concentrated together in immediate view, these elements are merely distracting. Particularly in a small area, limit the number of design *and* colour sensations, or the results are visually restless and exhausting.

One recourse is to combine the different elements into a cohesive overall plan. If you want a rockery, design it so that it links a change in levels and takes the place of a retaining terrace wall. A 'natural' pond looks absurd artificially placed in a lawn by the house, but becomes appropriate if hidden round a corner among trees and shrubs. A stretch of formal light-reflecting water in a strict geometrical shape fits with horizontal lines or clipped shapes of hedges and topiary which form the framework for colour effects in coherent patterns, carefully arranged to manipulate perspective, increasing or diminishing dimensions, and giving sensations of warmth or coldness.

The type and the size of garden can be the starting-point in a quest for appropriate choice of colour. An inward-looking city garden might be mainly green, creating the effect of an oasis in a dazzle of urban colour; alternatively, as a contrast to the greyness of urban life, the inner garden might be full of vivid bright flowers and leaves, an opportunity to use exotic plant material inappropriate against a background of native woods and hedgerows.

To the viewer outside, colours are seen against the house; to the owner inside, garden colours must blend or contrast purposefully with a greater plan. (Even a windowbox in a town may be viewed from inside against the background of leafy foliage in a nearby square, and its theme will certainly need to relate to the framing colours of paintwork or window curtains.)

A suburban garden uses the trees and shrubs of neighbouring gardens as a background to the colours chosen, and specific schemes should fit appropriately into an 'open-plan' system where each private garden area must become part of an overall view. Like flower colours, the brighter-coloured foliage needs particularly careful placing so that purple, gold or glaucous blue do not jar in a natural landscape; a bird's-eye view of a country garden should find that the garden perimeter blends with the countryside without a sharp dividing line, while the more exotic plants in 'artificial' colours are best placed nearer the house, where they relate to man-made surfaces. Transfer the garden to another region and reverse the use of plants; the sober greens and greys of a temperate landscape are replaced with ochre-coloured earth, and native trees have strong blue-toned leaves.

Our subject is colour in *your* garden. Yours is the canvas; you the reader are the garden artist painting in your chosen style with the colours you prefer: you create the picture. (In a large garden you may produce a number of different pictures.) This chapter explores some practical activities behind the aesthetics, from the decisions that concern how to use the site, how to translate colour ideas into practice, how to design, plan and plant – and then maintain the planting successfully through time.

The examples I have given offer a few guidelines – rules of thumb – for approaching design. Since too much causes confusion, be selective. This does not inevitably mean using only a few colours, or choosing monochrome schemes; but combining colours carefully, in limited compositions. Keep them apart spatially, in different compartments or in garden areas separated by neutral foliage; keep them apart in time, making them feature in different seasons. When combining colours in a multicoloured scheme, study the kaleidoscope of ways shown in the pictures in this book and look at gardens of all kinds for inspiration – and then translate the ideas for yourself.

Chapter II offers some theory and suggests reliable colour combinations to choose, both harmonies and contrasts. It also offers explanations that help understand how they work and why. But bear in mind always the size, style and scope of your canvas – your context.

You can plan colour but not always control it, since colour in growing plants will sometimes surprise you. Besides, the most memorable and enchanting of garden pictures can sometimes arise by happy accident: your eyes are often opened by chance to some new colour sequence which inspires and enriches your colour sense.

Gardens themselves offer sources of inspiration to the gardener seeking some starting-point for introducing new colour schemes into his site. Look at pictures of them, read accounts of them in books, but above all visit as many gardens as you can, in as many different seasons as possible. Great gardens open to the public may seem at first sight to have little in common with the average domestic plot. But apart from noting down plant names and colours, and making sketches showing some pleasing relationship between plants, or the way a trailing plant softens a wall (and noting the colour of the wall) – in other words finding the colour associations in grander schemes that can be reproduced at home – these famous gardens offer a wealth of information about style, formality, scale, balance: all of which gradually sharpen the observer's understanding of design and composition. Many great gardens derive from some classic or traditional style, some present a synthesis of ideas from different historical periods and up-to-date plant colour, others are products of an individual mind.

The ideas these garden visits produce will doubtless have to undergo a fair amount of translation to suit the imitator's circumstances. They may not work at all: an imitation of Capability Brown demands vast scale and is not effective if the landscape beyond the garden perimeter is an urban one. You may have to précis a vast colour scheme into a mere incident in a small garden, to interpret the colour scheme in terms of different plants because your soil type is different or

In the limited space of a small town garden, an atmosphere of surprise and mystery is achieved by a good marriage of architecture and planting. The lines of masonry, softening leaf shapes and vertical emphasis of both pillars and planting create a graceful complexity which allows a lot to happen in a small space. The cool biscuit-colour of the bricks does not reduce dimensions, and its effect is tonally matched by the flower scheme of gentle pinks. Pelargoniums, *Polygonum bistorta* and white balls of *Viburnum × carlcephalum* all keep the mood restrained without fussiness. Foliage of polygonum, hosta and alchemilla contribute interest all through the season, and drama is added by the tall fuchsia towering above the geranium-filled container.

your aspect incurs different amounts of sun, or to alter colours slightly to harmonize with the different materials of your walls and paths.

In most gardening climates the natural landscape resolves itself into a series of greens, greys and pale browns. The gardener shapes this landscape, introducing scale and dimension with the careful placing of strong, heavy forms, soaring evergreen verticals and varying leaf texture and shape. This can be done formally: gardens inspired by Italian tradition are architectural compositions in greens and greys. Textured foliage of box, evergreen oak and smooth-leaved lemon contrast with silvery olive trees and dark green cypress spires. Terraces and balustrades are linked by grey stone steps; blue unclouded skies reflect in water, leaving garden areas restful and shaded.

A different approach to creating a peaceful and spacious atmosphere is seen in the English park: in the eighteenth century the natural setting was used as inspiration, then, moulded land masses and planted groves of trees 'improved' on nature. Tree outlines gradually fusing and paling in the middle distance, and grassy slopes, make the parkland picture one of light and shadow rather than one based on either flower colour or geometrical form.

The Japanese gardener might use natural features in the green of a pine tree or the brown or grey of gravel and rock to reproduce a landscape in miniature. Interest and meaning is given by the pattern of raked gravel and the ripples on reflected water, each feature symbolic and carefully placed.

As for the colour schemes which grand and municipal gardens display to the visitor, styles still derive from the nineteenth century, when newly introduced plants of the brighter hues prompted new interest in the art of colourful

gardening. Beds were often planted in geometrical patterns with little regard for colour associations or harmonies. Intricate design, concentric colour circles, swirls of coloured gravel were seldom 'aesthetic', but were the forerunners of splendid municipal 'bedding out' in modern parks, where nowadays colour sense is more carefully developed. Planting schemes of bulbs, half-hardy annuals and tender plants for flower and foliage are changed three times annually, giving scope to the plant-breeder and nursery seedsman to provide the materials for experiment. Here the private gardener who lacks space and scope can study colour associations and then use them on a small scale as incidents in his own garden.

The best of the annual bedding in parks – the epitome of brightly coloured planting – 'works' when colours are paired in exciting or subtle combinations, when the geometry of the beds are simple shapes with firm lines. Close planting gives the illusion of solid slabs of contained colour. Bedding fails when plants are too far apart for the colour to be 'read' across the intervening patches of earth, or when plants are scattered in small groups, or sometimes even singly, and lose their colour emphasis. Compare the generous quantity of massed plants in a good park bed to the half-dozen plants set in a line in the suburban front garden – often blue lobelia alternating with salmon begonia – and producing little more overall impression of colour than the greyed tones of the earth of the flower-bed. Better to mass plants in one powerful block of colour that will read from a distance than to waste dots of colours along a border.

The antithesis of the artificial geometric beds of flat colour may be the three-dimensional herbaceous border, bulky with shrubs and perennials in different colours, and contrived to look natural. Perhaps the greatest influence on the borders we see in gardens today is that of Gertrude Jekyll: her garden colour theories were a reaction to the brash and often thoughtless colour arrangements of the Victorian period, where good plants were often used in ugly ways.

She developed colour schemes for gardens as an 'art' ethic, making use of her own training as a painter and designing borders as three-dimensional 'pictures', their colours carefully graded and selected and arranged in contrived sequences for close-up or distant views. Using her artist's eye, and her sound knowledge of plants and their needs and behaviour, she placed them unerringly in series of 'themes' based (where there was space for separate garden compartments) on seasonal colour, or on strictly orchestrated colour borders. She made borders and gardens of closely related colour patterns using subtle gradations of hues; one might be

Colour schemes that work perfectly in context are a matter of scale and proportion as well as choice of appropriate plant colours and shapes. It may be worth taking a cue from the style and colour of near-by buildings. The tone of the brickwork, for example, can be the starting point for a harmonizing scheme of interrelated flower colours; any paintwork visible in the garden area needs to fit comfortably into the garden picture.

OPPOSITE In an urban garden, cream roses become dramatic as the only plants visible beside the front door. Their cream tints associate gently with the cream-coloured walls and the white door and seat. The picture is deliberate and satisfying, and the substitution of a more colourful rose might threaten the simplicity of this scene. In another season, to evoke a new mood, exchangeable containers might offer new possibilities: spring bulbs might be in dramatic red or softer pink, and later-summer bedding could include trailing blue lobelias under scented cream-coloured tobacco plants.

RIGHT In many gardens, neighbours' plants become part of the framework. A section of weathered brick wall has its own textures, its redness further softened by proportionately large swathes of climbers. The strong red flowers of *Clematis* 'Ernest Markham' climb above the wall into an overhanging bush in the garden beyond. Below, creamy-white pompon chrysanthemums echo the cream variegation in the leaves of *Hedera helix* 'Goldheart', which clings tightly to the wall.

yellow, orange and red; another, moving farther round the spectrum, might extend into the colours of sunset, flower and foliage in hot bright hues gradually turning to deeper crimsons and dark violets, to give effects like a Turner painting. Quieter schemes could be in softer blues and violets with grey-green or glaucous leaves.

Often she planted in drifts rather than blocks of colour, so that tapestry effects were achieved with one colour touching many other adjacent ones, and being correspondingly 'altered' in appearance in the different ways described in the next chapter, sometimes tinged with the complementary shadow of one, sometimes another. Just as in any pictorial or architectural composition balance is achieved by careful arrangement of pale and dark features, upright or rounded shapes, distributed to best effect, so Miss Jekyll also used floral and foliage colour in careful gradations of tints and shades to build up a picture. A focal point to dominate a view would be in bright eye-catching colour, while areas of massed lower-toned or paler colour would make a quiet background for a vivid patch of contrasting hue.

She planned gardens of monochrome colouring, each one approached through or viewed initially from an area where the scheme was contrasting, in this way preparing the eye for maximum impact. A chain of garden compartments each dominated by a single colour – orange, grey, gold, blue and green – were separated from each other by evergreen hedges. The central garden, filled with golden and variegated foliage plants, framed the view towards the blue or grey compartments, where the eye would find the complementary blues and misty greys at their most vivid and bright.

Many of the greatest English gardens are Jekyll inspired: Hidcote, Sissinghurst and the smaller Tintinhull all have separate colour areas where hardy flowering and foliage plants are woven into related or contrasted colour schemes. Sometimes one colour is predominant for one season only, and a bed or border can change gear in mid-season: an area of stimulating blues and yellows in spring might become by midsummer a misty picture of blues, violets and pale grey leaves. Another border of spring flowers may later be white, pink and grey. Miss Jekyll worked when gardens were large; seasonal gardens and separate colour themes were possible, to be visited only when at their best. The modern gardener working in a more limited area can still apply many of her colour 'rules', but as incidents rather than whole schemes.

While Gertrude Jekyll was applying the colour theories of Goethe, Chevreul and the Impressionists to English gardens, Claude Monet, himself one of the earliest Impressionists,

was taking his easel out into the open to capture the continuous colour changes through the weather and seasons, as well as the constantly changing atmosphere and light during the course of a single day. When the viewer steps back from the picture, the jumble of incongruous colours assembled on the flat canvas arrange themselves into a work of art representing Monet's vision of nature or of his own garden. Monet used his knowledge of colour relationships, tonal values, harmonies and contrasts to produce a final completed canvas, but he first composed the painting in terms of areas of darkness and light, of shadow and sunlight, before elaborating the colour tones, and adding strong brush strokes to indicate foliage or petal texture. We can compare his technique to that of the gardener building up a balanced framework of 'greens' on which to hang his colour network.

Monet's garden became an obsession. He chose his plants and colours in order later to paint them, and made the garden itself, as much as the paintings of it, become a work of art. His famous water lily pictures, painted to be arranged round a room, each had long sweeps of canvas dominated by a single related colour scheme. Like visiting a garden, the observer then moved round to another canvas and different colours.

As he got older Monet saw colour in his mind, capturing its essence from the imagined colours of his garden and extending the colours over a new range. Similarly, as Miss Jekyll grew older, almost blind, she became obsessed with abstract colours, creating plans for gardens of deeper, richer hues, ever closer to Turner's final studies, where his pictures ceased to be representational and became abstract studies of colour relationships.

What is inspiring is ultimately a question of personal vision and taste, and I am naturally drawn to recommend the types of garden that seem to me to use colour most excitingly. But a word of warning, perhaps most simply summed up by the formula 'Avoid using *too much* colour'. This is the impression given when colours are not set into the green or grey framework that holds a design together, and is even more applicable to coloured foliage than to flower colours. I know one country garden where the overall design is excellent, the lines and masses clear and structural. However, in almost every case a plant with coloured leaves – in purple, glaucous, gold or variegated tones – has been used in preference to green. The individual colour associations in each of the separate groups is telling, but a sense of overall unity is missing. How much more effective would it have been to divide the garden into distinct colour areas or themes, linked and framed by contrasting green shades.

Here in *Le Jardin à Giverny* Monet placed on his canvas the extreme colour contrasts of massed orange nasturtium, violet-mauve asters and banks of mixed red, pink and white dahlias. Afternoon sun filters through leaves and flowers to fall on these strong colours in an alternating pattern of light and shade formed by yew trees and their overhanging branches. Sweeping brush strokes of green and reddish-brown portray the textured yew foliage. Monet loved to use almost pure hues in his paintings and toned down neighbouring shades to make a balanced colour composition. Few gardeners succeed with such bold vision since plant colours cannot be manipulated as with the stroke of a paint brush. Monet wanted to capture a fleeting moment in his garden in an impressionistic sense – a painting of the same scene at another time of day would show different light conditions and colour relationships. For most gardeners colour perception becomes confused in their own garden with what the mind knows of the detailed planting; the casual visitor is better able to receive a distinct colour sensation and store it in his visual memory like a painting.

A second lesson to be gained from looking at gardens large and small, public and private, is summarized by the concept of 'appropriate planting'. Many stylistic approaches to garden design, especially those that minimize maintenance, were originally conceived for a particular context and fail to be sympathetic in a new setting, or when interpreted in a new way. Sweeps of coloured foliage taking their cue from local earth tones or building materials and following natural contours can make effective foils to modern architecture, especially in enclosed urban areas, where bright leaf colour does not seem out of place. Translate them to a country garden, though, whose perimeter fence is surrounded by a different type of vegetation, and they look absurd. In the same way steep banks bordering city motorways can make good use of massed ground cover of varied foliage plants; once the motorway reaches the open countryside, however, plants which blend into the rural environment should be used. Some limitation in the colour range is desirable, too, in the popular conifer or heather garden where prostrate textured foliage is given vertical interest by small punctuating conifers – a labour-saving style very much suited to single-storey buildings. Combined with grey rock slabs, gravel and simple graphic paved surfaces, such planting can approach the simplicity of the Japanese garden, but it loses its effect in a clash of idioms if viewed against too close a background of landscape dominated by grass and broad-leaved trees and shrubs.

Underlying the aesthetic limits to what is 'appropriate' in planting are the more fundamental practicalities of climate, site and garden aspect. The indoor flower arranger can choose any leaf or flower to build an attractive picture of colour and texture, combining feathery plumes of astilbe, majestic hosta foliage, fleshy-leaved sedums and silvery artemisia or achillea – plants which could not grow together in a single garden bed. Similarly in the past nurserymen have prepared colourful displays of growing plants at horticultural shows, regardless of their different habits and growing conditions in the garden. To an experienced gardener, however harmonious the colour associations, a planting will not 'look right' if the plants come from widely different habitats; nor, ultimately, will the plants all survive. When planning to introduce a new colour scheme, the limitations of climate, aspect and soil in your garden may actually make the task of choosing from a bewilderingly large range of plants simpler. When moving to a new area, besides consulting zoning charts and analysing your soil type, look at the plants which thrive in the locality: both the natural vegetation and the garden plants growing there will indicate the possibilities open to you. You may not be able to use the exact planting associations you have used successfully elsewhere or seen and admired in another garden, but a similar effect can be achieved by choosing plants appropriate to the new site. Garden colour planning is not only arranging harmonies around existing garden features; in many cases you decide on a definite colour scheme and then choose the plants which will make it live. In fact much of the basic colour arranging *depends* on both factors, rearranging plants to make better compositions and finding plants to perfect a colour picture as yet on paper or even still an image in your mind. As you work, save time and disappointment by studying where a plant comes from and giving it conditions as similar as possible to those of its native habitat. If you can't do this, make another choice of plant. Many climatic factors (discussed in more detail in the appendix on 'Climate and growing conditions') can be influenced and controlled by gardening skills and equipment. Pockets of favourable microclimate can exist in a garden within a climatic zone, or can be artificially created. Slopes can extend the growing season and help frost drainage; bricks and stone reflect extra heat to ripen and harden the wood of tender plants. Raised beds ensure drainage for alpines and Mediterranean plants which can withstand low air temperatures but cannot endure water freezing round their roots and crown. Many plants, tender when young, can withstand much more extreme temperatures if given early protection.

Similarly soil type and texture can be partly controlled. It is possible to make lime-free beds in an alkaline area for plants which need an acid soil of low pH. This is done frequently and successfully for containers, less well for whole garden areas where plants often look inappropriate, especially if the surrounding countryside has a very different sort of vegetation. This decision is subjective, and is carried to extremes by the ecologist who will grow *only* indigenous plants in his garden. However, soil-changing tricks and other adaptations which make it possible to grow a new range seem to work in a garden isolated from a natural environment. Exotics in pots used as garden features placed near the house do not look out of context, but such devices fail when plants are intended to look natural in the outer garden, in woodland glades or near the perimeter fence, close to native undergrowth – with the result that you see plants growing together in a way impossible in natural conditions.

Adapt your planting schemes to your environment. Don't plant silver- and grey-leaved plants in shade; give them full sun and free drainage, and instead choose ferns with delicate lacy leaves which love darkness. Don't plant rich feeders next

to plants which prefer stony infertile soil; even well-loved combinations of roses and lavender bushes give cultural difficulty, because their needs differ. Grow them to be seen together, but discreetly plant the lavender in stony well-drained soil. Don't plan a colour scheme which depends on golden foliage in full sun; most plants with this type of leaf colouring need shade or the leaves shrivel and burn. Don't feed variegated plants with rich food; their leaves will form new chlorophyll and become green. Many lily species which would make colourful groupings next to hardy herbaceous plants in open borders crave cool woodland conditions in deep (often acid) soil, and a protective low plant canopy for their emergent shoots. The colour schemes you choose are limited by your garden conditions, and their results and the satisfaction you get from them do depend on appropriate planting and plant associations. As you adapt plants to your environment remember how light affects the colours you choose. In a country where bright sunlight will fade even the

Red tulips under the boles of trees line a cobbled path which leads to a firm architectural focal point. Colour as much as linear perspective defines space, and this monochrome planting accentuates axial direction. The strong colour and simple forms of the massed tulip flowers stand out clearly against the other colours in the picture: grey stonework and low-toned sculptural green leaves of the tulips themselves, and the patterns of light and shade on the flower forms, show that the bold use of a single colour need not be monotonous. The hand of the real artist resists the temptation to add other colour elements in this season, which would distract the eye and reduce impact; the glimpses of white from neighbouring colour schemes does not interfere with the reds.

Firm architectural planting such

as this depends for effect on its conviction: a generous number of tulips, thickly massed, makes this a strong seasonal picture which would be weakened by less dense planting.

strongest colours, planting associations can be made with the brightest colours possible – colours which, under grey northern skies, look out of place and garish. In a humid atmosphere, pale pastel flower colours and subtly textured leaves glow and look appropriate; under fierce sunlight they fade to insignificance.

The use and the enjoyment that any garden provides will vary from season to season, from family to family. In winter a garden is mostly seen from indoors, with brisk visits out to examine the details of a leaf or flower or to capture the scent of some perhaps petalless bloom. In summer, depending on climate and family habits, the garden becomes an extension of the house – or is ignored while everyone goes away on holiday. Where there is space for separate seasonal or colour effects, relate the accessibility of each area to its most attractive period. In winter a garden is enjoyed near the house, but hide a formal rose garden then, when it is hard-pruned and unsightly. Make screens of later-flowering plants to conceal spring areas when they have become dull. A traditional herbaceous border is for viewing in summer rather than spring. Plan seats for warm weather in a restful green spot, with a prospect towards the garden's most colourful area or – if work allows leisure to sit out only at dusk – beside white or pastel flowers and pale silvery-grey foliage, which glow luminously in the dark.

Decide first when your garden area – defined by its basic framework – should look its best. Make strong and purposeful associations rather than using colour so discreetly that no definite impression is made: massing seasonal colour is more effective than separate spots of interest with large expanses where nothing is happening. Isolate different colour schemes with bands of quiet foliage to increase impact, but if two or more colours are chosen for their simultaneous effect, concentrate them together – or you might just as well have them perform in different seasons.

A large garden offers the luxury of individual compartments each with its own seasonal or colour impact at the appropriate time, and together providing someone exploring the garden with the visual impact of distinct changes in atmosphere – from vivid to quiet colour, from warm to cool. In the small garden where such variety is impossible, it may be most satisfactory to concentrate on stunning plants which perform for distinct short periods, and generally to pay more attention to continuity of foliage and textural effects 'out of season'.

Even with ample space for separate compartments, the type or situation of the garden may well dictate the periods of

One gardener may dismiss as dull the picture another acclaims for its subtlety; one may call garish the colourful planting his neighbour sees as bright and cheerful. These two borders against backgrounds of trees have similar scale and planting proportion, but differ widely in colour impact, and appeal to different tastes and moods. Muted colour tints and shades, ABOVE, demand close attention to yield their charms. Indistinct flower forms of gentle creams, pinks, mauves and muted blues blend together with textured leaves of grey and green to a muted contrast of dark foliage and flowers at the end of the border.

Colours from the opposite side of the spectrum combine in the second border, RIGHT, and call for an almost conscious effort to refocus the eye on their stimulating warmth. Patches and blocks of solid colour and pure hue remain distinct, balancing but not blending. Look closely to appreciate how the linked yellows are enhanced by the deep velvet-reds, while a block of white flowers and clumps of silver foliage make the colours seem even more vivid and deep.

On dull days the misty, muted border is more alive with colour, while the bright border of 'hot' colours becomes almost too bright. Sunlight fades and yellows all colours, sometimes, in hot climates, generating a heat haze which blurs colour divisions, fading the brightest colours and giving the muted tones even less emphasis. Plan your colour borders in sun or shade to take account of this phenomenon wherever possible.

maximum colour effects. Woodland gardens, for example, tend to have a burst of colour from bulbs and shrubs in spring and early summer, followed by a long green summer interval before the glorious hues of autumn foliage.

Many traditional hardy plants of the sort found in cottage gardens are at their most effective when flowering in early or midsummer, but lavender bushes, peonies and iris all have leaves which give good architectural form through the rest of the season. In another garden, where 'herbaceous' borders carry colour into the autumn, spring-flowering bulbs planted in drifts will help to hide the necessary staking of these late-flowerers before their own foliage billows out to disguise sticks and string.

For most of us the amount of time available for maintenance affects the types of plant chosen for any specific area. Generally speaking the more effort given to dividing and replanting perennials, lifting and drying off bulbs temporarily replaced by flowering annuals or bedding-out plants, and even almost daily chores such as dead-heading – not only to improve the appearance of a scheme, but also to conserve the energy of a plant which might otherwise set seed, tidying of dying leaves and weeding – the more effective and prolonged will be the results.

The most time- and labour-saving planting is that of permanent trees and shrubs above broad sweeps of ground-covering material, possibly paving or gravel, but often either grass or shrubs and perennials which grow together and prevent weed germination. The canopy of shade cast by the highest plants must not be too dense for the grass and low-growing plants to thrive. Even paving and gravel need attention: at least annual application of weedkiller, brushing or raking, and constant removal of dead leaves and debris. Grass needs mowing about 28 times a year for a smooth lawn, or a minimum of three or four to get a textured surface not too full of weed. The best grass needs feeding, selective weed-killing, scarifying and raking. Plants used as ground cover take several years to grow together; perennials often stop flowering well unless frequently lifted and divided. In the meantime weeds must be kept to a minimum by hand-weeding, using contact herbicides, and by deep mulching; this last speeds the plants' growth and controls germination of annual weeds.

This sort of gardening limits the possibility of many different colour effects. Choose plants which have as many qualities as possible: winter aspect, flowering season, foliage character and perhaps autumn colouring and fruit, but spectacular effects may have to be confined to specific seasons of tree or shrub flower. A single low-growing shrub or perennial carpeting the ground may offer only one season of flowering interest. The quality of a plant and its foliage appearance throughout the year becomes of vital interest, and colour effects may depend on subtle foliage differences in tones and textures.

Between this sort of gardening and the most labour-intensive styles where bulbs and bedding are changed two or three times a year, are infinite modifications, incorporating ideas from both. Some permanent planting is mixed with perennials which need more or less frequent division; bulbs planted under deciduous shrubs will thrive for years and need not be lifted annually. Most plantings are a happy blend depending on the owner's plant preferences and the time available for maintenance.

In an average garden today, much of the area is mixed planting. Trees and shrubs give scale, height and interest all year, casting shade on neighbouring plant groups. Shrubs as single specimens or clumps give winter structure and seasonal colours. Between them in blocks or drifts of suitable scale are perennials and bulbs with different flowering seasons. The bulbs that should be 'baked' each summer will gradually deteriorate, and may have to be renewed fairly frequently to maintain a reliable display. If time permits, a seasonal burst of colour may be accentuated by a clump of annuals – or an entire new season of colour may be introduced.

A border for winter effect depends on evergreens and elegantly shaped deciduous shrubs that flower then – or even in another season. But if later in the year you want more than one definite period of interest, try to use temporary plants which replace each other for the specific moments of optimum effect, as well as the permanent plants which not only give structure but need to be left in the ground to develop. Spring bedding colour, whether bulbs or hardy annuals, can be lifted to make room for new annuals or tender plants designed to coincide in flowering beauty with another time of the year. If no annuals are grown it is all the more important to consider the contribution of each plant to the whole scheme in its 'quiet' period. Permanently sited spring bulbs can be interplanted with groups of summer-flowering agapanthus, which hide dying bulb leaves, and strong sturdy perennials with attractive leaves early in the summer, such as Japanese anemone, can fill in gaps between bulb clumps and contribute flowers much later. Spring-flowering shrubs coincide with the first bulbs. Lavender bushes with violet spikes and grey foliage link the seasons until the agapanthus are in flower, and a late-summer ceanothus, clerodendrum,

Eupatorium ligustrinum or mallow extend effects into a third distinct season to coincide with the Japanese anemone and other late-flowering perennials.

Where space is limited, perhaps to one border visible from the house all through the seasons, the choice of colours and how they are used becomes correspondingly more important. The border may be colourful during as much of the year as possible, or during only one or two seasons. Some colour schemes are more appropriate to a confined area than others. Different ends of a relatively small border may effectively be devoted to separate colour themes, each one perhaps at its best in a different season. The part nearest the house might be planned predominantly as a winter garden, the next area along for spring flowers, and so on, ending with late-summer colour where a warm sitting area is most used at that season.

How does the choice of colour affect the seasonal aspect of the area being considered? In many ways a disciplined approach to colour effects simplifies and dictates the choice

Planting beside natural water should be of appropriate moisture-loving plants; here well-chosen feathery white astilbe, yellow lysimachia and paler yellow *Primula florindae* are reflected in still water to give an extra dramatic dimension to the picture. Iris leaves provide contrast of form and texture, and their flowers announced the yellow theme in earlier summer. Yellows and greens are closely linked in the spectrum, and the white here is creamy, not too pronounced a contrast. The whole effect of this planting is of colours that are as restful to the eye as the still water.

of the actual plants. Choose a season, then make a list of the plants that flower in one or more colours at that time; do the same for another season, remembering that colour themes can easily change throughout the year. A blue and yellow spring border can become predominantly yellow in summer, pink and grey or full of hot colours in late summer. Or just the reverse. Plant vivid red and scarlet tulip bulbs and orange or crimson wallflowers for spring, setting the plants or bulbs in autumn between the clumps of blue and pink Michaelmas daisies.

As you decide on plants for your wished-for colour effects, consider also their contribution during the other seasons, their habits and cultural needs. Shrubs which give necessary structure do not like to be moved, and each year they grow in height and spread, casting shadows on neighbouring areas, affecting the growing potential of near-by plants as well as altering the aesthetic balance of heights and shapes. Just as colour masses are distributed through a scheme in contrasting association or in carefully contrived gradations of related tints and shades, so the size of the colour area and relative heights of plants affect the composition. In a narrow border too many tall plants will make it seem even narrower; in a broad expanse too many plants at similar level give a flat two-dimensional effect, like a painting without the subtlety of cast shadows, as plants in different planes screen or expose each other. Yet each shadow alters colour relationships as well as affecting how a plant may thrive. A background hedge in a narrow border may give the desired architectural stability, its visual continuity and strong colour framing the grouped plants in front of it, yet it may equally well compete for light and air, and take much of the nutrition out of the soil. At the front of a border low planting with good evergreens will stabilize a scheme, linking a bed with lawn or pavement. Higher architectural plants link the area with trees or hedges of the garden framework yet compete for allotted space with plants chosen purely for limited seasonal effects. Remember as well as these three-dimensional effects, relative areas of plant colour and their tonal and lightness/darkness contrasts can be as important as the actual colour associations used – and that each individual composite scheme must equally fit in

The appearance of colours changes with distance and has an additional influence on a planting scheme designed to emphasize linear perspective. Pink roses lining a path, LEFT, draw the eye deep into the picture as their fading misty colouring extends the apparent length of the path – an effect exaggerated by extreme contrast with the dark yew of the framing arch. Their light colour and indistinct forms give the pathway an illusion of width. Dark colours, on the other hand, tend to narrow dimensions, and a solid evergreen hedge around a garden or bordering a path can reduce the feeling of space.

The Irish yews punctuating the approach to the house, RIGHT, define the edges of the flower-strewn paved path, but are perfectly in scale. The carpet of helianthemums in weaving reds and pinks glows with colour at midday, and whenever the sun shines. The brightest reds are in the foreground; the colours blending and weaving and becoming paler with distance.

to the whole background structure of garden and house.

Before beginning a plan on paper, carefully consider any other factors which will influence the actual plants chosen to implement the seasonal or colour scheme. Colours and shapes can become focal points to dominate and attract, or increase space by fading into the background. A golden-leaved tree or shrub may be an eye-catcher among more sober foliage, yet in a dark north-facing garden may cheer and give the effect of light and sunshine. Remember from which direction you approach a bed or border as well as whether you see it all at one glance or move slowly along it. Is it most often seen from the windows of the house, or observed in the closest detail of leaf and flower, colours following one another as the observer moves along its margin?

Before filling in the plants make a three-dimensional sketch which relates the area to the whole garden. Consider the areas of sun and shade in the bed, and how much seasonal variation will occur in light and shadow. Some section which is permanently shady in winter may well have sun through much of the day in high summer, and these differences can be exploited when choosing plants for each season.

Except in the tropics, nature has distinct seasonal colour associations which have traditionally affected garden planning and even now, when nature has been manipulated to provide a choice of spectral colour for most of the year, some expectation of garden colours in almost defined seasons does affect our attitudes. Many plants have been especially bred to extend the flowering period, to withstand extremes of cold and heat, of moisture and drought. Plants introduced from foreign countries, garden cultivars and hybrids in new and different colours, 'improved' plants where the proportion of flower to leaf and stem have been altered, all change the relationships between nature's colours and those available for garden use. Nevertheless we do *expect* spring colours to be light and cheerful, signifying annual re-awakening as soil warms up, and later colours to become darker and richer, symptomatic of maturing leaves and preparing the mind for fiery autumn shades which are the climax before winter colours of dead or dying plant material.

Optimum flowering and foliage times for all plants through the five gardening seasons of this book are very variable, depending on the individual garden's climate and on other conditions. However strictly you try to place plants' perform-ance in chronological sequence, they often overlap; however you mean them to coincide in flowering, one will sometimes finish early, another be late in beginning. Choose flowers and leaves for the optimum moment when they 'work' best together, but their appearance in their less good moments is also important. Even evergreens shed their leaves, and the tender silver and grey shrubs are scruffy in winter and need severe pruning in early summer, making unsightly woody shapes. The elegant leaves of many herbaceous plants are untidy, even ugly, as they wither. When plants begin to flower their leaves often lose their glossy sheen, and not all seed-heads and dying stems are attractive. As you plan for seasonal or separate colour effects try to visualize each plant through *all* the year; remember how pruning, staking, tying and general feeding and maintenance will also affect what you see. The gardener intent on providing the conditions neces-sary for each plant may see the garden not so much in seasonal colours as in terms of seasonal jobs which have to be done to ensure that his plants perform at their best in season, and do not fade away in too unsightly a fashion.

In winter, nature's low-toned background colours are little different from those within the garden framework. Evergreen trees and bushes and low undergrowth are dark and solid: their leaves can sparkle with ice-crystals or shine with dew and dampness. Grass is paler but glows emerald-green against grey skies, its after-image colouring the adjacent bare grey branches with a pinkish glow. In dark woodland shadows become purplish on misty days as tree trunks recede into the humid atmosphere and blue depths of landscape. When snow covers the ground the garden merges with the background, only the continuous lines of hedge and wall and the arrange-ments of tree or bush silhouette revealing the hand of the garden planner. Inspected closely, the surface quality of some evergreen leaves reveals subtle differences in texture and colour, and some fruit and seeds from the previous season give more pronounced colour than the low tones of the winter tree buds. The buff and brown seed-heads and stems of perennials as well as deciduous shrubs are ornamental even after foliage has withered, and give height and perspective in borders through the bleaker winter months. Indeed many of the less hardy herbaceous plants actually benefit from the extra protection given by overhead stems during severe weather, and some gardeners wait till spring for final tidying, removing only the most unsightly rotting leaves. Earth, where visible in beds, is dark and rich, colour deepened by protective mulches and blending with the paler tones of decaying foliage. In the kitchen garden, as in ploughed fields, newly turned earth reveals darker textured particles of soil, and vegetables in strict rows make patterns as precise as any formal parterre.

As growth begins in spring colours multiply and a period of

intense gardening activity begins. Young buds and foliage shoots are pale, sometimes golden, pink and almost translucent. Low-growing bulbs are in drifts of the traditional colours of spring: cool blue and glimmering yellow. Garden shrubs, except for woodland evergreens, tend to have flowers in yellow or white, or white tinged with pink.

Jobs in the garden include the careful dividing and replanting of the clumps of perennials which were not dealt with in the autumn and the final pruning of frost-burnt shrub tips. The success of the colour effects planned for later depends on maintenance and feeding now. Planning for the change from spring-flowering biennials or hardy annuals and bulbs for new colour effects means preparing seeds, seedlings and

An herbaceous border on the grand scale will offer different colour pictures according to where you stand; it may be taken in at a glance from a distance, or will unfold its details and individual colour associations only as you walk along its length. Gertrude Jekyll perfected the art of orchestrating colours so that the gaze travelled naturally from one area of planting to the next without abrupt transition, and built up exciting colour combinations gradually from areas where the eye had been prepared by restful greens and greys. In this wide border colours are arranged in a sequence

reminiscent of Jekyll's practice. Subdued grey and silver-leaved plants with cool cream and white flowers progress towards the hotter colours of the spectrum in the centre, where drifts of related yellow, orange and red flowers glow in front of a purple-leaved cotinus. Colours pale again towards the far end of the border. The white and cream flowers in the foreground are just beginning to bloom. When they are fully out they will compete for dominance with the brightly coloured flowers which draw the viewer into the present picture.

As pure hues, red and blue make too harsh a contrast, and one or both should be paled or toned down. In spring, LEFT, the distinct forms of pink tulips grow through a sea of blue forget-me-nots in a soft and gentle contrast where unequal 'weighting' of area makes a satisfactory composition. The blue blends with green leaves into a restful low-toned background.

The same colour combination in early summer, RIGHT, contrasts pink *Rosa* 'La Follette' and the evergreen shrub raphiolepsis with powdery-blue ceanothus. A stone wall in achromatic grey makes an ideal background for the delicate colours and gives protection to these tender, sun-loving plants.

PAGE 31 In a bog-garden planting, contrasts of foliage texture and form are as telling as those of colour; indeed, where moisture-loving plants make appropriate neighbours, colour combinations seldom jar. In early summer, giant umbrella-like grooved leaves of gunnera make a canopy over pink candelabra primula and yellow *Iris pseudacorus*. Reflecting light on their upper surface and revealing a tracery of strong veins underneath, gunnera leaves on their own make a satisfactory garden composition.

tender perennials for planting when the last frosts permit. As well as planning colour for the rest of the year, spring borders themselves may need adjusting. Some spring bulbs like to be lightly shaded by the canopy of deciduous shrubs through the summer but many need a more open situation and gradually flower less reliably as neighbouring bushes grow and increase the area of shade. Similarly, the space available for spring-flowering bedding plants diminishes each season, and decisions should be made while colour effects can be recorded as to which plants to sacrifice. Of all garden planning that of spring bulbs is most difficult, as within a few weeks they vanish; photographs provide the best records of colour drifts, and ensure wise re-assembly in the autumn at planting time.

Early summer brings intense garden activity as well as a burst of new colour. Shrubs and bulbs continue to flower, but the earliest bulbs already have untidy leaves which cannot be removed until they die down. In the place of tulip bulbs, summer-flowering annuals or tender bedding plants are planted after the last frost, needing pinching out of tips to encourage bushy growth. Earlier flowering plants in containers such as wallflowers and tulips can also be changed to a new colour scheme: have ready inner pots already filled with plants in flower, brought on in a greenhouse or garden centre, to ensure continuity. Most of these half-hardy plants need massing, since individually they do not qualify as specimen plants; but being specially bred for continuous summer flowering, they contribute a precise colour effect for a long period.

Herbaceous perennials now making emergent clumps need careful staking and tying: hazel or willow sticks, bamboos or garden stakes in discreet colours will be quickly covered by the growing foliage. Later, use tarred string or twine in muted tones – not electric-green or orange binder-twine, free from the neighbouring farmer. Net or wire mesh panels for climbing plants can also be obtrusive spots of colour, so use materials which fade into the background walls or weave into the foliage.

Protective mulches – coverings of dark peat, sawdust, mushroom compost, forest bark or farmyard manure – are added now to preserve moisture, improve the texture and workability of the soil and suppress annual weed germination; they also act as a cosmetic covering blemishes and making a strong surface link between plant colours: by stressing uniform colour at ground level, each bed seems larger, as well as looking neat.

The paler new growth of evergreen plants is starting to make a tapestry of colour as it weaves in with the older darker shades. The more tender shrubs, many with grey leaves, need firm pruning far back into the wood; they will look unsightly until soft new growth appears by midsummer. While elegant leaves of peonies remain attractive all summer, those of oriental poppies die down ungracefully, and other plants must be planned to hide the fading leaves.

Colour in open borders is generally white, yellow and pink, with the bright blues of the tender American ceanothus making stronger splashes of colour against warm walls. The earliest rose species are in soft yellow, quickly followed by pink, reds, magenta, and crimson: the more vermilion and scarlet hues of modern roses indicate how seasonal colour associations are ceasing to have much relevance. Many bush roses, unsightly in winter, come into glossy healthy leaf in early summer and even before flowering contribute to mixed planting and begin to make the formal rose garden attractive. Use preventive sprays in early summer: don't wait until the

leaves are disfigured if incidence of disease is common in the region: healthy well-fed roses are less affected.

Lawns are intensely green after spring fertilizing: later closely cut grass becomes brownish and tired-looking after weekly mowing. In long grass dying leaves of colchicums and daffodils look untidy and prevent mowing, but the contrast between these shaggy areas and the smooth green of shaven grass can provide useful texture and colour interest.

By summer the foliage of many shrubs which have finished flowering will be in full colour, already deeper and richer. Purple-leaved shrubs are at their darkest, excellent foil to neighbouring crimson or violet-blue flower colour. Deciduous golden and pale-leaved plants without the protection of some shade are becoming less effective as they scorch in the summer sun. Herbaceous hardy perennials are at their best, foliage hiding unsightly stakes and ties: there are dead-heads to remove or to leave to contribute pale browns and buffs to a later colour scheme. Some perennials will flower again much later if cut to the ground now, perhaps weakening their physic but giving a welcome burst of colour at the end of the season, and in the short term making clumps of fresh healthy leaves.

Helianthemums, penstemons and many brightly flowered annuals continue to perform well only if regularly dead-headed: an easy, if time-consuming task. Pick sweet peas daily to prevent their setting seed and ceasing to flower. Remove dead rose flowers and cut back the shoots to encourage new foliage and growth which will later bear flowers. Dead-heads of conventional packed and folded rose petals are unattractive spots of colour, but the dying wide-open single flowers of many species should be endured for the later benefits of colourful fruits.

Some border plants now need additional water and feeding if the weather is dry, sometimes urgently before they come into flower to prevent promising buds from shrivelling up in hot sun. Even annuals, reasonably drought-resistant if well established, may need water to encourage growth; other sun-loving plants need surprisingly moist soil and in an abnormally hot summer will refuse to flower at all.

It is too late to make major alterations to colour schemes which are not a success. The most you can do is to cut off offending flower-heads, and make notes for transplanting in the appropriate season. Hardy perennials seldom suffer from being moved or divided in autumn or spring, but try to give shrubs a permanent setting. If unavoidable, move evergreens in early autumn or spring, and deciduous shrubs any time of open weather during the winter. At the same time as noting disappointing colour associations, make use of flower-heads from other parts of the garden to experiment with new harmonies and contrasts, placing one colour next to another and watching it through the changing light of a whole day: if the combination 'works', plan it for next year. Playing the same game with the flat colours of panels or catalogue reproductions gives a far less realistic picture: use 'live' material whenever possible.

Many of the late-flowering hardy perennials have the traditional hot colours associated with late summer; in fact the range of the purest spectral hues is greatest now. Earlier maintenance has prepared these plants to survive vicissitudes of weather through the summer months; it is self-evident that healthy plants, growing in conditions which suit them, best survive freak periods of storm or drought, of cold or extreme heat, and are also best equipped to withstand disease. Equinoctial gales can ruin the fragile plants chosen to make late colour events and leave sad gaps in a deliberately planned sequence of colour. A well thought out border will have a balanced mixture of plants which thrive in the possible extremes of the local climate so that if there is a particularly dry or wet season there will always be *some* plants which perform well. Plants which are temperamental should at least have elegant foliage which will compensate for failure to contribute to the planned colour sequence. Plants you would not normally call 'first-class' may well earn a position because they are sturdy and reliable. Many of the rather coarse-leaved daisy-flowered perennials come in this category, but beware the mildew-prone Michaelmas daisy and look for old-fashioned types or modern disease-free hybrids. Remember also that the silvery-grey foliage which has been at its best since midsummer continues to contribute and will enhance and enrich pale-flowered neighbours. Make features of grey leaves and cool pale pastels to emphasize how nature *can* be manipulated in the garden.

Maintenance continues and planning for next season's colours is now essential. Some earlier-flowering perennials already need lifting and dividing, as it is essential to get them re-established before the first cold spells. Bulbs for next season's display need planting; fortunately tulips can be planted late in place of the tender bedding plants and annuals which continue flowering well into the autumn.

The flame colours of autumn leaves are eye-catching, lengthening the period of effective garden colour as herbaceous perennials pass their best. Even in the smallest space plan to include at least one tree or shrub that will contribute splendid colour in the autumn.

There are many ways of approaching making a planting plan for a specific area of the garden; individual gardeners with different inspiration may set about creating their schemes in a series of different stages. Sometimes a measured plan is first drawn on squared paper, colour areas are painted in and plant names follow. Other gardeners may begin with their basic choice of plants, deciding at least on feature plants which will dictate not only the colour scheme but also the season when the planting will be at its most interesting. Personally, I will think of a season and a dominant plant and colour all at once, and then build up my garden picture from that point. By the time the plan is almost complete, I may even take away some of the original plants.

The relationship of the specific planting area to the design and balance of the whole garden, and – of course – its aspect and soil type, are also taken into consideration before any firm decisions are made; these limiting factors often make choosing appropriate plants easier rather than more difficult.

For the sake of simplicity, let us consider designing the planting for an empty bed. The area is small enough to be taken in at a glance from a convenient standpoint, close enough for the chosen blocks or drifts of colour to remain distinct rather than blending optically over a distance.

The stages outlined here are numbered, but the order in which they are executed will not be the same for every gardener, nor will all the points necessarily apply in every situation. Use them as a checklist to make sure that every factor has been considered at some point during planning.

Stage 1: site Consider the relationship between this limited area, the house and buildings, and the rest of the garden. This may be the exact spot where a tree is needed, where sober greens should prepare the eye for a more vivid area, where formality is needed after freer woodland planting, or vice versa. The context is almost certain to give some hint of the appropriate style. If possible, make a sketch of the area.

Stage 2: aspect The basic climatic factors, the degree of sun and shade, soil type and drainage factors will all affect (and may even dictate) the type of plant that will thrive here.

Stage 3: season Think when you would like the area to be at its best. Concentrate on strong effects for a limited season rather than trying to make an area interesting all year round.

Stage 4: colour scheme Choose a dominant colour or colour combination for this limited season. Inspiration may

come from a garden you have seen, whose colour terms can be translated to this new situation using plants which are suitable for the site. Other inspirations come from pictorial images, oriental carpets, landscape or any decorative art.

Considerations from stage 1 may influence the way you deploy colour. Think of perspective: choose cool, receding colours to increase apparent dimensions or warm vibrant colours to diminish the sense of space. Considerations of colour behaviour from Chapter II may help you decide on harmonizing colours, contrasts or monochrome schemes; examples from the 'colour chapters' may help you decide on a predominant theme.

Check that the chosen theme works in the site: that the plant colours will marry well with any building materials, background foliage, etc. Check also that predominant colours look their best at the time of day when they will be seen: e.g. pastels and white glow flatteringly in twilight.

Stage 5: outline plan Now make a detailed plan on graph paper, including any existing features. Fill in your first key plants, chosen in stages 1 to 3, and introducing the colour decided upon in stage 4. This will set the scale for the whole planting.

Stage 6: colour plan Colour your plan, or make a sketch, in crayons or watercolours to carry through the considerations of colour harmony and balance in stage 4: this is vital for a multicoloured planting in order to see how the colours are distributed, but is less so for single-colour or harmonious schemes. Your rough drawing will not represent plant colours accurately, but is useful to indicate overall pattern.

The sketch book opposite shows the initial planning stages in the colour scheme for an imaginary border. The south-facing site is protected by a high wall of modern brick of a dull pinkish-grey. The tree which shades the eastern end of the border is a *Malus × hupehensis*, providing the initial structural element and the reference point for scale. Where an evergreen would cast dense shade and preclude an underplanting of bulbs, the malus has a light canopy. It also offers the bonus of autumn fruit, but more importantly provides the colour keynote – pink – and its early-summer flowering gives the first hint for the timing of the scheme.

A prostrate juniper towards the other end of the bed links the border with the lawn and gives structural balance.

Having decided on a pink theme (stage 4), an initial list of possible key plants is considered. All are pink-flowered, but their foliage qualities and form as well as requirements will need checking.

The first plant to look for is a climber to soften the bare expanse of dull brick; clematis is considered but rejected in favour of actinidia, which can be pruned back to make a patterned winter framework.

From the shortlist of possible shrubs, kolkwitzia is chosen: one of my favourites, whose delicate flowers and pale foliage seems just right with the graceful actinidia.

Stage 1 - Bed / south-facing - 9 x 2·5 metres (30 x 8 ft)
            wall - 2·5 metres (8 ft)

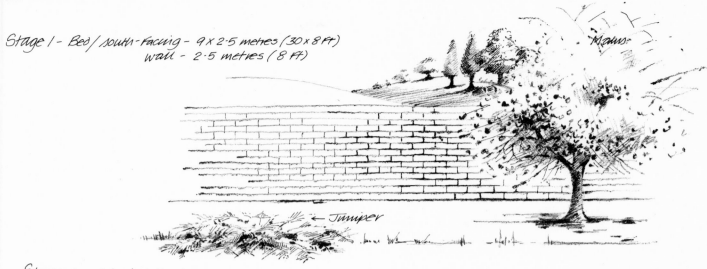

Malus

← *Juniper*

Stage 4 : pink/white theme - early summer

Key plants -   for wall ——— <u>Clematis montana</u> ? - too large and spreading
          (A) ——— <u>Actinidia</u> - better, to 'soften' wall
      feature shrubs — <u>Escallonia</u> ? good structure - too definite an outline
                <u>Camellia</u> ?   } no - too 'exotic': and rhodos best in
                <u>Rhododendrons</u> ? } woodland
pink and white in early (B) ——— <u>Kolkwitzia</u> - nice fluid lines (good with Actinidia)
        summer   <u>Weigela</u>
           pink <u>Syringa</u> } too solid/heavy

Stage 5 : Outline plan

(B)   (A)   Malus

Juniper

Stage 6 : Colour sketch
     <u>N.B.</u> Remember deeper pinks for emphasis

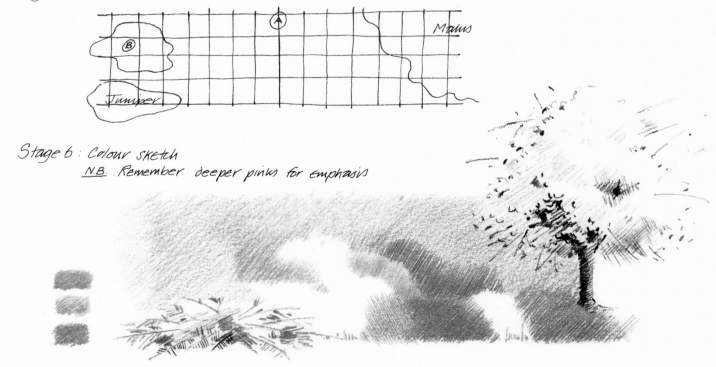

Stage 7: plant list Make a list of plants that are appropriate in terms of season and colour: Chapters III to IX are specially organized to help, but necessarily include only a selection of the plants that I find most useful and are my personal favourites. Don't underestimate the importance of plant structure and foliage in your choice.

Stage 8: plotting Fill in the planting areas of the chosen plants on the plan. (If you are planning effects for more than one season, it might be worth making a second or third plan for the other periods, marking in plants as they appear in their 'off' seasons.) As you draw in the areas of the plants on your list, consider all their attributes and try to indicate how they will interrelate to fill the border with a well-structured composition. Remember, yours is not a flat canvas: planting is in different planes. Moreover, plants are constantly growing and changing, casting shadows and screening other plants. Even if your final image is to be a pictorial one, much of your time may be spent close to the plants, where detail of dying foliage, unsightly stakes and ties and well as the garden's 'flow' through the seasons, will be readily visible. (Besides, you may wish to reconsider the labour involved in looking after some of the subjects on your initial list.) Picture plants at the back against their background hedge or wall; plants in the front will link the bed with foreground grass or paving. Decide how many plants will make a balanced group of the proportions you want, and plant in uneven numbers.

Stage 9: filling gaps Apart from the aesthetic balance, have you left any space for temporary and seasonal planting? Spring bulbs and bedding can extend a seasonal colour effect, or contribute interest in a season not at first considered important. At this point add any companion plants that will take over from neighbours that become dull after flowering, or to disguise dying leaves. However, as you allocate areas for these infillers, remember that permanent plants will alter their relative scale every year. Trees and shrubs resent being moved; many perennials perform best if not divided too often. Spaces and shapes left for bulbs and annuals will therefore become smaller each year, drifts will become narrower, and colour relationships dependent on balance and scale will alter and change what you see.

Stage 10: winter framework It may be useful to adjust some planting to improve the winter appearance of the bed, altering plants towards evergreen or structural shapes. I prefer to do this now rather than only at the beginning.

Stage 11: streamlining What further improvements can be made for other seasons? Rather than removing plants, this may mean adding bulbs and perennials that thrive among and around permanent planting. Low-growing spring bulbs and lilies for later flowering, for instance, can push their way through the low foliage carpet of early-flowering shrubs; Japanese anemones will spread into gaps – but might eventually prove too invasive.

Stage 12: overall structure Check that the design is held together by a firm structure. The colour schemes should already be harmonious, but to give the design unity, colour blocks may need to be repeated at regular intervals or repositioned, or stronger evergreen shapes may need to be chosen for emphasis.

Having decided on the key plants, actinidia and kolkwitzia, plants C to J on the list are filled in – in that order – balancing colours and forms, and keeping the climbing actinidia as focal point on the wall. Plants are chosen with foliage characteristics as well as flower colour in mind: glaucous dianthus leaves, grey anthemis and green-leaved achillea. All are fairly labour-saving permanent plants; achillea is potentially invasive. All are quick-growing, too: the border will look effective by the second season, but quite colourful in the first.

Stage 9 provides an opportunity to take stock, to fill gaps in the bed and to compensate for moments of 'off-peak' performance. A climbing rose and a clematis are planted flanking the actinidia to improve effects as the actinidia's leaves fade to plain green. Similarly, the deep red form of *Eccremocarpus scaber* is planted around the actinidia roots and will be allowed to seed freely to climb among its leaves, contributing rich colour later in the summer.

There is no space for annuals in the bed, but tulip bulbs may be squeezed in behind the edging plants to state the pink theme early in the year. Two dull spaces are filled at this stage: helleborus is planted as ground cover under the malus, and *Anemone blanda* around the roots of the kolkwitzia. Blue anemones are chosen: it seems pedantic to pursue the pink theme too remorselessly all year round.

When winter structure is assessed, the bare branches of the neatly pruned actinidia, the brown peeling bark of the kolkwitzia and the trunk of the malus make a framework above the mounds of green juniper, grey anthemis and glaucous dianthus. At this stage, *Iberis sempervirens* is substituted for one of the clumps of anthemis: it contributes white flowers at the apropriate season, and its green foliage balances better with the juniper. Picture the bed in winter, with the perennials cut to within a few inches of the ground, which is covered with a good deep even mulch to make an attractive dark background.

The bed has now filled up with planting, leaving little space for further additions. Finally, *Lilium regale* bulbs are interplanted with the tulips. (For late summer, *Galtonia candicans* and japanese anemones are alternative possibilities.) For a moment the felicitous combination of dark lavender flowers and regale lilies springs to mind: but shortage of space overall would mean the sacrifice of some other plant, such as the earlier-flowering iberis. On reflection, the latter contributes best to the period chosen for greatest impact, and no changes are made.

pinkish

Stage 7/8: Basic plants

Malus

Juniper

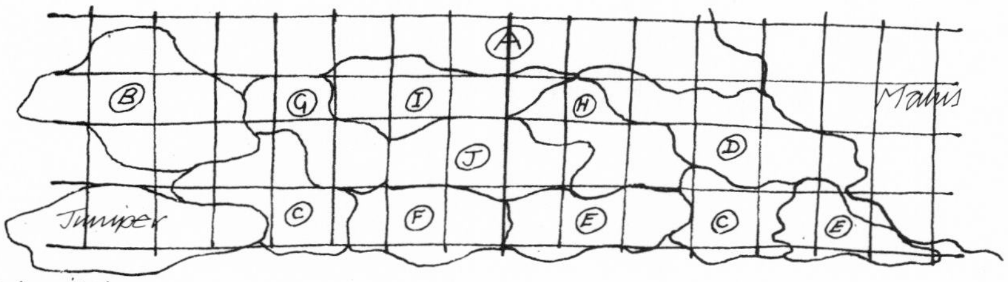

7/8 basic plants

Ⓐ *Actinidia kolomikta*
Ⓑ *Kolkwitzia amabilis*
Ⓒ *Anthemis cupaniana* (white) - 2 clumps
Ⓓ pink ROSE — ? Hybrid musk 'Penelope'
Ⓔ *dianthus* - glaucous foliage - 'Highland Queen' or 'Excelsior'
Ⓕ *Lychnis flos-jovis* ? (grey leaves) or *Dictamnus albus purpureus* — or Heuchera for foliage texture?
Ⓖ pink PEONIES
Ⓗ red Penstemon 'Garnet' (in drifts) ⟵ deeper colour
Ⓘ *Achillea ptarmica* 'The Pearl'
Ⓙ *Cistus x skanbergii*

Ⓚ pink climbing ROSE 'NEW DAWN' ⎫ to mingle with
Ⓛ *Clematis viticella* 'Abundance' ⎬ Actinidia
Ⓜ pink TULIPS: 'Queen of the Bartigons' ⎭
        (2 groups of 12)
Ⓝ *Eccremocarpus scaber* ⟵ deeper colour
    (deep crimson seedling: plant 3 under
                        Actinidia)
Ⓞ *Helleborus orientalis* - group of 3 under malus
Ⓟ *Anemone blanda* (blue) - under kolkwitzia,
        for early spring - maybe 25 bulbs

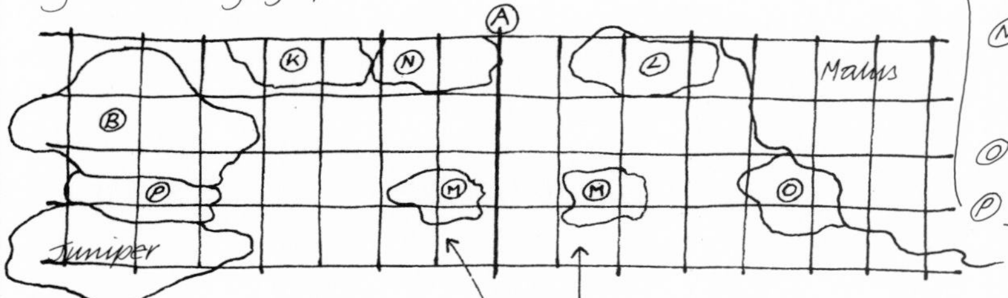

Filling gaps

Stage 9: filling gaps

Malus

Juniper

Stage 10: Winter structure

prune tidily (FRAMEWORK ON WALL)

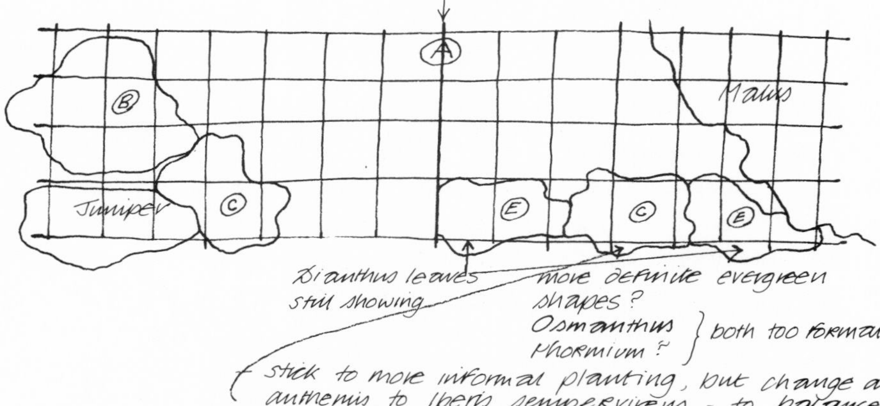

Malus

Juniper

Dianthus leaves   more definite evergreen
still showing   shapes?
                      Osmanthus ⎫ both too formal
                      Phormium? ⎭
stick to more informal planting, but change one
anthemis to *Iberis sempervirens* - to balance
            with green juniper.

Stage 11: Streamlining
    interplanting possibilities:
Ⓠ *Lilium regale* - plant 9 bulbs in with tulips - add lavender too??
    Acidanthera murielae ? ⎫
    Galtonia candicans ? ⎬ no space!!
    Japanese anemones   ⎭

N.B. interplanting of annual PETUNIAS (pink and white) while
permanent plants grow to mature size.

—The Nature of Colour—

Nature paints with light using living pigments, textures and coloured shadows - a far richer palette than that available to the artist who colours a canvas. The gardener, like the painter, combines colours to create harmonious and satisfying effects. He cannot change colours by mixing pigments as the painter does, but like the painter he will affect the appearance of a colour by where he places it. No colour is seen in isolation; each is perceived in relation to some other colour or colours and is constantly modified not only by its neighbours but by *all* colours immediately visible at a glance, and by those which were seen a moment before. These colour effects depend also on the relative size of the different areas of colour and the distance from which they are seen. A painter arranging his paints on the canvas, which is to be viewed from a certain optimum distance, can make use of colour theory which teaches him how neighbouring colours blend and change so he can control the result. The gardener, on the other hand, equally aware of colour phenomena, has all sorts of extra considerations. Leaves and flowers are sometimes viewed close to, at other times from much farther away; indeed, the observer's viewpoint is constantly altering. Sometimes garden colour is seen unfolding as you walk along a border, when each successive colour is affected not only by its neighbour but by the colour you have just passed. Other plant associations are seen as a static picture, perhaps glimpsed across a lawn, or studied in a container, situations where distance determines how the colours remain distinct or blend and alter. The painter Monet *chose* to depict a scene at different times of day or at different seasons to show how the colours he captured on canvas were altered by the light; a gardener sees his colours alter hourly as the sun emerges or disappears, as leaves moving in a breeze make changing patterns of light and shade minute by minute, and as the changing light of day alters in the atmosphere. The gardener cannot consider the success of his plant colour arrangements only for an hour or even a day, as if captured on a canvas or in a colour photograph; he has to think of colour relationships through all the garden seasons, making use of his knowledge of plant behaviour as well as scientific colour language.

Painters and gardeners both know that colours may not only be arranged in pleasing associations (painters, of course, can also arrange colours representationally), but that colours can imply weight and solidity or lightness and fragility. Colours can emphasize the architectural properties of a shape and can underline the effectiveness of linear perspective and focal points. Colours can also be made to trick and deceive spatially, changing apparent distance and altering dimensions. Cool blues and violets and dull browns and greys appear to recede, giving an impression of distance, and the painter can easily make objects seem farther off by using either a paler version of a foreground tone, or a colour in this 'cool' range. The warmer colours, yellow, orange and red, generally appear to advance, foreshortening distance, but even these, when used as paler versions of colours in the immediate foreground of paintings, will give some illusion of greater depth and distance. The painter can choose the exact colour mix he knows will create these desired effects; garden colours are far less predictable, and constantly changing colour relationships in constantly fluctuating daylight are likely to make carefully planned exercises of aerial perspective unpredictable in the garden. Yet the broad principles are available to the gardener who wants to exaggerate the length of a border or seem to alter the shape of a garden area to play down some dull area or to draw attention to a focal point. Sometimes, for example, the eye is prepared for bright colour by making a quiet approach through shade and greenness which, by contrast, accentuates the more vivid hues.

There are both painters and gardeners who seem instinctively to understand colour, placing pigments on a canvas or plants in a flower-bed with unerring discretion, which, often, they find difficult to explain. For most of us, however, under-

standing and appreciation come from a combination of observing what actually happens in nature with a study of theory. Artists have turned to science to explain their observations of colour behaviour. The physicist teaches about light and the composition of light rays; the chemist can demonstrate how pigments which reflect light rays are organized. The physiologist can show how the brain deciphers colour 'messages' received from the eye. The gardener planning his garden and arranging his plants to form satisfying pictorial images draws on the aesthetic theories of colour harmony evolved by painters, weavers and all other colour craftsmen – theories which are themselves often rooted in this body of scientific knowledge.

To make use of colour language in a practical way in the garden it is worth looking at the various disciplines which have shed light on the nature of colour itself. By defining colour terms as precisely as possible, this knowledge helps us understand what we see and thus enables us to work with colour more skilfully.

What, then, is colour? Colour is a sensation which occurs only when there is illumination. The colour perceived depends on the quality and brightness of the light in which it is viewed as well as on the texture and form of the coloured surface. Light rays reflected back to the retina are sent as messages to the brain to be recognized and decoded. The human eye is capable of seeing only a narrow waveband of the radiation emitted by the sun: rays longer than red are invis-

ible, and the ultraviolet rays shorter than violet are visible to bees, but not to humans.

To the physicist, light is the raw material of colour. Newton first established that 'white' sunlight contains all the colours of the spectrum. Long before the true nature of light's wavelengths and rates of vibration were understood, he observed that white light could be split through a prism into its component parts. For convenience this visible spectrum is graphically portrayed in the shape of a wheel, most usefully nowadays with six segments (though Newton's original one showed the seven hues he discerned in the rainbow). The physicist is further interested in the way that the colour perceived depends on the nature of the object, which reflects and absorbs light rays selectively. A 'white' surface reflects nearly all light rays, which combine to appear white to the eye. A 'blue' surface absorbs red, orange, yellow, green and violet rays, but the reflected blue rays reach the eye and are perceived as blue. A leaf is green because the pigment chlorophyll which it contains reflects green rays; however, the appearance of that green is affected by additional physical factors: a smooth surface looks darker and purer in colour than a matt or dull surface where hairs or roughness interfere with the direct reflection of light (see Appendix I: Colour in plants). In practice, white light – daylight – is more often than not already biased towards one of the spectral colours. The effect of this is to influence our perception of intrinsic pigment colour. The illumination of bright sunlight tends to faintly yellow all flower colour: in countries with especially fierce midday sun, even intensely vivid flowers in scarlet or bright orange appear faded. For this reason, in tropical countries, the brightest colours are needed to satisfy the cravings for strong garden colour. In a temperate climate under grey skies, on the other hand, muted low-toned green leaves glow more brilliantly, white and pastel-coloured flowers shine, but the brightest hues become garish. The soft grey-green needles of a pine tree are luminous against a grey stormy sky, and in winter mown lawns become a glowing emerald green in the grey light. Humidity in the atmosphere makes light soft and pearly, and gives the grey tones characteristic of northern landscapes.

As the sun's rays redden at evening, strong bright garden colours become mellowed and rich, eventually, as dusk falls, moving towards violet and blackness. Just as in sunlight flower colours are yellowed, in shade they tend towards violet, at the opposite end of the spectrum; deep reds, blues and greens are, however, more easily sobered by shade than are whites, yellows and pastel colours, as the presence of

PAGE 37 Sunlight pierces the panicles of wisteria like the prisms of a chandelier. Strong light blurs creamy-white and pale greens to seem translucent; in shade, the white flowers retain distinct form. Monet studied and painted such subtleties here at Giverny.

OPPOSITE An east-facing border in the evening sun shows how light filters through leaves to enhance the colour scheme. Contrast of light is added to the complementary purple and gold foliage. The prunus is dark where it is silhouetted against the western sky, but relieved by the bluish matt leaf surfaces that catch the light, and by the stained-glass effect of a few translucent leaves. It is always worth while positioning richly coloured foliage where you will see it illuminated by the low rays of the sun. But the thick yew hedge remains impenetrably in shadow.

Where the red rays shine directly into the corner of the garden and warm the honey-coloured stone walls, RIGHT, strong and pale yellow flowers, which can seem harsh and dazzling in full daylight, are mellowed, while violet verbena fades into dark shadows to the right of the picture. Evening light throws long complementary shadows, and gives colours a mysterious richness.

muted shade in the visual field makes the pale colours more brilliant by contrast.

The human eye uses light completely mechanically. Exactly as in a camera, a crystalline lens allows images in miniature to fall on the retina, from which 'messages' reach the brain for codification and classification in terms of colour, relative lightness and form. All vision depends on learning to focus the eye, but ultimately the brain will use its judgement, perception and experience to decide what it actually sees, and then what to call it. The eye notices colour in an object before it sees shape; a fleeting glimpse of a flower suffices to register the impression of its colour. It appears that the eye's mechanism is so ordered as to perceive four colours distinctly: red, yellow, blue and green. Each gives a unique sensation; they in no way resemble one another. Orange, somewhere between red and yellow in the spectrum, has no such individuality, since it contains a hint of both. Violet contains a mixture of blue and red, and similarly eludes simple recognition and clear definition.

The eye's natural focal point seems to coincide best with green or, in sunlight, a greenish-yellow. Red, the longest of visible light rays, needs a refocus of the lens, and short blue and violet rays force a similar adjustment. Such differences of focus partly explain the readily observable phenomena that red objects appear to advance and to foreshorten distance, that green is 'restful', since it calls for no lens adjustment, and that blue and violet seem to recede into the distance. Distant colours in a landscape or garden tend to fade, due to the atmosphere's scattering of light rays. For the same reason while bright red and orange objects in the foreground tend to retain their defined form even while distance from them increases, dark-toned blues and violets more quickly blend and blur as the observer moves farther away. These attributes can be exploited by the painter and the gardener as colour perspective.

After first registering hue, the eye also decodes colours in terms of other properties: lightness or darkness, dullness or brightness, for which the convention of 'the dimensions of

THE SPECTRAL WHEEL

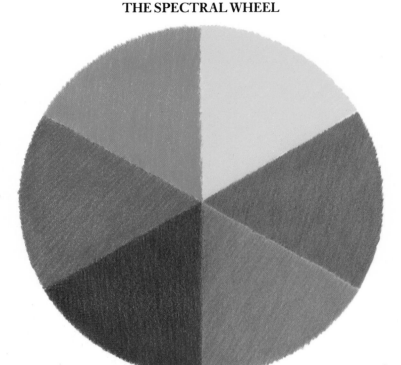

The graphic wheel chosen for our discussion of garden colour is based on three primary hues: red, blue and yellow, and three secondary hues: orange, green and violet. The gradations of colour can be represented by further subdivisions of the wheel, showing blending colours in ever narrower segments, although in the continuous band of the spectrum of light rays, neighbouring hues grade and blend into one another infinitely.

Other wheels may use four primaries (including green), may derive primaries from light rather than from pigment, and in print may show the spectral hues in colours with perceptibly different bias.

The wheel usefully identifies complementary colours as pairs of diametrically opposite hues (e.g. red and green). It also defines harmonizing colours as hues adjacent on the wheel and thus sharing a pigment (e.g. red–violet–blue). Contrasts share no pigment.

Colour theorists have evolved ingenious diagrams to represent their conception of the three 'dimensions' of colour – on the two dimensions of the page, and in the medium of printing inks on white paper. Intricate colour 'solids' and interlinking charts may go some way towards demonstrating the complexity of colour theory, but they involve considerable space, and elaborate explanation. However, since some visual image usually helps distinguish the different qualities of colour, the three principal gradations of colour are illustrated here in coloured pencil sketches, OPPOSITE. They help define the commonly used terms which have in fact precise application in colour language, and are vital to the colour descriptions used throughout this book.

colour' provides useful descriptive terms. The eye tends to exaggerate the differences between adjacent colours – an optical phenomenon which deserves closer attention in due course – and quantifiable explanations of the effects produced by colour are invariably confused by such subjective and psychological factors as what the brain assumes the eye is seeing, by emotional mood and also by personal and cultural associations. One answer from science is the systematic measurement of the light and pigment in the whole range of colours available in a medium such as paint, printing ink, dyestuffs – or plant materials. This analysis produces a series of colour swatches and reference numbers by which any example can, in the appropriate light conditions, be matched and classified.

The laboratory conditions in which such colour identification should take place are outlined in the notes to the Colour Chart of the Royal Horticultural Society of London. To match a petal or leaf colour to the chart (which is, incidentally, based on the concept of the dimensions of colour), the specimen needs to be examined indoors, in a good north light, against a white background. Samples should include a bud just before breaking, an open flower that is as near perfect as possible, and a flower fully out to fading. Such classification is, of course, valuable to the plant breeder, who allocates a code summarizing the three dimensions of the

colour of every plant tested. But the artificial controlled conditions in which plant colour is identified simply illustrate by contrast some of the very real differences in the situation of the practising gardener. Even when every leaf and flower has been carefully catalogued with a number consistent with the RHS panels, the gardener will have to take into account the variations in flower colour that naturally occur in different soil conditions, the fluctuations of light that are part of the everyday garden scene, and the influence of neighbouring colours on what is perceived.

A parallel limitation characterizes the gardener's use of flower catalogues – and even books – in search of a particular colour for a proposed scheme. Both photographs and colour reproduction in printing impose some degree of distortion on 'true' colour (most obviously inaccurate in the cyan range, where pure blues shift easily towards violet and purple). No single printed image can illustrate the succession of colour as a leaf or flower opens and fades through a season, and reproduced colour is flat and even, giving only a hint of texture and of the way an individual petal, for instance, contains an almost imperceptible gradation from its 'basic' hue into the adjacent colours in the spectrum.

Such subtleties of living colour are difficult to capture and hold in the mind; the artistic challenge of planning harmonies and contrasts in garden schemes, this constantly changing

THE DIMENSIONS OF COLOUR

1 HUE

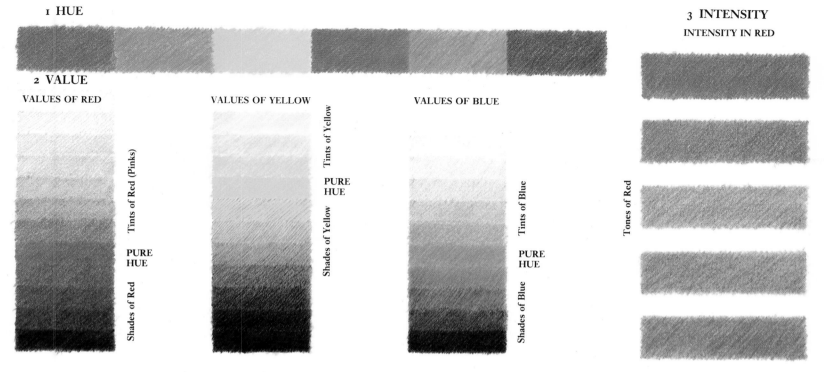

INTENSITY IN RED

2 VALUE

VALUES OF RED

Tints of Red (Pinks)

PURE HUE

Shades of Red

VALUES OF YELLOW

Tints of Yellow

PURE HUE

Shades of Yellow

VALUES OF BLUE

Tints of Blue

PURE HUE

Shades of Blue

Tones of Red

HUE, the first dimension, is the quality that distinguishes a named colour such as red from orange, its neighbour, and from green, its complementary. Conventionally, six hues (red, orange, yellow, green, blue and violet) are shown in separate segments, although in the continuous band of the spectrum, neighbouring hues grade into one another infinitely. Hue is by definition pure colour, containing no white, black or grey.

Pure spectral hues are rare in nature: most colours have some element of pigment from a neighbouring hue, and are influenced by one of the other 'dimensions'.

VALUE, the second dimension, is the degree of a colour's luminosity: the quality that differentiates between lightness and darkness.

Colour values which are graded towards white – lighter colours – are generally known as tints; those graded towards black – darker colours – are called shades.

The hues do not all have the same value. In the spectral wheel, yellow, the lightest colour, has a higher value than that of any other pure hue. Violet, the darkest colour, has the lowest value.

Any single hue also varies in value. A light yellow has a higher value than a dark yellow: this relative luminosity differentiates two examples of the same hue.

INTENSITY, the third dimension, gives some measure of the quality of relative colourfulness or greyness: it differentiates the dull from the bright colour. Also known as chroma, purity or saturation, we see this dimension all around in the muted colours of the landscape, although it is perhaps the most elusive to grasp and to depict in diagrammatic form. The spectral hues are pure colours; as they become 'greyer', we speak of them as tones, or desaturated colours, which are dull rather than bright.

Above is a representation of successively diminishing intensity in red, as the pure hue (top) loses brilliance and becomes increasingly dull and grey-toned.

RIGHT A colour is influenced in all three dimensions by its neighbours, and seems to become as different as possible from an adjacent colour. Here pairs of spectral hues are surrounded by different contrasts, demonstrating hue and value changes.

SIMULTANEOUS CONTRAST

quality of growing plants adds yet another factor to be considered. But just as the theory of the dimensions of colour provides a conceptual tool for colour discussion, so colour charts and photographs are undoubtedly a useful reminder – provided the user allows for their limitations.

The gardener is working with something far more ephemeral than the paint pigments of an artist – which, when placed together, change appearance optically, though not physically; yet, here again, a discussion of artists' pigments can provide a useful tool towards making a more precise definition of some aspects of what we see as plant colour.

The painter can produce an infinite number of colour values by adding white or black pigment to any of the spectral hues on his palette. In a monochrome band of reds, for example, colour value will vary between the pure spectral red – represented in the garden by a scarlet rose or an oriental poppy – lightening towards the paler reds of pink-flowered Japanese anemones, and to white with a mere tinge of pink in flowers such as peonies and spring-flowering prunus. Towards the lower end of the colour-value scale, a crimson rose is darker than the spectral hue, and increasingly tending towards black are the magnificent black-centred *Geranium sanguineum* and the almost black flowers of the mourning geranium, *G. phaeum*, and of *Veratrum nigrum*. (In fact these darker reds contain violet or dark blue pigment rather than literal 'black'.)

In terms of their colour value, some hues – such as yellow and orange – alter much more radically than others when becoming paler or darker. Red fading to pink always retains its distinct 'redness'. Yellow with white added changes to apricot; yellow with black becomes olive-green; orange plus black becomes brown. Green, like red, does not change its character, simply becoming richer when it appears to contain black, especially in the colour of a leaf whose surface is glossy and glowing, for example *Acanthus mollis* or *Fatsia japonica*. Blue has so little luminosity that it easily becomes black when it is darkened, as in *Tulipa* 'Queen of the Night', the rare *Fritillaria camtschatcensis*, or the almost black leaves of the little grass-like *Ophiopogon planiscapis* 'Nigrescens'. Blue can, however, have a lot of white added without losing its essential 'blue' character.

So far, in spite of our awareness of changing conditions in the garden, we have been talking about these colours as if each was perceived in isolation. The picture is further complicated, however, by various optical phenomena that constantly give a dynamic quality to vision: they seem, in fact, to take place in the brain rather than in the mechanism of the eye, and paradoxically they continue to evade full explanation by physiologists or psychologists.

Stare for a few seconds at a vivid red object and then transfer the gaze to a blank sheet of white paper – or the margins of this page: a greenish shape will appear. A violet object will evoke a yellow after-image; a blue shape an orange after-image. The eye which has been staring at a given colour has a strong tendency to evoke an image of its complementary – the colour diametrically opposite on the spectral wheel. Since the reaction involves an element of time – perhaps 20 to 40 seconds – it is known as 'successive contrast'.

A related phenomenon, 'simultaneous contrast', is immediate: it occurs when two colours side by side are each simultaneously affected by the after-image of the other. In effect each colour becomes 'tinged' with a new colour, as if a film or haze of a colour's complementary was being imposed on its neighbour: the result is to drive the colours farther apart in terms of the spectral wheel, and to make them seem as different as possible from one another. Take a juxtaposed blue and yellow: a 'film' of violet (complementary to yellow) will tinge the blue, while a corresponding film or haze of orange appears to deepen the yellow. If the pair of juxtaposed colours is already complementary, they will simply each appear intensified, and their degree of contrast will be exaggerated.

This rather theoretical information is of interest to the gardener choosing to put distinct blocks or patches of colour together. It may be subjective whether a colour is 'improved' or is 'injured' by its neighbour, but it is a fact that it is altered; some forewarning of the fact that a planting may turn out to be more garish than intended, or less harmonious, can help the gardener to compensate in advance for the effects of such optical phenomena – for instance by choosing a scarlet rather than a crimson among the reds, or perhaps a violet- rather than a greenish-blue. Colours retain their truest appearance beside white, so white flower groups can be useful for separating colours which are likely to injure one another. Grey reflects all light rays, but does so less strongly than white. Grey foliage quickly appears lighter or darker as neighbouring colours become darker or lighter; at the same time grey leaves accentuate the purity and brightness of adjacent flowers. Next to grey, pure hues glow even more vividly, while pale pastel tints brighten. The grey leaves themselves do not meanwhile remain neutral: they become tinged with the 'haze' of the complementary reaction. (It is important to distinguish this optical effect of juxtaposing other colours with grey from the so-called 'greying' of colours within the

Although colour behaviour is relative, depending on neighbouring colours and on the quality of light, red is almost invariably the most advancing colour. Set against a mid-green background, a pure red bloom can seem detached from its own foliage and stalk, and foreshortens distance. However, pure hues are rare in nature, and in the poppy-fields beloved by painters, the green is usually low-toned, presenting less of an optical challenge.

We are constantly advised to look to nature for inspiration, but gardening is an art, and to make a satisfying picture we may analyse in colour terms what is happening in nature and translate this into a gardening context.

The odd poppy-head in the foreground here does look disembodied where its contours are not clearly illuminated. Where sunlight makes the petals shining or translucent, however, the pure hue stands out in relief and the picture becomes three-dimensional. Silvery-green textured grass-blades and seed-heads and dark shadows stitch the pure hues together and demonstrate that areas of equal colour value need such links of lighter and darker colour to display all their textural nuances.

SIMULTANEOUS CONTRAST

Juxtaposing two hues has the optical effect of exaggerating the difference between them and 'driving them farther apart'. Each colour appears to be tinged with the complementary of its neighbour; paired complementaries seem more brilliant. The other two dimensions, value and intensity, further affect the apparent changes in the pairs of pure hues listed here.

change due to contrast	pairs of pure spectral hues	change due to contrast
more greenish ◄	YELLOW/ORANGE	► more reddish
more yellowish ◄	ORANGE/RED	► more purplish
more orange-red ◄	RED/VIOLET	► more bluish
more purplish ◄	VIOLET/BLUE	► more greenish
more purplish ◄	BLUE/GREEN	► more yellowish
more bluish ◄	GREEN/YELLOW	► more orange
more greenish ◄	YELLOW/RED	► more purplish
more orange-red ◄	RED/BLUE	► more greenish
more violet ◄	BLUE/YELLOW	► more orange
more yellowish ◄	ORANGE/VIOLET	► more bluish
more purplish ◄	VIOLET/GREEN	► more yellowish
more bluish ◄	GREEN/ORANGE	► more reddish
more brilliant ◄	YELLOW/VIOLET	► more brilliant
more brilliant ◄	ORANGE/BLUE	► more brilliant
more brilliant ◄	RED/GREEN	► more brilliant

COMBINING COLOURS FROM THE SPECTRUM

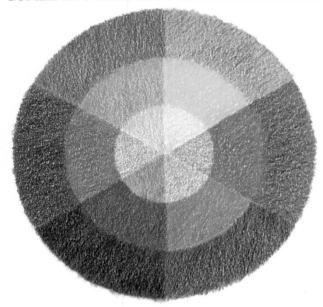

As a starting point for discussion, the spectral wheel offers a selection from the palette available to the gardener. Omitted from this wheel with its tints and shades are the infinite gradations between adjacent hues, and intensity, the third dimension, which is better observed in nature than in the most ingenious of 'colour solids'.

HARMONIES FROM RELATED COLOURS

The eye is not forced to refocus when sunset colours are planted in spectral sequence. Grey and green leaves exaggerate contrasts: purple foliage tones down contrast and gives weight and balance.

Colours linked by blue pigment blend easily into subtle misty pictures, whether tinted or shaded. Grey and blue foliage brightens the more sombre violets and purples and works well with the pastel tints.

The possible permutations of colour combinations are infinite, if we include all the dimensions, the effects of light, relative areas of colour, multicoloured compositions, the qualities of texture and mass – all of which influence each other and change what we see.

The diagrams and suggestions here are, then, only the starting point, using the graphic device of the wheel and the colour swatches opposite as a visual reminder. Implicit in the use of spectral hues in these diagrams are the other possible dimensions or qualities of that colour, just as in the shorthand of language we use the word 'red' to encompass a whole range of different mental images.

There are broadly speaking two approaches to combining colours: working with colours that are related by shared pigment to make harmonious compositions, or using contrasts which share no common element to compose a potentially more lively picture. However, the distinction is not cut and dried, and contrasts may be modified so that they share a pigment, become less different, and are by definition harmonious.

The distribution of colours in the wheel can help the artist build up balanced colour pictures. The wheel seems to split along various axes into hemispheres of contrasting character – providing ready-made colour schemes, or the elements to balance.

The hemisphere with red at its centre seems 'warmer'; the opposite side, with blue/green/yellow, seems relatively cooler. A diametrical split running between green and blue gives lighter colours on one side and darker, lower-value colours on the other. An axis equally bisecting the red and the green segments creates the simplest choice of harmonious schemes: the crimson/violet/blue/blue-green of one hemisphere share a pronounced blue pigment; scarlet/orange/yellow/yellowish-green on the other side all share a distinct yellow bias. Plants chosen exclusively from on either side of this imaginary line will be harmonious together, and many gardeners base their colour schemes on this simple division.

terms of the dimensions of colour: a 'greyed' colour is measurable objectively as a hue that is desaturated, or of diminished intensity. Perhaps the best example would be the muted 'greyed' tones of green in a distant landscape.)

The degree to which adjacent colours appear to affect one another also depends on relative area: isolated flower-heads against a larger expanse of foliage, for example, will be much more altered than the leaves, although where the colours touch, the leaves will be significantly altered by the complementary of the flower colour. And so far the influence of optical phenomena has been considered as if each separate colour group was clearly distinct. But in a garden any colour arrangement tends to be seen from both near and far: from a distance, and depending on the size of the blocks or drifts of colour, the elements may blend visually rather than remaining separate. Pointillist painters made use of this principle, as in a cottage garden or alpine meadow scattered multicoloured flowers blend together and lose distinction. Larger blocks of colour, however, blend in this way only when seen from far away, but colours perceived are already modified by distance, which alters each colour pattern.

A gardener who is aware of these principles of colour and colour changes is equipped with the grammar of colour

Spectral hues combined in equal amounts may create a colourful impression, but can confuse the eye with a scene that is dazzling and disruptive. It is largely a question of taste, but there are different tactics for using combinations of these strong colours successfully. (Of course, 'changing' the colour of an actual plant or flower is impossible: you modify the scheme at the planning stage, or substitute a different plant to make a more pleasing effect.) These examples use the six spectral hues to demonstrate extremes of contrast.

Adjusting proportions: balance a smaller amount of a more intense colour – perhaps the pure hue – against a larger expanse of lower tones. This usually means flower-heads or clumps of the more advancing reds or eye-catching yellows against the mistier tones, shades and tints of greater areas of the relatively receding violets, blues or greens.

Alter both colours to a higher or lower value or to a different intensity. As pastel tints, both colours are linked by mutual lightness or whiteness. As shades,

both have darkness in common. Lower-toned versions of colours are less dazzling, since they share a degree of 'greyness'.

Alter the value of *one* colour, but to avoid uncomfortable and sometimes almost sickly combinations, maintain the 'natural order': i.e., make higher-value colours lighter, and relatively lower-value colours darker. The deepest yellow will look 'wrong' with a pink, lavender or pale blue (all tints of darker spectral hues) if it becomes higher in value – and competes with the more normally luminous yellow.

This principle holds when combining colours adjacent on the spectral wheel, too: with orange/red associations, deepen the already darker red instead of the orange, rather than risking a fight between pink and cinnamon; with red/violet associations, tint the red to pink, which harmonizes with any shade of violet, rather than paling the violet into a lavender that clashes with pure red.

language. Let us look at the way in which this knowledge can be used to create planned colour arrangements.

Arranging colours in the garden involves combining harmonies between closely related colours and contrasts between those as different as possible, and observing the relationship between these chosen associations and the more general background garden colours. These elements may all be carefully deployed to create architectural balance, which is as vital to a pleasing picture as the more personal aesthetic decisions about which colours enhance or injure one another. Changing the 'weight' of a colour, for instance from light to dark, or altering its intensity from bright to dull, and changing the relative areas of colour visible at one glance, as if in a painting, all influence the final result almost as much as the original choice of colours. A painter finishing a canvas may decide to blur a bright colour, or blend its edges with a neighbouring pigment, or to introduce tonal gradations to indicate distance, light and shadow to accentuate perspective and form, or even a note of 'warmth' and 'coldness' to perfect the work. The gardener works in more than one plane, makes pictures to be viewed and appreciated from many angles, and chooses his colour schemes far ahead. As the visitor moves through the garden, his eye seeks both rest and the constant

BASIC COLOUR ASSOCIATIONS

Bright/dazzling as pure hues. Interpose yellowish-orange as link, or deepen orange/lighten yellow. Balance with larger expanse of muted complementaries.

Works as part of gradated sunset sequence, especially if the red is deepened to magenta. Beware of tints in this combination: too pale a pink can look sickly.

A strong, hot combination that can be overpowering. Add blue to make the red crimson for closer harmony; this works very successfully as tints, i.e. pinks and mauves.

Optically confusing, especially when different in intensity. Best when pure blue moves towards violet, and used as drifts of shimmering low tones. Grey foliage.

A 'natural' combination, but to retain true quality of pure blue, low-toned greyish-greens are less distracting than bright greens.

Yellowish-greens of foliage make a restful and easy transition for the eye. To keep the yellows truer, substitute grey or greenish-blue foliage for plain green.

Link with orange tones in sunset sequence or combine toned-down greenish-yellow with velvety red. With tints, pink should be deeper than yellow: use grey foliage.

Difficult to combine as pure hues. Good when both colours tinted or shaded (when the red becomes blued), and when proportions of colour areas are altered.

Prevalent green foliage usually links these contrasts reliably. Most tints and shades work well together. Adding tones of orange or violet makes richer picture.

A nearly complementary pair, almost overpowering as pure hues. Lighter orange goes with most deeper violets. Avoid converse, where pale lavender has higher value.

Pure hues lack differentiation: highlight plant forms to create relief. Alternatively, use greyer leaves, when toned-down colours harmonize with violet tints.

As with violet/green, two hues similar in value need strong shapes for interest. Link with yellow-pigmented flowers or leaves; greys and whites only distract.

Maximum value difference prevents too vivid complementary contrast: keep the yellow pure/pale, and lighten/tone down violet for less drama. Low-toned foliage.

Versatile and reliable: even equal blocks of pure hue can work as isolated incidents. Otherwise, tint or shade both or either. Add neighbouring yellow or violet into picture.

Equal areas of pure red and green are optically exhausting; tone down or blue both for a more harmonious effect, and/or tint the red. Or use purple or red-tinged foliage.

have a fixed relationship in the spectral wheel. Triads of colour based on rotating a triangle round the wheel so that the original three painter's primaries – yellow, red and blue – become desaturated and harmonious mixes as citrus/russet/slate or as buff/plum/sage combine in muted harmony. Another, more analytical, recommendation requires the visual field to add up to white light, drawing on the concept by which the light primaries of red, blue and green mix additively as light rays to become white light. Yet the triads are perhaps more suitable for textile design or interior decorating than for the garden, where greens in vegetation almost invariably predominate. Choosing a spectral wheel based on four 'primary' points – red, blue, green and yellow – will increase the relative area of 'cool' colours at the expense of the 'warmer' reds, oranges and yellows, and may be helpful and more realistic for the gardener, but still offers only a schematic guideline. The scientific theory of 'white' light seems of little practical application for the gardener gazing at a sunlit border and noting the dynamic quality of the colours as they seem to alter one another and as the light changes them. But if we dismiss the more abstract theories of colour harmonies as of little practical use in garden planning, we should not ignore their value as part of the gardener's intellectual equipment. His grasp and understanding of them may help him to make what seem to be instinctive or intuitive judgements.

The most useful and more immediately practical tools seem to be simpler. We have already mentioned the somewhat vague concept of 'balance'. One key to understanding it may lie in considering how nature composes a 'picture'. Strong incidents of intense colour, in nature, are usually seen against a larger background area of lower-toned contrast. Bright red poppies in a field would seem glaringly bright if the grass surrounding them was a pure green; in fact the larger grassy expanse is low-toned, composed of infinite gradations of greenishness, thus preventing blobs of red colour from appearing to be in a different and nearer planting plane. One can immediately think of successful colour contrasts of the same sort in the garden; perhaps a group of oriental red tulips surrounded by a haze of toned-down (i.e. darker, lighter or desaturated) blue massed forget-me-nots. Bright blue ceanothus might be underplanted with orange or bronze wallflowers of a low 'greyed' tone. In nature there are in fact relatively few pure hues, so it is not difficult for the gardener to surround a bright colour with larger areas of less intensity. In practice, it seems most satisfactory to team the lighter colours in tints with the darker colours in shades, rather than the other way round. It also works better to make the larger

stimulation of change, and perhaps on leaving the garden the visitor carries with him in his memory a series of impressions of colour rather than any analysis of the separate colour effects and associations he has seen. Yet these separate colour pictures are the tools of the garden artist or designer. Colour theorists have come up with a thousand recommendations to help people to combine colours in a pleasing way. Operating within the context of different cultures, and often strongly influenced by passing fashion (think of 'blue and green should never be seen'), they have brought to their task their personal predilections, as we all do, responding positively to some colour combinations, negatively to others. Just as the dimensions of colour have qualities which can be reduced to mathematical formulae, so some theorists have attempted to give scientific exactitude to aesthetics. There are systems which claim that the most pleasing colour combinations come from putting together certain colours which

OPPOSITE **This picture of a planting scheme in firm compartments demonstrates two tactics for combining a number of contrasting colours in one visual field. Horizontal lines of clipped box divide separate flower blocks and prevent their blending. The colours chosen are modified pure hues: spectral red has been paled to pink, blue is desaturated and covers a larger area, and cream tulips soften the glare of pure shining yellow. As the palest and most luminous of the spectral hues, yellow is instantly visible, demanding recognition and forcing the pink tulips to recede into the misty background of blue forget-me-nots.**

ABOVE **In a border of perennials, contrasts blend in cool drifts. Yellow thalictrum, dark blue salvia, misty mauve catmint and pinkish-mauve *Lythrum salicaria* have flower forms which weave together; the clearer shapes of bright yellow hemerocallis and the delphinium spires give the grouping definition.**

The effect is hotter, RIGHT, when the yellow has warmed almost to orange and the mauves have deepened into crimson phlox and violet *Salvia nemorosa* 'Superba'. Here the colours in solid blocks even if viewed from a considerable distance remain distinct and offer optical effects of simultaneous contrast rather than a gradual transition from one to another. Pale greenish-yellow alchemilla and solidago in the left foreground link the planting scheme with the lawn.

Complementary yellow and violet placed together as pure hues tend to look as different as possible and to make one another seem more brilliant, effects magnified by lightness and darkness contrast. Make a satisfying garden picture by modifying one or both of the pair of complementaries.

In the lacy web of climbers, ABOVE, the yellow and violet are tinted almost to maximum paleness, the flowers retaining just a hint of the spectral colour. *Clematis* 'Nellie Moser', cream climbing roses and *Wisteria floribunda* 'Macrobotrys' combine in an incident of garden colour that

weaves together the more substantial expanses of yellow-leaved *Robinia pseudoacacia* 'Frisia' to the left, the mass of wisteria foliage and the border planting below.

A far heavier and more dramatic contrast occurs BELOW, in a juxta-position of solid blocks of santolina, with tinted flowers of almost creamy-yellow, and *Salvia nemorosa* 'Superba', with deep rich velvety violet flowers. The exaggerated contrast due to the yellow's being in sunlight and the violet in shadow demonstrates the 'natural order' – where low-valued colours look best deepened beside those of lighter, high values.

area in any visual field low-toned, leaving pure hues to make the eye-catching but smaller incidents.

The most useful and reliable 'systems' for combining garden colours are based on the one hand on harmonies and on the other on contrasts. Remember that apart from any aesthetic implications, 'harmonies' in technical colour language means colours which are closely related because they share a pigment. The diagram of the spectral wheel is the most useful tool displaying these colours in their pure hues, but always remember that using pure colour as a basis for comparison creates an oversimplified situation. It is *all* the infinite variations in the qualities of colour, particularly those influenced by texture of flower or leaf, which interact with the constantly changing light to give the viewer more subtle and far-ranging impressions. A sequence of colours that are adjacent on the spectral wheel will – in theory – go together harmoniously. 'Contrast' sounds more dramatic: using two colours unrelated by mutual pigment implies a disruptive and perhaps restless effect, confusing the eye with conflicting demands. Among contrasts are those between complementary colours. Again, in the technical sense, these do not necessarily flatter each other: being opposites on the spectral wheel, each simply intensifies the other – for better or worse.

Describing the quality of colour is one of the most difficult and fascinating aspects of the subject. The observer is faced with a challenge whenever he tries to talk about, depict or reproduce the constantly changing colours that he sees. The layman is apt to scatter colour names and modifying terms such as shade, tint, tone and complement throughout his language, unaware that these terms have precise definitions and applications.

For everyday purposes it is often enough to say 'a green bush'. In doing so, the brain is simplifying the messages from the eye, which may be relaying patterns of silver light-reflecting leaf surfaces, almost black leaf-shadows – as well as a gamut of different greens in between. The brain selects as its standard the 'average' leaf seen in normal daylight, and chooses for convenience to remember this and to disregard the visual information about the shining silver and shadowy black elements of the picture, instead imposing this impression of 'average' greenness on the bush as a whole.

(The artist, on the other hand, may choose a range of different paints from his palette, running through the greens from near-black to white itself to depict each separate leaf surface and so convey his impression of the sunlit bush.)

The observer may further describe his bush or its leaf as olive-, sage- or bottle-green, or use other qualifying words to

A group of violet *Echinops ritro*, beloved by bees, stands out in clear contrast of form and colour against a cloud of golden rod. The yellow is luminous and bright, virtually the pure spectral hue, and the violet, although strong, pales and fades to a light steely mauve in the foreground, where it blends with foliage colours. The eye instinctively recognizes and appreciates contrast of dark violet and gleaming yellow, choosing to overlook the less effective foil where the large flower-head of pale mauve silhouetted to the right of the picture has become as pale as the yellow. If all the echinops heads appeared this pale, the colour association would seem weak and unsatisfactory.

specify the green quality, but such adjectives will evoke subjective images and associations in different observers, and precise colour-matching from such loose descriptive terms is invariably unreliable.

One answer from science is the systematic measurement of the light and pigment in the whole range of colours available in a given medium of paint, print, dye – whatever – which produces a series of colour swatches and reference numbers to which any sample can in the appropriate conditions of light be matched and classified. A side-effect of this scientific approach is some degree of standardization of descriptive terminology. The dimensions of colour, as we have seen, define the spectral colours in terms of three different dimensions – hue, value and intensity – and provide definitions of the terms shade, tint and tone.

Systems of colour measurement provide laboratory-controlled guidelines to the plant breeder and to the professional, but gardening is also an art, and for verbal descriptions of plant colour, we should perhaps be allowed a degree of metaphor. Very few words in the language pertain in the first place to colour: hue, dark and pale are examples. Few colour names, too, belong properly to the spectral hues: red, blue, green, and yellow – plus black, grey and white. All the remaining colour vocabulary draws in one way or another on analogy. Most names like orange, violet, gold and apricot are borrowed from other objects. Some of this process has become so familiar that we forget that harmonies, tones, chords and dissonant notes are images derived from music, and it is sometimes argued that these borrowed terms have measurable parallels with the original musical terms. Like a note in music, for example, the impression of a colour is indeed impossible to catch and to hold.

Colours adjacent on the spectrum may in principle be easier to use than contrasts, since they offer an easier transition for the eye, and it does not necessarily follow that these related combinations are less exciting and vibrant. Blued colours are renowned for their relatively gentle and receding qualities, unlike the optically demanding reds and yellows. Yet the group of delphinium, *Campanula lactiflora* and *Geranium psilostemon* in the border, LEFT, is as intense as possible. Simultaneous contrast pushes the blue and magenta farther apart, intensifying their differences. The dense forms of all three types of flower-head and the shapes of the plants themselves all reinforce the colour impact.

The colour incident, RIGHT, is a far subtler exercise in the use of much the same colour range, in an entirely different kind of planting. The common element is again blued pigment: in the muted green foliage, the crimson rose and the purple *Clematis × jackmanii* that wanders into the picture over the coppery leaves of *Berberis thunbergii* 'Atropurpurea'. Both pictures sing in dull or evening light, when blues always come into their own.

Some flowers have themselves contributed colour names: lavender, mauve, violet, lilac and rose are instances. Colours on shade cards are often prefixed by a more or less agreed qualifying term: forget-me-not-blue, olive-green, buttercup-yellow are derived from plants; fruits, other foods (salmon-pink), precious stones (turquoise), and everyday minerals (slate-grey), place names and even animal life contribute further elements of colour vocabulary.

However, even if we have accurate descriptions of flower and of leaf colour, they are hardly adequate if they allude to colour without mentioning texture, and the illusion created by mass or density, too, often forms an integral part of a description. In its material appearance a petal may be papery, shiny, velvety, thick, translucent; a leaf's surface texture may be glossy, matt, downy, corrugated, wax-coated. Both flower-heads and leaves may be held in dense clumps that reinforce the 'solid' appearance of their colour, or they may by their form or their shimmering movement incorporate a good deal of light – making their overall effect 'lightweight' and airy. A description of a plant's colour calls thus not only for some reference to its 'flat' or measurable shade-card colour, but also for some allusion to any textural or light-reflecting properties. To some extent the language of plant colour must be impressionistic: analogy and metaphor are admissible, as when trying to find ways to convey the elusive taste of a wine.

Colours can be filmy and atmospheric, like a crimson evening sky; in a garden, the crowded tiny heads of white gypsophila or a cloud of blue flax flowers have this quality. Colour can also have the depth and volume of a glass of red wine or the tightly packed and folded petals of a rose. Colour can be translucent, as in stained glass, or transparent, as in the paper-thin petals of romneya or cistus. Colour looks luminous when surrounded in a garden by lower and darker tones, and white and pale flowers glow like lamps in the dusk. Colours can be dull and matt-surfaced like suede, as in the felted hairy leaves of plants adapted to control respiration in hot climates, lustrous like velvet pansy petals, or metallic as in the tinsel-blue head of a garden thistle.

Nuances of colour are sometimes hinted at in the botanical Latin of a plant's specific epithet or cultivar name. There are nine or so terms for white other than the usual '*albus*'. *Candidus* describes an especially pure or shining white (*Lilium candidum, Galtonia candicans*); *dealbatus* suggests leaves slightly dusted with white, as in *Acacia dealbata*; *Salvia argentea* has silvery leaves. In the lower colour values, *nigrescens* moves towards black *niger*, and the prefix *atro-* suggests the subtle muted 'greyed' tones of the deep mysterious reds, for example *Cosmos atrosanguineus* and *Berberis thunbergii* 'Atropurpurea'. Other Latin adjectives such as *fulgens, metallicus* and *coruscans* denote some form of shining brilliance, while *tristis* and *sordidus*, discouraging though they sound, represent the gentler, subtler tones so necessary in garden pictures. The quality of colour as manifested in leaf texture is there in names such as *Dorycnium hirsutum* (implying hairiness), *Salix lanata* (woolliness) and *Populus canescens* (with a shining grey leaf).

The names of colours are no more than an aid to fix in the mind and memory the transient impressions of what one sees, and a tool to make easier and more accurate the comparisons between plants which may be the 'same' measurable colour, but which look quite different. It is perhaps more important to develop one's own private system of observing and memorizing, but any such process can only enrich and deepen the enjoyment of looking at garden colours.

CHAPTER III

THE WHITES

Pure white results when all light rays are reflected from a surface. Whiteness is maximum lightness; theoretically, the opposite is blackness, in a surface absorbing all light rays. Midway between the two, grey absorbs and reflects all light rays in equal proportions. The white surface of a page, a room with white walls or a landscape of snow creates an incomparable feeling of space, and neighbouring colours seem deeper and more glowing in contrast. The appearance of white depends on the texture; white paper can be rough or smooth, matt or shining, paint on walls can be glossy with highlights or matt-surfaced like whitewash on a garden wall. Snow appears white because of innumerable air spaces formed by ice crystals: a snow landscape yellowed by the sun's rays has complementary blue shadows, which gradually turn to green as the rays of evening light redden.

Nature uses white in some of its most beautiful pictures. On a grand scale magnificent white clouds shining in sunlight seem solid in deep blue sky, although we know them to be insubstantial. The jagged outlines of chalk cliffs, formed over millions of years by layers of minuscule shells, tower above the changing blues and greens of the sea – yet distance and atmosphere make their hardness seem soft and creamy. In a more domestic landscape, white fruit blossom in an orchard, white moon daisies in a green field and white florets of Queen Anne's lace in a hedgerow will shimmer like spangled silver to make unforgettable impressions. These satisfying pictures in the natural world suggest creating garden schemes where the only flower colour is white, seen at its best against a background of textured green and grey leaves.

Are white gardens popular because they are fashionable or because, as in interior decorating, white is considered 'safe'? Or is it that they strike a cool chord of simple restfulness away from the harsh discords of pure spectral colours and man-made dyes of garish hues?

Excessive hybridization by nurserymen in search of ever-brighter colours in flowers, often at the expense of form, fragrance and subtle gradation of colour, has led many a sophisticated gardener to search for a quieter mood, with plantings of white flowers weaving among textured leaves of silver, grey and green. Perhaps the idea of a white garden appeals for its simplicity; practically every common garden flower has a white form. But the sensitive gardener discovers that a white garden is not just a garden exclusively of white flowers marching in time through the flowering seasons. In the first place, the quality of whiteness is worth looking at. The eye can discern changes in whiteness by tiny degrees, and the very term 'white' comprehends its own spectrum of tints. Subtle gradations of colour and texture, shape and form, combine to transmit a variety of light reflections: white flowers are easily tinted by 'violet' shadows or by the complement of a neighbouring colour, challenging the very description of 'monochrome'. Even the rich whiteness of the 'Iceberg' rose – or the even more solidly white 'Frau Karl Druschki' – may be relieved by the tinted shadows of reflected light from neighbouring colours; a background of green yew makes white flowers seem pink-tinted, and all neighbouring flower colour in bright pure hues will similarly 'shadow' the whites with complementary tints.

Moreover, comparatively few flowers are pure white: most have faint touches of pink, creamy-yellow, ivory, soft grey or lavender, a petal gradating from pure white to stronger tints which blend to give an overall impression of these gentle soft colourings. Examined closely a white foxglove has purple guide-marks, a white mallow has delicate pink-veined petals, white iris have creamy-yellow falls, and California poppy (*Romneya coulteri*) has bright orange stamens, all colourings which faintly tinge the white with complementary shadows. Other 'whites' are subtle pale grey: *Campanula* 'Burghaltii' has large tubular bells of lilac-grey, and the spikes of *Lysimachia ephemerum* are the palest of greys, held above translucent grey-green leaves.

Texture, too, gives white flowers varying degrees of light reflection and absorption. Some petals, like those of tulips, are shining; others, like trumpet daffodils, are papery; flowers like cistus have petals resembling crumpled tissue paper – they are almost transparent and last only a day in the hot sun. A matt white surface becomes pearly, almost silver, when covered with minute velvety projections, and clouds of gypsophila, crambe and *Clematis recta* give a fragile, airy impression of white haziness. Lilies are waxy to the touch and glow with surface brightness, exciting even in the fierce light of a midday sun, and especially luminous when dusk falls, only relieved by tinted shadows of reflected light.

There are white flowers, though, whose effect when grouped in a clump is dazzling in its purity, and can make a contrast as harsh as any between bright hues. Containers of white petunias or white bedding *Lavatera* 'Mont Blanc' make solid white incidents in garden grouping. A pure white phlox draws the eye to the patch of bright, light colour it introduces into a border scheme. The form of the 'Iceberg' rose is reduced to a white glare when the contrast of a dark background is too strong. In general, light colours look better with white than dark colours which create too great a contrast. When using 'whites' formally to give architectural balance and symmetry, however, this contrast is exactly what is needed, although it would be out of place where soft delicate tints build up a whole garden picture. Pure whites strengthen and deepen but do not necessarily brighten neighbouring colours; white flowers can separate contrasting hues without altering their colour appearance and make seemingly garish or 'difficult' associations pleasing and acceptable. Bright white will light up a corner of woodland shade. With grey, white softens and lightens the heavy green foliage of high summer, whose very maturity and lushness can seem almost oppressive.

White flowers are an excellent choice for a garden that is visited on summer evenings, white flowers glowing like lamps

PREVIOUS PAGE **Sunlight and shadow give depth to the creamy clusters of** *Rosa longicuspis* **arching gracefully over an iron canopy and contrasting with the more solidly packed petals of the bush rose** *R.* **'Iceberg'. Box hedging makes a firm structural framework to contain the free-flowing flowers and mingling foliage greys.**

Informal white gardens that are based on no regular design rely on other elements for interest and structure. A block of white is so emphatic that repetition along a border instantly establishes a formal pattern; where 'natural' planting makes an asymmetrical design, the whites must form good overall shapes and be backed by a supporting cast of foliage plants.
RIGHT **Green and grey-leaved plants are tightly packed to give a feeling of luxurious growth. A bank of small white flowers of** *Campanula lactiflora* **makes a frothy cloud above equally ethereal lime-green plumes of** *Alchemilla mollis* **and feathery** *Artemisia canescens.*
OPPOSITE **Silhouetted delphinium spikes and drifts of unsophisticated cottage-garden valerian and** *Achillea ptarmica* **'The Pearl' are linked by** *Artemisia absinthium* **to make a more insubstantial effect.**

as dark colours fade to violet and blackness. At twilight when the eye gradually responds less to colour than to the degree of illumination, orange and red flowers and green leaves seem black, while blue and white flowers appear brighter and luminous. As darkness falls, white and pale pastels remain distinguishable until all light has gone.

White flowers, then, can be used in a garden in several different ways. How you use them will depend on your own inclination and training. White flowers can accentuate rigidity or soften and mellow the harshest conflicts. In some planting schemes they give emphasis and strong contrast. In other, more gentle and restful designs, white and tinted flowers are linked to background foliage by intermediary textured greys and greens which blend extremes of white and green in the eye to make a pool of light and soft intermingling texture. In an all-white garden clumps of isolated white flowers can stand out against a background of hard dark green yew or appear softer against a hedge of feathery

tamarisk or juniper. The background foliage may be interwoven greens and greys, enlivened like a tapestry by young foliage of yew and box, pale and shining against their own darker mature evergreen leaves. A clump of lilies or a white rose will stand out as an incident against mid-greens or in deliberate contrast to a dark colour in a border scheme. Contrasting clumps can be repeated as symmetrical accents to make planting more formal. At the opposite extreme you can intermingle white and pale-tinted flowers with greys and silvers so that they lose their individuality. Frothy clouds of creamy artemisias, *Crambe cordifolia*, giant gypsophila and ivory *Aruncus dioicus* give height. They may be linked with the silver foliage of a weeping pear, *Pyrus salicifolia* 'Pendula', or wavy-edged grey-leaved elaeagnus. Silver onopordon and lacy *Artemisia arborescens* and the pewter *A.* 'Powis Castle' may be interposed between 'white' and background colours. At lower levels little tanacetum, with leaves like feathers, and the much-loved *Stachys olympica* link white-flowering plants

with a foreground of green lawn, brick paths, paving or gravel. Foliage plants and grasses are as effective as white flowers in breaking firm decisive outlines and diminishing contrast: leaves and grasses variegated with white or cream give new textures and subtle pale shapes.

Formality comes from repetition of colour as much as from firmly cut geometric hedging or topiary, and a white garden can be intensely formal. White flower blocks emphasizing corners and dimensions will regulate an all-white garden; white flower blocks (or clumps of the 'white' effect of variegated foliage) can make a less structured garden scheme balanced and symmetrical. A rectangular bed of dwarf box may be starkly bedded out with massed white petunias or permanently planted with ground-hugging *Lamium maculatum* 'Album', the variegated leaves of which mingle with the white flowers. Further emphasis is given with white tulips in the spring. White bedding verbena and white tobacco plants look lovely in the same setting for later summer. A border of mixed planting will be given direction and coherence when clumps of white flowers are repeated at regular intervals.

White flowers are sympathetic to almost any garden materials. Climbing white-flowered clematis, roses and the tender white potato flower, *Solanum jasminoides* 'Album', look equally at home against painted trellis, walls of mellow brick, or climbing into the branches of an old fruit tree.

Cream and white variegated green leaves can be used in the same way as white flowers to make shimmering effects of light and shade, particularly effective when arching fronds are stirred by gentle breezes. In winter variegated evergreen shrubs such as buckthorn (*Rhamnus alaterna* 'Argenteo-variegata'), privet, Portuguese laurel (*Prunus lusitanica* 'Variegata') and variegated hollies will thrive in deep shade, while the rare variegated *Fatsia japonica*, as well as being evergreen, flowers in early autumn, its creamy panicles of globular flower-heads a welcome addition at this time of year. Where low-growing plants are desirable, variegated periwinkles (*Vinca major* and *V. minor*) need little full light, *Pachysandra terminalis* 'Variegata' (more interesting than its green form) and the aptly named new cultivar *Lamium* 'Beacon Silver' will glow in dark corners. In open positions the pale variegated leaves of deciduous dogwoods (*Cornus*), elder, kerria, philadelphus and weigela make attractive clumps behind white flowers, some of their leaves margined with cream and white, others with a central pale stripe, all most effective if given a contrasting background. Variegated perennials, too, are appropriate foils to white flowers, emerging at their most striking in early summer. Alpine strawberry (*Fragaria vesca*

Two pairs of associated plants making chiaroscuro patterns of texture and form provide a study in the qualities of whiteness. Substantial waxy petals with smooth light-reflecting surfaces seem whiter-than-white, their purity exaggerated by contrast with shadowed greens so dark they are almost black. Some intermediate flower or leaf tones are needed to link these two extremes and soften the hard monochrome effect.

Graceful massed florets of *Astrantia major*, ABOVE, contrast with the clear sculptural forms of *Lilium regale* flowers. Perfect companion plants, both thriving in moist rich soil, they each demonstrate that 'white' may be an oversimplified description. The lilies have distinct deep yellow centres, and their

pronounced three-dimensional form means that their whiteness is relieved by violet shadows. The astrantias are tinged with pink, a colour which is enhanced by contrast with complementary green, and the delicate shadows among the filigree dome of florets make a soft greyness to connect the extremes of light and dark. A twist of bindweed adds an unexpected link, too, between the plants.

Gleaming *Zantedeschia aethiopica* flowers, RIGHT, make an almost disembodied drift of shining white shapes, but their stark contrast is linked in both line and colour by spikes of creamy *Sisyrinchium striatum* in a dramatic but ephemeral display.

'Variegata'), semi-evergreen ajuga, astrantia, hosta and symphytum all have well-marked foliage, and often if firmly cut back in midsummer send up new fresh creamy or green shoots.

With such a profusion of white flowers to choose from, there is little difficulty in extending a white scheme over a long season. In late winter, as the days lengthen again, there are the honey-scented flowers of sweet box (*Sarcococca*) and the precious white form of the Algerian iris (*Iris unguicularis*) opens in mild spells. Snowdrops, crocus and leucojums spread in clumps under deciduous trees and shrubs, and make drifts in lawns. As spring arrives, white honesty, forget-me-nots and daffodils make informal clumps near early-flowering viburnums and in woodland *Anemone nemorosa*, both single and double forms, spread in deep leaf-mould, interplanted with the more exotic trilliums and erythroniums from North America. White tulips, white Brompton stock and the annual grey-leaved navelwort (*Omphalodes linifolia*) can be used more formally in beds or containers. The summer snowflake *Leucojum aestivum*, which confusingly flowers in spring, will make a green and white sheet among rose bushes, invasive but not damaging to their roots and vigour. In sheltered spots the daisy-flowered *Leucanthemum hosmariense* and *Anthemis cupaniana* begin their long flowering season, both with attractive grey leaves, those of the latter strangely musk-scented. They like to tumble forward over paving, making a rounded contrast to the sword-like leaves of iris which fan above them.

In an orchard, pear or cherry blossom makes white froth against the sky, while in the garden the weeping Japanese cherry, *Prunus* 'Shimidsu Sakura', with its dangling double white flowers, makes an accent of colour against a background green hedge or as a free-standing specimen is a focal point on a green lawn. In a villa garden in Tuscany, a white banksian rose clambers into a tall grey cedar, both silhouetted against the blue Italian sky.

As the season progresses, many shrubs come into flower, magnolias, spiraeas, scotch roses, more viburnums, and the indispensable *Choisya ternata*, with dense but glowing foliage. From earliest spring there are white and creamy clematis, small-flowered species which drape themselves like curtains over walls and trees. Double and single peonies (some *lactiflora* types with central orange stamens of eye-catching colour), iris, bearded and species, often with shading of lilac-blue or creamy bronze, are succeeded by campanulas, crambes and white dictamnus. In a white garden, grey, silver and glaucous foliage plants recover from the winter frosts and early pruning, and weave and intermingle to soften the strong contrast between white flowers and plain deep green leaves.

Stuartias, styrax and deutzia flower in summer and in sheltered gardens *Drimys winteri* and *Carpentaria californica* thrive against warm walls. The ghostly handkerchief tree, *Davidia involucrata*, is covered by its strange white bracts as the summer season of roses sets in, their first flush of flower completed before the main flowering period for hardy herbaceous perennials arrives. In mixed beds the scented philadelphus, with cistus and olearia, will give variety of form to companion hardy perennials, and self-seeding white valerian will flower in nearby paving or gravel giving a feeling of age and maturity.

Hebes, starting to flower a little later but continuing well into autumn, make useful rounded shapes and have glaucous or fresh green leaves to accompany their long white racemes. Hoherias, eucryphias and hydrangeas follow each other in flowering progression and white-flowered hostas look ethereal in deepest shade. Most lilies prefer woodland conditions, but can make clumps of colour in well-nourished open beds, or thrive in containers filled with suitable compost. The Madonna lily (*Lilium candidum*), however, prefers to be baked in full sun; in contrast the giant cardiocrinum needs cool rich loam and protection from the sun's rays. There are hardy white agapanthus as well as more tender types which need winter protection. They do not flower readily after replanting and like to be tightly packed in pots and left undisturbed for many years. Dimorphotheca, grey-leaved *Chrysanthemum foeniculaceum* and white petunias prolong seasonal colour, although a cream form of the latter, if seed can be obtained, is less glaring and solid. The soft grey leaves of *Helichrysum petiolatum* and those of its lime-yellow variants intermingle pleasantly with low-growing 'whites'. *Acidanthera murielae* (now sometimes *Gladiolus callianthus*) is a tender late-flowering bulb of elegant beauty, only matched by the spring-flowering *G. tristis* with its cream-flushed-green flowers of great delicacy. Both are very different in character from the coarse hybrids of the large-flowered class.

As summer fades, daisies, asters and another bulbous plant, *Galtonia candicans*, with colchicums, give a last burst of bloom. *Clematis flammula* and the creamy *C. rehderana* have small star-shaped cowslip-scented flowers and deserve a warm situation next to a tender evergreen shrub such as *Eupatorium ligustrinum*, which flowers until the end of the year, its flat clusters of white daisy-flowers faintly tinged with pink. The fragrant flowers of *Clerodendron trichotomum* last well and are followed by turquoise berries.

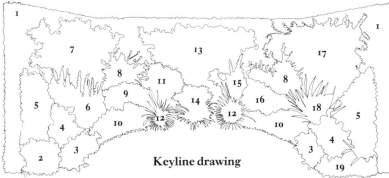

Keyline drawing

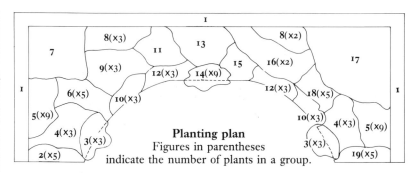

Planting plan
Figures in parentheses
indicate the number of plants in a group.

This planting for the sunny half of a 14 m (45 ft) square garden is at its best at midsummer. Grey and silver foliage separates the white flowers from the strong contrast of the surrounding yew hedge. The aromatic leaves of anthemis, artemisia, santolina and tanacetum give a Mediterranean flavour to a garden area planned for all-year-round interest. In well-drained soil these 'greys' keep form and colour even in harsh winters; in summer they become billowing feathery masses in contrast with the more solid outlines of the weeping grey pear, spiky iris and silvery thistles.

White is seen here in many different textures, and as soft creamy or lavender tints rather than as pure laundry-white. Two groups of tall nicotiana which replace early-flowering ivory-white tulips give symmetry round a central planting of agapanthus. Lichen-covered grey stones and a circular lily-pond help to give the garden structure, since planting is mainly informal. Clouds of filmy gypsophila balance the ethereal bushes of the tender *Chrysanthemum foeniculaceum* on the opposite side of the garden (not shown), where *Hydrangea arborescens*, late-flowering white hostas and eucryphias continue the theme in shade.

Plant key
1 *Taxus baccata*
2 *Dianthus* 'Mrs Sinkins'
3 *Anthemis cupaniana*
4 *Rosa* 'Moon Maiden'
5 *Nicotiana sylvestris* interplanted with earlier *Tulipa fosterana* 'Purissima'
6 *Lysimachia ephemerum*
7 *Hoheria glabrata*
8 *Onopordon acanthium*
9 *Gypsophila paniculata*
10 *Santolina neapolitiana*
11 *Artemisia arborescens*
12 *Helictotrichon sempervirens*
13 *Rosa* 'Pax'
14 *Agapanthus campanulatus* 'Albus'
15 *Artemisia* 'Powis Castle'
16 *Romneya coulteri*
17 *Pyrus salicifolia* 'Pendula'
18 *Iris florentina*
19 *Tanacetum haradjanii*

Nymphaea odorata 'Minor' in pool. *Lunaria annua* 'Alba' is allowed to seed in the background, and drifts of white *Viola septentrionalis* carpet the ground in spring.

WINTER

CAMELLIA

C. sasanqua has the glossy dark green leaves characteristic of the camellias (see Foliage framework: green). A warm frost-free climate suits the plant best, although hot summer sun and a sheltered site encourage the formation of buds in colder latitudes. Small fragrant flowers are carried from late autumn through the winter months. There are several good garden varieties, mainly Japanese bred, with single and double blooms of pink and rich red as well as white. *C.s.* 'Narumi-gata' has wide single petals, white with the edges tinted pink; 'Blanchette' is smaller and pure white.

SMALL EVERGREEN TREE FULL SUN ZONES 8-9

CHIMONANTHUS WINTER SWEET

C. praecox has rather waxy creamy-yellow flowers with purple-stained inner petals which are intensely fragrant, their heavy spicy scent almost overpowering when branches are brought into a small room. Plants take several years to flower. The cultivar *C.p.* 'Grandiflorus' has larger flowers, which are quite yellow in colour.

LARGE DECIDUOUS SHRUB FULL SUN ZONES 7-9

ERICA HEATH

Hardy ericas vary from prostrate mat-forming shrubs to the taller and more elegant tree heaths of the Mediterranean type. Most need a soil with low pH but are adaptable to alkaline areas with suitable peaty soil preparation and water-retentive mulches to build up humus. Many flower through the winter months giving valuable white and pink colour on grey days, when few other plants offer such consistent effects. The flowers are weather-resistant. After flowering is over, use sharp shears to trim into compact shape.

E. carnea (perhaps now correctly *E. herbacea*) 'Springwood White' is known as winter heath or snow heath. It carries white flowers in profusion from early winter to spring, and its spreading and ground-hugging nature prevents weed germination in summer.

SMALL EVERGREEN SHRUB FULL SUN OR HALF SHADE ZONES 5-8

GALANTHUS SNOWDROP

The characteristic white drooping flowers with green markings are familiar harbingers of spring. Easy to establish, especially if planted when beginning to grow or after flowering, snowdrops may be naturalized in drifts and clumps under deciduous trees and shrubs. They need light and air as flowers and leaves develop but require shade to keep roots cool in summer. The specialist will grow a number of species, but most gardeners grow single and double forms of the common snowdrop, *G. nivalis*.

BULB 7.5-15 CM (3-6 IN) HALF SHADE OR SHADE ZONES 4-8

IRIS

I. unguicularis 'Alba', the charming white form of the Algerian iris, is still rare, perhaps thriving less than the lilac-coloured type (see The blues: winter). A bed at the foot of a hot wall is a delight in winter, but certainly the best results are obtained in climates similar to that of its native Algerian hills.

EVERGREEN RHIZOME 38 CM (15 IN) FULL SUN ZONES 7-9

JASMINUM JASMINE

This is a large genus of mainly twining climbers, most with fragrant white, pink or yellow flowers. The common white jasmine, *J. officinale*, flowering in summer, is completely hardy. *J. polyanthum*, however, is generally grown as a conservatory plant, or pot-grown for bringing into the house from a frost-free glasshouse. The scented white flowers open from pink buds. Prune hard after flowering and feed during the summer.

EVERGREEN CLIMBER FULL SUN ZONES 9-10

LONICERA HONEYSUCKLE

A bushy shrub rather than a climber, *L. fragrantissima* carries highly scented flowers on bare twigs in late winter. Its flowers, and those of the very similar *L. standishii*, are tubular, carried in bunches and creamy-white.

MEDIUM DECIDUOUS SHRUBS FULL SUN OR HALF SHADE ZONES 6-9 See also Clear yellows: summer.

SARCOCOCCA

CHRISTMAS BOX, SWEET BOX
These little evergreen shrubs all flower in midwinter. The delicious vanilla fragrance from the tiny blooms wafts across a garden.

S. confusa and *S. ruscifolia* are similar in appearance, the former bearing black berries during the summer and the latter red ones. Glossy foliage which glows in the darkness beneath taller plants and a dense spreading habit make these shrubs attractive all year.

SMALL EVERGREEN SHRUBS SHADE ZONES 7-9 See also Foliage framework: green.

VIBURNUM

V. tinus, laurustinus, can flower almost all winter, the white flowers opening from pink buds. The flat corymbs are held above glossy green leaves. In mild gardens a laurustinus hedge is always decorative with metallic blue fruit, slightly concealed by the strong leaf growth in summer, and with its covering of attractive bloom in winter. It thrives in shade.

MEDIUM EVERGREEN SHRUB FULL SUN OR SHADE ZONES 6-9

Viburnum tinus

SPRING

AMELANCHIER SNOWY MESPILUS
A. laevis, sometimes confused with
A. canadensis or *A. lamarkii* (of gardens),
flowers in spring, white racemes appearing as
pink-tinted foliage unfurls. The foliage
assumes rich tints in autumn. It prefers acid
soil.
SMALL DECIDUOUS TREE OR LARGE SHRUB
FULL SUN   ZONES 5-9

ANEMONE WINDFLOWER
A. nemorosa, the European wood anemone,
thrives in woodland conditions under
deciduous trees or shrubs. Mulch with water-
retentive material. The rhizomes spread
rapidly and the plants also seed freely. The
white flowers, 2.5 cm (1 in) wide, rise above
deeply cleft leaves. Forms with pale blue
flowers are also attractive.
DECIDUOUS RHIZOME   15-23 CM (6-9 IN)
SHADE   ZONES 7-9

ARABIS
A. caucasica 'Flore Pleno' is the double form of
the little mat-forming white-flowered arabis,
so suitable for making neat cushions at the
front of sunny borders, or effective if allowed
to trail over the edge of a container planted
with mixed spring bulbs or antirrhinums. The
grey-green leaves are hoary. It needs to be
clipped and dead-headed after flowering is
over.
EVERGREEN PERENNIAL   23 CM (9 IN)
FULL SUN OR HALF SHADE   ZONES 6-9

BERGENIA
B. stracheyi has pink flowers in the rarely seen
species, but is more generally seen as the white
B.s. 'Alba'. The flowers are held above pretty
rounded leaves, much less coarse and invasive
than most bergenias, and worthy of a choice
site in semi-shade.
EVERGREEN PERENNIAL   23 CM (9 IN)
HALF SHADE   ZONES 6-9
B. 'Silberlicht' has pure white flowers which
turn pink as the flower-heads mature. The
leaves are large and untidy, but the flowers are
among the most attractive of the genus. Plant
to edge a bed of lenten hellebores and
intermingle with the little black-stemmed *Aster
divaricatus* which has white daisy-flowers in
late summer.
EVERGREEN PERENNIAL   30 CM (12 IN)
HALF SHADE   ZONES 6-9
See also Foliage framework: green.

CHOISYA
C. ternata, Mexican orange, is a splendid
glossy-leaved shrub (see Foliage framework:
green) which in spring is covered with sweet-

scented flowers resembling orange-blossom.
The flowers often appear again in late summer.
In a cold garden it needs to grow against a
warm wall. Alternatively, grow it in a pot to
bring indoors for early flowering.
MEDIUM EVERGREEN SHRUB
FULL SUN OR HALF SHADE   ZONES 7-9

CLEMATIS
Clematis prefer their roots in shade in rich
fertile soil, allowing twining stems to reach into
the light for maximum flowering. Protect
against slug damage in early spring and spray
when giving regular doses against botrytis to
peonies and lilies. Even so, mysterious 'wilt'
can kill a well-established plant. Species
clematis usually have small nodding flowers of
white or muted pale colours; large-flowered
hybrids are very decorative with wide open
stronger-coloured flowers of blue, violet and
deep red. Guide the climbing stems with
careful tying and encouragement to make
elegant fan-shapes on walls rather than
bunched untidy stems. In general, species and
spring-flowering clematis need little pruning;
others, including large-flowered hybrids,
flower best if winter-pruned.
    In a favoured site the evergreen *C. armandii*
and *C. cirrhosa balearica* will prosper.
C. armandii has glossy leaves composed of
three long leaflets, and creamy-white axillary
clustered flowers. Seedlings often grow into
insignificant plants, so take internodal cuttings.
Give a sheltered site where a plant may
scramble into a small tree. *C. cirrhosa balearica*
has ferny leaves; the creamy drooping bell-
shaped flowers have insides spotted in purple.
They begin to appear in winter and are
followed by silky seed-heads which look
attractive all summer.
EVERGREEN CLIMBERS
FULL SUN, ROOTS IN SHADE   ZONES 7-9

ERYTHRONIUM DOGTOOTH VIOLET
E. revolutum has several good forms of white
and yellow. Beautiful mottled leaves of shining
green and bronze appear in early spring. *E.r.*
'White Beauty' has white reflexed petals on
stiff stems. Clumps of these hardy small plants
from north-west America are among the most
desirable early flowerers in any garden.
Anemone nemorosa, the wood anemone, makes
an attractive companion plant in cool soil, and
arching stems of Solomon's seal can rise
behind, its white lily-of-the-valley flowers
extending the season. Interplanted drifts of
blue anemone (forms of *A. blanda*, *A. nemorosa*
and *A. apennina*) also look harmonious.
CORM   23 CM (9 IN)   HALF SHADE
ZONES 5-9

FRITILLARIA FRITILLARY
The white form of the beautiful snake's head
fritillary, *F. meleagris*, appears almost as
frequently as the type with its purple
chequered markings. Bell-shaped flowers
dangle singly or in pairs on long, slim stalks
with scattered grey-green leaves. A European
native, it is found in damp meadows but grows
well in dry gardens. Grow it in grass or
scattered through shrubberies; effective with
bright carmine *Cyclamen repandum*, blue scilla
or omphalodes, or, perhaps best of all, alone in
drifts in grass.
BULB   30 CM (12 IN)
FULL SUN OR HALF SHADE   ZONES 6-9

Erythronium revolutum 'White Beauty'

Anemone nemorosa

Helleborus orientalis

Iberis sempervirens

HELLEBORUS HELLEBORE

H. corsicus has pendent creamy-green clustered flowers above superb grey-green leaves. It revels in cool, rich soil and flowers over a long period, seeding freely *in situ*. It and the hybrids of the lenten hellebore, *H. orientalis*, grow well together, the latter having wide-open nodding flowers that may be white, blush-pink to purple or purple-spotted. Lilies are excellent companion plants, their young shoots enjoying the low shade created by hellebore foliage.
SEMI-EVERGREEN PERENNIAL
45-60 CM (18-24 IN)   SHADE   ZONES 6-9
See also Foliage framework: green.

IBERIS CANDYTUFT

I. sempervirens is a low spreading plant, its dark green leaves covered in white (sometimes pink-tinted) flowers for many weeks. Trim it after flowering to make a tidy compact shape. The dark leaves make it a valuable 'anchor' plant all year; the white flowers are a welcome block of spring colour.
EVERGREEN PERENNIAL   23 CM (9 IN)
FULL SUN   ZONES 5-9

LEUCOJUM SNOWFLAKE

L. aestivum, the summer snowflake, thrives in damp water meadows, producing white flowers, marked in green, on long stems. It is at its best naturalized in grass, each plant readily increasing in rich soil. A form 'Gravetye Giant', selected many years ago by William Robinson, is probably the best.
BULB   60 CM (24 IN)   HALF SHADE
ZONES 7-9

LUNARIA HONESTY

L. annua 'Alba', the white form of the common biennial honesty (see Strong reds: early summer), has typical, rather coarse, green toothed leaves and cross-shaped cruciferae flowers. It seeds true, and so is a useful background plant in a white garden. The papery seed-pods are attractive for indoor decoration.
EVERGREEN BIENNIAL   60 CM (24 IN)
FULL SUN OR HALF SHADE   ZONES 6-9

MAGNOLIA

M. × soulangiana is perhaps the best loved, deservedly, of spring-flowering shrubs. The large tulip-shaped white flowers, opening before the leaves unfurl, have rose-purple stains at their base. Though tolerant of town pollution, it prefers acid soils, as do most magnolias. As a lawn specimen it grows to be a small spreading tree; against a wall it will double its size over the same period of years. Grow a carpet of spring bulbs or autumn-flowering *Cyclamen hederifolium* at its feet.
SMALL DECIDUOUS TREE   FULL SUN
ZONES 7-9
M. stellata is a rounded bush taking many years to grow large, but flowering when still young. It is most useful in a small garden, the white star-shaped flowers opening from grey hairy winter buds and covering the branches. Underplant it with the later-flowering primrose-yellow Welsh poppy, *Meconopsis cambrica*, and allow autumn-flowering blue gentians to glow under its light canopy of green foliage.
MEDIUM DECIDUOUS SHRUB   FULL SUN
ZONES 7-9
See also Foliage framework: green.

NARCISSUS

Choose miniature *N. bulbocodium*, *N. cyclamineus* or their hybrids for special positions where they will be undisturbed. Most have creamy-white petals, and larger, more robust hybrids, from the Triandrus division, have pale cream back-swept petals and white rounded cups: *N.* 'Thalia' and 'Tresamble' make lovely groups for naturalizing in drifts in grass. For a cool greenhouse, or for forcing, the Tazetta narcissus 'Paper White' has clustered heads of cream and papery-white.
BULBS   10-30 CM (4-12 IN)
FULL SUN OR HALF SHADE   ZONES 6-8
See also Clear yellows: spring.

OMPHALODES

O. linifolia, Venus's navelwort, is now rather rare. It is an annual, best sown in early spring from the previous year's seed. It is inclined to damp off if overwintered and is often eaten by slugs if put outside too soon. The flowers are charming, a sort of almost bluish-white, and the leaves are a pale silvery-grey. Grow it in a pot to make a white froth of delicate blossom.
ANNUAL   30 CM (12 IN)   FULL SUN
ZONES 6-9

ORNITHOGALUM

O. umbellatum, star of Bethlehem, bears a corymb of white star-shaped flowers with strange green outer stripes on the petals. Plant in October in beds or naturalize in short grass.
BULB   10-30 CM (4-12 IN)
FULL SUN OR HALF SHADE   ZONES 6-9
O. nutans has nodding, bell-shaped flowers on erect stems, silvery-white with a broad green stripe on the outside of each petal. Very easily grown, allow to form clumps in shrubberies.
BULB   20-45 CM (8-18 IN)
FULL SUN OR HALF SHADE   ZONES 7-9

OSMANTHUS

O. delavayi has dark glossy leaves and a neat, compact habit. The small white flowers are very fragrant, smothering the shrub in late spring. The flowers are tubes 1.2 cm (½ in) long and similarly wide at the mouth, held in axillary clusters. The plant is hardy and adaptable, preferring an open situation but not fussy about soil.
MEDIUM EVERGREEN SHRUB   FULL SUN
ZONES 7-9

PAEONIA PEONY

P. emodii has graceful arching stems, pure papery-white flowers with golden stamens and luxuriant green leaves. Grow it behind strong clumps of hellebores where a canopy of light foliage protects it from fierce sun.
DECIDUOUS PERENNIAL   90 CM (36 IN)
HALF SHADE   ZONES 6-9
P. lactiflora and the earlier-flowering *P. officinalis* both have white forms, and thrive in rich well-manured soil. *P.l.* 'Duchesse de Nemours' is double, white and very fragrant.
DECIDUOUS PERENNIAL   60-90 CM (24-36 IN)
FULL SUN   ZONES 6-9
P. suffruticosa 'Rock's Variety' has typical elegant Moutan foliage and semi-double white

Prunus 'Shirotae'

flowers with a maroon-crimson blotch at the base of each petal. Try to obtain this rare plant which fits into any scheme.
MEDIUM DECIDUOUS SHRUB   FULL SUN
ZONES 6-9
See also Foliage framework: green.

PIERIS
White pitcher-shaped flowers are held among bright red or pink juvenile foliage (see Strong reds: foliage). Flowers and young growth need protection from late frost.

P. 'Forest Flame' has brilliant red young leaves which gradually turn pink, then green. The white flowers are in large terminal panicles. One of its reputed parents, *P. japonica*, is hardy and frost-resistant, with glossy, coppery foliage, and forms exist with pink flowers. One of the best whites is *P.j.* 'Purity'.

P. *formosa forrestii* has different clones such as 'Jermyn's' and 'Wakehurst', with larger white flowers than the type.
MEDIUM EVERGREEN SHRUB   HALF SHADE
ZONES 7-9

PRIMULA
P. japonica 'Postford White', a candelabra type with flowers arranged in whorls up the tall stems, has broad crinkled green leaves and white flower tiers. Like most Japanese plants, it needs acid soil. Plant in drifts in damp, rich ground and make sure it does not dry out in summer.
DECIDUOUS PERENNIAL   60 CM (24 IN)
FULL SUN OR HALF SHADE   ZONES 6-9

PRUNUS FLOWERING CHERRY
Prunus covers a wide range of evergreen and deciduous flowering shrubs and small trees, but here we consider the flowering cherries, which are perhaps best known as the very free-flowering Japanese hybrids, indispensable small trees for modest-sized gardens. Careful choice will ensure steady flowering progression from midwinter right into the summer season.

P. 'Shimidsu Sakura' (syn. *P. serrulata longipes*) is a small spreading tree with drooping branches from which are suspended long-stalked pendulous clusters of double white flowers, pink-tinted in bud. Plant as individual lawn specimens or, if scale permits, in pairs to frame a path or doorway.

P. 'Shirotae' has large double or semi-double white flowers, held in drooping clusters, among fresh, young green leaves. 'Tai Haku' has large, single white flowers and rich copper-red young foliage. It grows more upright than the former two, which have almost a weeping habit.
SMALL DECIDUOUS TREES
FULL SUN OR HALF SHADE   ZONES 6-9

PYRUS PEAR
P. communis is the common or garden pear, still to be seen in old gardens and orchards. With black bark, glossy green leaves and white blossom in spring, it rivals many ornamental small trees for charm. It is now difficult to obtain, new modern hybrids being more valuable for fruit quality and quantity. Grow some of the old forms such as *P.c.* 'Doyenne du Comice' and 'Pitmaston Duchess' as espaliers, trained on wires to give formality.
SMALL DECIDUOUS TREE   FULL SUN
ZONES 6-9

RHODODENDRON

R. 'Fragrantissimum' is tender, needing a conservatory or cold greenhouse. The flowers are held in umbels of three or four and are funnel-shaped, richly scented, white flushed rosy-pink. The leaves are dark green and corrugated.
MEDIUM EVERGREEN SHRUB   FULL SUN
ZONES 8-9
R. 'Loder's White' is dome-shaped, handsome foliage clothing the bush to the ground. Flowers form conical trusses of about twelve, pink in bud, opening to white edged with pink, with a scattering of mauvish spots.
LARGE EVERGREEN SHRUB   HALF SHADE
ZONES 7-9
R. 'Mount Everest' is very vigorous and flowers freely. Narrow bell-shaped pure white flowers with brown specks are held in a thick truss.
LARGE EVERGREEN SHRUB   HALF SHADE
ZONES 7-9
R. decorum is one of the most desirable of this wide-ranging genus. Funnel-shaped spotted fragrant flowers can be white or shell-pink and are carried freely in lax trusses. The leaves, up to 15 cm (6 in) in length, are glabrous.
LARGE EVERGREEN SHRUB   HALF SHADE
ZONES 7-9
See also Pinks and mauves: spring.

SMILACINA

S. racemosa, also known as false Solomon's seal, is a woodlander needing rich, deep soil. Arching stems bear veined pale green leaves.

Smilacina racemosa

Fluffy cream flower-plumes have a delicious lemon scent. A most desirable plant associating with spring bulbs to give extra foliage interest and height. Grow in half shade or in moist soil, with companion planting of emerging rodgersia leaves.
DECIDUOUS PERENNIAL   60-90 CM (24-36 IN)
HALF SHADE   ZONES 8-9

SPIRAEA

Spiraeas are hardy, undemanding shrubs thriving in any soil, in sun or shade. One of the best, and most well known, is *S.* × *arguta*, the bridal wreath, which has arching branches, conspicuously brown in winter, studded with pure white clustered flowers in spring. Prune the flowering shoots hard as blossom dies. *S. thunbergii* is similar, with paler foliage and a more twiggy, compact habit.
MEDIUM DECIDUOUS SHRUB
FULL SUN OR HALF SHADE   ZONES 6-9

TULIPA TULIP

Blocks of creamy-white tulips for a separate garden area are formal and dramatic, heralding a new season of colour planting quite different from the natural drifts of snowdrops in woodland or carpets of early crocus on a green lawn. There is nothing casual about the planting of highly bred, aristocratic tulips. Shapely leaves of green or grey-green and sculptured flower-heads make a deliberate garden impact, improved by a formal repetition of the blocks of colour in beds or containers, or

Zantedeschia aethiopica 'Crowborough'

alongside a path to emphasize direction.
T. fosteriana 'Purissima', 38 cm (15 in), has large outer petals of milky-white to cream. The grey-green leaves are attractive long before the flower-stems emerge. Single Early *T.* 'White Hawk', 30 cm (12 in), has tighter globular heads of white petals. Double Early *T.* 'Schoonord' is a large-flowered pure white, 30 cm (12 in). The taller Mendel tulip, *T.* 'White Sail', is a creamy-white, 40 cm (16 in).
BULBS   FULL SUN   ZONES 5-9
See also Clear yellows: spring.

VIBURNUM

V. × *burkwoodii* is one of the best hybrids, with scented pink-tinted white flowers carried in profusion for many weeks. Dark green leaves are brownish-grey and felted on the undersides. It is quite hardy, and happy in acid or alkaline soils. A warm wall and protection from cold winds will ensure optimum performance. There are various clones derived from it, but it remains an outstanding asset in any garden.
MEDIUM EVERGREEN SHRUB
FULL SUN OR HALF SHADE   ZONES 7-9
See also Foliage framework: green.

VIOLA
PANSY, VIOLET, HEART'S EASE
Bedding pansies may be sown the previous summer for winter and spring flowering. They make ideal pot plants, surviving extremes of cold, and if planted in good time before the first frosts will continue in flower for six months. Certainly they are among the best plants for spring show in cold climates.
V. 'Mount Everest' has large, plain white flowers, unmarked with typical pansy patterns. Sow in midsummer, prick out and establish in flowering site before autumn.
BIENNIAL   23 CM (9 IN)   FULL SUN
ZONES 4-9
V. septentrionalis has low-growing green leaves attractive in midsummer and beautiful, but scentless, white flowers.
DECIDUOUS PERENNIAL   15 CM (6 IN)
HALF SHADE OR SHADE   ZONES 5-9

ZANTEDESCHIA

Z. aethiopica, the hardy arum, is usually seen in its 'Crowborough' form, which grows splendidly in rich, moist soil. Leaves often get nipped with frost but, once well established, the white arum flowers are pure and beautiful, especially by the side of natural or ornamental water. Cover the crowns with a protective mulch in winter.
DECIDUOUS PERENNIAL   100 CM (40 IN)
FULL SUN   ZONES 8-10

EARLY SUMMER

ANTHEMIS
A. cupaniana needs a dry sunny well-drained site, where it can sprawl, its white daisy-flowers carried over a very long period above silver dissected leaves. It gets untidily woody after a few seasons, so look out for self-sown seedlings, or overwinter easily rooted cuttings, for replacements. Plant with white tulips or close to other 'silvers', where contrasting leaf textures make a pattern of silver and grey.
SMALL EVERGREEN SHRUB   FULL SUN
ZONES 7-9

CAMASSIA QUAMASH
C. leichtlinii, normally blue (see The blues), has a garden form with delicate creamy flowers. Grow between later-flowering herbaceous plants, which obscure the withering laxly bending leaves.
BULB   90-120 CM (36-48 IN)
FULL SUN   ZONES 6-9

CAMPANULA
There are white forms of many of the different blue border and creeping campanulas (see The blues: summer). *C. carpatica, C. latifolia, C. latiloba, C. persicifolia* and *C. cochlearifolia* all have 'Alba' forms.
C. 'Burghaltii' has grey hooded flowers, perfect to tone with purer whites and purples. Large drooping bells sometimes need support for their slender stems. It is rare and desirable.
DECIDUOUS PERENNIAL   60 CM (24 IN)
FULL SUN   ZONES 7-9

CARPENTARIA
C. californica produces lovely saucer-shaped pure white flowers with conspicuous yellow anthers. In a good year this wall shrub is covered with bloom; after a hard winter the green leaves are unsightly and need careful pruning so as not to lose flowering shoots.
MEDIUM EVERGREEN SHRUB   FULL SUN
ZONES 8-10

CENTRANTHUS VALERIAN
C. ruber 'Albus', the white form of ordinary red-flowering valerian, is lovely if allowed to seed haphazardly in cracks and crannies. An old wall with scattered plants in flower gives a feeling of maturity to a garden. Tiny flowers are grouped on long heads above fleshy leaves.
EVERGREEN PERENNIAL OR BIENNIAL
60-90 CM (24-36 IN)   FULL SUN   ZONES 7-9

CERASTIUM
C. tomentosum, snow in summer, makes a low mat of silver, densely covered in short-stemmed saucer-shaped white flowers. Grow it to drape a wall, in paving, or at the front of a bed. It is charming but spreads fast.
EVERGREEN PERENNIAL   7-15 CM (3-6 IN)
FULL SUN   ZONES 5-9

CISTUS SUN ROSE
The sun roses, as well as having attractive evergreen foliage (see Foliage framework: green), flower very freely with lovely white or pinkish papery flowers. Many species or hybrids have flowers with basal blotches or stains on the petals. Flowers smother bushes and open with the sun. Plant these sun-lovers on sloping dry banks. None have a long life-expectancy, but cuttings strike easily in grit.
C. × *corbariensis*, one of the most hardy, has crimson-tinted buds which open pure white. It has hairy leaves. *C. populifolius*, one of its parents, has larger poplar-like leaves, and flowers have yellow stains at the base.
C. *ladanifer*, the gum cistus, has sticky green metallic leaves; flowers are white with chocolate-purple stains on each petal.
C. *laurifolius*, tall and tough, the leaves dark green and glabrous above and white-felted below, has yellow-centred white flowers. Probably the hardiest cistus.
SMALL OR MEDIUM EVERGREEN SHRUBS
FULL SUN   ZONES 7-9

CLEMATIS
Early-summer clematis, which require little seasonal pruning (only enough to keep a vigorous plant from spreading beyond its allotted space) make curtains of blossom over high walls or will cascade out of trees. Twining stems quickly cover unsightly sheds or stumps.
C. *chrysocoma* and its variety *C.c. sericea* (syn. *C. spooneri*) grow to only 3 m (10 ft) and flower freely. The white flowers, delicately tinged pink, are produced on single stalks. The latter, although hardier and more rampant, has a shorter flowering season while the species, flowering also on the current year's wood,

Anthemis cupaniana

Cistus ladanifer

Crambe cordifolia

Convolvulus cneorum

extends its beauty for many weeks.

C. montana in the species has pure white flowers, each individually wider and more showy than those of *C. chrysocoma.* It is completely hardy, as are its varieties and cultivars, many of which have pink-tinted petals. For any garden of reasonable size this clematis is a must; its white curtain is the perfect foil to neighbouring glossy green foliage and to 'silvers', or forms a backcloth to yellow flowers of the early-flowering shrub roses.
DECIDUOUS CLIMBERS
FULL SUN OR HALF SHADE, ROOTS IN SHADE
ZONES 4-7
See also spring, above.

CONVALLARIA LILY OF THE VALLEY
C. majalis needs shade and well-prepared and enriched soil. *C.m.* 'Fortin's Giant' is a slightly taller, strong-growing form. The plants are slow to establish but once satisfied will thrive. The flowers are deliciously fragrant and are often grown for picking; later the leaves make impenetrable cover.
DECIDUOUS PERENNIAL   23 CM (9 IN)
SHADE   ZONES 6-9

CONVOLVULUS
C. cneorum has pink buds opening to ivory-white single flowers above silver leaves. Its delicate subtle colouring makes it a perfect foil to all garden colour. A warm sunny site with excellent drainage is essential, or grow plants in pots, and give winter protection.
SMALL EVERGREEN SHRUB   FULL SUN
ZONES 7-9

CORNUS DOGWOOD
C. kousa and *C. nuttallii* have conspicuous white bracts above typical veined leaves. Making small trees or large shrubs in an average garden, both these dogwoods prefer deep, lime-free soil, but *C. kousa* has a Chinese form, *C.k. chinensis*, which is more lime-tolerant. Plant in woodland with some light shade from the fiercest summer sun.
LARGE DECIDUOUS SHRUB OR SMALL TREE
HALF SHADE   ZONES 6-9
See also Clear yellows: foliage.

CRAMBE KALE
C. cordifolia, colewort, with its huge rough cabbage-shaped leaves and tall stems of cloud-like tiny white flowers, is a wonderful perennial. It flowers early, needs no staking, and contributes architectural quality, so often lacking in flowering border plants. Grow it on a corner, at the back of a border, and against a dark background. The roots are deep and it needs several years to establish before performing at its best.
DECIDUOUS PERENNIAL   1.8 M (6 FT)
FULL SUN   ZONES 6-9

CRATAEGUS THORN
C. × lavallei is a small tree with a dense head and long glossy leaves; it is smothered in season with white single open flowers, followed by orange-red fruits. Lovely at the edge of a garden; one of the best small trees to tolerate wind and drought.
SMALL DECIDUOUS TREE   FULL SUN
ZONES 6-9

DAVIDIA
HANDKERCHIEF, DOVE OR GHOST TREE
D. involucrata takes a few years to establish and flower. Thereafter it is usually covered annually with strange, unequal-sized, paired white bracts; unusual as well as beautiful. One at Hidcote in Gloucestershire is quite famous. It is best as a specimen tree, too splendid and ephemeral to fit into a colour scheme. Any decent soil suits it.
SMALL DECIDUOUS TREE   FULL SUN
ZONES 7-9

DEUTZIA
Deutzias are easily grown mostly hardy garden shrubs with white or pink flowers. All need the flowering shoots cut out as they wither. Ordinary soil and plenty of moisture-retentive compost encourage flowering.
D. chunii has flowers with petals white inside and pink outside, in panicles held along elegant arching branches. It tends to flower later if grown in shade.
D. gracilis flowers early and may be forced, in a greenhouse, to flower for the house in late winter. Outside in cold gardens it may be damaged by late spring frosts.
MEDIUM DECIDUOUS SHRUBS   FULL SUN
ZONES 5-9

DICENTRA
D. eximia 'Alba' bears nodding white flowers above decorative glaucous ferny leaves. Use it in a white and grey garden.
DECIDUOUS PERENNIAL   30-45 CM (12-18 IN)
FULL SUN   ZONES 6-9

DICTAMNUS
D. albus, burning bush, has aromatic leaves and white flowers carried in erect spikes. It is worthy of a choice site in a white garden, or will eventually make a sturdy clump in a mixed border. Leaves in spring may be attacked by slugs.
DECIDUOUS PERENNIAL   45-90 CM (18-36 IN)
FULL SUN   ZONES 7-9
See also Pinks and mauves: early summer.

DRIMYS
D. winteri, Winter's bark, is a most handsome plant for a sheltered garden. Grown in the open it will make a pyramid shape, but against a wall the branches may be encouraged to grow horizontally and extra heat encourages flowering. A form *D.w. latifolia* is hardier, with wider green leaves, copper-tinted when young. In both, flowering is free, white scented flowers with creamy edges covering the bushes after a mild winter.
LARGE EVERGREEN SHRUB   FULL SUN
ZONES 8-9

GERANIUM CRANE'S BILL
The hardy herbaceous geraniums are mostly deciduous and among the most decorative and useful garden plants. Happy in ordinary soil, in sun or light shade, they cover a wide range of flower colour from blue, violet, purple and pink to white. Most make mounds, spreading under deciduous shrubs, or may be planted in groups in border colour schemes.
G. renardii has grey-green velvety leaves and white, almost grey, flowers with maroon veins.

Plants are slow to establish and prefer full sun.
DECIDUOUS PERENNIAL   23 CM (9 IN)
FULL SUN   ZONES 6-9
G. sylvaticum 'Album' has fresh green leaves and white flowers, is tough and spreads fast.
DECIDUOUS PERENNIAL   60 CM (24 IN)
FULL SUN OR SHADE   ZONES 6-9
G. pratense, meadow crane's bill, has a double white form, *G.p.* 'Plenum Album', of great charm. The flowers of 'Striatum' are speckled and pale grey. Increase by division; seedlings may be pale violet-blue, as in the wild type.
DECIDUOUS PERENNIAL   90 CM (36 IN)
FULL SUN OR SHADE   ZONES 6-9

HALESIA SNOWDROP TREE
H. carolina drapes its branches with white bell-shaped flowers. It needs a lime-free soil and generally flowers before the leaves emerge.
SMALL DECIDUOUS TREE   HALF SHADE
ZONES 6-9

HESPERIS
H. matrionalis, sweet rocket, is a tall plant for open shrubberies. Branching stems carry sweet-scented flowers, especially fragrant in the evenings. Sow seed the previous summer; flowers vary from white to shades of lilac-pink. A double form is now regrettably rare.
SEMI-EVERGREEN PERENNIAL
90-120 CM (36-48 IN)
FULL SUN OR HALF SHADE   ZONES 5-9

IRIS
I. orientalis (*I. ochroleuca* of gardens) makes clumps of stiff sword-like stems. Plants quickly increase and spread once established in good rich moist soil. The flowers are white with a broad yellow stripe in the recurving falls. If possible grow it where foliage will hide the dying iris stems later in the season. Rodgersias and rheums love similar conditions.
DECIDUOUS PERENNIAL   60-120 CM (24-48 IN)
FULL SUN OR HALF SHADE   ZONES 6-9
There are several good forms of Bearded iris with white-tinged green, blue or cream flowers, which look soft and harmonious among pure intense whites. To avoid staking, choose one of medium height, such as the old *I.* 'Helen Mackenzie'.
DECIDUOUS RHIZOMES   75-150 CM (30-60 IN)
FULL SUN   ZONES 6-9
See also Foliage framework: silver and grey.

MAGNOLIA
M. wilsonii has pendulous saucer-shaped white flowers with red stamens. Plant on a bank in order to look upwards into the hanging flowers. A wide spreading shrub, tolerant of lime, and happiest in light shade, it will flower when quite small, especially if not allowed to dry out in summer, so keep well mulched.
LARGE DECIDUOUS SHRUB   HALF SHADE
ZONES 7-9
See also Foliage framework: green.

MALUS FLOWERING CRAB
M. hupehensis grows stiffly into an upright branched tree. Pink-tinted buds open to white scented flowers which are very freely carried. It is in the top class of flowering crabs. In spring the young leaves are purple-tinted and in autumn the small fruits are yellow blushed red.
M. × 'John Downie', perhaps the best fruiting crab, has white flowers and conical orange and red fruit, perfect for jam-making, and very ornamental in late summer.
SMALL DECIDUOUS TREES   FULL SUN
ZONES 6-9

MYRRHIS
M. odorata, sweet Cicely, has lovely divided ferny leaves and white cow-parsley flowers carried in flat umbels. It seeds freely and will colonize a rough corner. It smells of liquorice.
DECIDUOUS PERENNIAL   60 CM (24 IN)
FULL SUN OR HALF SHADE   ZONES 5-9

OLEARIA
Most of the olearias with their excellent evergreen foliage (see Foliage framework: silver and grey) have attractive white daisy-flowers that make a good contribution to a white scheme.
O. × *scilloniensis*, a garden hybrid, has pale grey-green leaves and white flower trusses, the small daisy-flowers carried very freely. One of the hardier olearias, it may make a pleasant

Clematis montana

Myrrhis odorata

contribution on the edge of a shrubbery or in a border scheme. The leaves are valuable in winter, and the habit shapely.
MEDIUM EVERGREEN SHRUB   FULL SUN
ZONES 8-10
O. cheesemanii has grey-green leaves with white or buff undersides. It is also tough and a very ready flowerer.
SMALL EVERGREEN SHRUB
FULL SUN OR HALF SHADE   ZONES 8-10
O. × mollis, with almost silver leaves, needs hot sun but the roots must be kept moist in summer. A good ornamental plant for a 'silver' border, white daisy-flowers mingling with the leaves.
SMALL EVERGREEN SHRUB   FULL SUN
ZONES 8-10

Trillium grandiflorum

Sanguinaria canadensis 'Flore Pleno'

PHILADELPHUS MOCK ORANGE
All philadelphus have white scented flowers and are a most useful genus for woodland and open border planting. The many species and hybrids vary greatly in size and cover a two-month flowering span, so, if space permits, try an assortment to ensure a fragrant garden through many weeks. Most will thrive in shade or in full sun. Tolerant of any soil, they love rich feeding before flowering. Trim flowering shoots back fiercely as soon as flowering is over to encourage new growth. Philadelphus survive neglect but carry flowers less freely.
P. coronarius has creamy-white richly scented flowers; perhaps the best 'doer' in poor soils, continuing to flower annually even if neglected. Golden-leaved *P.c.* 'Aureus' and the variegated-leaved 'Variegatus' add interest; plant both in half shade.
MEDIUM DECIDUOUS SHRUB
FULL SUN OR HALF SHADE   ZONES 5-9
P. delavayi has large green leaves, grey-felted on the undersides. The heavily scented white flowers are carried in dense racemes. It is one of the best for a mixed open border, as the leaves and habit are attractive out of the flowering season.
LARGE DECIDUOUS SHRUB   FULL SUN
ZONES 5-9
See also summer, below.

PITTOSPORUM
P. tobira, a tender Asiatic species, much used for hedging in Mediterranean-type climates, can be grown in colder climates in containers with a minimum of protection from severe frosts. The flowers are cream-coloured, orange-blossom-scented and are carried among the glossy leaves. It is a wall shrub in coastal areas, needing a southerly aspect, but in a hot climate it thrives in cool shade.
LARGE EVERGREEN SHRUB
FULL SUN OR SHADE   ZONES 8-10

POLYGONATUM SOLOMON'S SEAL
P. × hybridum is a lovely woodland plant, loving shade, and its long arching stems and horizontally poised leaves are the perfect accompaniment to late spring bulbs such as *Anemone apennina* and fritillaries, the stems leaning over fading flowers. The white bells hang in clusters, a greeny tinge relieving the purity of flat white. Plant next to *Smilacina racemosa* and to glossy-leaved shrubs such as *Viburnum davidii* and the little sarcococcas, and to contrast with the lacy foliage of ferns. After flowering the leaves are sometimes eaten by pests: spray with an insecticide.
DECIDUOUS PERENNIAL   90 CM (36 IN)
SHADE   ZONES 6-9

PYRACANTHA FIRETHORN
These strong, mainly evergreen, shrubs may be planted as windbreaks in an exposed garden, or can be tightly and formally trained against a wall. They also make solid spiny hedges. The hawthorn-like flowers are a froth of foaming white, while yellow, orange or red berries last well into the winter months.
P. coccinea 'Lalandei' has toothed oval leaves and is tough and vigorous. If pruned after flowering, there are few autumn fruits – but sometimes these must be sacrificed to keep the bush shapely. Hedges may be carefully cut to allow as many berries as possible to form. Ordinary soil, not too rich, suits this plant.
LARGE EVERGREEN SHRUB   FULL SUN
ZONES 7-9

RHODODENDRON
R. 'Snow Queen' is a hardy hybrid, lovely and free-flowering. Its trusses of funnel-shaped flowers are dark pink in bud, opening to pure white with a brown basal blotch. *R.* 'Sappho' has a rounded or domed habit with handsome conical trusses, mauve in bud, opening pure white with a mauve-black blotch.
LARGE EVERGREEN SHRUBS
FULL SUN OR HALF SHADE   ZONES 7-10
See also Pinks and mauves: early summer.

ROSA ROSE
R. pimpinellifolia (syn. *R. spinosissima*) is densely suckering, has fern-like leaves and is thicket-forming, with double or single white or pink flowers. It makes a charming hedge where its root spread may be contained, thriving in sandy soil. Flowers are followed by black hips.
R. × alba 'Maxima' has grey-green leaves and carries arching sprays of flat white double flowers. It is lovely against a dark background, and the greyish leaves fit it for a 'silver' garden (see Foliage framework: silver and grey).
R. rugosa 'Blanc Double de Coubert' has typical rugose foliage: crinkled leaves of fresh green. Scented white flowers are carried spasmodically through the summer after the first flowering flush. It is pest- and disease-resistant.
MEDIUM DECIDUOUS SHRUBS   FULL SUN
ZONES 6-9
R. 'Iceberg', or nowadays 'Schneewittchen', is a bush rose for flower-beds, but may be pruned very lightly and allowed to grow more naturally for the edge of shrubberies. A double white scented flower is held in trusses over dark green glossy leaves. It flowers brilliantly, twice if carefully dead-headed and cut back.
DECIDUOUS BUSH ROSE   FULL SUN
ZONES 6-9
R. × paulii, a very prickly, sprawling vigorous

rose, has single wide-open flowers, with crinkled, papery petals. One of the few roses willing to trail downwards, it will drape over a wall, or make dense ground cover in wild areas.
LARGE DECIDUOUS SHRUB
FULL SUN OR HALF SHADE   ZONES 6-9
See also Pinks and mauves: early summer.

RUBUS BRAMBLE
R. × tridel 'Benenden' has single white flowers carried along arching branches. They have conspicuous golden-yellow stamens. Plant in light woodland, undercarpeted with *R. tricolor* with its mat-forming stems and glossy leaves.
MEDIUM DECIDUOUS SHRUB   HALF SHADE
ZONES 5-9

SANGUINARIA BLOODROOT
S. canadensis from Canadian woodlands thrives in well-drained rich acid loamy soil. Creamy-white flowers emerge from between the folds of the leaves, which later open out flat to show their handsome deep lobes of grey-green. The leaves die down in summer, and this is the moment to transplant if desired. A double form, *S.c.* 'Flore Pleno', is commonly grown in gardens, its tightly packed cup-shaped petals very freely carried among the unusual leaves.
DECIDUOUS PERENNIAL   30 CM (12 IN)
HALF SHADE   ZONES 5-8

SISYRINCHIUM
S. striatum, with its grey iris-like leaves, contrasts with rounded and feathery shapes. The creamy flowers are just pale enough to fit into a white colour scheme.
EVERGREEN PERENNIAL   60 CM (24 IN)
FULL SUN   ZONES 7-9

SYRINGA LILAC
S. vulgaris 'Alba' is just one of the good white-flowered garden forms of this well-known shrub (see The blues: early summer). Plant it in light woodland or in a sunny bed; flowers are regularly produced in richly scented, pyramidal panicles. It benefits from pruning of spent flower-heads and rich feeding. It prefers an alkaline-based soil.
LARGE DECIDUOUS SHRUB
FULL SUN OR HALF SHADE   ZONES 5-9

TIARELLA
T. cordifolia, foamflower, needs a position in shade, where it makes an attractive ground cover, the rich green leaves bronze-tinted in winter. Creamy-white feathery spikes cover the plant in early summer, and quickly spreading roots prevent germination of seedling weeds.
EVERGREEN PERENNIAL   15-30 CM (6-12 IN)
SHADE   ZONES 5-9

TRILLIUM WAKE ROBIN
T. grandiflorum has shining leaves with pronounced veins. It spreads by underground roots, slowly at first, but in cool humus eventually makes a large clump. Funnel-shaped pure white flowers top the dome-shaped plant. Plant in drifts between hostas and erythroniums.
DECIDUOUS PERENNIAL   30-45 CM (12-18 IN)
SHADE   ZONES 5-9

TULIPA TULIP
Early-summer varieties sustain the impact of the spring tulips (see above). Triumph *T.* 'Pax' is a solid pure white on a sturdy stem, 45 cm (18 in). Even taller is the Cottage or Single Early *T.* 'Cazzara', another substantial pure white flower on a strong stem, 50 cm (20 in). Lily-flowered *T.* 'White Triumphator' has beautiful creamy-white reflexing petals and flowers over a long period, 70 cm (28 in).
BULBS   FULL SUN   ZONES 5-9

VIBURNUM
V. opulus 'Sterile' (syn. *V.o.* 'Roseum') is a garden form of the woodland guelder rose or water elder. Its large 'snowballs' are composed of sterile flower-heads at first creamy-white, ageing to pink tints. All *V.o.* cultivars have white flowers; many of these are followed by glistening red or yellow fruits (see Hot colours: fruits and berries).
LARGE DECIDUOUS SHRUB   SHADE
ZONES 6-10

V. plicatum 'Mariesii' throws out tiers of horizontal branches as it grows, each branch covered in lacy white flowers, actually a mixture of sterile and fertile florets. The leaves are well formed, and often colour bronze-red in autumn. Plant as a focal point, where its interesting structure draws the eye, or use it on a corner or a bank, where its tabulated branches emphasize garden features.
LARGE DECIDUOUS SHRUB
FULL SUN OR HALF SHADE   ZONES 7-10
See also Foliage framework: green.

WISTERIA
The white form of the Japanese wisteria, *W. floribunda* 'Alba', has long pendulous flowering racemes borne just as the leaves unfurl. Each flower is subtly lilac-tinted. Smaller than the vigorous Chinese wisteria, it is ideal for a modest-sized garden.

The Chinese wisteria, *W. sinensis* 'Alba', has long white racemes of flowers and is perhaps the noblest climber of all, suitable for an ordinary garden. It may also be trained to make a spiralling upright shrub or after many years a small tree; a pair framing a path or view is breathtaking.

Tidy back after flowering, shortening the new shoots again in winter. Feed richly when young; it is hardly necessary after the plant is well established.
LARGE DECIDUOUS CLIMBERS, SHRUBS OR
SMALL TREES   FULL SUN   ZONES 6-10
See also The blues: early summer.

Sisyrinchium striatum

Wisteria floribunda 'Alba'

SUMMER

ACHILLEA YARROW
A. ptarmica 'The Pearl', with double white button flowers and green leaves, is an old well-tried favourite. The stalks are sturdy and neither wind nor rain will bend or break them. Plant it in a mixed colour border where it will both link and separate bright contrasts.
DECIDUOUS PERENNIAL   60 CM (24 IN)
FULL SUN OR HALF SHADE   ZONES 5-9

Achillea ptarmica 'The Pearl'

Campanula pyramidalis 'Alba'

ARTEMISIA
A. lactiflora, white mugwort, one of the few garden artemisias with green rather than grey leaves, is a useful border plant; cream plumes of tiny flowers tower upwards, and a clump spreads quickly. Use at the back of a main border next to pure white clouds of *Crambe cordifolia* or pale yellow fluffy thalictrums. The cream is subtle enough to mix with pure bright blues, so use in a blue and grey garden to enhance the effects. It seems a dull plant on its own, but is invaluable as a neighbour.
DECIDUOUS PERENNIAL   1.8 M (6 FT)
FULL SUN   ZONES 7-9

ARUNCUS GOAT'S BEARD
A. dioicus (syn. *A. sylvester*) is handsome with broad coarse fern-like leaves, making an attractive green hummock all summer. Its tall creamy-plumed flower-heads last for many weeks and look attractive even when fading. Surely no garden should be without a clump? Plant with pale blue *Campanula lactiflora* or with brighter delphiniums for contrast, or harmonize with cream or pale yellow lilies, to give a cool restful effect.
DECIDUOUS PERENNIAL   2.1 M (7 FT)
FULL SUN OR SHADE   ZONES 6-9

ASTILBE
A. rivularis has elegant leaves, very deeply divided and luxuriant (see Foliage framework: green). Above them, the arching plumed panicles of small greenish-cream flowers last for many weeks, and are useful even as the seed-heads become buff-brown. Best in a moist site, the emergent leaves look splendid with pink candelabra primulas flowering in early summer, and contrast with hairy rodgersia foliage.
DECIDUOUS PERENNIAL   1.8 M (6 FT)
FULL SUN OR HALF SHADE   ZONES 7-9
A. × arendsii 'Bridal Veil' is a garden hybrid, demanding less space. It is attractive, with pure white flowers opening from green buds and turning cream with age.
DECIDUOUS PERENNIAL   75 CM (30 IN)
FULL SUN OR HALF SHADE   ZONES 7-9

ASTRANTIA MASTERWORT
Flower-heads of these umbelliferous plants are charming: a central group of tiny florets is surrounded by a 'collar' of bracts like an old-fashioned posy. The green divided leaves make a basal rosette. Spreading by underground runners, astrantias like to be kept moist in summer. In *A. major* the florets are whitish-green with a green surrounding collar.
DECIDUOUS PERENNIAL   60 CM (24 IN)
FULL SUN OR HALF SHADE   ZONES 7-9

CAMPANULA BELLFLOWER
Two summer-flowering campanulas are valuable for indoors or out.

The white form of *C. isophylla*, *C.i.* 'Alba', with delicate grey-green leaves and large starry flowers, is a trailing plant for containers or hanging baskets in full sun. Take cuttings in the autumn or protect the plant from frost.
SEMI-EVERGREEN PERENNIAL   23 CM (9 IN)
FULL SUN   ZONES 8-10
C. pyramidalis, the chimney bellflower, with blue flowers, is described in The blues; the white-flowered *C.p.* 'Alba' is equally attractive. Place a group of flowering pots against a background of dark yew, or in the corner of a room, and it will shine luminously, lasting many weeks even if deprived of light after it starts to flower. It is perennial in favoured sites, but more often biennial.
BIENNIAL OR SEMI-EVERGREEN PERENNIAL
1.8 M (6 FT)   FULL SUN   ZONES 6-9

CARDIOCRINUM
Once classified as a lily, *C. giganteum* differs mainly in the large glossy heart-shaped leaves which certainly add to the decorative value of this tall plant through early spring weeks. Needing rich well-worked and mulched soil, moist yet well drained, and light shade; an open glade in woodland is ideal for a natural setting. In a smaller garden space may surely be found at the back of a shrubbery for these magnificent plants. Bulbs take several years to mature and flower; the main bulb actually withers away after flowering, leaving small offsets. It will take time to get a flowering progression established but every effort, especially the rich, lush feeding, is worth while.

Known as the giant lily, *C. giganteum* soars upwards, heart-shaped leaves decreasing in size towards the top of the stalk. Long trumpets of greenish-white hang downwards, their scent wafting a considerable distance.
BULB   1.8-3 M (6-10 FT)
HALF SHADE   ZONES 8-10

CHRYSANTHEMUM
C. foeniculaceum, a tender shrub, is best treated as an annual, cuttings taken at the end of each summer. Its deeply divided fennel-like foliage of silvery-grey (see Foliage framework) and white daisy-flowers are superb, especially in large pots. Although a separate species, it is like the Paris marguerite, *C. frutescens*, in flower but with more elegant leaves.
SMALL EVERGREEN SHRUB   FULL SUN
ZONES 8-9
C. maximum, the Shasta daisy, has many good garden forms with semi-double and double white and cream flowers. Perhaps a little dull

and coarse, nevertheless clumps make effective splashes of strong white where needed. Little trouble to grow, it is an ideal plant for a busy gardener, since it needs no staking.
DECIDUOUS PERENNIAL   60-90 CM (24-36 IN)
FULL SUN OR HALF SHADE   ZONES 6-9

CISTUS SUN ROSE
C. × *cyprius* is vigorous and one of the hardiest; white papery flowers have conspicuous crimson blotches at the base of each petal.
MEDIUM EVERGREEN SHRUB   FULL SUN
ZONES 8-10
See also early summer, above.

CLEMATIS
C. recta, an upright-growing herbaceous clematis, has white single flowers (a rare double form exists), carried on tall stems if staked; alternatively, grow it to trail forward over earlier-flowering plants, such as delphiniums or campanulas. A purple-leaved form (see Strong reds: foliage) looks lovely with pink-flowered neighbours.
DECIDUOUS PERENNIAL   1.2 M (4 FT)
FULL SUN, ROOTS IN SHADE   ZONES 6-9
C. 'Marie Boisselot', a large-flowered hybrid, has beautiful pure white, flat petals, that look almost double. They are pink-tinged as they unfold. Grow it through an early-flowering shrub, or train it in a fan shape on a wall.
DECIDUOUS CLIMBER   FULL SUN OR SHADE,
ROOTS IN SHADE   ZONES 6-9
C. 'Huldine' has slightly cupped white flowers, faintly mauve outside; each petal is almost translucent. Greenish stamens relieve the pure central whiteness. It flowers on the young wood, so cut back fiercely in winter, and give it plenty of space to spread, the roots shaded by neighbouring plants and its head reaching to the light.
DECIDUOUS CLIMBER   FULL SUN,
ROOTS IN SHADE   ZONES 6-9
See also spring, above.

CLETHRA
C. alnifolia, the sweet pepper bush, has white racemes with wafting fragrance. It requires lime-free soil but is otherwise undemanding. Grow it in semi-shade. There is a form with larger flower-heads, *C.a.* 'Paniculata', and also one with pale pink flowers, *C.a.* 'Rosea'.
MEDIUM EVERGREEN SHRUB   HALF SHADE
ZONES 7-9
C. arborea is tender but most desirable. In a warm garden it merits a prime position, huge white lily-of-the-valley flowers carried in panicles to catch the eye.
LARGE EVERGREEN SHRUB OR SMALL TREE
FULL SUN   ZONES 7-9

DEUTZIA
D. setchuenensis bears corymbs of closely packed small white flowers on rather vertical branches. It is supposed to be a little tender, young shoots subject to late frosts, but it is usually safe in a mixed border, where its pale green leaves and brown peeling stems make it a feature during its non-flowering period, and its upright habit prevents it from encroaching on neighbouring plants. Most often found in gardens is *D.s. corymbiflora* with larger flower-heads.
MEDIUM DECIDUOUS SHRUB   FULL SUN
ZONES 6-9
See also early summer, above.

DIANTHUS PINKS AND CARNATIONS
D. 'Mrs Sinkins', perhaps the favourite pink of all, has fringed white scented double flowers. It is very vigorous, and it may be used to make a delightful grey carpet under and around roses, where the white flowers prolong the flowering season. Try not to give it the rich feeding the roses need.
SEMI-EVERGREEN PERENNIAL   23 CM (9 IN)
FULL SUN   ZONES 6-9
See also The blues: foliage.

DIGITALIS FOXGLOVE
These woodland plants seed freely and white forms look ghostly at dusk when darker garden colour fades. Plants of *D. purpurea* 'Alba' have spikes of white tubular flowers with spotted markings to attract pollinators. As with the yellow evening primrose, *Oenothera biennis*, it is best to allow haphazard natural seeding. Do not plant in formal groups.
EVERGREEN BIENNIAL OR PERENNIAL   1 M (3 FT)
FULL SUN OR HALF SHADE   ZONES 5-9

DIMORPHOTHECA CAPE MARIGOLD
Dimorphotheca is often classified as *Osteospermum. D. ecklonis* (syn. *Osteospermum ecklonis*) is a South African daisy, tender, but easily rooted from cuttings at any time of year. It is ideal for troughs and containers with pale mauvish or white flowers for different colour schemes. *D.e.* 'Prostrata' spreads and weaves through other plants; white flowers have outer petals distinctly blue-tinged, and the centres are dark navy-blue.
DWARF SUB-SHRUB   FULL SUN   ZONES 7-10

EUCRYPHIA
Eucryphias are shrubs for deep acid soil; highly ornamental with glossy leaves and creamy-white flowers opening to show bright yellow stamens.
E. glutinosa, deciduous and free-flowering, makes a pyramidal regular shape, a feature or

focal point in a small garden and appropriate in any woodland shrubbery.
E. × *intermedia* 'Rostrevor' is evergreen and more lime-tolerant, while *E.* × *nymansensis* 'Nymansay', also evergreen, is able to grow in alkaline clay soils as long as the texture is improved by plenty of humus.
EVERGREEN AND DECIDUOUS SMALL TREES OR
LARGE SHRUBS   HALF SHADE   ZONES 7-9

Clematis 'Huldine'

Clematis 'Marie Boisselot'

Houttuynia cordata

FILIPENDULA MEADOWSWEET
F. hexapetala (syn. *F. vulgaris*), dropwort, unexpectedly thrives in dry chalky soil, so may be planted in an arid part of the garden. The finely divided fern-like leaves make a green hummock. Fluffy white meadowsweet flowers are held on branched stems. A double form, *F.h.* 'Plena', is good.
DECIDUOUS PERENNIAL   60 CM (24 IN)
FULL SUN OR HALF SHADE   ZONES 5-9

GYPSOPHILA
G. paniculata is loved for its cloud of frothy white flowers which bury withering stalks and flowers of neighbouring perennials. Plant behind oriental poppies and train forward over decapitated delphinium stalks, as Miss Jekyll advised at the turn of the century. The pure white cultivar, *G.p.* 'Bristol Fairy', has tiny double flowers. Grow from cuttings quickly rooted as shoots appear in late spring.
DECIDUOUS PERENNIAL   90-120 CM (36-48 IN)
FULL SUN   ZONES 7-9

HEBE
SHRUBBY VERONICA, SHRUBBY SPEEDWELL
H. recurva makes a neat shrub, with short white flowering racemes carried over a long period. It is hardy. The cultivar *H.* 'C.P. Raffill' grows to 90 cm (36 in), is long-lived and produces flowers earlier and carries them into late summer.

H. albicans, *H. glaucophylla* and *H. pinguifolia* 'Pagei' all have slate-grey leaves and white flowers. They thrive in full sun and need plenty of moisture. Plant in groups for front edging, intermingling with flowers of pastel-tints or of dark blue or violet. Try *Viola labradorica* creeping under *H. glaucophylla*, and tall *Salvia guaranitica* towering over the prostrate *H. pinguifolia* 'Pagei'. Hebe cuttings strike easily, so experiment with the reputedly tender species.
SMALL EVERGREEN SHRUBS   FULL SUN
ZONES 8-9
See also Foliage framework: silver and grey.

HERACLEUM HOGWEED
H. mantegazzianum, giant hogweed or cartwheel flower, like an immense cow parsley, stands up to 3 m (10 ft), stems bearing flat heads 60 cm (24 in) across. It is spectacular, best in a wild damp garden but, if carefully dead-headed to prevent seeding, may be planted in a quite modest area. Leaves are large and decorative, but sap from broken or cut stalks is dangerous and produces blisters and extreme irritation to tender skin.
DECIDUOUS BIENNIAL   3 M (10 FT)
FULL SUN OR SHADE   ZONES 7-9

HOHERIA
Hoherias belong to the mallow family, white flowers, nestling among green leaves, cover the branches in summer in the deciduous species, a little later in the more tender evergreen varieties. They are easy to grow in any fertile soil; it is strange that they are not more familiar. *H. glabrata* and *H. lyallii* flower within a few weeks of each other. Very alike, their flexible branches are crowded with flowers.
LARGE DECIDUOUS SHRUBS   FULL SUN
ZONES 8-9

HOUTTUYNIA
H. cordata loves a cool moist root run. Green, bronze-tipped leaves set off strange little white flowers with cone-shaped centres. A double form, *H.c.* 'Flora Pleno', is less invasive. Its central cone is densely packed with white petals.
DECIDUOUS PERENNIAL   30 CM (12 IN)
HALF SHADE OR SHADE   ZONES 6-9
See also Strong reds: foliage.

JASMINUM JASMINE
J. officinale, old-fashioned jessamine, thrives in poor soil but revels in sun. Nevertheless, good feeding will increase luxuriant growth, though not necessarily flowers, and it will then cover pergolas and arbours, the white clustered blooms scenting the garden with a delicious

subtle fragrance. Give it a host plant to climb into or trellis work to twist about. There is a form, *J.o.* 'Aureovariegatum', with creamy-yellow variegation in the leaves.
DECIDUOUS CLIMBER   FULL SUN   ZONES 7-9

LATHYRUS
L. odoratus, the garden sweet pea, with its scented flowers has traditionally been grown for cutting in kitchen gardens. Try growing it up formal tripods or frames to give tall spires of colour in borders. Spencer cultivars are popular and *L.o.* 'Swan Lake' and 'White Ensign' have plain white flowers on long stalks. Some of the *grandiflorus* varieties, derived from the everlasting pea, *L. latifolius*, are still obtainable; in fact are now much in demand for their fragrance. Sow in early spring, or late autumn, in individual pots, putting out in late spring. They appreciate rich soil and plenty of moisture. Keep cutting regularly, or flowering will cease.
ANNUAL CLIMBERS   FULL SUN   ZONES 5-9

LILIUM LILY
These desirable bulbs are not all easy to grow and some of the best species do not thrive when lime is present in the soil. Liable to late frost damage, grow them among low-growing plants which give protection to emerging tips. In general they like a rich well-drained soil, so plant each bulb in sharp grit if soil is heavy. Protect from slugs and in spring spray against botrytis. Lovely planted in groups in light woodland to look natural among informal shrub and tree planting, they can equally successfully be grown in borders for specific colour effects. The lilies most fussy about soil and cultivation can be effective grown in carefully prepared compost in containers, where they can be moved from the light shade beneficial in early growth to a more open situation for flowering.

L. candidum, the Madonna or white lily, prefers a hot position in front of a warm wall, to the usual rich deep soil sought by Asiatic and American species. A temperamental plant, it will succeed in some gardens and fail elsewhere. Spray regularly against botrytis, especially in damp warm weather.
BULB   90-150 CM (36-60 IN)
FULL SUN   ZONES 7-9
L. regale is perhaps the most popular and, except for martagon types, the easiest lily to grow. It is suitable for pots or for making picturesque clumps in an herbaceous border. Protect the emergent tips from late frosts and give frequent top-dressings of loam, leaf mould and compost. I feed regularly as flowering time approaches. The creamy-white

funnel-shaped blooms, borne in loose clusters, have sulphur-yellow centres, and the backs of the petals appear as if lightly brushed and shaded rosy-purple. Sow seed as soon as it is ripe; after three years bulbs will be mature and ready for planting out in a permanent place in the garden.
BULB   75-180 CM (30-72 IN)
FULL SUN OR HALF SHADE   ZONES 7-9

LYCHNIS CAMPION
L. coronaria 'Alba' seeds true although the type, known as dusty miller, has crimson or pink flowers. Grey felted leaves, on stems rather sprawling in habit, make the plant fit nicely under tall bush roses or flop over stone edging. It is a plant which enhances all neighbouring flower colours; best of all perhaps in a white and grey garden.
DECIDUOUS PERENNIAL   60 CM (24 IN)
FULL SUN   ZONES 5-9

MALVA MALLOW
M. moschata, musk mallow, behaves rather like a shrubby perennial, but seldom lives for more than a few seasons. Allow it to seed and it will always find a corner in which to thrive. It is too

pretty, with either pink flowers or white in *M.m.* 'Alba', to be excluded from a main border. The flowers cover the bush, which has deeply cut and lobed green leaves, and a tidy, rounded symmetrical shape. If you had space it might be lovely interplanted with the earlier-flowering yellow tree lupin, the whole bed undercarpeted with low-growing *Stachys olympica* 'Silver Carpet', *Cerastium tomentosum* or the little grey-leaved hebes.
DECIDUOUS PERENNIAL   60-75 CM (24-30 IN)
FULL SUN   ZONES 6-9

NICOTIANA TOBACCO PLANT
The flowering tobacco plant, *N. alata* (syn. *N. affinis*), is grown for its deliciously scented flowers, most fragrant on a warm summer's evening. The pale colours and white shaded with green are most noticeable at dusk. *N.a.* 'Grandiflora' has larger flowers shaded with yellow. The tubular flowers open late in the day, and green sticky leaves are effective weed-smotherers when it is used for bedding out. Grow as an annual.
ANNUAL OR DECIDUOUS PERENNIAL
60-90 CM (24-36 IN)   FULL SUN   ZONES 8-10
N. sylvestris is tall with very large leaves and

long white funnels; almost as beautiful as a lily. Take seed and grow as an annual; in well-drained soil plants survive an average winter.
ANNUAL OR DECIDUOUS PERENNIAL
1.8 M (6 FT)   FULL SUN   ZONES 8-10

NYMPHAEA WATER LILY
N. odorata 'Minor', a form of the original wild American species, is good for formal pools in a small-scale garden. Narrow-petalled white flowers have a haunting fragrance, noticeably after rain. This compact plant is happy in shallow water, or any depth to 45 cm (18 in).
DECIDUOUS WATER PERENNIAL   FULL SUN
ZONES 8-9

OLEARIA DAISY BUSH
O. macrodonta is magnificent; its grey-green holly leaves are silvery-white on the undersides (see Foliage framework: silver and grey). The broad panicles of tight daisy flower-heads cover the bush in season. An excellent seaside plant, withstanding fierce winds and salt sprays and reasonably hardy inland, it is especially useful in town gardens.
LARGE EVERGREEN SHRUB   FULL SUN
ZONES 7-9

Lilium regale

PETUNIA

Petunias are sun-loving plants for bedding out and for containers. Grow them from seed sown in early spring, pricked out into large trays with a rich compost, and put in the garden after the last frost. Many good colours in white, cream, pale yellow, blue, burgundy and pale pink are obtainable, and modern garden hybrids in stripes, with frilled petals and two colours. It is hardly necessary to add that the simple beauty of one appropriately chosen single colour is to be preferred. Needing little water and loving warmth, they do need constant dead-heading. A good large-flowered white petunia is *P.* 'Snow Cloud'.

ANNUAL   30 CM (12 IN)   FULL SUN   ZONES 4-9

PHILADELPHUS MOCK ORANGE

Philadelphus of different heights come as later-flowering successors to those mentioned above in early summer. Many Lemoine and modern hybrids are excellent and floriferous.

  P. 'Avalanche' and 'Belle Etoile' are small compact shrubs, the former with single flowers of pure white, the latter white, opening wide to display the centre of dark maroon. 'Innocence' grows tall, the flowers single, and the leaves are prettily variegated in cream and white. Spray young shoots and buds against blackfly. 'Manteau d'Hermine' is small, too, with cream double flowers.

DECIDUOUS SHRUB   FULL SUN OR HALF SHADE
ZONES 5-9

POTENTILLA SHRUBBY CINQUEFOIL

P. fruticosa 'Manchu', formerly known as *P.f.* 'Mandschurica', is a shrubby potentilla with silvery-grey leaves and a spreading habit. Grow it for edging where the brown sprawling stems are attractive in winter, and the white flowers are carried for many weeks in summer.

SMALL DECIDUOUS SHRUB   FULL SUN
ZONES 7-10

RODGERSIA

R. aesculifolia, as its name denotes, has leaves like a horse chestnut. Crinkled bronze leaves set off its own white clustered flowers. Plant in boggy ground. Pink-flowered neighbours will harmonize with the purple-bronze tints in the young leaves.

  R. podophylla has triangular-shaped leaves with jagged lobes and fine cream flowers. It is one of the few rodgersias which thrive in relatively dry conditions, and continues to spread.

DECIDUOUS PERENNIALS   90-120 CM (36-48 IN)
FULL SUN OR HALF SHADE   ZONES 7-9
See also Foliage framework: green.

ROSA ROSE

Up to date classification puts the non-recurrent summer-flowering climbers into ramblers. Some, like *R. longicuspis, R. filipes* and *R. rubus*, are species; most are garden plants, occasionally with exact parentage unknown, as with the excellent *R.* 'Bobbie James'. The famous *R. filipes* 'Kiftsgate' may still be seen in the garden from which it took its name, climbing and rambling high and wide.

  These roses open just as the first June flowering of bush types comes to an end, *R. longicuspis* being even a week or so later. Picturesque and very floriferous, small flowers, white but often pink-tinted in bud, held in trusses and clusters, roses of this character are not for a small garden. Cascading branches of scented white bloom make features where space allows. Grow them up an old apple or pear tree or over stumps. They make surprisingly good woodland plants, flowering in light overhead shade, reaching always to the light above.

DECIDUOUS CLIMBERS   TO 9 M (30 FT)
FULL SUN OR HALF SHADE   ZONES 7-9
See also Pinks and mauves: early summer.

THALICTRUM MEADOW RUE

T. aquilegifolium, with pink-mauve flowers, has a white form, *T.a.* 'Album', held above grey-green leaves. It is outstanding and worthy of a place in any sunny border. Even better, if obtainable, is the taller white form of *T. delavayi* (*T. dipterocarpum* of gardens), with large more open panicles of flowers, and smaller more elegant leaves.

DECIDUOUS PERENNIAL
60-150 CM (24-60 IN)   FULL SUN   ZONES 6-9
See also Pinks and mauves: early summer.

TRACHELOSPERMUM

These evergreen climbers need a hot climate and a warm wall. Self-clinging climbers *T. asiaticum* and *T. jasminoides* both have fragrant small creamy-white flowers, resembling jasmine. The former is the hardier, and is neat and compact. Both are suitable for growing in a protected summerhouse, or in a large pot to bring into the house when carrying the scented flowers. *T. jasminoides* will cover a house wall with self-clinging twining stems in favoured climates.

EVERGREEN CLIMBERS   FULL SUN
ZONES 8-10

Rosa 'Bobbie James'

Rosa filipes 'Kiftsgate'

LATE SUMMER

ACTAEA BANEBERRY
A. alba, white baneberry, bears clusters of white marble-like berries above its ferny leaves. Give it a cool woodland site, and plant in groups.
DECIDUOUS PERENNIAL   90 CM (36 IN)
HALF SHADE OR SHADE   ZONES 4-8

AGAPANTHUS BLUE AFRICAN LILY
One of the most desirable late-summer flowers is the white form of *A. campanulatus*, *A.c.* 'Albus'. The petals are pure white but the clustered flowers in flat heads give a deliciously creamy-green impression, as flower stalk, buff calyx and white petals blend together above the fresh strap-like leaves. It seems completely hardy and its soft colouring, desirable enough during a long flowering period, continues as flower-heads fade to pale straw-colour.
DECIDUOUS PERENNIAL   75-100 CM (30-40 IN)
FULL SUN   ZONES 8-10

ANAPHALIS PEARLY EVERLASTING
A. triplinervis has grey-white leaves covered in pearly-white yellow-centred everlasting flowers. It makes an attractive grey foliage plant, and leaf and flower together look silvery.
DECIDUOUS PERENNIAL   30 CM (12 IN)
FULL SUN   ZONES 7-10
A. cinnamomea (syn. *A. yedoensis*) is taller and very invasive, spreading by underground roots. Plant it in dry shade where little else will thrive. Impossible not to like it for its white bunched flowers and almost white foliage.
DECIDUOUS PERENNIAL   45 CM (18 IN)
FULL SUN OR SHADE   ZONES 7-10

ANEMONE WINDFLOWER
Among the Japanese anemones, *A. × hybrida* 'Honorine Jobert' has pure white flowers with a conspicuous bunch of yellow stamens. It flowers for months rather than weeks, and is lovely in a pink and white scheme in sun, or at the edge of woodland with dark-leaved shrubs. Unfortunately it spreads very quickly.
DECIDUOUS PERENNIAL   1.5 M (5 FT)
FULL SUN OR SHADE   ZONES 6-9

ASTER
A. divaricatus, a Michaelmas daisy with wiry lax black stems, prefers cool shade to an open sunny border. The tiny white daisy-flowers will fall over neighbouring plants, a tendency much used by Gertrude Jekyll with her favourite bergenias. In spring young growth is fresh bright green. It should be planted more often in 'difficult' sunless town gardens, brightening dark corners for many weeks.
DECIDUOUS PERENNIAL   60 CM (24 IN)
SHADE   ZONES 5-9

A. umbellatus, with white flowers and yellow centres, together mixing to give a gentle creamy effect, the opposite to the laundry-white of Japanese anemones. It seems to be free of typical Michaelmas daisy mildew.
DECIDUOUS PERENNIAL   1.2 M (4 FT)
HALF SHADE   ZONES 5-9

CHRYSANTHEMUM
C. uliginosum (syn. *C. serotinum*), the Hungarian daisy, flowers very late, perfect for mixing in large clumps with pastel-coloured Michaelmas daisies. It is a little coarse for a white and silver garden where much depends on delicate ferny foliage and small light flowers of pale creamy-whites and papery textures. This daisy is a solid plant and a good 'doer'.
DECIDUOUS PERENNIAL   1.5-2.1 M (5-7 FT)
FULL SUN   ZONES 6-9

CLEMATIS
C. flammula, fragrant virgin's bower, is bushy with delightful creamy-white, sweetly scented flowers. Grow it to twine through trellis or old balustrading. Try letting it clamber through low deciduous shrubs that flower in spring, but give it as much sun as possible.
 C. viticella 'Alba Luxurians' has green tips to white petals, sometimes almost entirely green. It is elegant, in habit very much resembling the species, *C. viticella*, purple virgin's bower, with long stalks and a nodding head, although different in flower colour. Grow it through an early-flowering clematis; make sure the unusual flowers are readily visible. Prune both these late flowerers in late winter.
DECIDUOUS CLIMBERS
FULL SUN, ROOTS IN SHADE   ZONES 6-9

CLERODENDRUM
C. trichotomum is a strong-growing, suckering shrub, with white, very fragrant – almost too sweetly scented – flowers enclosed in maroon calyces and are held in erect clusters. Later, turquoise fruits last well into the winter months. Plant it as a specimen rather than in a mixed border where suckers become a nuisance. *C.t. fargesii* is even more free-flowering and has fruits in pink calyces.
LARGE DECIDUOUS SHRUB   FULL SUN
ZONES 7-9

ESCALLONIA
E. 'Iveyi' has decorative glossy leaves and large panicles of white flowers. A good corner plant or focal point in the smaller garden, this escallonia has a regular pyramidal shape. In mild areas it will make a towering hedge; in colder areas give it a warm situation against a south-facing wall.
LARGE EVERGREEN SHRUB   FULL SUN
ZONES 8-9
See also Foliage framework: green.

Anemone × hybrida 'Honorine Jobert'

Anaphalis cinnamomea

EUPATORIUM

E. ligustrinum (syn. *E. micranthum*) has flat pinky-white flower-heads composed of tiny daisies, much loved by butterflies. It continues to flower against a wall sheltered from frosts well into autumn. Like other tender evergreens it will often shoot from the base after a severe winter, catching up, with speedy young growth, to flower in season quite normally.
MEDIUM EVERGREEN SHRUB   FULL SUN
ZONES 7-9

FATSIA

F. japonica, revelling in dry shade, is the perfect shrub for an enclosed town garden or for a dark corner with a northern aspect. The glossy aralia-like leaves (see Foliage framework: green) are a foil to the cream panicles that terminate the stems throughout autumn. It has an exotic sub-tropical appearance and does not fit into a conventional planting scheme. Plant above a carpet of variegated periwinkle.
LARGE EVERGREEN SHRUB   SHADE
ZONES 8-10

GALTONIA SUMMER HYACINTH

G. candicans has erect flower stems bearing bell-shaped white flowers, shaded or marked with green. It fits into a white garden, stems soaring upwards through light grey foliage. Plant bulbs in spring, or in pots in the autumn for forcing.
BULB   90 CM (36 IN)   FULL SUN
ZONES 7-10

GLADIOLUS CORN FLAG

G. callianthus (for long known as *Acidanthera bicolor* or *A. murielae*) flowers late, its long grassy leaves carrying arching flower-heads, pure white with dark violet blotches inside. Plant beneath a warm wall, with neighbouring pink-flowered nerines and *Amaryllis belladonna*. A few corms quickly increase by little 'cormlets', which should be grown on in a frame or pots.
CORM   90 CM (36 IN)   FULL SUN   ZONES 8-10

HOSTA PLANTAIN LILY

Grown primarily for their leaves (see The blues: foliage), some hostas make a timely contribution to the white flower garden.

H. plantaginea 'Grandiflora' has young foliage of golden glowing green, darkening through the season. The white trumpet-shaped flowers, lily-like in appearance and fragrance, come just when many summer flowers fade. It needs a warm spot to ensure reliability of flowering and is a perfect pot plant if well watered through the hottest months.

H. 'Royal Standard' is similar but the flowers are lilac-tinted, subtle in colour and in fragrance.
DECIDUOUS PERENNIALS   60-90 CM (24-36 IN)
HALF SHADE   ZONES 6-9

HYDRANGEA

Hydrangeas need generous feeding and plenty of moisture. They are woodland plants needing light shade, but are surprisingly adaptable to being grown in containers, and often make features in small town backyards. Their flowers are composed of fertile and sterile inflorescences sometimes in a dome shape and sometimes in a flattened head. In the former, known as hortensias, the mop heads are of sterile florets only in colours of greenish-white, pink, low-toned red and blue. In acid soils 'blue' flowers can be almost turquoise. In alkaline soils the 'blues' fade to pink; 'blueing' powder will correct this, but colours will always remain muted. In fact most hydrangeas are happier in a deep acid loam than in one containing lime. The lacecaps with sterile florets surrounding central flat corymbs of tight fertile flowers are the more attractive plants, less artificial and fitting more appropriately into mixed borders.

H. arborescens is a lax shrub with greeny-white sterile florets forming a globular head. Its cultivar *H.a.* 'Grandiflora' is one of the best. A sub-species, *H.a. radiata*, has a conspicuous white undersurface to the leaves; desirable but perhaps a little less hardy.

H. involucrata 'Hortensis' is dwarf with charming double pinky-white florets.

H. paniculata has two good forms. One, *H.p.* 'Grandiflora', is showy with large creamy-white panicles of sterile florets; 'Praecox' has flatter corymbs and flowers earlier.

H. quercifolia, the oak-leaved hydrangea, is exciting with very large leaves which colour magnificently in autumn, peeling buff bark and round-topped panicles of white flowers. It is best against a wall; protect from wind, and shade from midday sun.
SMALL TO LARGE DECIDUOUS SHRUBS
HALF SHADE   ZONES 5-9

LATHYRUS

L. latifolius 'Albus', the white perennial pea, will form a large sprawling mass growing forward to drape itself down a bank or trained to cover and conceal earlier-flowering perennials. The pink type is tougher but once established in an open site, in full sun, the white form is much more beautiful, in fact spectacular. Grow from seed or delve deeply in spring to find black roots to divide and move.
DECIDUOUS PERENNIAL   3 M (10 FT)
FULL SUN   ZONES 5-9

LEPTOSPERMUM

L. grandiflorum has silvery foliage (see Foliage framework) and wide white flowers. Probably a variety of the species *L. flavescens*, it appears to be one of the hardier of the genus, well worth trying in an average garden.
LARGE EVERGREEN SHRUB   FULL SUN
ZONES 8-10

Lysimachia ephemerum

Hydrangea arborescens

Hydrangea quercifolia

LYSIMACHIA LOOSESTRIFE
L. clethroides is a running plant in damp soils, more restrained in dry. Its white flowers are carried in gently arching spikes.

L. ephemerum has glaucous grey leaves in spring, later turning green, above which tall flower stems bear slender spikes of delightful grey-white flowers. Grow it in thick clumps in a 'white' garden. Foliage and flower between them give value all summer.
DECIDUOUS PERENNIALS   90 CM (36 IN)
FULL SUN   ZONES 6-9

MYRTUS MYRTLE
Myrtles love hot sun and stony soil, not too rich. On *M. communis* the glossy aromatic leaves are densely held and small white flowers are followed by black berries. Plant at the base of a warm wall for profuse flowering. It is useful as a seaside shrub. It has broad oval leaves, while the hardier form *M.c. tarentina* has narrow hard foliage and decorative white berries.
MEDIUM EVERGREEN SHRUBS   FULL SUN
ZONES 8-10

PHLOX
The taller phlox are useful late-flowering plants for an open border, but also thrive in half shade. They like rich feeding and should be split up (discarding the central crown) every few years. All phlox tend to get eelworm,

identifiable by swollen shoots and twisted, wispy leaves so, if necessary, propagate from root cuttings, burning old diseased stock.

P. maculata has a lovely form, *P.m.* 'Omega' – white with a lilac eye, and scented.
DECIDUOUS PERENNIAL   100 CM (40 IN)
FULL SUN OR HALF SHADE   ZONES 6-9
P. paniculata 'Mother of Pearl' is white suffused pink, very healthy and vigorous.
DECIDUOUS PERENNIAL   1.2-1.5 M (4-5 FT)
FULL SUN OR HALF SHADE   ZONES 6-9

PLATYCODON BALLOON FLOWER
P. grandiflorus 'Mariesii Albus' has white balloon-like buds opening white, faintly tinged with pink or blue. A perfect late flowerer for the white garden, but equally pretty with bright fuchsias and late-flowering colchicums.
DECIDUOUS PERENNIAL   45-60 CM (18-24 IN)
FULL SUN   ZONES 6-9
See also The blues: late summer.

POLYGONUM
P. baldschuanicum, the Russian vine, is a vigorous climber, scrambling into old trees or quickly covering a trellis or arbour. It will cover 3-4 m (10-13 ft) in one season and eventually 15 m (50 ft) or more. White fluffy panicles are faintly tinged pink. Make it a feature in a garden; it will swamp most neighbours.
LARGE DECIDUOUS CLIMBER
FULL SUN OR HALF SHADE   ZONES 7-9

SANGUISORBA BURNET
S. canadensis has white flowers held above elegant fresh green pinnate leaves. The bottle-brush flowers arch with the stems, but seldom need support. It is a choice plant, not often grown.
DECIDUOUS PERENNIAL   1.2-1.8 M (4-6 FT)
FULL SUN   ZONES 4-8

SAXIFRAGA SAXIFRAGE
S. fortunei is outstanding. Grow it in shade at eye-level in a raised bed where mahogany stalks and red undersides of the glistening bronze leaves are visible. The flowering shoots are delicate and airy; plant next to red-berrying actaeas (see Hot colours: fruits and berries). *S.f.* 'Wada's Variety' and 'Windsor' are both strong cultivars.
DECIDUOUS PERENNIAL   30-40 CM (12-16 IN)
HALF SHADE   ZONES 5-9

SORBUS
S. hupehensis, an Aucuparia sorbus from west China, has white fruits, subtly tinged with pink, which hang conspicuously on the purple-brown branches into winter. It always looks neat and elegant.
MEDIUM DECIDUOUS TREE
FULL SUN OR HALF SHADE   ZONES 4-8

SYMPHORICARPOS SNOWBERRY
S. × *doorenbosii*, a hybrid snowberry, has a form *S.* × *d.* 'Mother of Pearl' which is a most decorative and useful garden plant. It is much to be preferred to the suckering common snowberry, *S. albus*, which although attractive in shady woodland, should not be allowed in the garden. *S.* × *d.* 'Mother of Pearl' bears heavy crops of subtly rose-flushed white berries, the size of marbles. Plant it where you pass in early winter; it is quite charming.
SMALL DECIDUOUS SHRUB   HALF SHADE
ZONES 5-8

FOLIAGE

'White' foliage is interpreted as green leaves variously marbled, veined or variegated with white, cream or silver. At a distance the markings blend with green pigment to give a light, fragile effect contrasting with the solid weight of plain leaves. But since markings are often subtle, allow plants to trail out of pots or to flop out over border edgings, where details can be easily examined.

Most evergreen whites and silvers retain their colour variation through the year and in sun or shade; deciduous plants thriving in sun form new chlorophyll and by midsummer, especially with rich feeding, the leaves become green.

Plants with yellower variegation are found in the next chapter. See also information on leaf variegation in Appendix I: 'Colour in plants'.

ACER MAPLE
A. negundo 'Variegatum', the variegated form of the American box elder, has broad white irregular margins to the pale green leaves. Its bushy head, seen against a dark background, has a light airy effect, giving a feeling of space.

A. platanoides 'Drummondii' has leaves of dark green edged with white, the two colours firm and contrasting. A less vigorous form of the Norway maple, this is a tree for a small garden, and green-foliaged plants below should match the green of the inner leaf.

MEDIUM DECIDUOUS TREES   FULL SUN
ZONES 7-9

ACORUS
A. calamus 'Variegatus' has long iris-like leaves neatly striped with cream. It thrives in boggy ground beside streams. Plant it next to bronze-tinted rodgersias or the purple-leaved rheum.

DECIDUOUS PERENNIAL   90 CM (36 IN)
FULL SUN   ZONES 7-9

ACTINIDIA
A. kolomikta is a hardy climber with distinctive foliage. From a distance it appears variegated white and cream; close examination reveals heart-shaped leaves banded with white, pink and green. Later they fade to brownish-green after flowering in summer.

DECIDUOUS CLIMBER   FULL SUN   ZONES 7-9

AJUGA
A. reptans, bugle, carries whorls of bright blue flowers above prostrate evergreen leaves which may be green, purple-bronze, variegated or tricolour in bronze, pink and green. The green form is the most vigorous for ground cover, but the coloured forms look pretty in appropriate associations. *A.r.* 'Variegata' has grey-green leaves with cream variegation, perfect under the light shade cast by a purple-leaved plum, the blue bugle flower further enriching the colour scheme in season.

EVERGREEN PERENNIAL   10 CM (4 IN)
FULL SUN OR SHADE   ZONES 5-9

ARALIA
A. elata 'Variegata' has leaves with pale cream variegation, lighter and more shimmering than the gold-variegated plant (see Clear yellows: foliage). Grow a smooth green-leaved plant round its feet for quiet contrast: the shrubby *Pachysandra terminalis* or perennial *Alchemilla mollis*.

LARGE DECIDUOUS SHRUB
FULL SUN OR HALF SHADE   ZONES 7-9

ARRHENATHERUM
A. elatius bulbosum 'Variegatum' is a beautiful little spreading form of onion couch grass, with thin leaves striped and margined silvery-white. Grow it at the front of a white and silver border. Little basal bulb-like swollen stems formed during the summer will make new plants.

DECIDUOUS RHIZOME   90-120 CM (36-48 IN)
FULL SUN   ZONES 7-9

ARUM
A. italicum 'Pictum' has arrow-shaped glossy leaves, the edges undulating and margined with an even band of green. The central and radiating veins are a distinctive pale creamy-green. Leaves first appear in autumn, and new growth continues until it reaches its maximum height and lushness in early spring. Plant in a circle round a deciduous tree where small crocus flowers may push through the foliage in spring.

DECIDUOUS TUBER   30-45 CM (12-18 IN)
FULL SUN OR HALF SHADE   ZONES 7-9

ASTRANTIA MASTERWORT
A. major 'Sunningdale Variegated' has greeny-white subtle-coloured flowers and yellow- and cream-splashed leaves which glow in spring, especially close to the purple-tinged leaves of *Clematis recta* 'Purpurea', or the shrubby purple-leaved *Weigela florida* 'Foliis Purpureis'.

DECIDUOUS PERENNIAL   60 CM (24 IN)
FULL SUN   ZONES 7-9
See also summer, above.

AZARA
Azaras are attractive evergreens with small glossy leaves and vanilla-scented flowers in spring and early summer. All natives of South America, few are reliably hardy.

A. microphylla 'Variegata' prefers deep acid woodland soil and a sheltered site. The green 'type' plant is hardy, glossy green leaves just concealing pale yellow puffs of fragrant petalless flowers in very early spring. Unfortunately, the variegated form lacks its vigour, and is slow to grow, often succumbing to hard frosts during its first winter seasons.

Actinidia kolomikta

However, when well grown it makes a picture of delicately poised beauty, cream-splashed leaves shining against dark foliage backgrounds.

TALL EVERGREEN SHRUB   FULL SUN OR SHADE
ZONES 8-10

BRUNNERA

B. macrophylla 'Hadspen Cream' has leaves prettily marked and edged with cream. It is not so bright in colour contrast as *B.m.* 'Variegata', but the spreading clumps are less inclined to revert to dull green. It is one of the most choice variegated plants; increased only by annual division, it is unfortunately slow to make clumps.

DECIDUOUS PERENNIAL   30 CM (12 IN)
HALF SHADE OR SHADE   ZONES 7-10
See also The blues: spring.

BUDDLEIA

B. davidii 'Harlequin' has creamy-white variegated leaves and reddish-purple flowers, a pretty combination. Smaller than the type, *B. davidii* (see The blues: late summer), it fits snugly into a border scheme, and responds to fierce early spring pruning. If space permits, grow in a group.

MEDIUM DECIDUOUS SHRUB   FULL SUN
ZONES 7-9

CAREX SEDGE

C. riparia 'Variegata' has long arching narrow and distinctly striped grass leaves, some almost white. It spreads quickly in damp soil, and is ideal cover for a natural pond edge, a foil to big-leaved gunnera or rodgersia.

DECIDUOUS PERENNIAL   60-90 CM (24-36 IN)
FULL SUN OR HALF SHADE   ZONES 6-9

CORNUS DOGWOOD

The dogwoods are a genus of small trees, shrubs and herbaceous perennials grown for many differing qualities. Trees and tall shrubs have elegant shapes and green or variegated foliage, and flower in early spring to summer. Often they have coloured autumn tints. Some have red, green or russet-gold stems in winter, colours brightest when pollarded each spring.

C. *alba* 'Elegantissima', this variegated-leaved form of the red-stemmed dogwood, has bright white leaves, sometimes showing almost no green. Although quite common, this is a marvellous foliage shrub; groups planted at the edge of water or woodland are pale and beautiful on sunlit days.

MEDIUM DECIDUOUS SHRUB
FULL SUN OR HALF SHADE   ZONES 7-9
C. *alternifolia* 'Argentea' grows in tiers, with horizontal branches at intervals up the 3 m

(10 ft) stems, eventually making a flat-topped shrub. The leaves are green and white. It is one of the handsomest variegated shrubs, delicately posing like a ballet dancer. Grow it on a corner or by a doorway, plain green leaves near by enhancing its beauty but not competing.

LARGE DECIDUOUS SHRUB
FULL SUN OR HALF SHADE   ZONES 7-9
C. *controversa* 'Variegata' is like a larger version of the previous shrub, eventually making a medium-sized tiered tree like a giant wedding cake. The leaves are long and irregularly splashed with white, slightly yellow on the margins. Brunnera, blue-flowered in early summer and its rough green leaves making a sober underplanting later, is a perfect companion plant, thriving in the canopy of its light shade.

MEDIUM DECIDUOUS TREE   FULL SUN
ZONES 7-9

COTONEASTER

C. horizontalis 'Variegatus' has prettily marked green and white leaves, which turn pinkish in autumn. It is rather less vigorous, and more compact, than the type.

MEDIUM EVERGREEN SHRUB   FULL SUN
ZONES 6-9
See also Foliage framework: green.

CYCLAMEN

By careful planting it is possible to have flowers of the small hardy cyclamen in bloom at almost any time of the year. Developing from corms, the species are distinct not only in flowering time but also in their dormancy period. Leaves, too, vary in shape but are all marked in silvery-green, the markings varying not only between species but also between individual plants of one species. Coming from the Mediterranean, all cyclamen like high summer temperatures, but they vary in their need for sun and shade.

C. *hederifolium*, sowbread, has ivy-like leaves, patterned with silver on a green base, slightly pinkish on the undersides. It has charming mauve, pink or white flowers in late summer, the leaves thickly covering the ground from early autumn to early summer. The leaf colouring is more pronounced in an open position, and a colony benefits from a mulch while dormant in the summer.

C. *repandum* has arrow-shaped leaves with toothed margins, usually patterned with silver and dark green, and palest at the edge. The pink to carmine-red flowers of the commonly cultivated form, with strange twisted petals, appear in late spring.

CORMS   15 CM (6 IN)
FULL SUN OR SHADE   ZONES 6-9

Cornus alba 'Elegantissima'

Arum italicum 'Pictum'

ERYNGIUM

E. variifolium has spiny green toothed leaves, with conspicuous white veins, forming a handsome rosette through all the seasons. Although the thistly pale blue flowers in late summer are not exciting, its foliage brightens up a winter border.

EVERGREEN PERENNIAL   45 CM (18 IN)
FULL SUN OR HALF SHADE   ZONES 7-9

Glyceria maxima 'Variegata'

EUONYMUS SPINDLE TREE

Evergreen euonymus make attractive foliage clumps or hedges, especially at the seaside or in urban areas. Those with leaves variegated, in silver or gold, keep their colour in sun or shade. Deciduous species often have bright berries, seed or split capsule visible as red and yellow, and their leaves assume brilliant autumnal tints. They are not particular about soil, if anything preferring it alkaline.

E. fortunei radicans 'Silver Queen' has shallow-toothed leaves with a broad creamy-white margin. Young leaves unfolding all through the summer have a yellow tinge which adds interest. Since this little shrub responds to tight clipping, it may be used to make a formal edging, or planted in groups to make dense ground cover. Self-clinging against a wall, it will grow upwards making a sizeable plant. It is attractive in full sun and even in sunless backyards where little else will flourish.
SMALL EVERGREEN SHRUB OR CLIMBER
FULL SUN OR SHADE   ZONES 8-10

FATSIA

F. japonica 'Variegata' has its handsome glossy leaves tipped and margined with white. Unfortunately it is very expensive, since plants are grafted on to the green form and grow slowly.
MEDIUM EVERGREEN SHRUB   SHADE
ZONES 8-10
See also Foliage framework: green.

FRAGARIA STRAWBERRY

F. vesca, the alpine strawberry, has a less invasive form, *F.v.* 'Variegata', with charming variegated leaves, green heavily splashed with white. Mature leaves last through the winter and make a delightful fresh-looking patch of colour under dark hedges or bushes.
EVERGREEN PERENNIAL   23 CM (9 IN)
SHADE   ZONES 6-9

FUCHSIA

Where climate allows, fuchsias make colourful hedges, or simply clumps of colour in the front of borders. Flowering is continuous in summer and the leaves of some forms have attractive markings.

F. magellanica 'Versicolor' has striking grey-green leaves, with pronounced pink markings and creamy-white variegation. Forms differ widely in the strength of their colouring so look for one with good markings. It is lovely underplanted with glaucous grey dicentra or making an impact beside dark purple foliage.
MEDIUM DECIDUOUS SHRUB   FULL SUN
ZONES 7-9

F. 'Sharpitor' has pale green or white variegated leaves and very pale pink, almost white, flowers. It is probably a sport of *F. magellanica molinae.* Unfortunately it is tender, but looks lovely in containers. Take cuttings in late summer.
SMALL DECIDUOUS SHRUB   FULL SUN
ZONES 7-9

GLYCERIA GREAT WATER GRASS

G. maxima (syn. *G. aquatica*) is very vigorous in water, equally happy with its feet in an ornamental pond or at stream edges. It is extremely palatable to horses and cows. The variegated *G.m.* 'Variegata' is less invasive, leaves boldly striped white and creamy-yellow, emerging in spring almost pink. It grows happily in ordinary soil and is a useful water and border plant.
DECIDUOUS PERENNIAL   75-120 CM (30-48 IN)
FULL SUN   ZONES 7-9

HEBE
SHRUBBY VERONICA, SHRUBBY SPEEDWELL

H. × *andersonii* 'Variegata' is a sport with a very beautiful leaf, margined ivory-white, the centre grey-green splashed with darker green. The flowers are bluish-purple, a particularly fine association of leaf and flower. Though tender it may survive some frost, but it grows quickly from cuttings and it is more satisfactory to have new plants annually than to protect and cherish woody ones.
MEDIUM EVERGREEN SHRUB   FULL SUN
ZONES 8-10

HEDERA IVY

H. canariensis 'Gloire de Marengo' has wide triangular leaves carried on long pink leaf-stalks. Cream margins, wider at the base, surround grey and dark green centres. The plant will make excellent cover or will climb, but is a little tender; best in town microclimates.

H. colchica 'Dentata Variegata' is very similar but larger in all its parts, out of scale for a small garden, but magnificent where space permits.

H. helix has so many forms with cream and white variegation that it is difficult to choose. Decide whether a subtle grey-green toning leaf is appropriate or one on which the white and green are sharply defined. *H.h.* 'Glacier' has a glaucous leaf outlined with a thin silver line. 'Harald' has a stronger, brighter two-colour leaf. 'Silver Queen' comes somewhere in between, with the white tinged pink in winter.
EVERGREEN CLIMBERS   FULL SUN OR SHADE
ZONES 7-10
See also Foliage framework: green.

HEMEROCALLIS DAY LILY

H. fulva 'Variegata' is a rare foliage plant, but worth searching for. The leaves, particularly in spring, have a wide white stripe, brightening up some dull corner or contrasting with plain green and purple foliage plants.
DECIDUOUS PERENNIAL   1.2 M (4 FT)
FULL SUN OR SHADE   ZONES 6-9
See also Foliage framework: green.

HOLCUS

H. mollis 'Variegatus', the white and green striped form of the invasive creeping soft-grass, may be planted to make a patch of bright 'white' in a silver and grey garden, or as neat edging to a border. Trim it annually, in summer, with shears to prevent flowering and to encourage new growth.

DECIDUOUS PERENNIAL   20 CM (8 IN)
FULL SUN   ZONES 6-9

HOSTA PLANTAIN LILY

H. albomarginata, one of the smaller hostas, has green leaves with a narrow white margin. Useful for planting in groups in small gardens.

   H. fortunei 'Marginato-alba' has sage-green leaves, broadly edged with white, and with grey undersides. It is outstanding, good as a specimen, effective in drifts, or in a pot. It has lilac flowers in summer.

   H. ventricosa 'Variegata' has dark green leaves margined with creamy-white.

DECIDUOUS PERENNIALS   45-75 CM (18-30 IN)
HALF SHADE OR SHADE   ZONES 6-9
See also The blues: foliage.

HYDRANGEA

H. 'Tricolor', a lacecap hydrangea, has leaves variegated in green, grey and cream. It is quite hardy and vigorous, but it should not be given rich food or the leaves will revert to green.

MEDIUM DECIDUOUS SHRUB
FULL SUN OR SHADE   ZONES 7-9
See also Foliage framework: green.

ILEX HOLLY

I. aquifolium 'Ferox Argentea', silver hedgehog holly, is a rounded bush whose very prickly leaves have spines on the leaf surfaces as well as round the edge. The centre of the leaf is green and the crinkled margin is creamy-white. It is easy to see why it is given its name, the whole effect a blurred and fuzzy outline of cream.

   I.a. 'Argenteo Media-picta' (syn. *I.a.* 'Silver Milkboy'), the silver milkmaid holly, has leaves of glossy green with a pure white centre. It has spiny leaves and may be used for hedging, making an impenetrable boundary.

LARGE EVERGREEN SHRUBS
FULL SUN OR SHADE   ZONES 6-9
See also Foliage framework: green.

IRIS

I. pallida dalmatica 'Variegata' has yellow or, for the white garden, cream-edged grey leaves. It spreads more slowly than the ordinary form.

EVERGREEN RHIZOME   75 CM (30 IN)
FULL SUN   ZONES 7-9
See also Foliage framework: silver and grey.

Kerria japonica 'Variegata'

KERRIA JEW'S MALLOW

K. japonica 'Variegata' is a charming suckering bush for open positions. It can be trimmed to make a compact mound or allowed to grow loosely and weave in among neighbouring plants. The pale green and white leaves are a foil to its primrose-coloured single flowers.

SMALL DECIDUOUS SHRUB
FULL SUN OR HALF SHADE
ZONES 7-9

LAMIUM DEAD NETTLE

L. maculatum is normally variegated in gardens: a green leaf with a central white splash. It has dull mauve flowers, is well known and tends to be an invasive garden pest. Its pink and white forms, respectively *L.m.* 'Roseum' and 'Album', are much prettier. Mass them within the formality of a low box hedge surround, and the effect is stunning, the fresh golden-green of the box contrasting with the silver, white and green of the ground cover. The planting is trouble-free and permanent: the plants simply need clipping with shears once a year.

   L. 'Beacon Silver' has more shining silvered leaves and thrives in light shade, young growth being particularly bright in spring. I have found it good in pots, and an attractive foil to tulips allowed to push up through the foliage in early spring.

EVERGREEN PERENNIAL   20-40 CM (8-16 IN)
HALF SHADE   ZONES 6-9

Hedera canariensis 'Gloire de Marengo'

OSMANTHUS

O. heterophyllus 'Latifolius Variegatus' has broad leaves edged with silver. Individually the leaves are beautiful and the upright habit of the bush is distinctive.

MEDIUM EVERGREEN SHRUB
HALF SHADE OR SHADE   ZONES 7-9
See also Foliage framework: green.

PELARGONIUM 'GERANIUM'

Pelargoniums are mainly tender sub-shrubs for pots or summer bedding. Cuttings are easy to take each autumn, kept frost-free all winter and put out again after the last spring frost.

Prunus lusitanica 'Variegata'

P. crispum 'Variegatum' has fragrant crinkled variegated leaves and small pale pink flowers. The leaves are lemon-scented. It is a charming winter pot plant.

EVERGREEN SHRUB   90 CM (36 IN)
FULL SUN   ZONES 9-10

PHALARIS

P. arundinacea 'Picta', the ribbon grass or gardener's garters, has leaves longitudinally striped in white. Dense and quickly spreading, it is best planted where it can be contained by paving or some other constraint. Cut it down in mid-season and new, young growth will be shining white.

DECIDUOUS PERENNIAL   90 CM (36 IN)
HALF SHADE   ZONES 6-9

PHILADELPHUS MOCK ORANGE

P. coronarius 'Variegatus', although very pretty, is a poor performer, slow to grow and difficult. The tall *P.* 'Innocence', when in flower in midsummer with its leaves almost as creamy-white as the blossom, is most attractive and the flowers are sweetly fragrant. Unfortunately it is gaunt and dull later, after the severe pruning it needs to ensure free flowering in the following year.

TALL DECIDUOUS SHRUB
FULL SUN OR HALF SHADE   ZONES 5-9
See also early summer, above.

Phalaris arundinacea 'Picta'

PHORMIUM

The small *P. cookianum* 'Variegatum' has its variegation in the centre of the leaf, sometimes broad and creamy, at others narrow. *P. tenax* 'Variegatum' has broad leaves margined with a thin line of white. It is best to choose an individual plant, since even named clones vary considerably.

SMALL TO MEDIUM EVERGREEN SHRUBS
FULL SUN   ZONES 8-10
See also Foliage framework: green.

PITTOSPORUM

P. tenuifolium 'Garnettii' has small leaves flushed pink and white. It is hardier than the more open-growing *P.t.* 'Silver Queen', which has silver-suffused margins to its leaves, and becomes denser and more bush-like in shape. Both are beautiful foliage plants, needing a warm wall in exposed gardens.

MEDIUM EVERGREEN SHRUB
FULL SUN OR SHADE   ZONES 8-10
See also Foliage framework: green.

POPULUS POPLAR

P. candicans 'Aurora' has startling leaves, pink and creamy-white when young, gradually turning pale green throughout the summer. Grow it to attract attention in a small garden, or plant groups to blend among more sober foliage colour. Cut it back in early spring to make the leaves even paler and larger.

TALL DECIDUOUS TREE   FULL SUN
ZONES 6-9

PRUNUS

P. lusitanica 'Variegata' has glossy green leaves discreetly flecked with cream, irregularly along the edges. Smaller in all respects than the green Portugal laurel, it is an excellent choice for a small garden. Mauve and white flowers look lovely with it.

MEDIUM EVERGREEN SHRUB
FULL SUN OR SHADE   ZONES 7-9

RHAMNUS

R. alaternus 'Argenteovariegata' is a lovely evergreen, the leaves marbled grey-green and with silver margins. In shade the plant glows, the white and green mixing to look ghostly and luminous. It has an upright habit, small leaves and twigs intermingling, no part clearly defined. Plant it next to glossy-leaved fatsia.

LARGE EVERGREEN SHRUB   SHADE
ZONES 7-9

SAMBUCUS ELDER

The ordinary European elder, *S. nigra*, has several good sports with coloured and variegated leaves. *S.n.* 'Albovariegata' has pale

leaves irregularly margined with white. It is a useful large shrub, broad flower-heads matching the white-toned leaves and making a quiet and cool background to almost any planting. Early bluebells, bright blue brunnera and summer lithospermum all look lovely at its feet. At the end of the season the hardy deciduous ceanothus give the same pure blue, but in paler tints, and makes an excellent companion. Allow evening primroses to seed and flower between these bushes.
LARGE DECIDUOUS SHRUB   HALF SHADE
ZONES 6-10

SAXIFRAGA SAXIFRAGE
S. stolonifera, mother-of-thousands or strawberry geranium, is obliging, preferring damp shade under a north wall. The leaves of *S.s.* 'Tricolor' are smaller, multicoloured in marbled grey, white and a sort of dark pink. It is the ideal plant to carpet the ground under a dark holly hedge. Neither plant is fully hardy, 'Tricolor' less so. They are colonizers, but not difficult to control. The overground runners, equipped with little plantlets at their ends, are bright pink.
EVERGREEN PERENNIAL   23 CM (9 IN)
SHADE   ZONES 8-10

SCROPHULARIA
S. aquatica 'Variegata', the variegated water figwort, has toothed thick leaves, patterned cream and green. Preferring moist shade, companion plants are pink-flowered astilbe, bronze-tinted rodgersia or the brown-purple leaves of *Ligularia dentata* 'Desdemona'.
DECIDUOUS PERENNIAL   60 CM (24 IN)
HALF SHADE   ZONES 6-9

SILYBUM
S. marianum, the milk thistle, has dark glossy leaves, spiny and lobed, the veins boldly marked in white, giving a marbled appearance. It is an attractive oddity, its purple thistle-flowers appearing on branched stems in late summer. Usually a biennial, and self-seeding after a hot summer.
EVERGREEN BIENNIAL   60-120 CM (24-48 IN)
FULL SUN   ZONES 8-10

SYMPHORICARPOS SNOWBERRY
S. orbiculatus 'Variegatus' is a lovely garden plant, its green-leaved form best in rough woodland where allowed to spread. The variegated snowberry thrives in full sun, the small green and white leaves neat and pretty in a border of mixed colours. It suckers freely and so must be watched.
MEDIUM DECIDUOUS SHRUB
FULL SUN OR HALF SHADE   ZONES 5-9

SYMPHYTUM COMFREY
S. × uplandicum 'Variegatum' has typical hairy borage leaves, very beautiful, large and pale green, with a wide margin of rich creamy-white. A plant spreads slowly to make a clump, but is most desirable. Grow it as a specimen: a little shade prevents late-summer leaf-scorch and if cut down in midsummer it throws up handsome new foliage. If it must be divided, do this in early spring.
DECIDUOUS PERENNIAL   90 CM (36 IN)
FULL SUN OR HALF SHADE   ZONES 6-9

VIBURNUM
V. tinus 'Variegatum', the variegated laurustinus, has delightful pink leaf-stalks and green and creamy-white leaves. Grow it against a wall and it will make a symmetrical pyramid shape. It is less hardy than the green-leaved type (see winter, above).
MEDIUM EVERGREEN SHRUB   FULL SUN
ZONES 7-9

VINCA PERIWINKLE
V. major 'Variegata' is a tall straggling plant with clearly defined green- and cream-patterned leaves. It hardly grows densely enough for ground cover, but massed together it makes a good splash of colour in deep shade.
SMALL EVERGREEN SHRUB   SHADE   ZONES 6-9
V. minor has creamy or yellowish variegated forms, the best of which has white flowers. This is a low ground cover, dense and weedproof, under shrubs.
DWARF EVERGREEN SHRUB
HALF SHADE OR SHADE   ZONES 6-9

WEIGELA
Weigelas are a group of hardy deciduous shrubs, suitable for an open border or for light woodland. Pink rather short foxglove-shaped flowers are held in clusters in early summer. There are red- and white-flowered forms.
    W. florida 'Variegata' has arching branches with lightly wrinkled leaves of pale green, widely margined with cream. Pale pink flowers are carried very freely. Prune hard after flowering; the leaves often look unsightly as summer proceeds, so position where late-flowering perennials will screen it.
MEDIUM DECIDUOUS SHRUB
FULL SUN OR HALF SHADE   ZONES 6-10

ZEA
Z. mays, maize, has an excellent variegated form, one of the few variegated plants loved by Gertrude Jekyll. *Z.m.* 'Gracillima Variegata' has arching striped broad leaves.
ANNUAL   90 CM (36 IN)   FULL SUN
ZONES 8-10

Saxifraga stolonifera

Scrophularia aquatica 'Variegata'

CHAPTER IV

CLEAR YELLOWS

To pass from the cool restfulness of green- and grey-leaved shrubs into a bright pool of yellow flowers and golden foliage is to experience the same sudden cheering of the spirit as when the sun emerges unexpectedly from behind leaden clouds. These pale yellows are serene and softly exciting, yet warm and bright; satin and even velvet textures give yellows the richness of gold. (The very word 'yellow' comes from the Indo-European *ghelwo*, meaning 'related to gold'.) The most luminous of colours, yellow is perceived by the eye most readily, before other colours. It lacks the disembodied advancing quality of red, or the receding attributes of the 'blues', yet attracts and dominates, drawing the eye irresistibly. Like a spotlight on a stage, yellow attracts attention, placing deeper colours in a metaphorical shadow.

In the garden, yellow flowers and pale young foliage evoke the spirit of spring. Pale yellow aconites, winter jasmine and primroses are eye-catchers among the low-toned greens of evergreen foliage, fallen leaves and brown earth which are nature's colours at the start of the season. Lower-toned yellows in the 'golden' greens of spring foliage are in harmony with winter's olive-greens and russet colours and with the plum-tinted colours of tips of new leaves.

In this chapter we consider the yellows close to the clear pure hues, and flowers and leaves of pale gold and lime-green, in all their dimensions. The hotter yellows moving towards orange and scarlet are considered with these other flame colours in Chapter VIII: there emphasis falls on later borders dominated by these rich colours, which complement the lush summer green foliage and harmonize with autumn leaf colour. Clear yellow flowers gleam rather than glow; matched by the almost translucent golden leaves of deciduous shrubs, they seem light and ephemeral.

In the spectrum these yellows lie between closely related harsher yellow and deep orange shades on one hand and yellowish-greens and green on the other. Harmonious planting schemes can scale through to the darker, hotter shades of orange and red, or can with lime-green and citron flowers and golden and gold-variegated foliage merge into pale and then darker green leaf colour. Pale luminous yellows harmonize too with low-toned greens and browns which move towards desaturated grey tones and neutral achromatic foliage colours. These yellows find their complements in blues, violets and mauves, but impact and contrast are not startling and dazzling, as when a bright green is placed next to a saturated red. Yellow, even when at its purest, remains the palest colour; its complementary, violet, is the darkest of all hues. We have seen that contrast effects are greatest when hues have much the same value. Yellow and gold, then, used in contrast with violets and mauves, do not dazzle as much as many other complementary associations; there is less imperative need to lower one of the tones or to alter relative areas of colour.

In the creative arts it is thought that in any one scene a relative proportion of yellow to violet of about three to one is quiet and cheerful, not too brilliant. With our gleaming yellows, innumerable separate garden pictures can be created by using golden leaves associated with violet and mauve flowers, or dull purple foliage as a foil to pale primrose flower colour, or yellow with mauve-to-violet flowers in planting harmonies with green leaves as a linking background. Plant a carpet of hardy summer-flowering mauve, magenta or violet geraniums under the branches of the golden *Robinia pseudo-acacia* 'Frisia', in front of *Philadelphus coronarius* 'Aureus', or in the shade. Purple-leaved cotinus, berberis or plum-coloured filbert (*Corylus maxima* 'Purpurea') can have casual plantings of pale yellow foxgloves or *Oenothera biennis* between them, or, more formally, they can be grouped with pale yellow shrub roses and underplanted with *Alchemilla mollis* or *Crocosmia* 'Solfatare', which flowers late in the season. Flowers that are yellow, cream, ivory, yellow-tinted, blushed with pink to subtle apricot, or buff-tinted as in *Rosa*

PREVIOUS PAGE *Solidago* × *hybrida* makes a pool of light in the foreground of a flower group of blending yellows. The flat flowers of achillea and the tall verbascums at the back are in fact a stronger and deeper yellow when viewed close to, but here the paling effect of distance prevents them from stealing the picture. Creamy plumes of *Artemisia lactiflora* subtly link these gleaming yellows with the greens of accompanying leaves; pure white flowers in that role would be too eye-catching. The blueness of a clear sky can become part of a colour picture, here brightening contrasting yellows even as the sun fades them.

RIGHT *Bupleurum falcatum* softens the transition between the pale daisies of *Chrysanthemum* 'Jamaica Primrose' and the dark background hedge. The 'measurable' yellow of the tiny bupleurum is not dissimilar to that of the daisy, but petal form and texture and neighbouring colours influence our impression so that these two yellows appear quite different from one another. The airy umbels blend into lime-green, while the flat petals, seen against complementary blue-green leaves, reflect their true colour more accurately.

These greens and yellows are cool; *Curtonus paniculatus* flowers bring a note of warmth into the right-hand side of the picture. Although the colours have shared yellow pigment in common, the curtonus is so intense a red that its effect against the pale yellows and dark Irish yew background is one of contrast rather than of related colour harmonies.

A contrast in mood with this studied economy of subtle colour is the sunny border, OPPOSITE. Mixed daisy-flowered groups of rudbeckia in the background, helenium to the right and inula in the foreground, and spikes of invasive *Lysimachia punctata*, demonstrate a wealth of different yellows in varying forms and textures, in a more relaxed planting which warms the senses and attracts the eye. As the spectator moves away, these yellows pale and intermingle, losing the definition of their separate planting planes.

Bright yellow and violet-blue, opposites on the spectral wheel, make a classic combination of complementaries, especially when as here, FAR LEFT, the almost acidic *Antirrhinum* 'Yellow Triumph' is accompanied by heleniums in a related deeper yellow. Colour perspective is exaggerated as the receding purple-blue tones of the delphiniums make them fade farther into the background, while the mass of eye-catching yellow has a foreshortening effect. In a smaller bed such an assertive yellow might be a small accent against a much larger area of the misty desaturated blue tones.

CENTRE Many green leaves contain sufficient yellow pigment to make related colour harmonies with yellow flowers. Here drifts of alyssum and lime-yellow alchemilla are grown in and against a stone wall with bright glossy foliage of *Bergenia crassifolia*. Apart from the powdery yellow flowers, contrasting leaf forms fill this picture with textural interest.

LEFT A yellow azalea glimmers in a woodland glade, enhancing the effect of dappled sunlight. Yellow, the palest of the pure hues, readily becomes luminous when surrounded by lower and darker tones. Here even the shade of the surrounding trees darkens the greens of the neighbouring foliage and allows the yellow to gleam even more brightly.

ruffles the leaves and gently disturbs existing patterns.

Strips or focal points of yellow foliage enhance a garden's formal layout. Golden or variegated box or even dwarf *Thuja* 'Rheingold' can be clipped to make a formal edging. Yellow-leaved low-growing perennials such as creeping Jenny, *Lysimachia nummularia* 'Aurea', marjoram and thyme can spill forward on to gravel paths or pavement for a softer effect. In deep shade golden-leaved ivies and the herbaceous climbing golden hop, *Humulus lupulus* 'Aureus', will glow with bright colour.

Many deciduous trees and shrubs as well as herbaceous plants have golden or pale-leaved variants, usually softer in texture than those of evergreens; among them are acers, elders, cornus, philadelphus and physocarpus. These leaves often become greener (or if in full sun are liable to scorch) by late summer, but by then there are plenty of yellow-flowered perennials which carry a garden theme into early autumn; helianthus, rudbeckia, pale solidaster and self-seeding evening primrose (forms of *Oenothera*) make vivid clumps. In autumn deciduous trees and shrubs often have leaves which colour to pale yellow before falling and are enriched by neighbouring foliage of evergreens such as the Japanese *Cryptomeria japonica* 'Elegans', which turns a rich bronze-brown, making a splendid background to yellow flowers and the buff colours of dying flower stalks and seed-heads.

Through the flowering season yellow flowers can become the background flower colour to many border schemes, blending with most colours, clashing with few. Among them feathery plumes of *Thalictrum speciosissimum*, creamy *Aruncus dioicus*, ivory-tinged *Artemisia lactiflora* are excellent border

This border illustrated in two seasons has been carefully built up into a balanced harmony based on varied contrasts with yellow tones. It consists of a series of colour incidents, each one a contrived association of yellow and blue flowers with appropriate foliage accompaniment, which combine to make a highly impressionistic picture when glimpsed as a whole. Where harsher yellows are used, grey and green leaves tone down and soften extreme opposites. However, yellows predominate in the picture as spots of pure hue against larger expanses of de-saturated blues, greens and greys.

The design for this bed was sketched out first with crayons. The two main seasons were coloured in, and then evergreens such as piptanthus, ceanothus and grey-leaved old English lavender were added for winter structure and to link the bright contrasts during quieter periods.

The shrubs and climbers respond to shapely pruning, so that areas of colour and plant proportions stay reasonably constant. Lime-green nicotiana, daisy-flowered *Felicia pappei* and annual ageratum fill in the gaps where tulips provided colour in early summer.

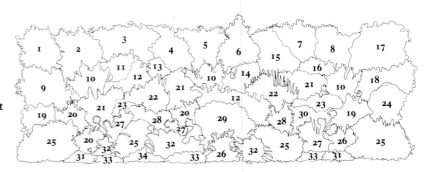

Keyline drawing

plants. These light yellows injure no companion flower groups, are injured themselves by very few. Perhaps pure spectral yellow shouts most persistently beside the purest red with no hint of orange or blue; yet choose yellow flowers in pale tints or lower tones and even red with yellow can seem harmonious. Red with orange pigment is a flame-coloured relation, linked by orange-yellow shades; yellow with blue-toned red looks pale and light. There are few flowers of such a pure intense red that they shock with the brightest yellow. With bright crimson and magenta, yellow can be rich and glowing, especially when both colours are toned down by evening light or grown in shade, and linked by violet. Yellow flowers even as bright as lily-flowered tulip 'Mrs Moon' can be grown in front of a red brick wall, since most terracotta colours have a measure of mellow orange tinting. Yellow looks clear and clean against a white trellis or near any white paint in a garden. Yellow flowers find harmony with their own leaves, becoming more 'orange' against dark green, darken-

ing in shade with pale leaves, glowing with leaves of blue-green. Many glaucous and grey-leaved plants have yellow flowers, sometimes a harsh yellow, which the strong hints of complementary blue make more brilliant. Mix soft yellows with the harsher ones making a whole garden area of grey-textured leaves, some matt and hairy, others shining silver and feathery, allowing a riot of related flower colour to cheer the mind, especially on a dull sunless day. Yellow is always active, the colour nearest to light, a colour which as the sun's rays 'yellow' a landscape or a flower group, brings a sense of well-being.

Spring flowers are predominantly yellow. Winter jasmine, golden aconites, small yellow species *Iris danfordii* come with warmer winter days and are followed by daffodils, pools of pale colour set among grass in drifts and abstract shapes or in formal panels to line an avenue or edge a driveway. Pale *Coronilla glauca* has primrose-coloured blooms among its blue-green leaves, against a sheltered wall. Wild primroses

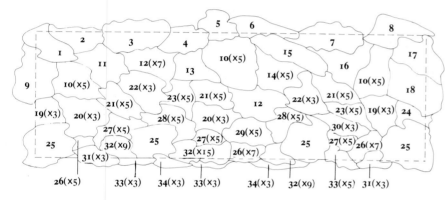

Planting plan. Figures in parentheses indicate the number of plants in a group.

Plant key

1	*Clematis orientalis*	18	*Rosa* 'Canary Bird'
2	*Rosa* 'Frühlingsgold'	19	*Aster frikartii* 'Mönch'
3	*Ceanothus* × 'Autumnal Blue'	20	*Hemerocallis citrina*
4	*Celastrus orbiculatus*	21	× *Solidaster hybridus*
5	*Lonicera tragophylla*	22	*Salvia farinacea* 'Victoria'
6	*Abutilon* × *suntense*	23	*Aquilegia alpina*
7	*Ceanothus thyrsiflorus* 'Cascade'	24	*Clematis flammula*
8	*Fremontodendron californicum*	25	*Lavandula angustifolia*
9	*Piptanthus laburnifolius*	26	Blue Dutch iris
10	*Iris sibirica*	27	*Agapanthus* Headbourne Hybrids
11	*Phlomis fruticosa*	28	*Lilium* 'Limelight'
12	*Nicotiana* 'Lime Green'	29	*Ceratostigma willmottiana*
13	*Teucrium fruticans*	30	*Caryopteris* × *clandonensis*
14	*Campanula latifolia*	31	*Felicia pappei*
15	*Cytisus battandieri*	32	*Tulipa fosterana* 'Candela'
16	*Artemisia arborescens*	33	*Ageratum houstonianum*
17	*Clematis tangutica*	34	*Helianthemum* 'Wisley Primrose'

are scattered in hedgerow banks. Wallflowers make patches of sunshine in containers or under the walls of a house, filling the air with rich scent, which in itself is intensely evocative of spring. In favoured gardens mimosa (*Acacia* species) have pale yellow flower puffs and a rich fragrance matched by shrubs such as corylopsis and hamamelis, for the half-shade of light woodland, and revelling in acid soil. The common yellow azalea, *Rhododendron luteum*, has flowers in rounded trusses, and later the bronze-red leaves give colour in a shady dark corner. Winter-flowering mahonias give way to spring-flowering but less scented species, between them covering a period of flowering from early autumn to early summer. Some of the tender mahonias from Texas and Mexico flower in summer and have glaucous or redcurrant berries above blue-green veined leaves.

As the season progresses into summer there is no shortage of yellow-flowering plants: pale bracts of dogwood, pale yellow shrub roses, yellow flag iris (*Iris pseudacorus*), bright pea-flowers of *Piptanthus laburnifolius*. Yellow verbascum next to velvet-red *Rosa* 'Frensham' or scarlet *Monarda didyma* can be linked by a background hedge of darkest yew. Dark foliage helps to anchor the light floating influence of a luminous yellow, so use glossy green leaves for foreground planting, anchoring paleness firmly to the ground. Bergenias, box, holly and yew are green all the year and give the necessary stability; in full summer grey leaves link yellow flowers with the bright emerald green of mown lawns.

In late summer forms of St John's wort flourish in half-shade while heleniums, through a range of yellows, give patches of light, bright colour in sunny borders. In a warm situation lime-green nicotiana contrast with blue-flowered agapanthus and later-flowering ceanothus of powder-blue or intense blue. In damp soil the maple-leaved *Kirengeshoma palmata* has soft, cool yellow flowers and in a dry, sunny spot the last flowers of pale yellow kniphofias are borne until the nights get cool.

WINTER

CORONILLA

C. glauca and its variegated form *C.g.* 'Variegata' flower intermittently all winter, perhaps at their best in early spring. *C. glauca* has delicate grey-green leaves and delightful pale cool yellow pea-blooms. The variegated form is less hardy. Both can be grown in containers and will flower well in a summerhouse or cold greenhouse.

MEDIUM EVERGREEN SHRUB
FULL SUN   ZONES 8-10

ERANTHIS

E. hyemalis, the winter aconite, will make a glowing flowering carpet of golden-green in midwinter. Individual bare stems end in a ruff of divided leaves enclosing a single yellow buttercup-flower. As the flowers wither, deeply cut green leaves make attractive clumps, which can be tidily mown in spring. Plant under a deciduous tree such as lime or chestnut or beneath shrubs.

DECIDUOUS PERENNIAL   5-10 CM (2-4 IN)
HALF SHADE   ZONES 4-9

HAMAMELIS WITCH HAZEL

H. mollis, the Chinese witch hazel, has typical strap-like petals which withstand frost. They are golden-yellow and sweetly fragrant, ideal for picking for the house as well as lasting for many weeks in the garden. A form *H.m.* 'Pallida' has paler blossoms. In autumn the leaves, particularly in a rich acid soil, turn buttercup-yellow.

LARGE DECIDUOUS SHRUB
HALF SHADE   ZONES 6-9

JASMINUM JASMINE

These are climbers and shrubs, mainly hardy, and grown for their very fragrant yellow, pink or white flowers. Most prefer full sun, but do not need rich feeding.

J. nudiflorum, winter jasmine, flowers all through an average winter, bearing yellow flowers along leafless stems. Fortunately it will thrive in shade, as summer appearance is dull. Prune immediately after flowering is finished.

MEDIUM DECIDUOUS SHRUB
HALF SHADE OR SHADE   ZONES 6-10

MAHONIA

M. 'Buckland' and 'Charity', both seedlings of *M. lomariifolia* and *M. japonica*, are superb upright-growing mahonias with long spiny leaflets and terminal clusters of spreading and ascending racemes carried during midwinter. *M. lomariifolia* is less hardy but has distinct erect stems with long leaves composed of numerous pairs of narrow leaflets. The racemes of yellow flowers are long and stiffly upright.

MEDIUM EVERGREEN SHRUBS
FULL SUN OR SHADE   ZONES 7-10

M. japonica has deep green large pinnate leaves, and arching racemes of very fragrant lemon-yellow lily-of-the-valley flowers. The leaves often assume bronze tints in autumn.

MEDIUM EVERGREEN SHRUB
HALF SHADE   ZONES 7-10
See also Foliage framework: green.

Mahonia 'Buckland'

Eranthis hyemalis

Acacia dealbata

SPRING

ACACIA

A. dealbata, silver wattle, a small tree with pale silvery fern-like foliage, is covered in early spring with clouds of clear yellow scented flowers, making a delightful combination. Originally from Australia, it is now a florist's tree grown commercially as 'mimosa' in favoured areas, but well worth attempting in a garden microclimate where, thanks to rapid growth, it may have many seasons of flowering before succumbing to an exceptionally cold spell.

SMALL EVERGREEN TREE
FULL SUN   ZONES 8-10

A. pravissima, Ovens wattle, has unusual flattened grey leaves and larger globular heads and prefers reflected heat from a wall to encourage flowering.

LARGE EVERGREEN SHRUB
FULL SUN   ZONES 9-10
See also Foliage framework: silver and grey.

CALTHA MARSH MARIGOLD

C. palustris 'Plena', the double form, bears its numerous deep yellow flowers on short branched stems above shining green leaves. Preferring to grow in shallow water or in deep moist soil by a natural stream or pond, a flowering group makes a pool of luminous colour matched by the reflecting water.

DECIDUOUS PERENNIAL   30 CM (12 IN)
FULL SUN OR HALF SHADE   ZONES 4-9

CHEIRANTHUS WALLFLOWER

Usually grown as biennials, the seed sown in the previous summer and plants moved to the site for flowering in early autumn, forms of *C. cheiri* make attractive splashes of early spring colour in a range which goes from ivory and cream through all the yellow-red fire colours (see Hot colours) to deepest blood-red. They continue to flower until after the last frosts, when summer bedding plants can take their place and contribute to later colour schemes. They should be planted in groups and drifts between spring bulbs and early-flowering perennials, where their green leaves look attractive even in winter.

C. cheiri 'Primrose Bedder' contributes pale yellow spikes on short stems, an excellent companion for golden daffodils and for blue forget-me-nots or brunnera.

EVERGREEN BIENNIAL   30 CM (12 IN)
FULL SUN   ZONES 6-9

CORYLOPSIS

C. pauciflora, a relative of witch hazel, hamamelis, is one of the most attractive early spring-flowering shrubs. The flowers are bell-shaped and fragrant, of pale primrose colour,

Corylopsis pauciflora

Fritillaria imperialis

borne freely but liable to be nipped by frost or searing winds. It prefers acid or neutral soil. Its habit is spreading, and under its canopy small bulbs or early violets thrive.
MEDIUM DECIDUOUS SHRUB
HALF SHADE   ZONES 6-9

CROCUS

A small cormous plant, some of the more tender species need specially prepared drainage in troughs or alpine houses, but most are suitable for naturalizing in short grass. The green leaves with their central white stripe wither quickly, permitting the grass to be mown within a few weeks of flowering. Drifts of early flowers appear to replace aconites (*Eranthis hyemalis*) as they begin to fade. Apart from the yellows, white, mauve and violet crocus can be planted to harmonize with different colour schemes.

C. chrysanthus 'E.A. Bowles' has rich golden-yellow flowers in the first days of spring, at the same time as the smaller *C. angustifolius* (syn. *C. susianus*), known as the 'cloth of gold' crocus.
CORMS   7.5-12.5 CM (3-5 IN)
FULL SUN   ZONES 5-9

DORONICUM LEOPARD'S BANE

D. austriacum is a most useful early-flowering daisy, carrying its bright yellow blooms freely even in shade. Adaptable and easy to cultivate,

it thrives with companion plantings of wood anemone (*Anemone nemorosa*), erythronium, bright blue brunnera and omphalodes.
DECIDUOUS PERENNIAL   60 CM (24 IN)
HALF SHADE   ZONES 6-9

EUPHORBIA SPURGE

Attractive as grey-green foliage plants (see Foliage framework), euphorbia 'flowers' are insignificant: it is the petal-like bracts that in fact contribute the colour.

E. myrsinites has trailing stems, 40 cm (16 in) long or more, of blue-grey leaves, bearing attractive sulphur-yellow bracts. Needing hot sun and good drainage, it is best grown in raised beds or to fall over the edges of troughs.
EVERGREEN PERENNIAL   15 CM (6 IN)
FULL SUN   ZONES 7-9
E. polychroma (previously *E. epithymoides*) makes a bright yellow-green spreading clump, giving colour for many weeks in late spring. Seed is easily gathered and germinated.
DECIDUOUS PERENNIAL   45 CM (18 IN)
FULL SUN OR HALF SHADE   ZONES 6-9

FORSYTHIA

F. suspensa is a rambling shrub with interlacing branches, much more attractive than the more frequently grown forms of *F.* × *intermedia*, most of which are inelegant in shape and bear harsh yellow flowers. For a more subtle

colouring, the pale primrose blooms of *F. suspensa*, borne on leafless branches, look lovely undercarpeted with blue, white or yellow spring flowers.
TALL DECIDUOUS SHRUBS
HALF SHADE   ZONES 6-9

FRITILLARIA FRITILLARY

F. imperialis, the crown imperial, flowers freely in good soil which is not too moist or alkaline. A ruff of green leaves surrounds the stem which bears at the top a hanging cluster of bell-shaped flowers of yellow, orange or red. Unfortunately the bulbs are often expensive and plants increase slowly. *F.i.* 'Lutea Maxima' has lemon-yellow flowers and makes an attractive picture with the early-flowering species *Paeonia mlokosewitschii* and scented Lily-flowered tulip 'Mrs Moon'.
BULB   90 CM (36 IN)   FULL SUN   ZONES 7-9

KERRIA JEW'S MALLOW

K. japonica, the single-flowered species, is preferable to the often-seen old cottage-garden shrub with double orange blooms. A suckering small shrub with pale yellow blooms, it, and its variegated form (see The whites: foliage), have a delicate elegance. It makes a good neighbour to small bulbs, its sparse leaves casting little shade in summer.
SMALL DECIDUOUS SHRUB
FULL SUN OR HALF SHADE   ZONES 7-9

Lysichitum americanum

Tulipa 'Monte Carlo'

Primula vulgaris

LYSICHITUM SKUNK CABBAGE

L. americanum, yellow skunk cabbage, and the white *L. camtschatcense* are the only representatives of this genus, from different continents but requiring similar growing conditions. They thrive at the edge of natural streams or ponds, producing striking arum-like spathes, followed by massive glossy green foliage. *L. americanum* has wide green-tipped yellow spathes, a spreading root system and seeds freely, if conditions suit it.
DECIDUOUS PERENNIAL   60-90 CM (24-36 IN)
FULL SUN OR HALF SHADE   ZONES 4-9

NARCISSUS DAFFODIL

Most narcissi thrive in grass; the European *N. pseudonarcissus* is found in damp meadows. They always look beautiful naturalized in drifts under deciduous trees or in open glades. In deep loamy soil, preferably slightly acid, the bulbs multiply. Where space is limited, selected narcissi may be planted annually in containers, like other spring-flowering bulbs.

N. bulbocodium, hoop-petticoat daffodil, has wide-open 2-3.5 cm (about 1-1½ in) trumpets.

It needs looking after, for at only 10-15 cm (4-6 in) tall, it is so small that it is easily lost. *N. cyclamineus* is another dwarf of great merit, the flower resembling that of a cyclamen and 15-20 cm (6-8 in) high. It is rich golden-yellow.

N. pseudonarcissus, the Lent lily, has pale nearly white petals with lemon-yellow trumpets on stems 20-35 cm (8-14 in) tall. If thriving, it increases rapidly.

N. 'Golden Rapture' and *N.* 'Kingscourt' are golden and lemon-yellow respectively, trumpets and petals all being the same colour, and both up to 45 cm (18 in) tall. *N.* 'St Keverne', with a shorter central cup, is of rich gold throughout, and stands 50 cm (20 in) high. *N.* 'April Tears' is a Triandrus daffodil with pendent flowers and back-swept petals of creamy-white. Another, similar, *N.* 'Thalia' is taller at 25 cm (10 in), and is creamy-yellow.

The deeply scented wild jonquil, *N. jonquilla*, has given rise to many good garden forms. *N.* 'Trevithian' is a clear buttercup-yellow, 40 cm (16 in) tall.
BULBS   FULL SUN OR HALF SHADE
ZONES 6-8

PAEONIA PEONY

P. lutea ludlowii, one of the shrubby tree peonies, has deeply segmented green leaves and yellow single flowers. Although not in the top rank among tree peonies its ability to thrive in a shady north-facing border makes it exceptionally useful. There, as the muted cream and mauve flowers of the Lenten rose (*Helleborus orientalis* hybrids) fade at the end of winter, this shrub will extend the season of flower.
MEDIUM DECIDUOUS SHRUB
HALF SHADE   ZONES 7-9
The soft grey-green leaves of the perennial *P. mlokosewitschii* emerge early, and the cool lemon-yellow single flowers are a delight in a sunny border. The foliage remains elegant throughout the summer and pods open to reveal red seeds completing the picture in autumn.
DECIDUOUS PERENNIAL   60 CM (24 IN)
FULL SUN   ZONES 7-10

PRIMULA

P. vulgaris, the wild European primrose, and the flower most evocative of a new season, opens in sheltered ditches and woodland in midwinter. In shrubberies, with snowdrops of subtle white and green, the pale yellow flowers express the spirit of unsophisticated natural gardening, simple spring colour 'unimproved' by the hybridizer in search of vivid impact.
DECIDUOUS PERENNIAL   10-15 CM (4-6 IN)
FULL SUN OR HALF SHADE   ZONES 5-9
See also Pinks and mauves: spring.

PRUNUS FLOWERING CHERRY

P. 'Ukon', Japanese cherry, bears creamy tinged-green semi-double flowers, set among bronze leaves. It is seen most effectively against a dark background. Its flowers reliably last many weeks unless devastated by storms.
SMALL DECIDUOUS TREE   FULL SUN
ZONES 6-9
See also The whites: spring.

ROSA ROSE

R. banksiae 'Lutea' is a semi-evergreen climber for warm walls, where the wood is well-ripened the previous summer. The charming double yellow rosettes have a delicate fragrance. Prune immediately after flowering.
SEMI-EVERGREEN CLIMBER
FULL SUN   ZONES 7-9
See also Pinks and mauves: early summer.

TROLLIUS GLOBE FLOWER

Trollius prefer moist rich soil in borders or at the edge of streams, where their deeply cleft leaves look attractive all summer. The garden

EARLY SUMMER

hybrids *T.* × *cultorum* (the *T.* × *hybridus* of some plant catalogues) have big globe-shaped flowers resembling double buttercups. They vary in colour between pure clear yellow and deep orange. *T.* × *cultorum* 'Canary Bird' (*T. ledebourii* of gardens) has pale yellow flowers and those of 'Goldquelle' are deeper golden-yellow.
DECIDUOUS PERENNIAL 60-90 CM (24-36 IN)
FULL SUN OR HALF SHADE ZONES 5-9

TULIPA TULIP
One of the essential bulbs for spring flowers (as well as popular for earlier forcing in the house). Choice from the huge range must depend on personal preference, and the exact shade needed for a particular scheme. Plain colours, vivid or pale, are easier to associate with other plants than are the stripes in two colours or the streaky patterns of fringed petals. In municipal gardens tulips are planted in strong contrasting blocks of colour; in smaller gardens they provide emphatic touches of early colour in mixed borders or make focal points in containers. Like poppies in a cornfield, tulips scattered through the rough grass in orchards, meadows or country gardens shimmer like colours in a pointillist painting.

A progression of different tulips provides flowers from mid-spring well into early summer. Early and late species, blowsy doubles, scented Lily-flowered, with reflexed petals, and long-stemmed elegant Darwins are available. When choosing tulips, beware the short-stemmed varieties: their thick heavy heads can distort elegant proportions.

In a small garden the bulbs can be lifted, dried and stored, to give space for annuals; in the larger garden most tulips can be left *in situ* and will continue to flower satisfactorily for many seasons. They like full sun and rich soil.

Grow the clear yellow tulips in drifts to contrast with blue spring bulbs or to relate to the delicate lime-green bracts of euphorbias.

One of the earliest, *T. kaufmanniana* 'Chopin', 20 cm (8 in), has shortish stems, brownish leaves and clear yellow open flowers.

Single Early *T.* 'Bellona' has deep golden-yellow flowers, 30 cm (12 in) tall, and 'Mon Tresor' is a gentle yellow, 25 cm (10 in). Double Early *T.* 'Monte Carlo' is lemon-yellow outside, deep yellow inside, and 40 cm (16 in) tall. *T. fosterana* 'Candela' is a soft yellow, 40 cm (16 in) high.
BULBS FULL SUN ZONES 5-9
T. sylvestris is a European species with grey-green leaves and delicately fragrant pale yellow flowers, suitable for half shade under deciduous trees and shrubs.
BULB HALF SHADE ZONES 5-9

ALYSSUM
Alyssums thrive in ordinary soil, making clumps of colour at the front of borders. *A. saxatile*, the well-known gold dust, is now placed in the genus *Aurinia* by some authorities. Its cultivar *A.s.* 'Citrinum', with soft grey-green leaves, has lemon-yellow flowers. *A.s.* 'Compactum' is smaller, with golden flowers. Both should be trimmed after flowering.
EVERGREEN SHRUBBY PERENNIALS
15-30 CM (6-12 IN) FULL SUN ZONES 6-9

CEPHALARIA
C. gigantea (*C. tartarica* of gardens) has magnificent dark green divided leaves and large scabious-like primrose-yellow flowers on tall stems. A statuesque plant for the back of a border, lovely to contrast with blues or harmonize with darker yellows.
DECIDUOUS PERENNIAL 1.5-1.8 M (5-6 FT)
FULL SUN ZONES 4-9

CYTISUS BROOM
Brooms have arching branches with flattened stem-like leaves of no great significance, but they are spectacular when covered in flower. They thrive in poor sandy soils. *C.* × *praecox* 'Warminster' has a mass of rich creamy-yellow flowers. Ideal for a shrubbery or for the back of a border.
MEDIUM DECIDUOUS SHRUB FULL SUN
ZONES 7-9
C. scoparius 'Cornish Cream' is an attractive form of the common broom, the flowers cream and freely carried.
MEDIUM DECIDUOUS SHRUB FULL SUN
ZONES 6-9
C. × *kewensis* is semi-prostrate, the creamy-yellow flowers falling over steps or paving.
SMALL DECIDUOUS SHRUB FULL SUN
ZONES 7-9

ERYTHRONIUM
E. revolutum hybrids have white or yellow flowers with brown markings carried on stems above mottled or bronze leaves. *E.* 'Kondo' has pale yellow flowers, and the taller 'Pagoda' is a more vivid luminous yellow. Clumps of erythroniums thrive in rich woodland soil, the glossy richly marked foliage appearing early. If dividing is necessary, complete after flowering, preventing the corms from drying off.
CORM 30-45 CM (12-18 IN)
SHADE ZONES 5-9

EUPHORBIA SPURGE
E. characias and *E.c. wulfenii* are very similar, the flower of the former having a black eye, while those of *E.c. wulfenii* are pure greenish-yellow with a yellow centre. They are short-lived plants but valuable for flower and grey-green or glaucous leaf (see Foliage framework: silver and grey). Cuttings of good forms are easy to strike and seedlings occur naturally, but are variable. Ordinary soil which is not too rich and good drainage ensure success.
MEDIUM EVERGREEN SHRUBS
FULL SUN ZONES 7-9
E. robbiae, Mrs Robb's bonnet, is a suckering spreader, very valuable for covering areas of poor soil, with long-lasting pale yellow bracts above dark green leathery foliage (see Foliage framework: green). It is happy in moderate shade but flowers best in full exposure, lovely with other yellows and bright blues, and even with drifts of purple honesty.
EVERGREEN PERENNIAL 30-60 CM (12-24 IN)
FULL SUN OR HALF SHADE ZONES 7-9
See also spring, above.

Cytisus × *kewensis*

Erythronium 'Pagoda'

Hemerocallis flava

Potentilla × 'Elizabeth'

Rosa 'Golden Wings'

HEMEROCALLIS DAY LILY
H. flava (syn. *H. lilioasphodelus*) has lily-like recurving petals of clear yellow, very fragrant. The leaves are thinner and less coarse than those of the later-flowering day lilies.
DECIDUOUS PERENNIAL   30-60 CM (12-24 IN)
FULL SUN OR HALF SHADE   ZONES 6-9

LABURNUM
L. × *watereri* 'Vossii', a small green-leaved tree, has long flowering racemes of yellow pea-flowers. Suitable for all types of soil. Grow it over supports to make an arbour.
SMALL DECIDUOUS TREE   FULL SUN
ZONES 6-9

MECONOPSIS
M. cambrica, the Welsh poppy, may easily become a weed but, if massed under flowering magnolias and the dying flower-heads removed before seeding, it is effective with its pale flowers shining above fresh ferny foliage.
DECIDUOUS PERENNIAL   20-60 CM (8-24 IN)
FULL SUN OR SHADE   ZONES 6-9
M. chelidoniifolia, from China, has beautiful lobed hairy leaves and branching stems bearing pale yellow papery flowers. Lovely in cool woodland, it prefers moist deep acid loam.
DECIDUOUS PERENNIAL   90 CM (36 IN)
HALF SHADE   ZONES 6-9

PIPTANTHUS
EVERGREEN LABURNUM
P. laburnifolius (syn. *P. nepalensis*) has bright yellow pea-flowers, smothering the bush with colour. Plant it where sheltered from cold winds and prune after flowering. It may be trained against a wall.
MEDIUM SEMI-EVERGREEN SHRUB
FULL SUN   ZONES 7-9

POTENTILLA SHRUBBY CINQUEFOIL
These useful hardy shrubs flower over a long period and brown stems and seed-heads are attractive all winter.
P. arbuscula has sage-green leaves and brown and shaggy stems in winter. Large rich yellow flowers are borne until the autumn.
SMALL DECIDUOUS SHRUB
FULL SUN OR HALF SHADE   ZONES 6-9
P. × 'Elizabeth' is dome-shaped with rich canary-yellow flowers, very freely carried. Grow it as a hedge or in groups.
P. fruticosa 'Katherine Dykes' has similar rich yellow flowers but a taller, more lanky habit, suitable for the back of a border.
MEDIUM DECIDUOUS SHRUBS
FULL SUN OR HALF SHADE   ZONES 6-9
See also Foliage framework: silver and grey.

RHODODENDRON
R. falconeri has trusses of creamy-yellow bell-shaped flowers, which, with its exciting and magnificent leaves (see Foliage framework: green), makes it a most desirable plant for a favourable climate, where soil is acid and moist.
TALL EVERGREEN SHRUB
HALF SHADE   ZONES 8-10
R. luteum, the old *Azalea pontica*, is still one of the best, with fragrant trusses of rich yellow tubular flowers, and brilliant orange or scarlet autumn colour. When happy in light woodland it will sucker freely and spread.
MEDIUM DECIDUOUS SHRUB
FULL SUN OR HALF SHADE   ZONES 6-9
See also Pinks and mauves: spring.

ROSA ROSE
Some of the earliest roses to flower are shrubs often with yellow or white flowers, fitting appropriately into light woodland shrubberies or into open borders.
R. hugonis and *R.h. cantabrigiensis* have arching branches and small fern-like leaves with single creamy-yellow flowers, followed by black and orange hips respectively. *R. omeiensis* 'Lutea' has strange translucent crimson thorns and four-petalled yellow flowers. Perhaps best of all in this group is *R.* 'Canary Bird' with arching brown stems and fresh green ferny

SUMMER

leaves, and large single yellow flowers. *R.* 'Frühlingsgold' has pale green leaves and semi-double clustered flowers of pale yellow, more fragrant than many of these early roses. All look lovely with underplantings of blue-flowered omphalodes and lithospermum, or of creeping ajuga with blue flowers above green, bronze or variegated leaves.

MEDIUM DECIDUOUS SHRUBS
FULL SUN OR HALF SHADE   ZONES 6-9
The earliest of the climbing roses to flower is the slightly tender *R. banksiae* 'Lutea', described earlier under spring. *R.* 'Gloire de Dijon', a nineteenth-century hybrid-tea type with buff-yellow scented double recurrent flowers, is still one of the best and will grow to 4.2 m (14 ft) against a warm wall. *R.* 'Lawrence Johnston' has scented semi-double cupped blooms of bright yellow, freely carried but not recurrent. *R.* 'Mermaid' has wide single flat fragrant flowers of sulphur-yellow and glossy almost evergreen leaves. It needs no pruning, but continual tying in for an elegant shape. *R.* 'Golden Showers', a modern climber, bears clusters of large yellow flowers over a long period. Very floriferous, but seldom grows beyond 1.8 m (6 ft).

DECIDUOUS CLIMBERS   FULL SUN   ZONES 7-9
Later-flowering roses which bloom well into summer and again later include *R.* 'Allgold', a bush rose with a compact shape, glowing green leaves and unfading double yellow flowers held in trusses. Well looked after and regularly dead-headed, this rose is a vigorous repeat-flowerer. Plant in groups of three in a mixed border to complement blue flowers, or to blend with creams and whites. The clear strong yellow of the petals makes a definite impact.

SMALL DECIDUOUS BUSH ROSE
FULL SUN   ZONES 6-9
R. 'Golden Wings', a modern shrub rose, has pale yellow flowers with deeper centres and amber stamens. Recurrent and fragrant, and more ethereal than the former, use it in more natural planting schemes.

LARGE SHRUB   FULL SUN   ZONES 6-9
See also Pinks and mauves: early summer.

TULIPA TULIP
Following on from the spring-flowering tulips, Darwin *T.* 'Niphetos' is a soft sulphur-yellow, long-stemmed above good leaves, and 65 cm (26 in) tall. Less desirable, but very similar and more easily available is Lily-flowered *T.* 'Mrs Moon', 60 cm (24 in), whose canary-yellow flowers have a wafting scent. Another Lily-flowered tulip, 'West Point' has long pointed petals in a good clear yellow, 50 cm (20 in).
BULBS   FULL SUN   ZONES 5-9
See also spring, above.

ACHILLEA YARROW
A. × 'Moonshine' with its silver-grey pinnate leaves and flat pale sulphur-yellow flowers is an excellent mixed border plant, a comfortable foil to almost any flower colour, and its grey foliage enhancing pastel colours.
DECIDUOUS PERENNIAL   60 CM (24 IN)
FULL SUN   ZONES 4-9

ALCHEMILLA LADY'S MANTLE
A. mollis has lime-green flowers, held on drooping stems, making a froth of colour above grey-green foliage (see Foliage framework: green). A rapid colonizer, but an indispensable plant. Grow under purple-foliaged shrubs.
DECIDUOUS PERENNIAL   30 CM (12 IN)
FULL SUN OR HALF SHADE   ZONES 5-9

ANTHEMIS
A. tinctoria, ox-eye chamomile, is generally grown now in hybrid form. *A.t.* 'E.C. Buxton' has lemon-yellow daisy-flowers through early and midsummer, held above deeply lobed green leaves. It is an excellent decorative plant thriving in any good border soil, complementing delphinium blues, and harmonizing with almost every other colour.
DECIDUOUS PERENNIAL   75 CM (30 IN)
FULL SUN   ZONES 6-9

CYTISUS BROOM
C. battandieri, the Moroccan broom, has deliciously pineapple-scented yellow pea-flowers, borne in racemes from among the silver leaves. It responds happily to being wall-trained and the heat ensures free flowering.
LARGE SEMI-EVERGREEN SHRUB
FULL SUN   ZONES 8-9

GENISTA BROOM
G. aetnensis, the Mount Etna broom, has golden-yellow flowers carried on green rush-like arching branches. It is beautiful during its long flowering period, a little dull out of season. Needs underplanting with low-growing shrubs, and its yellow cloudy effects are a foil to nearby purple-foliaged plants.
LARGE DECIDUOUS SHRUB   FULL SUN
ZONES 6-10

HEMEROCALLIS DAY LILY
H. citrina has pure lemon-yellow lily-shaped flowers, making a dense ground-covering mound with its elegant grassy leaves. The hybrid *H.* 'Marion Vaughn' has larger flowers of the same clear yellow. Use for massed architectural planting or for glowing colour.
DECIDUOUS PERENNIAL   90-120 CM (36-48 IN)
SUN OR SHADE   ZONES 6-9

Cytisus battandieri

Oenothera missouriensis

Lonicera japonica 'Halliana'

HYPERICUM ST JOHN'S WORT

H. calycinum, rose of Sharon, is an excellent carpeter for dry shady soil (see Foliage framework: green), but flowers more freely given an open position. Trim to 15 cm (6 in) in the late spring to get maximum flowering and to remove untidy growth. The yellow saucer-flowers set among the green leaves last for many weeks.
SMALL EVERGREEN SUB-SHRUB
FULL SUN OR HALF SHADE   ZONES 6-9
H. olympicum 'Citrinum' makes a mounded shape in well-drained soil. The small pointed grey-green leaves have erect stems carrying large lemon flowers. Grow it to seed in grey-coloured pavement.
DWARF EVERGREEN SUB-SHRUB
FULL SUN   ZONES 7-9

KNIPHOFIA RED HOT POKER

Although red hot pokers almost by definition epitomize the blazing 'hot' colours, many cultivars are available in cooler yellows.

K. 'Goldelse' has narrow rush-like leaves with light yellow flowers. 'Maid of Orleans' is paler, with creamy flower-spikes. 'Wrexham Buttercup' and 'Yellow Hammer' both have more vivid yellow flowers overlapping in season with the later-flowering species. These pale clear colours fit into any theme.
SEMI-EVERGREEN PERENNIAL
75-120 CM (30-48 IN)   FULL SUN   ZONES 7-10

LILIUM LILY

L. szovitsianum (syn. *L. monadelphum szovitsianum*) will thrive in alkaline soil. The clear yellow flowers are scented. Plant deeply, in a handful of sharp grit to aid drainage. A most desirable and hardy lily. I have seen it grown formally in the light shade of a pleached lime walk. Its petals become luminous in the dappled shade cast by the frond-like leaves of laburnum or gleditsia.
BULB   100-150 CM (40-60 IN)
SHADE   ZONES 6-10
L. 'Destiny', one of the Mid-Century hybrids, has single lemon-yellow flowers, brown-spotted with reflexed petal tips. It is easy to grow, looking its best in woodland glades.
BULB   75-100 CM (30-40 IN)
FULL SUN OR HALF SHADE   ZONES 7-10
L. 'Limelight', an Aurelian hybrid trumpet lily, has narrow, funnel-shaped fragrant pale yellow flowers, and is also lime-tolerant.
BULB   100-165 CM (40-66 IN)
FULL SUN OR HALF SHADE   ZONES 7-10
See also The whites: summer.

LONICERA HONEYSUCKLE

Shrubs and woody climbers in this attractive genus make excellent garden plants, a species or hybrid flowering in every season of the year. Most are fragrant, and some of the more exotic, although not particular about soil, are tender. The climbers need their heads in full sun but are happy with roots in shade. Spray against aphis which disfigure leaves and flowers. Although few of the flowers are solely yellow, these honeysuckles make a perfect background where yellow is the dominant hue.

L. japonica, Japanese honeysuckle, has a form *L.j.* 'Halliana' which is particularly free-flowering and fragrant. Plant it to clamber into a tree or over an old stump. The flowers are white fading to yellow.
SEMI-EVERGREEN CLIMBER
SHADE   ZONES 6-10
L. periclymenum 'Belgica', early Dutch honeysuckle, continues to flower through early to late summer, the reddish-purple to yellow flowers curtaining a wall in fragrant blossom.
DECIDUOUS CLIMBER
FULL SUN OR HALF SHADE   ZONES 6-10

NYMPHAEA WATER LILY

N. odorata 'Sulphurea', a primrose-yellow North American water lily with bright green leaves slightly spotted with red, has flower petals which stand well out of the water. It needs a warm situation, sheltered from cold winds. In shallow warm water flowering begins earlier, and when plants are dug straight into a pond bottom, rather than suspended in containers, they grow more vigorously. Water surface reflection may be spoiled by too many leaves, so choose appropriate plants for the area of water. The small *N.* × *helvola* (syn. *N. pygmaea helvola*) can thrive in 15 cm (6 in) of water, although frost damage is possible unless it is containerized and given winter quarters. The olive-green leaves support wide flowers of soft creamy-yellow.
DECIDUOUS WATER PERENNIAL
FULL SUN   ZONES 8-10

OENOTHERA EVENING PRIMROSE

All oenotheras are sun-lovers for warm borders. The well-known biennial *O. biennis* seeds freely, its pale yellow flowers glowing at dusk. Grow to flower next to blue Ceanothus and purple-leaved cotinus.
DECIDUOUS BIENNIAL   50-100 CM (20-40 IN)
FULL SUN   ZONES 6-9
O. missouriensis has great single flowers up to 10 cm (4 in) across, of clear yellow, held on prostrate stems clothed with dark green ribbed leaves. Makes a splash of contrast next to brighter blue-flowered *Salvia patens*.
DECIDUOUS PERENNIAL   23 CM (9 IN)
FULL SUN   ZONES 6-9
O. tetragona fraseri has produced many named seedlings, all with richly tinted spring foliage, reddish buds opening to vivid yellow flowers.
DECIDUOUS PERENNIAL   45 CM (18 IN)
FULL SUN   ZONES 6-9

PHLOMIS

P. chrysophylla and the better known *P. fruticosa*, Jerusalem sage, have whorls of yellow flowers, held among the grey upper leaf axils. The former has a yellowish tinge to the grey-green felted leaves. Use in 'silver' gardens or even in a white garden, where these flowers soften pure solid whites.
MEDIUM EVERGREEN SHRUB
FULL SUN   ZONES 7-9
See also Foliage framework: silver and grey.

SEDUM STONECROP

S. acre, wall pepper, is a mat-forming invasive creeper for drystone walls or pavement. Overlapping yellow-green leaves support stems bearing flattened yellow flower-heads composed of clusters of tiny stars. Try to

LATE SUMMER

establish to look haphazard and natural: this sort of free-seeding plant quickly softens the hard lines of new masonry.
EVERGREEN PERENNIAL   5 CM (2 IN)
FULL SUN   ZONES 7-9

× SOLIDASTER
A bigeneric hybrid between *Aster* and *Solidago*, × *S. hybridus* has open heads of light canary-yellow daisy-flowers. Not too vigorous and spreading, it fits easily into modest surroundings, a pale receding colour rather than one attracting and dominating.
DECIDUOUS PERENNIAL   60-75 CM (24-30 IN)
FULL SUN   ZONES 5-9

SPARTIUM SPANISH BROOM
S. junceum has erect green rush-like stems, and grows into a bush of open habit. When in flower the fragrant yellow pea-flowers cover the bush. Prune hard in early spring to keep a compact shape. An excellent seaside plant, needing sun, poor soil and good drainage. Not entirely hardy and may be damaged in severe winters. Plant at the back of a border.
MEDIUM DECIDUOUS SHRUB
FULL SUN   ZONES 7-9

THALICTRUM MEADOW RUE
T. speciosissimum (*T. flavum glaucum* of gardens) has splendid glaucous divided foliage, beautiful from early spring to autumn, even after flowering is well past. The fluffy yellow flower-heads are also valuable in any colour scheme linking blues and harsher yellows. It is most effective against a hedge of sombre yew.
DECIDUOUS PERENNIAL   1.5 M (5 FT)
FULL SUN   ZONES 5-9

VERBASCUM MULLEIN
Verbascums with large basal leaves of leathery green or felted grey have stout stems bearing flower-spikes in various yellows and sometimes white, pink and purple. They are all useful in sunny mixed borders, even the tallest seldom needing staking, and each plant or group has an architectural quality lacking in more mundane herbaceous perennials and biennials. Watch out for caterpillars in midsummer, which can decimate the foliage overnight.

V. chaixii and *V. vernale* seem, in gardens, synonymous. Towering spikes of vivid yellow flowers give colour for months, branching stems from low down continually succeeding earlier blooms. Large leaves form ground-covering clumps, attractive and important in their own right. Avoid planting next to brighter pinks, but ideal with violet shades.
SEMI-EVERGREEN PERENNIAL   TO 1.8 M (6 FT)
ZONES 6-9

ANTIRRHINUM SNAPDRAGON
Usually grown as annuals for bedding or containers, these easily cultivated plants have fragrant flower-spikes in many shades of subtle colour. Intermediate or semi-dwarf Nanum cultivars of *A. majus* are popular and rust-resistant; one of the best of the Nanums, of a good creamy-yellow, is *A.m.* 'Yellow Monarch'.
ANNUAL   45 CM (18 IN)
FULL SUN   ZONES 5-9

BUPLEURUM THOROUGHWAX
B. fruticosum, shrubby hare's ear, has beautiful glaucous sea-green leaves above which stiff stems carry yellowish-green umbels in summer; later the seed-heads remain yellow-buff through the winter months. Shape the bush in late spring to encourage new growth. Foliage and flower together make a blending grey-green-gold effect.
MEDIUM EVERGREEN SHRUB
FULL SUN   ZONES 8-9
See also Foliage framework: green.

CALCEOLARIA
C. integrifolia bears corymbs of very bright yellow pouch-shaped flowers above greeny-grey leaves. It is not reliably hardy but can be used for effective 'bedding out'. It looks lovely with the grey leaves and powder-blue flowers of *Parahebe perfoliata*, and with lavenders and silver-leaved artemisias. The yellow flowers are eye-catchers, dominating any colour arrangement.
SEMI-EVERGREEN SUB-SHRUB   30 CM (12 IN)
FULL SUN   ZONES 8-9

CHIASTOPHYLLUM
C. oppositifolium (syn. *Cotyledon simplicifolia*) with its attractive bronze-tinted green foliage makes a lovely edging plant, freely bearing 20 cm (10 in) sprays of yellow flowers on pinkish stalks. It spreads quickly and tolerates poor conditions.
EVERGREEN PERENNIAL   10 CM (4 IN)
HALF SHADE   ZONES 6-9

CLEMATIS
C. orientalis is very vigorous with green ferny leaves, the pendulous yellow star-like flowers being succeeded by silky seed-heads of silver-grey. 'Bill Mackenzie' is one of the best forms.

C. rehderana flowers late, having almost died back to the ground in the winter, but needing plenty of space to develop each season. The flowers are bell-shaped, soft primrose-yellow and scented like cowslips. *C. tangutica*, possibly a form of *C. orientalis*, has rich green divided leaves and strong yellow lantern-flowers, growing densely over low fences or trellis.
DECIDUOUS CLIMBER
FULL SUN OR HALF SHADE, ROOTS IN SHADE
ZONES 5-9
See also The whites: spring.

COTONEASTER
C. × watereri 'Rothschildianus' has a distinctive spreading habit and bears large clusters of creamy-yellow fruits. Perhaps it is the best yellow-fruited plant, with the green leaves carried through winter the perfect foil.
LARGE EVERGREEN SHRUB   FULL SUN
ZONES 6-10

Clematis tangutica

Helianthus × multiflorus

Rudbeckia fulgida deamii

Tagetes patula

GLAUCIUM HORNED POPPY
G. flavum has bright yellow cup-shaped paper-textured flowers on short stems above pale grey-green lobed leaves (see Foliage framework: silver and grey). It is happy at the front of a border sprawling out over a stone edging or path. A raised bed to ensure drainage is even better and will ensure that the poppy is perennial. Allow it to self-seed; seedlings flower the same year.
ANNUAL, BIENNIAL OR EVERGREEN PERENNIAL
23 CM (9 IN)   FULL SUN   ZONES 6-9

HELENIUM SNEEZEWEED
Numerous garden hybrids, mainly from *H. autumnale* crossed with other species such as *H. bigelovii*, make sturdy clumps in well manured soil but usually they need some support. The pure yellow, orange or brown-toned daisy-flowers (see also Hot colours) are very freely carried and associate well with those

in the same yellow-orange-red range, or are softened by creamy neighbouring blooms. The foliage is poor, so plant close to clumps of macleaya, thalictrum or acanthus to give early seasonal interest. Choose the exact colour and shade from observation of a good border.
H. autumnale 'Golden Youth' is a clear yellow.
DECIDUOUS PERENNIAL
75-120 CM (30-48 IN)   FULL SUN   ZONES 5-9

HELIANTHUS SUNFLOWER
Far from elegant, these tough coarse annuals and perennials do extend a flowering season and will strengthen a colour scheme. Most have large brilliant yellow daisy-flowers held on tall stems above an invasive root system.
H. × multiflorus 'Capenoch Star' is a pale, cool yellow.
DECIDUOUS PERENNIAL   1.5 M (5 FT)
FULL SUN   ZONES 5-9
See also Hot colours: late summer.

HYPERICUM ST JOHN'S WORT
H. 'Hidcote' is a superb hardy suckering but not invasive shrub for an open or shady situation. It bears its large saucer-shaped yellow flowers unfailingly and freely for almost three months. Few shrubs are so valuable for late-summer colour.
MEDIUM EVERGREEN SHRUB
FULL SUN OR SHADE   ZONES 6-9
See also Foliage framework: green.

KIRENGESHOMA
K. palmata with its beautiful palmate leaves loves moist rich soil. Its pale cool shuttlecock flowers coincide with dark flowers of *Aconitum napellus* and the superb Japanese anemone *Anemone × hybrida* 'Honorine Jobert', with pure-white golden-centred flowers.
DECIDUOUS PERENNIAL   90 CM (36 IN)
FULL SUN OR HALF SHADE   ZONES 6-9

LILIUM LILY
L. auratum, the Japanese golden-rayed lily, needs rich acid soil, and seldom increases reliably. It is so beautiful that it should be grown in pots if soil is unsuitable. Brilliant creamy-white petals have golden rays or bands and spots of wine colour scattered over the surface. Shade is essential for emergent stems. Grow them behind spring-flowering hellebores or clumps of small evergreen shrubs. Auratum lilies need no flowering companions; enjoy them alone as glorious groups of colour.
BULBS   1.2-2.1 M (4-7 FT)
FULL SUN, BULBS IN SHADE   ZONES 6-9
L. henryi 'Citrinum', a stem-rooting and lime-tolerant lily, has glossy arching stems and recurved flowers of pale almost apricot-yellow, lightly spotted chocolate. It thrives in a mixed border, light shade protecting emerging shoots.
BULB   1.2-2.4 M (4-8 FT)
HALF SHADE   ZONES 6-9
See also The whites: summer.

LONICERA HONEYSUCKLE
L. periclymenum 'Serotina', the late Dutch honeysuckle, is similar to *L.p.* 'Belgica' (see summer, above), but the yellowish flowers are splashed with purple on the outside.
  L. × tellmanniana has coppery-yellow flowers, reddish in bud, and succeeds in full shade. Its foliage is outstanding, inherited from one parent, *L. tragophylla*, bronze and glowing from early spring. Unfortunately it has also inherited the lack of fragrance.
  L. tragophylla itself is very tolerant of shade and has flowers in yellow terminal clusters. It is one of the prettiest, scent only being absent.
DECIDUOUS CLIMBERS
FULL SUN OR SHADE   ZONES 6-9

FOLIAGE

RUDBECKIA CONEFLOWER
R. fulgida has several varieties and cultivars, including *R.f. deamii*, *R.f. sullivantii* and its cultivar *R.f.s.* 'Goldsturm'. All have daisy-flowers with drooping bright yellow petals and dark brown, almost black, central cones. They make showy border clumps, ideal for an autumn yellow and brown-red colour scheme and for the hotter scarlet-orange schemes (see Hot colours). *R. laciniata* and the closely related but lower-growing *R. nitida* have large flowers with green central knobs. Of the latter, *R.n.* 'Goldquelle' has late flowers of double yellow. Plant in groups of five or seven; the leaves with bristling hairs are attractive, too.
DECIDUOUS PERENNIAL   60-180 CM (2-6 FT)
FULL SUN   ZONES 6-9

SOLIDAGO GOLDEN ROD
S. 'Golden Gates' has pale yellow-green leaves and flowers late, with long feathery sprays of pale yellow. It will thrive in quite poor soil.
DECIDUOUS PERENNIAL   90 CM (36 IN)
FULL SUN OR HALF SHADE   ZONES 4-9

SORBUS
S. 'Joseph Rock' bears clusters of fruit which when first formed are cream, but deepen to amber-yellow as they mature. Grow it beside other yellow-fruiting shrubs such as *Cotoneaster* × *watereri* 'Rothschildiana' to give extra colour impact through the winter. Birds seem to prefer red fruits, so yellow berries hang on longer.
MEDIUM DECIDUOUS TREE
FULL SUN OR HALF SHADE   ZONES 4-8

TAGETES MARIGOLD
T. erecta, the African marigold, is generally grown as an annual, planted out in the garden in late May. Some F₁ hybrids are particularly satisfactory. *T.* 'Yellow Climax' has double globular yellow flowers.
Some hybrids with the French marigold, *T. patula*, are rich golden-yellow and sturdy. Marigolds can be massed together for effect, or planted in drifts at the front of a border to give strong late-summer colour.
ANNUALS   20-75 CM (8-30 IN)
FULL SUN   ZONES 9-10
See also Hot colours: summer.

VIBURNUM
V. opulus 'Xanthocarpum', a garden form of the European guelder rose, has clear golden-yellow fruits in place of the scarlet ones of the type. A woodland garden for early winter might be devoted to yellow-berried shrubs and trees, with autumnal foliage a glowing background.
LARGE DECIDUOUS SHRUB
HALF SHADE   ZONES 3-9

'Yellow' foliage here covers leaves which are distinctly 'golden', either all year or at least when they emerge in spring, and also includes those variously marked and variegated in gold, yellow and creamy-yellow.
Most golden-leaved plants benefit from some shade; leaves may even scorch in full sun. Young evergreen foliage gradually becomes greener, and pale deciduous foliage is usually a sober green by late summer – when buttercup-yellow autumn foliage can take its place in a colour scheme. Variegated markings in evergreen leaves are the most reliable, remaining constant throughout the year in sun or shade.

ACER MAPLE
A. japonicum 'Aureum' is very slow-growing; count it as a shrub rather than a tree, although in due course it will reach 6 m (20 ft). The rounded slightly lobed leaves are golden-yellow, and turn fiery scarlet in autumn. It must have deep acid soil and some shade, but not too much or the leaves turn green.
SMALL DECIDUOUS TREE
HALF SHADE   ZONES 6-9

ARALIA
A. elata, the Japanese angelica tree, has huge doubly pinnate leaves, which in the variegated forms are irregularly splashed with yellow or creamy-white. As summer proceeds the leaves of these become more silvery and green, losing the golden glow. *A.e.* 'Aureovariegata' looks breathtaking in spring, the light glowing colour underplanted with blue brunnera or a clump of yellow or white *Erythronium*, dogtooth violets.
MEDIUM DECIDUOUS SHRUB
FULL SUN OR HALF SHADE   ZONES 7-9

ARUNDINARIA BAMBOO
A. pygmaea 'Viridistriata' is hardy and spreads slowly. Its leaves are striped rich golden-yellow, more yellow than green. The intensity of colour and size of the leaf are increased by annual cutting to the ground in autumn. Like all bamboos (see Foliage framework: green) it prefers moist soil but, strangely, adapts well to being grown in a container.
SMALL EVERGREEN BAMBOO
FULL SUN   ZONES 7-9

AUCUBA
A. japonica 'Gold Splash' has a butter-yellow centre to the leaf, only a thin rim of green remaining. The colour remains constant through the seasons in sun or shade. Too exotic for quiet woodland glades, this shrub makes an impact in an all-gold scheme.
MEDIUM EVERGREEN SHRUB
SUN OR SHADE   ZONES 7-9
See also Foliage framework: green.

CAREX SEDGE
The sedges are grassy plants with arching leaves and pendulous heads. The triangular stems help identification. All like moist soil, some in woodland and others in the open.
C. stricta 'Bowles' Golden' is lovely, the striped leaves turning to brilliant yellow in early summer, then fading to buff.
DECIDUOUS PERENNIAL   60 CM (24 IN)
FULL SUN   ZONES 5-9

CATALPA INDIAN BEAN TREE
C. bignonioides 'Aurea' has large soft leaves of rich yellow, the colour lasting all summer. It is slow to grow and late each season in coming

Acer japonicum 'Aureum'

Gleditsia triacanthos 'Sunburst'

so pale that it is almost white. Plant it in groups next to solid greens, or make a striking colour combination with heavy purple foliage plants and complementary blue flowers.
MEDIUM DECIDUOUS SHRUB
FULL SUN OR HALF SHADE   ZONES 4-9
See also The whites: foliage.

CORTADERIA PAMPAS GRASS
With luxuriant foliage and making immense clumps, pampas grasses bear creamy or pink-white plumes in late summer. *C. selloana* 'Gold Band' has a broad yellow stripe along the outer leaf edge. It is a beautiful arching plant, suitable for an eye-catching focal point or attractive in containers.
EVERGREEN PERENNIAL   1.5 M (5 FT)
FULL SUN   ZONES 8-10

ELAEAGNUS
E. pungens 'Maculata' has green leaves with a broad central splash of shining gold. It makes a magnificent bush, especially on a dull day when other leaves look matt and drab. On whole branches leaves sometimes revert to plain green and these should be removed.
LARGE EVERGREEN SHRUB
FULL SUN OR HALF SHADE   ZONES 6-9
See also Foliage framework: green.

FILIPENDULA MEADOWSWEET
F. ulmaria has a golden form, *F.u.* 'Aurea', the pinnate leaf of which is glowing yellow, perfect for waterside grouping or in a border with deep, rich soil. Unfortunately, in shade the leaves lose their vivid colour, as they also do after summer flowering.
DECIDUOUS PERENNIAL   90 CM (36 IN)
FULL SUN   ZONES 4-9

GLEDITSIA
G. triacanthos 'Sunburst', the golden-leaved honey locust, makes a vivid splash of colour among dark foliage. The pale, pinnate leaves emerge late, casting little shade over plants such as Solomon's seal, smilacina or blue-flowered brunnera, planted round the base. As summer progresses, the leaf fades to green, but in winter the brittle shining brown branches, armed with spines, make attractive patterns. Brown seed-pods stay on the tree until spring.
SMALL DECIDUOUS TREE   FULL SUN
ZONES 6-9

HAKONECHLOA
H. macra 'Aureola' has leaves with brilliant yellow stripes, spreading slowly from below ground. For quick effects, plant a group in moist well-worked soil. To make a strong, garish impact, plant next to the almost black

into leaf. Chestnut-like flower-spikes in summer are followed by long bean-like fruit-pods, from which the tree gets its name. It is best grown as a specimen tree in grass, with spring bulbs or a carpet of *Meconopsis cambrica* making a pale yellow circle at its feet.
MEDIUM DECIDUOUS TREE   FULL SUN
ZONES 7-9

CHRYSANTHEMUM
C. parthenium, ordinary feverfew, has a delightful golden-leaved form, *C.p.* 'Aureum', golden-feather, especially striking in early

spring when the leaves first emerge. Later, white button-flowers are carried on tall stems and the leaf colour turns to green. Seedlings come true so there is no problem increasing this plant. It is excellent in a dull corner, not fussy about soil or needing much light.
DECIDUOUS PERENNIAL   60 CM (24 IN)
FULL SUN OR SHADE   ZONES 7-9

CORNUS DOGWOOD
C. alba 'Spaethii', one of the red-stemmed dogwoods, has leaves marked in gold – so much gold that little green is evident, and that

ophiopogon: sometimes a visual shock stimulates by contrast with quieter planting, but should be in a hidden corner.
DECIDUOUS PERENNIAL   30 CM (12 IN)
FULL SUN   ZONES 7-9

HEBE
H. ochracea (still often called *H. armstrongii* in gardens), a whipcord hebe, has subtle colouring, best described as golden-yellow deepened and sobered into a greeny-brown honey-colour. The leaves and stems grow something like a small cypress, but the plant has a flat-topped appearance. The form *H.o.* 'James Stirling', with golden-brown almost straw-coloured foliage, seems hardy.
SMALL EVERGREEN SHRUB   FULL SUN
ZONES 7-9
See also Foliage framework: silver and grey.

HEDERA IVY
H. colchica 'Paddy's Pride' has large green leaves centrally splashed with golden and pale yellow. It is a wonderful town plant, covering sunless walls with bright colour, or happy to grow quickly as dense ground cover. *H. helix* 'Gold Heart' grows neatly and, branching at the base, vertical stems make symmetrical lines up a wall. The small arrow-shaped leaves have a central triangle of gold in the centre. *H.h.* 'Buttercup' and 'Angularis Aurea' have an all-over golden tint; the leaves in the former deeply lobed and in the latter simple.
EVERGREEN CLIMBERS
FULL SUN OR SHADE   ZONES 5-9
See also Foliage framework: green.

HELICHRYSUM
EVERLASTING, IMMORTELLE
H. petiolatum 'Limelight' has lime-green, almost yellow, hairy leaves. The surface of each leaf is so woolly that texture alone makes a complete visual contrast with that of a smooth leaf. This pale form, perhaps even more tender than the type, looks lovely with other summer bedding, in containers and in hanging baskets.
EVERGREEN SEMI-SHRUB   30 CM (12 IN)
FULL SUN   ZONES 8-10
See also Foliage framework: silver and grey.

HEMEROCALLIS DAY LILY
H. fulva 'Kwanso Flore-pleno' (syn. *H. disticha* 'Flore Pleno') has attractive green grassy leaves, brilliantly coloured pale gold as they emerge in early spring, shining like a patch of sunlight beyond a green lawn, as bright as golden aconites in midwinter.
DECIDUOUS PERENNIAL   1.2 M (4 FT)
FULL SUN OR SHADE   ZONES 6-9
See also Foliage framework: green.

HOSTA PLANTAIN LILY
H. fortunei 'Albopicta' has remarkable leaf colour in spring: each leaf-blade of butter-yellow is edged with pale green. Later the central yellow pales and the outer edge darkens, so that by midsummer the leaf is two-toned green, still subtle, but quieter. *H.f.* 'Aurea' emerges plain butter-yellow and fades to green. The flowers in summer are trumpet-shaped and lilac-coloured.
H. sieboldiana 'Frances Williams' has large grey leaves margined with a yellow band shading into the main leaf colour. It is a superb foliage plant, important enough to be a single feature in a pot.
H. tokudama 'Variegata' is the most spectacular; yellowish-green stripes break the blue corrugated leaves with subtle tints. It is difficult to place and is perhaps best grown alone as a specimen in a pot – as exotic as any tropical plant.
DECIDUOUS PERENNIALS   60-75 CM (24-30 IN)
FULL SUN OR SHADE   ZONES 6-9
See also The blues: foliage.

HUMULUS HOP
H. lupulus 'Aureus', the golden-leaved form of the perennial herbaceous twining climber, will grow to 6 m (20 ft) in one season. Colouring best in full sun, although the roots prefer shade, it quickly covers trellis, pergola or balcony, the pale vine-like leaves making a dense curtain.
DECIDUOUS HERBACEOUS CLIMBER
FULL SUN   ZONES 7-9

ILEX HOLLY
I. × altaclarensis 'Golden King' has broad almost spineless leaves, a gold band surrounding the green centre. It is slow-growing but spectacular against a dark background. It can be clipped into a solid shape or allowed to make a natural pyramid.
I. aquifolium 'Golden Milkboy' (syn. *I.a.* 'Aurea Mediopicta') has spine-edged leaves of the opposite variegation, gold in the centre surrounded by green. The resultant picture is less smooth, the green leaf edges, crinkled with the spines, gives a fuzzy, textured effect. It looks lovely making a group planted together for informal hedging.
LARGE EVERGREEN SHRUB
FULL SUN OR SHADE   ZONES 6-9
See also Foliage framework: green.

IRIS
I. pallida dalmatica 'Aureovariegata' has grey-green leaves striped in yellow. As flowering is poor, it is mainly a foliage plant (see Foliage framework: silver and grey). It is slow to

Hakonechloa macra 'Aureola'

Hosta fortunei 'Albopicta'

increase, but makes a nice patch of colour in front of a sunny border.
EVERGREEN RHIZOME   75 CM (30 IN)
FULL SUN   ZONES 7-9
I. pseudacorus 'Variegata', the yellow variegated sport of the ordinary green-leaved water-loving 'flag' iris, is beautiful in spring. Later the leaves turn wholly to green. Like all irises it needs frequent tidying of withering leaves and flower-stalks, an uncomfortable process in shallow water. It will grow in deep soil and is reputedly acid-loving, but perhaps more lime-tolerant than originally supposed.
DECIDUOUS RHIZOME   1.2 M (4 FT)
FULL SUN OR HALF SHADE   ZONES 5-9

LAURUS BAY LAUREL, SWEET BAY
L. nobilis 'Aurea' has golden-green leaves, attractive in winter. It is seldom seen, perhaps because it is more difficult to grow than the common bay, but in a favoured microclimate is valuable in winter when so much colour is low-toned.
TALL EVERGREEN SHRUB   FULL SUN
ZONES 7-10
See also Foliage framework: green.

Spartina pectinata 'Aureomarginata'

Origanum vulgare 'Aureum'

Philadelphus coronarius 'Aureus'

LIGUSTRUM PRIVET

L. ovalifolium 'Aureum', the golden privet, is brightly coloured. The glossy oval leaves are rich yellow, sometimes green-centred. It is a tough, coarse bush but the all-the-year-round colours make it useful in border or shrubbery. Underplant it with *Rubus tricolor* to create a shining picture in shady woodland.

MEDIUM EVERGREEN SHRUB
FULL SUN OR SHADE   ZONES 6-9

LONICERA HONEYSUCKLE

L. japonica 'Aureo-reticulata' has green leaves netted with golden variegated veins. It may be grown as a trailing climber, or clipped and shaped to form a golden mound at a border's edge. It is not free-flowering, but improves generally if well manured.

EVERGREEN CLIMBER
FULL SUN OR SHADE   ZONES 5-8

L. nitida 'Baggesen's Gold' has pale leaves all of one colour and texture. It is not pretty when examined closely, growing in a muddled twiggy fashion, but makes attractive mounded colour when grouped at the distant edge of a garden. It needs regular clipping to keep it dense and shapely, well-drained soil and full sun. It seems to lack personality; perhaps it is best used for block planting with modern architecture, but unlovable with favourite plants.

MEDIUM SEMI-EVERGREEN SHRUB
FULL SUN   ZONES 6-9
See also summer, above.

LYSIMACHIA LOOSESTRIFE

L. nummularia 'Aurea', golden creeping Jenny, covers the soil with trailing stems. The small golden-yellow leaves keep their glow in moderate shade and in summer the single yellow flowers intensify the effect. In the right place, in damp soil, perhaps linking stone with water, this is a valuable foliage plant.

TRAILING EVERGREEN PERENNIAL
23 CM (9 IN)   HALF SHADE   ZONES 5-9

MENTHA MINT

M. × gentilis 'Variegata' has leaves veined and blotched with yellow, and is smaller and more clump-forming than some mints. It may be a useful edging in a kitchen garden, but needs controlling.

DECIDUOUS PERENNIAL   20-90 CM (8-36 IN)
FULL SUN OR HALF SHADE   ZONES 6-9
See also Foliage framework: silver and grey.

MILIUM

M. effusum 'Aureum', Bowles' golden grass, is a lovely plant for a shrubbery, tolerating some shade. It is unsuitable for mixing with border plants. In spring the colour is brilliant, and although it becomes paler as it flowers, the leaf blades are still gold as they wither in autumn. It is beautiful beside blue flowers such as forget-me-not, brunnera and omphalodes.

DECIDUOUS PERENNIAL   40-150 CM (16-60 IN)
HALF SHADE   ZONES 7-9

MISCANTHUS

M. sinensis 'Zebrinus' has several broad yellow bands horizontally across the grassy leaf-blades. It makes a beautiful background plant for late-summer borders, and flower sprays of pinky-brown enhance its usefulness.

DECIDUOUS PERENNIAL   1.8 M (6 FT)
FULL SUN   ZONES 6-9

ORIGANUM MARJORAM

O. vulgare 'Aureum' is the golden-leaved form of the common culinary herb, making a low-growing carpet or ribbon at the edge of a border. Small purple flowers rise 15 cm (6 in) above the leaves in summer. The yellow colour is best brought out in sun, and becomes a pale-toned green mound in shade.

SEMI-EVERGREEN PERENNIAL   20 CM (8 IN)
FULL SUN OR SHADE   ZONES 7-9

OSMANTHUS

O. heterophyllus 'Aureomarginatus' has green holly-like leaves broadly edged with yellow. It is a beautiful shrub for the edge of woodland or for planting informally in a golden foliage area.

MEDIUM EVERGREEN SHRUB
FULL SUN OR HALF SHADE   ZONES 7-9
See also Foliage framework: green.

PHILADELPHUS MOCK ORANGE

P. coronarius 'Aureus' is one of the few members of this shrubby genus to have worthwhile leaves, most being grown for their scented flowers alone. Brilliantly bright gold in the spring, the leaves gradually fade (they will scorch in full sun) but still retain a faint glow even as they wither and fall. It is best massed in groups, effective next to contrasting purple foliage, or blending with many textured greens. The flowers are as fragrant as in the type.

MEDIUM DECIDUOUS SHRUB   SHADE
ZONES 6-9
See also The whites: early summer.

PHORMIUM

P. cookianum 'Yellow Wave' has a broad yellow stripe, edged with green. It is a low-growing plant suitable for a small garden and pretty in containers.

SMALL EVERGREEN SHRUB   FULL SUN
ZONES 8-10
See also Foliage framework: green.

PHYSOCARPUS

P. opulifolius 'Luteus' is a woodland shrub, liking moist soil. Its pale gold leaves contrast with purple foliage, such as *Ajuga reptans* 'Atropurpurea' with blue flower-spikes and bronze-purple leaves. Clumps of pale blue *Meconopsis betonicifolia*, in acid soil, make soft contrast with this golden shrub.
MEDIUM DECIDUOUS SHRUB
HALF SHADE   ZONES 5-9

RIBES FLOWERING CURRANT

R. sanguineum is a coarse shrub, some forms having rather dull pink flowers in early spring. Bring them into the house while they are still in bud, and the colour fades to an attractive tinted white. *R.s.* 'Brocklebankii' is a lower-growing shrub, making a mound of pale yellow leaves, gentle rather than startling in hue.
MEDIUM DECIDUOUS SHRUB
HALF SHADE   ZONES 6-9

ROBINIA FALSE ACACIA

R. pseudoacacia 'Frisia' has pinnate leaves of pale gold and is a small elegant tree shining with luminous colour. Like a shaft of sunlight in a wood, it makes all leaves near it dark and mysterious, deep-toned and shadowy. The small rounded leaflets keep their intense colour from spring to autumn and the deep furrowed bark makes it gaunt and distinctive even in winter, the brittle branches making a zigzag tracery. Fragrant white pea-flowers are freely carried on the green-leaved type, but are less striking among the golden leaves of *R.p.* 'Frisia' and sparse, sometimes only produced by mature specimens.
SMALL DECIDUOUS TREE   FULL SUN
ZONES 6-9

SALVIA SAGE

Its aromatic leaves used for flavouring stews and sauces, *S. officinalis* is a small evergreen revelling in full sun; grey-green leaves and violet-blue flower-spikes attractive and ornamental in the kitchen garden. There are several cultivars with different coloured leaves. *S.o.* 'Icterina' has leaves normally described as variegated green and golden-yellow. In fact the green is yellowish and the golden-yellow almost honey-coloured, giving the little bush a subtlety of hue which is softer and less glaring than many 'golds'.
SMALL EVERGREEN SHRUB   FULL SUN
ZONES 7-9

SAMBUCUS ELDER

S. nigra 'Aurea' has pale gold leaves, best if in full exposure, the colouring shading to darker gold and green to give a pleasant textured effect. It is commonly seen in wayside cottage gardens in Scotland, so probably comes true from seed. *S.n.* 'Aureomarginata' has leaflets with an irregular band of bright yellow.

S. racemosa 'Plumosa Aurea' is the best of all; its golden leaflets are fringed, giving a light airy effect quite different from the ordinary elder. The young leaves unfurl copper-coloured, gradually turning to pale yellow. Grow it in shade to prevent leaves from scorching. The conical white flower-heads are followed by dense clusters of scarlet berries.
MEDIUM TO LARGE DECIDUOUS SHRUBS
SHADE   ZONES 6-9

SPARTINA PRAIRIE CORD GRASS

S. pectinata 'Aureomarginata' has graceful narrow arching leaves striped with yellow, which rustle in the wind like bamboo. The pendulous flowers are draped with purple stamens. Grow it in dry soil to prevent it becoming invasive.
DECIDUOUS PERENNIAL   1.2-1.8 M (4-6 FT)
FULL SUN OR HALF SHADE   ZONES 6-9

SYRINGA LILAC

S. emodii, the Himalayan lilac, has a form, *S.e.* 'Aureovariegata', with large yellow leaves, the centres green. It keeps this variegation even in shade, and is a first-class foliage plant. It is rare in cultivation.
LARGE DECIDUOUS SHRUB
FULL SUN OR SHADE   ZONES 6-9

TAXUS YEW

T. baccata 'Aurea' and *T.b.* 'Elegantissima' are similar, if not identical. The young leaves are fresh golden-coloured, turning to green in the second year, the combination of young and old leaves giving a pleasant variegated effect. 'Dovastonii Aurea' has leaves margined in yellow, giving an overall gold impression. It is as vigorous as its green form, making a large wide shrub in due course, perhaps rather dominating in a modest garden, but a wonderful architectural feature when the scale is grand.
LARGE EVERGREEN SHRUB   FULL SUN
ZONES 5-9
See also Foliage framework: green.

THUJA ARBOR-VITAE

Thujas are generally small and slow-growing, rather similar to chamaecyparis, with pleasant aromatic leaves and conical shape. *T. occidentalis* 'Rheingold' is the golden-leaved form of the American arbor-vitae, a dense bush useful for winter colour and for edging.
SMALL EVERGREEN CONIFER
FULL SUN   ZONES 5-9

THYMUS THYME

T. citriodorus 'Aureus' has small golden leaves, deliciously lemon-scented. It grows best in a warm, well drained site.
DWARF EVERGREEN SUB-SHRUB
FULL SUN   ZONES 7-9

Sambucus racemosa 'Plumosa Aurea'

CHAPTER V

THE BLUES

Garden blues can be pale and luminous, dark and glowing, cool when pure or greenish, but warm and rich with added red pigment. The shining blue of lapis lazuli, like that of clear blue flowers, is bright and intense; the blues of distance and of shadows, on the other hand, are dull and muted, nearer in quality to the dark shades of the indigo dyes originally used in denim fabric. In the spectrum blue is essentially a dark colour, yet surrounding greyed colours of low intensity make the light blues luminous, and blues become especially glowing at twilight.

Blue is also a colour of emotional contradictions; it can be both stimulating and restful, perhaps because of its associations with the colours of the sky, the sea and distant landscape. The blue of the sky is calming and tranquil, the blue of the sea infers infinite depth, yet tranquillity can border on depression, and depth and distance can be disturbing. Scattered short wavelengths of light make the sky seem blue against the blackness of outer space, but 'sky-blue' is never an intense even blue, but one of infinitely graded tints and shades, since particles in the atmosphere interfere in varying amounts with the sun's rays. Blues in the distance draw the eye after them and compel motion, so garden boundaries are pushed out by banks of misty blue flowers melting into the blue distance. A 'sea' of garden blues – an expanse of interlocking drifts of different-toned blue flowers and leaves growing together – may be emotionally rich and exciting, but also restless, like the sea. Because blue does not define dimensions or set distinct limits, intermingling blues can even suggest a sense of insecurity and so are best placed in a garden where the illusion of space and distance they create can be used to advantage.

One of the sights characteristic of spring is that of a soft carpet of drifts of blue, the colours made luminous by contrast with low tones of earth or by the filtered light overhead. Scilla, muscari, pulmonaria, *Anemone blanda* and *A. apennina*

are all carpeters, giving their best if planted under protective deciduous trees or shrubs which shade them in later months. Both pure blues and violet-blues herald the spring, opening when leaves are fresh pale green and contrasting with the golden-yellows of daffodils. Later there are plenty of blue perennials, including anchusas and salvias as intense and pure as spring-flowering corms and bulbs, but by this time competition from other flowers is greater, and blues need separating from contrasting hot summer colours.

Known as cyanic colours, blues cover a range from blue-green and pure blues containing no hint of red to the deep purplish-blues and mauves, where strong traces of red give the blue warmth. Just as a red may be 'cold' when blue pigment gives a strong blue cast, so intrinsically cold blues increase in warmth as they become redder. Pure blue is rare in flowers, and even when it appears is likely to be qualified by a prefix such as clear, dark, intense or light. Periwinkle *Vinca minor* is clear blue; *Mertensia ciliata* is pale yet intense; *Salvia patens* is bright; *S. guaranitica* is dark, and *Veronica teucrium*, especially in its form 'Azureum', is an intense pure blue. *Campanula isophyllus* and *Convolvulus mauritanicus* are clear pale blues. Gentian blue is always bright but not always pure, often having violet or reddish tinges.

Some of the best examples of flower names borrowed for colour terms are among the blues: violet, lavender and lilac are all three strongly evocative of garden and household fragrance of a slightly old-fashioned sort. By definition, violet is a purplish-blue, almost as pale as mauve; lavender is pale blue with a hint of red, and lilac is a pinkish violet-like colour; but all names are liable to much confusion today, when the 'average' gardener has forgotten what violets, lavender flowers and lilac were like before they were 'developed' to cover a wider colour range. The colour of a scented wood violet is very different from the 'violet' of large hybrids. Few people now grow the original 'lilac' syringas, nowadays preferring darker shades or even white. Meanwhile, the old

PREVIOUS PAGE **Of all blue spring-flowering shrubs,** *Ceanothus thyrsiflorus* **'Cascade' must be the most spectacular. Above the shiny evergreen foliage of** *Choisya ternata,* **its bright blue panicles are so tightly massed that they make a blanket of almost solid colour. The glossy green leaves curtain the wall during the rest of the year. The presence of white** *Clematis montana* **'E.H.Wilson' deepens the blue, and prevents its being influenced towards violet by the neighbouring greens. However, to maintain the predominance of blue in this picture, the vigorous clematis may need occasional tough pruning.**

ABOVE **In a wild garden lupins in violet-blue and mauve related tones are colour incidents woven into a free-flowing tapestry of background foliage. The blending colours of the flowers themselves are made subtly more complex by the play of light and shade, the paling effects of distance and to some extent by the reddening after-image of the surrounding greens. The sheer expanse of the lupins and lushness of the vegetation make a rich and inviting garden picture, conjuring the sounds and scents of midsummer.**

ABOVE **Violas,** *Lavandula spica,* *Clematis* **'Perle d'Azure' and** *Solanum crispum* **'Glasnevin' are all low-toned desaturated violet or purplish-blues, their colour made more brilliant by grey lavender leaves and grey Dorset stone. The clump of pale campanulas to the right of the picture draws the eye as the other muted flower colours fade into the background. But the head of** *Lilium regale* **leaning into the picture from an adjacent planting is an intruder, demonstrating the potentially disruptive effect of pure white in a scheme based on gradations of colour. Cover the lily with a finger and see the difference.**

OPPOSITE **The violet-blue of the** *Iris sibirica* **and** *Geranium × magnificum* **are so similar that this is almost a monochrome planting. Grey stone, green foliage and the last of the pale wisteria blossoms are all quiet related colours. Where excitement and interest are not provided by colour itself, other factors become correspondingly more important in a design: here is contrast of form and texture between the key plants, and the two groups of iris frame the stone pedestal, which becomes a vital focal point.**

RIGHT A gentle spring triad of colour in a rose bed which will later offer a different colour theme. Dark blue *Muscari armeniacum* looks deep and bright, its blueness enhanced by the delicate pearly-white flowers and variegated leaves of *Lamium maculatum* 'Album' – a white which does not offer too stark a contrast – and by the muted complementary yellows of the primulas and auriculas.

OPPOSITE A sea of *Meconopsis grandis* floods a woodland glade between evergreen shrubs. Such a mass of pure blue flowers is almost as rare and precious as the much-prized lapis lazuli of the ancient world: most of the blues we see carpeting woodland in such profusion are the warm red-blues of anemones and bluebells, which deepen to violet in shadow, and easily become dark. The pure blues, on the other hand, can be luminous, especially when surrounded by deeper, lower-toned colours. The papery crinkled petals of these Himalayan poppies are translucent. Where the petals catch the light, they are pale blue and gleaming. Look at the rich pure blue of the closed poppy-heads and the petals that are in shade.

English or Dutch lavenders are largely superseded by darker-flowered cultivars such as *Lavandula* 'Hidcote' or *L.* 'Munstead'. Even 'forget-me-not' when used to describe a colour may well not refer to the traditional pale 'baby-blue' but to the more frequently grown darker forms whose stronger and more vivid flower is closer to the related brunnera or water forget-me-not. Cornflower-blue is bright, 'hyacinth' comes from the mineral conundrum rather than from the flower, and is a delicate violet-blue; 'sapphire' is deeper and stronger. Desaturated grey-blues are often described as metallic ('steely-blue'); slate-blue is a low-toned warm blue.

The red-blues are confused and particularly subjective, and will remain so until colour terminology is based on scientifically measured formulae. Even then accuracy will be difficult among the unstable blue-reds and reddish-blues: flower petals often turn blue with age, and all colours are sensitive to soil pH, most becoming pinker in acid conditions and bluer in alkaline. Descriptive words for blue are often misleading in garden books and catalogues, where both the camera and printing techniques distort the blues we see – so

the garden artist needs to draw from experience and create a personal colour memory of what tones will fit into his colour scheme and what plants to use.

Blue flowers can seldom be adequately described in terms of monochrome blues such as royal, navy, Oxford or Cambridge, although cultivars with such colour names convey a definite colour impression. The blue of a petal usually shades from dark to pale. Often the darker centre is brightened by complementary orange or yellow markings or stamens. Taking this example from nature, then, the gardener can learn to give interest by using drifts of blues in gentle gradations of colour intensity, subtly adding occasional complementary flower groups in ivory, pale or bright yellow or orange, to make each blue seem brighter.

Like any monochrome scheme, a 'blue' garden does not have to be confined to plants with blue flowers. Since the aim of any planting scheme is to be beautiful, any other flower or leaf colour which enhances the blueness is permissible. As Miss Jekyll wrote, 'It is a curious thing that people will sometimes spoil some garden project for the sake of a word. For instance a blue garden, for beauty's sake, may be hunger-

ing for a group of white lilies, or something of the palest lemon-yellow, but is not allowed to have it because it is called the blue garden, and there must be no other flowers.' She continues, 'Any experienced colourist knows that the blues will be more telling – more purely blue – by the juxtaposition of rightly placed complementary colour.'

By designing a blue garden to be reached through a garden where the foliage was predominantly gold, Miss Jekyll emphasized brilliance and purity. After-image effects guaranteed that 'surely no blue flowers were ever so blue before'. In the garden she recommended using only what she called 'pure' blues, with the exception of grey-blue eryngiums and the slate-blue flowers of herbaceous *Clematis heracleifolia davidiana*; she avoided the purple-blues of campanulas, but advocated the ivory-white *Clematis recta, Aruncus dioicus*, white tree lupins, and the bluish foliage of *Hosta sieboldiana*, yucca and rue. Elsewhere she used, if space permitted, the vivid blue-green lyme grass *Elymus arenarius* and, of course, *Euphorbia wulfenii* for glaucous leaves and lime-green flower trusses. The pale yellow feathery heads of tall *Thalictrum speciosissimum* above attractive blue-green leaves and variegated grass and maize (*Zea mays*) were also among her favourites for enriching 'blue' areas. Glaucous leaves push the bright pure blues towards purple into violet, so she found that to keep the distinct blueness it was important to plant only with the purest colour. If you do not wish to limit yourself so strictly, try combining your blues with silver and grey-foliaged santolina, giant onopordon and artemisias, which make all neighbouring colours more brilliant and do not alter the hue appearance: similarly, cream and white variegated leaves make the blues darker rather than redder. Clumps of glyceria, scrophularia and a carpet of creeping variegated ajuga between groups of blue flowers prevents insipidity.

Blues can so easily alter and injure each other and surrounding colours that a small variation in one group or flower colour can alter a whole garden picture. A garden with a sufficiently broad range of blues shading into misty, violet and purple colour is always restful and harmonious, seldom discordant. Even the presence of distinctly green-blues with these pure and warmer shades may simply recall the extraordinary range of colours in a landscape or seascape painting.

Schemes based on blue might choose flowers with colours moving in a carefully chosen gradation along the spectrum; all 'blues' from pure through deep violet to purples and warmer red shades. The darkness of violet might be represented by velvet-textured *Clematis × jackmanii* combined with purple-foliaged berberis or plum, moving on to crimson-flowered roses where bright red still contains a hint of blue pigment. Grow bright *Veronica teucrium* 'Azureum' or *Geranium × magnificum* as front edging, allowing the colours to move upwards together as a definite scale. Clumps of grey-foliaged santolina will make the dark colours more brilliant. A monochrome blue border can move from pale to dark blues and from deepest violet to paler warmer lavender and lilac tints. Start with the almost black *Viola* 'Bowles' Black', allowing it to seed freely where there is space and light between plants. Add lavender bushes and clumps of catmint and allow them to mingle with background planting of *Salvia turkestanica* or the taller paler-flowered *S. haematodes*. Later-season flower can be provided by misty slate-blue *Buddleia* 'Lochinch'. Since the blues are indistinct, this sort of gentle planting gives a feeling of distance if in the foreground, and adds dimension to a garden when a bed marks a perimeter.

Foliage schemes in blue-green can be composed where the 'pure' blue effects contributed by flower colour are not wanted. To add a dramatic element to a formal design plant *Melianthus major* in full sun for its important architectural pinnate leaves. In the wilder garden plant a sea of weed-proof lyme grass. If this is too invasive, try clumps of blue-green *Helictotrichon sempervirens*, a grass which keeps its modest clump-like shape and has arching fronds. For shade use blue-leaved hostas, preferably those with pale violet flowers. Complementary yellows and oranges carefully placed in 'blue' gardens enhance the picture: equally exciting are deliberately planted pairs of complementary colour. Make colour incidents by allowing bright blue ceanothus against a wall to be complemented by a clump of yellow lily-flowered tulips: 'Mrs Moon' is sweetly scented as well as bright and eye-catching. Bright blue scillas can undercarpet harsh yellow-flowered forsythia; bluebells make orange double-flowered kerria more glowing. Bright blue giant-headed *Scilla peruviana* under a warm wall will flower in front of the tender *Fremontodendron californicum*, and early ceanothus makes a neighbour to grey-leaved *Coronilla glauca*, with its glowing yellow pea-flowers.

As the summer season moves onward, blue *Iris sibirica* or *I. spuria* can make attractive clumps with yellow roses. Try pale *I. pallida dalmatica* in front of a climbing rose.

Harsher contrasts of orange lilies with blue delphiniums, pale yellow thalictrums and verbascums with violet campanulas will produce striking pictures, better passed and glimpsed briefly than made into a whole border scheme. Even dark blue with dark red, hues which at their brightest and purist are in violent contrast, can be rich and glowing if both colours are dark enough, or if viewed in mellow evening light.

In late summer link rich blues of agapanthus with the lime-green nicotiana, or plant pale slate-blue annual ageratum and pink-blue echium bedding plants in front of creamy roses. Allow *Verbena bonariensis* to seed between lavender bushes, in front of the spreading brighter blue ceratostigma, with a bush of pale yellow *Cestrum parqui* giving complementary colour against a neighbouring sunny wall.

White flowers contrast with the darkness of blues and make as great an impact as juxtaposed complementary hues. A clump of creamy-white lilies next to blue delphiniums can be incomparably beautiful and brilliant, but it should be an isolated incident in a garden. On the other hand, if the area covered with blue is increased, the blue paled or made lower in tone, then white-flowered clumps become less eye-catching and extreme in contrast. A sea of pale forget-me-nots can be interplanted with pure white tulip bulbs – or even with tulips of scarlet or deepest dark red. Creeping lithospermums, *Brunnera macrophylla*, omphalodes and woodland bluebells making beds of intermingling blue underneath spring-flowering *Magnolia stellata* or the white or pink-tinted tulip-flowered forms of *M. × soulangiana* are equally appropriate and attractive.

Similar effects can be achieved in the late summer using gentians such as *Gentiana septemfida*, *Salvia patens*, and the dark *S. guaranitica* to give glowing colour in shade where the soil can be kept moist. White- and cream-flowered eucryphias or *Hoheria sexstylosa* make stylish pyramids and enjoy the same conditions. Blue hydrangeas, in acid soil, make patches of colour in woodland for the wilder garden; and related hydrangea blues from bright almost turquoise to pale slate and violet-pink similarly make a textural contrast of solid colour in place of the misty lavenders and catmints of the earlier season. In full sun *Hibiscus syriacus* 'Coelestis' has flat open violet-coloured mallow blooms and looks warm beside the blue-green foliage of Jackman's rue. The very bright blue daisy flowers of the tender creeping *Felicia pappei* contrast with the taller herbaceous *Aster × frikartii* 'Mönch', whose arching stems carry large yellow-centred lavender-blue flowers. Both make companion plants for pink phlox and penstemon, particularly those with distinct blue pigment.

Keyline drawing

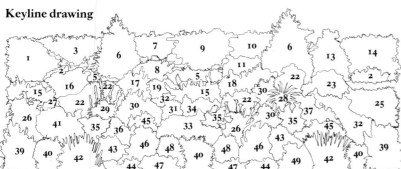

Planting plan. Figures in parentheses indicate the number of plants in a group.

This border of misty blues, at the peak of its flowering in high summer, is filled with pastel colours, which are delicate and clear when seen from near by, especially when made more vivid by neighbouring grey leaves, but which easily blend in the eye when seen from farther away. The 21 × 4 m (70 × 13 ft) bed is backed by a high wall where shrubs and climbers mingle to form a curtain of flowers and foliage. A narrow path between the wall bed and the border itself makes access easy and reveals to the explorer pockets of surprise colour accents.

The border is firmly structured with evergreens. Pyramids of bay (*Laurus nobilis*) are set against the warm wall. Dark-leaved iberis and three bushy mounds of pewter-grey *Artemisia* 'Powis Castle' are placed along the front of the border and give architectural stability. They link the billowing planting to

the lawn and provide solid contrast to the more filmy and fragile herbaceous plants. Foliage of Siberian iris, peonies and thalictrum contributes to the success of the border later, when grasses with rustling leaves and feathery plumes make blocks of muted colour between drifts of Michaelmas daisies in various colours. Bush roses flower on and off through the summer, and *Cotinus obovatus* gives a burst of fine autumn colour, a deliberate 'shock' to break the contrived prettiness of these predominantly pale receding colours.

This border is labour-intensive; shrubs increase in height and spread each season, distorting proportions, and the colour picture needs some adjustment almost annually when the herbaceous plants are divided. Tall perennials need staking each spring, as well as rich feeding.

Plant key

1 *Cytisus battandieri*
2 *Nerine bowdenii*
3 *Clematis rehderana*
4 *Camassia leichtlinii*
5 *Iris unguicularis*
6 *Laurus nobilis*
7 *Clematis orientalis*
8 *Eupatorium ligustrinum*
9 *Rosa* 'New Dawn'
10 *Clematis alpina* 'Frances Rivis'
11 *Daphne* 'Somerset'
12 *Viola labradorica* 'Purpurea'
13 *Abutilon vitifolium*
14 *Choisya ternata*
15 *Salvia turkestanica*
16 *Thalictrum speciosissimum*
17 *Geranium pratense*
18 *Ceanothus* 'Gloire de Versailles'
19 *Cytisus praecox*
20 *Paeonia lactiflora* 'Bowl of Beauty'
21 *Polemonium foliosissimum*
22 *Campanula lactiflora*
23 *Philadelphus* 'Innocence'
24 *Bergenia stracheyi*
25 *Cotinus obovatus*

26 *Eryngium giganteum* 'Miss Willmott's Ghost'
27 *Aster lateriflorus* 'Horizontalis'
28 *Miscanthus sinensis*
29 *Artemisia lactiflora*
30 *Aster umbellatus*
31 *Gypsophila paniculata*
32 *Clematis recta*
33 *Spiraea thunbergii*
34 *Thalictrum delavayi*
35 *Lilium regale*
36 *Paeonia* 'Globe of Light'
37 *Rosa* 'Buff Beauty'
38 *Anemone apennina*
39 *Acanthus mollis latifolius*
40 *Artemisia* 'Powis Castle'
41 *Rosa* 'Tynwald'
42 *Salvia farinacea* 'Victoria'
43 *Aster frikartii* 'Mönch'
44 *Iberis sempervirens*
45 *Hemerocallis citrina*
46 *Penstemon* 'Sour Grapes'
47 *Geranium renardii*
48 *Lysimachia ephemerum*
49 *Astrantia major* 'Sunningdale Variegated'

WINTER

Chionodoxa luciliae

Crocus tomasinianus 'Ruby Grant'

Scilla sibirica 'Atrocoerulea'

CHIONODOXA GLORY OF THE SNOW
As their name suggests, these little alpine plants are found near the snowline in their natural habitat and have an intense 'blueness' typical of mountain plants in full exposure. In gardens, in temperate climates, plant in short grass or in flower-beds in full sun, where the drifts of blue will take the place of fading aconites. Star-shaped flowers with white centres appear almost before the strap-shaped blunt-tipped leaves. Plant the bulbs in autumn: these accommodating plants can then be forgotten until their yearly flowering.

C. luciliae has light blue white-centred flowers; there are also white and pink forms. *C. sardensis* is sky-blue, sometimes with a small white eye.
BULBS   15 CM (6 IN)   FULL SUN   ZONES 6-8

CROCUS
C. tomasinianus develop buds long before the flower opens. Lavender to deep reddish-purple flowers cover a wide colour range; there is also a white form. It is a sturdy and hardy plant, happily naturalizing in short grass and seeding freely – sometimes too freely – in neighbouring flower-beds. The narrow leaves have a pronounced white rib.
BULB   7.5 CM (3 IN)
FULL SUN OR HALF SHADE   ZONES 6-9
C. vernus is a name used to cover the large-flowered Dutch forms, which have flowers of many shades. *L.v.* 'Queen of the Blues' is lavender-blue; 'Purpureus Grandiflorus' is purplish-blue.
BULB   10 CM (4 IN)   FULL SUN   ZONES 6-9
See also Clear yellows: spring.

IRIS
Small brightly flowered bulbous iris grown in prepared separate beds or troughs are very welcome in this season. Among the easiest and hardiest of these treasures, *I. histrioides*, in the reticulata section, bears its intense purplish-blue flowers with distinctive orange crests before the leaves emerge. The delicate petals seem unharmed by frosts. Plant in full sun.

Another reticulate iris, *I. reticulata*, is better known. In the wild, colours range between pale and deep blues and violets. Easy to grow and hardy, exact colour descriptions are difficult: like all 'blues' each named shade changes to being more or less blue or purplish when placed next to closely related blues, and blues printed as catalogue illustrations are even more chameleon-like. Look for variants where the name gives a clue. *I.r.* 'Cantab' is pale light blue and 'Royal Blue' is an Oxford-blue, both with little obvious 'red' pigment. 'J.S. Dijt' is a deep purple, distinctly red-toned. Good

SPRING

drainage and gritty soil ensure success, and bulbs increase readily by division.
BULBS   10-15 CM (4-6 IN)
FULL SUN   ZONES 7-9
I. unguicularis, the little Algerian iris, loves poor soil close to the base of a sunny wall. Try not to disturb, but cut down the grassy foliage in spring to allow the rhizomes to bake. If happy, the slightly scented violet flowers are borne all winter, but often each clump will have a seasonal flowering in a concentrated rush. *I.u.* 'Mary Barnard' has darker flowers, and a white form is very attractive and rare.
EVERGREEN RHIZOME   23 CM (9 IN)
FULL SUN   ZONES 7-9

SCILLA
Closely related to the genus *Chionodoxa* and to the English bluebell, *Endymion non-scriptus*, these blue-flowered hardy bulbs are at home in any well-worked soil, in rock gardens and in rough grass.
   S. bifolia has flowers varying in colour from a deep mauvish-blue to blue, and white and pink forms are not uncommon. It can be naturalized in grass.
BULB   15 CM (6 IN)
FULL SUN OR HALF SHADE   ZONES 7-9
S. sibirica has more than one stem rising from each little bulb with two to five brilliant deep blue or, in *S.s.* 'Taurica', pale blue nodding bell-shaped flowers. The leaves appear in very early spring, followed quickly by flowers carried over a long period. In very warm climates, plant in cool shade.
BULB   10-15 CM (4-6 IN)
FULL SUN OR SHADE   ZONES 3-8

VIOLA
PANSY, VIOLET, HEART'S EASE
V. × *wittrockiana* 'Azure Blue', grown as a half-hardy annual or biennial, always flowers well, especially if regularly dead-headed. Sow outside in the summer for all-winter performance, flowers hardly discouraged by severe frosts. Alternatively, sow in a greenhouse in early spring for summer flowers. 'Azure Blue' looks lovely in pots with silver-leaved *Tanacetum haradjanii* and white-flowering spring tulips. Use it for formal summer bedding; its regular shape and habit are excellent for geometrical patterns. Plant it with taller-growing greys or with white flowers; bright complementary orange and yellow would look good at a distance with grey or green foliage linking and separating the vivid contrasting colours.
ANNUAL OR BIENNIAL   23 CM (9 IN)
FULL SUN OR HALF SHADE   ZONES 5-9
See also Foliage framework: green.

ANEMONE WINDFLOWER
A. apennina has fern-like leaves and blue flowers with many petals. It loves to colonize in grass or in borders under deciduous shrubs, making drifts of colour. White and pink forms do exist but are rare. Plant the rhizome under purple-leaved plum and other purple- or bronze-leaved shrubs. Lovely, too, next to clumps of the dark burnished leaves of *Tellima grandiflora* 'Purpurea'. The pale blue flowers look equally good with the harsh yellows of early-flowering forsythia and the double kerria, and stunning under a white magnolia.
DECIDUOUS RHIZOME   15 CM (6 IN)
FULL SUN OR SHADE   ZONES 7-9
A. blanda flowers a little earlier than *A. apennina*, botanically distinguishable by the almost stalkless and hairless leaflets. The tuberous root is also more rounded. In a sheltered spot it may emerge from the soil and start to flower in very early spring, almost as the aconites fade. Its scale makes it perfect for the town garden where space is at a premium.
DECIDUOUS TUBER   10-15 CM (4-6 IN)
HALF SHADE   ZONES 7-9
A. nemorosa, white in the type (see The whites: spring), has several good colour forms. *A.n.* 'Allenii' has large pale silvery-lavender flowers. 'Robinsoniana' has lavender flowers and 'Royal Blue' is an almost intense blue, with a touch of lilac. They all make lovely drifts of colour, best not mixed but planted in isolated blocks of separate colours.
DECIDUOUS RHIZOME   15-23 CM (6-9 IN)
SHADE   ZONES 7-9

BRUNNERA
B. macrophylla has bright forget-me-not-blue flowers above rough hairy dark green leaves. It is an effective ground cover, although as a true perennial it loses its leaves in winter. Clumps quickly increase in size and self-sown seedlings flourish in shady corners. Apt to flag in periods of drought, moist soil and half shade suit it admirably. A drift of dark blue at the back of a shrubbery or under the canopy of a silver-leaved weeping pear is unforgettable.
DECIDUOUS PERENNIAL   45 CM (18 IN)
HALF SHADE OR SHADE   ZONES 6-9

CEANOTHUS CALIFORNIA LILAC
These sun-loving shrubs, especially the evergreen species, need a sheltered wall in most gardens, where they can grow as branching specimens or be rigidly trained back to get maximum heat from reflecting stone or brick. Deciduous types are, in general, hardier and make excellent border plants flowering later on when flowers are scarce: see also late summer, below.

C. impressus has small hard leathery leaves and deep blue flowers. Not very hardy and seldom long-lived, it amply repays a carefully chosen warm protected situation. Plant it behind Lily-flowered tulip 'Mrs Moon': the scented yellow flowers make a vivid contrast.
LARGE EVERGREEN SHRUB   FULL SUN
ZONES 7-10
C. arboreus 'Trewithen Blue' will ideally assume tree proportions in warm gardens. Deep blue panicles of scented flowers are carried among fresh green leaves. It is spectacular, especially if the not altogether frost-hardy foliage is free of unsightly brown scorch marks at flowering time. Make it a feature against the house wall and remember to stake carefully; since it is such a fast grower, the root system tends to be unstable.
LARGE EVERGREEN SHRUB   FULL SUN
ZONES 8-10

Brunnera macrophylla

Anemone blanda 'Atrocoerulea'

Omphalodes cappadocica

Myosotis alpestris

CLEMATIS

C. alpina is typically palish-blue and is a scrambler, happy over a low wall or over an old tree stump. The form *C.a.* 'Frances Rivis' is a deeper blue with sepals 5 cm (2 in) long. Grow it behind the yellow crown imperial, *Fritillaria imperialis*.

   C. macropetala 'Maidwell Hall' is a more solid blue than the *C. alpina* types, otherwise very similar in habit. None is over-vigorous or liable to strangle deciduous shrubs through which it may happily scramble. Mix them together to cascade over the edges of walls or large containers.

DECIDUOUS CLIMBERS
FULL SUN OR HALF SHADE, ROOTS IN SHADE
ZONES 3-9
See also The whites: spring.

IRIS

Hardy bulbous irises, usually divided into Dutch, Spanish and English, are tough plants needing little attention. Plant them to make colourful groups in a mixed border.

   The Dutch iris *I.* 'Wedgwood' is very popular, with pale blue flowers. It is tough and, planted in clumps in open borders, needs little attention apart from the removal of seed-pods as they form. There are several other good blue Dutch irises; they are mainly derived from *I. xiphium*.

   I. xiphium itself, Spanish iris, is usually smaller and flowers a little later. To fit into a pure blue or a violet-blue theme, choose a variety from named colours as catalogued by a reliable nursery.

   I. xiphioides, English iris, has a number of cultivars and hybrids varying in height and with larger, open flowers. Look for named varieties to find the shade and type of blue or violet that you prefer.

BULBS   60 CM (24 IN)
FULL SUN   ZONES 6-9

MUSCARI   GRAPE HYACINTH

Most of these little hardy bulbs have flowers in shades of deep purplish-blue to azure-blue. They thrive in ordinary soil, sometimes increasing almost too rapidly. Mass them below a specimen lawn tree, allowing the bulbs, mixed with a simple wood violet, to spread to the width of the canopy. They are much more effective like this than dotted about borders, where in time they become a pest.

   M. armeniacum has long racemes of bright blue. *M.a.* 'Cantab' is a pale form, 'Heavenly Blue' is brighter, and 'Blue Spike' has mid-blue flowers.

BULB   23 CM (9 IN)
FULL SUN OR HALF SHADE   ZONES 7-9
M. comosum (syn. *Leopoldia comosa*), the tassel hyacinth, has flower-heads where the upper flowers are purple, the lower and fertile ones olive-green. As they do not set seed, flowering continues over a long period.

BULB   45 CM (18 IN)
FULL SUN OR HALF SHADE   ZONES 7-9

MYOSOTIDIUM
CHATHAM ISLAND FORGET-ME-NOT

M. hortensia is an amazing plant, extremely difficult to grow successfully, even in favoured climates. It dislikes drought, yet must never be waterlogged, needs rich feeding of seaweed (which contains a high rate of potash and a wide range of trace elements), needs protection from full sun, yet loves heat, and will tolerate little frost. The advanced gardener who succeeds with this plant has a treasure. Deeply veined leaves similar to those of hosta, but evergreen, make a splendid clump from which rise bright blue forget-me-not flowers in large clusters. It should be planted in a quiet corner, where nothing else competes at flowering time.

EVERGREEN PERENNIAL   45 CM (18 IN)
HALF SHADE   ZONES 8-9

MYOSOTIS   FORGET-ME-NOT

M. alpestris, the wild European forget-me-not, has pale blue flowers. *M.a.* 'Royal Blue' has very bright blue flowers. Grow it from seed planted in summer to bloom the following spring. Allow to naturalize; not every seedling comes true, but the resultant mixture of tones is as attractive as the single colour. After a few years throw all plants away and start afresh.

BIENNIAL   23 CM (9 IN)
FULL SUN OR SHADE   ZONES 5-9
M. palustris, the water forget-me-not, for shallow ponds with a water depth of 7.5 cm (3 in), flowers for many weeks. *M.p.* 'Mermaid' has dark leaves, deep blue yellow-eyed flowers, and is tough and reliable.

DECIDUOUS PERENNIAL   15-45 CM (6-18 IN)
FULL SUN   ZONES 5-9

OMPHALODES   NAVELWORT

O. cappadocica, clump-forming with sprays of azure-blue flowers above long-stalked green leaves, can be planted in drifts at the edge of woodland. Superficially like forget-me-not, it is a true perennial and is more distinguished.

   O. verna, blue-eyed Mary, spreads more quickly, using rooting runners. It makes dense carpets of heart-shaped foliage above which are sprays of small blue flowers. It is earlier than *O. cappadocica*. Give plenty of moisture-retaining humus.

DECIDUOUS PERENNIALS   15 CM (6 IN)
HALF SHADE OR SHADE   ZONES 7-9

PULMONARIA   LUNGWORT

Ordinary pulmonarias (*P. officinalis*) can be dull and invasive, with undistinguished blue/pink borage flowers, but there are some more desirable species and forms.

   P. angustifolia 'Munstead Blue' has soft blue flowers opening from pink buds held above plain green slightly bristly leaves. Clumps make pools of blue beneath deciduous shrubs.

DECIDUOUS PERENNIAL   20 CM (8 IN)
HALF SHADE   ZONES 6-9

ROSMARINUS   ROSEMARY

Rosemary should be in every garden. Gaunt leggy bushes give a feeling of age and the pale mauvish-blue flowers can fit into any planting scheme. Bushes with greyish-green aromatic leaves used for flavouring link the ornamental and the kitchen garden. A small herb garden can be concealed by a rosemary hedge; an entrance can be framed by a pair of plants.

   R. officinalis flowers early and continues to do so spasmodically through the summer. New forms with darker flowers of lilac-blue and bright dark blue are attractive. *R.o.* 'Benenden Blue' is a slightly less hardy and smaller

EARLY SUMMER

rosemary than the type, but is worth risking for its bright blue flowers. Also tender is 'Severn Sea', a dwarf form with graceful arching habit and brilliant blue bloom. Neither grows very large, nor are they long-lived. A fastigiate type, 'Fastigiatus', can be grown tightly against a warm wall, and saves limited space.
SMALL TO MEDIUM EVERGREEN SHRUBS
FULL SUN   ZONES 7-10

SYMPHYTUM COMFREY
These rather coarse-leaved plants make splendid ground cover in shade. *S. caucasicum* is also a colonizer, spreading by underground runners. Grey rough-textured leaves which turn green later in the summer set off graceful loose sprays of pale blue forget-me-not flowers. Plant in light woodland. Alternatively, in a small garden, plant to disguise working areas, round garden sheds or oil tanks.
DECIDUOUS PERENNIAL   60 CM (24 IN)
HALF SHADE OR SHADE   ZONES 6-9

VINCA PERIWINKLE
V. minor, the dwarf periwinkle, has flowers in rich blue, plum or white. Double forms exist, too, and some have variegated leaves. It is usually grown in dry shade where it makes admirable weed-suppressing cover and is often neglected, never being fed or divided. However, when it is grown in the open and encouraged, it will flower much more freely.
DWARF EVERGREEN SHRUB
FULL SUN OR SHADE   ZONES 5-9

VIOLA
PANSY, VIOLET, HEART'S EASE
V. odorata, sweet violet, the little woodland plant with deliciously scented flowers, is a rapid colonizer spreading by runners and seed. Its late-winter and early-spring flowers do not set but, later, almost invisible flowers nestling under the leaves seed prolifically. Grow it as edging or at the base of a dark yew hedge or round a specimen tree set in a lawn and casting a heavy summer canopy. There are many 'improved' colour forms including white and pink. *V.o.* 'Czar' is a good violet-purple.
DECIDUOUS PERENNIAL   15 CM (6 IN)
HALF SHADE OR SHADE   ZONES 4-8
V. labradorica 'Purpurea' has bright violet-blue flowers and dark purple leaves (see Strong reds: foliage), which gradually change to green through the summer months. It is a delightful plant, eye-catching without being startling. Allow to seed at border edges, in gravel and in cracks of paving. Interplant clumps of it with grey foliage creepers or bushy silver artemisias.
DECIDUOUS PERENNIAL   15 CM (6 IN)
FULL SUN OR HALF SHADE   ZONES 3-8

ABUTILON
Two abutilons are valuable flowering shrubs with attractive grey-green semi-evergreen leaves, a regular pyramidal habit and bell- or saucer-shaped lavender-blue and pale mauve flowers. Plant against a wall for best effects and cut back hard after flowering. Both have white forms (see The whites: early summer).
   A. × suntense, a hybrid of *A. vitifolium* and the smaller, darker-flowered *A. oechsenii*, has cup-shaped dark violet-blue flowers, a strong enough colour to influence the choice of accompanying late-flowering tulips, such as *T.* 'Niphetos' with soft sulphur-yellow heads.
   A. vitifolium has wide saucer-shaped flowers, pale lilac to greyish-white.
LARGE SEMI-EVERGREEN SHRUBS
FULL SUN OR HALF SHADE   ZONES 8-10

AQUILEGIA COLUMBINE
A. alpina, although now available in many 'improved' strains with different flower colours, is itself of a pure sky-blue or blue and white, very pretty and delicate with its wing-like petals and tall spurs above grey-green leaves. Grow from seed and plant in light shade. It is just the right tone of blue to harmonize with the mauve-purple of *Erysimum* 'Bowles' Mauve' and honesty.
DECIDUOUS PERENNIAL   30 CM (12 IN)
FULL SUN OR HALF SHADE   ZONES 5-9

CAMASSIA QUAMASH
These plants, too, have been 'improved', increasing the size of flower and creating new shades between dark Oxford-blue and the pale washed-out blue of the original *C. quamash*. Another species, *C. leichtlinii*, has a deep blue form, perhaps the best. Plant in a clump in a mixed border, growing perennials to hide dying leaves.
BULBS   90-120 CM (36-48 IN)
FULL SUN   ZONES 6-9

CEANOTHUS CALIFORNIA LILAC
Among the ceanothus contributing flower colour in early summer are shrubs that are particularly valuable for their foliage form (see Foliage framework: green).
   C. dentatus has leaves with inrolled edges, making them appear smaller than they really are, and bright blue flowers. It needs a warm situation.
   C. 'A.T. Johnson' has rich blue flowers produced quite freely for the second time in autumn. When space is limited this seems a valuable quality.
   C. thyrsiflorus 'Cascade' is very floriferous. The powder-blue flowers held on arching branches give an almost weeping effect. I have found it one of the hardiest, and very fast.
LARGE EVERGREEN SHRUBS   FULL SUN
ZONES 7-10
C. × veitchianus, with glossy green wedge-shaped leaves, grey on the undersides, bears dense heads of bright blue flowers. One of the most free-flowering, it is sometimes confused with *C. dentatus*.
   C. prostratus and *C. thyrsiflorus repens*, creeping blueblossom, are more prostrate, making green mounds. The former is more mat-like, for a smaller garden, and has bright blue flowers; the latter has paler blue flowers.
MEDIUM EVERGREEN SHRUBS
FULL SUN   ZONES 7-9

CONVOLVULUS
These plants love to twine, but the small *C. mauritanicus* (syn. *C. sabatius*) from North Africa remains trailing. The flowers in bud are twisted, opening to wide tubes of intense blue. Give it good drainage and full sun. Grow to sprawl over the edges of containers and keep frost-free in winter if the garden is exposed, or if no suitable spot is available.
TRAILING DECIDUOUS PERENNIAL
15 CM (6 IN)   FULL SUN   ZONES 9-10

Abutilon × suntense

Convolvulus mauritanicus

Dwarf bearded iris with rosemary

GENTIANA GENTIAN

Gentians, generally with bright blue trumpet-shaped flowers, vary in their cultural requirements. Many species insist on acid soil; some are lime-tolerant. Most are prostrate-growing, trumpet flowers rising only slightly above green mat-forming leaf-clumps. Others grow taller in shady woodland conditions, revelling in moist soil.

G. acaulis can be unpredictable. Give it an open site and moist, humus-rich acid to alkaline soil, conditions it seems to require. It may still fail to flower for no apparent reason, though moving the plant, even a short distance, can solve this problem. In another garden the brilliant blue flowers are produced like clockwork every year, and the little gentian becomes invasive.

DECIDUOUS PERENNIAL   7.5 CM (3 IN)
FULL SUN   ZONES 6-9

IRIS

Irises vary so much in type and requirements as well as in appearance that it is best to give general descriptions in each group.

The Bearded German hybrids come in countless colours and varying heights. Dwarf forms, usefully, require no staking. I prefer those which are simple one-colour flowers, without frills or separate colour effects on the falls. Try to see them in flower at a local nursery and make a colour choice to suit your garden scheme. The leaves (see Foliage framework: silver and grey) are always useful for contrast with softer shapes.

DECIDUOUS RHIZOMES   45-150 CM (18-60 IN)
FULL SUN   ZONES 6-9

I. pallida dalmatica is a Bearded species with delicious pale almost lavender-blue flowers. Grey sword-leaves which are almost evergreen set off the pale flowers. Grow in large clumps. Full sun and good drainage are essential: allow the rhizomes, shallowly planted, to bake all summer. Plant, or divide, after flowering; roots must be allowed to re-establish before cold weather begins.

EVERGREEN RHIZOME   75 CM (30 IN)
FULL SUN   ZONES 7-9

I. douglasiana, I. innominata and various hybrids known now as Pacific Coast irises, are beardless, with coarse grass-like leaves and flower colours of blue-purple, lavender, yellow, orange and shades of white. They all need well-drained soil, preferably lime-free, and will thrive, unlike most irises, in light shade. Colours must be chosen directly from a plant: seedlings vary greatly. Plant them massed on a woodland bank or in a cottage garden under the canopy of a fruit tree.

DECIDUOUS RHIZOMES   20-30 CM (8-12 IN)
HALF SHADE   ZONES 7-9

I. sibirica, a beardless iris, is very accommodating, happy in moist soil beside a pond or thriving in a fertile soil in a mixed border. Branching stems bear flowers of many shades of blue, and hybridization has increased the range. The grassy foliage makes a compact tall clump, tending to become hollow and stemless in the centre after a few years. It should then be split up and replanted. Do this in autumn or as growth begins in the spring.

DECIDUOUS RHIZOMES   100 CM (40 IN)
FULL SUN   ZONES 6-9

LITHOSPERMUM GROMWELL

L. purpureocaeruleum (now for botanists *Buglossoides purpureocaerulea*), blue gromwell, sends out long arching tip-rooting stems which eventually form dark green mats. The flowers are of intense blue, forget-me-not-like and freely carried on upright stems but making a dense blue carpet under shrubs. A very beautiful ground-cover plant, dense and weed smothering, it thrives in a damp neutral soil. After flowering give it a sharp trim and pull or dig it out in winter if it exceeds its allotted space. Grow it with bluebells and *Brunnera macrophylla*, three shades of blue mingling delightfully. All being tough plants, they are ready to withstand invasive neighbours.

DECIDUOUS PERENNIAL   30-50 CM (12-20 IN)
HALF SHADE   ZONES 6-9

MECONOPSIS

M. betonicifolia (syn. *M. baileyi*), the blue poppy, has papery-textured almost transparent pale blue flowers on slender stems above grey-green bristly leaves. Asiatic meconopsis need a humid atmosphere and protection from drying winds, a rich, deep lime-free soil and part shade. In a woodland glade drifts of pale blue poppy, interplanted with drifts of yellow-flowering species, have an ethereal beauty: planted in drifts against low-toned greens they become luminous. Plant them only if you have the ideal conditions.

DECIDUOUS PERENNIAL   100-120 CM (40-48 IN)
HALF SHADE   ZONES 6-8

MERTENSIA SMOOTH LUNGWORT

M. ciliata, mountain bluebell or languid ladies, has dangling sky-blue bells and sprawling stems carrying grey-green leaves. Cool leaf mould and half shade are essential. The leaf appears late in spring and quickly withers after flowering: cover then with thick mulch, partly to enrich but also to mark the spot.

DECIDUOUS PERENNIAL   60 CM (24 IN)
HALF SHADE   ZONES 5-8

M. virginica, Virginia cowslip, has pale flowers almost violet in colour, drooping bells above grey foliage. It requires similar conditions.

DECIDUOUS PERENNIAL   30 CM (12 IN)
HALF SHADE   ZONES 5-8

NEPETA CATMINT

The lavender flowers of most catmints fit into soft colour schemes where pastel tints mingle with grey leaves, pink roses and startling pure whites. For many weeks grey-green hummocks are covered with arching flower-sprays. Cut back as soon as this first flowering is over and there will be a repeat performance in late summer. In cold gardens leave dead stems through the winter: they give some protection from severe frosts.

N. 'Six Hills Giant' can make a most attractive edging plant. Plant it between lavender bushes to extend flowering seasons, or line a bed of 'Iceberg' roses with it.
DECIDUOUS PERENNIAL   90 CM (36 IN)
FULL SUN   ZONES 6-9
In a small garden, plant *N.* × *faassenii* 'Blue Dwarf'.
DECIDUOUS PERENNIAL   35-40 CM (14-16 IN)
FULL SUN   ZONES 6-9
Another catmint, *N.* 'Souvenir d'André Chaudron', has almost bronze leaves and pale blue flowers. Treat it as an ordinary perennial, to occupy a place in a border, making an attractive once-flowering clump.
DECIDUOUS PERENNIAL   45 CM (18 IN)
FULL SUN   ZONES 6-9

PARAHEBE

Parahebe is confused somewhat between two other genera – *Veronica*, mostly herbaceous, and *Hebe*, mostly shrubby. These plants are very floriferous and cover the purple-blue-white range of flower colours. Botanists now often classify the following as *Veronica*, but gardeners still use *Parahebe*.

P. perfoliata, digger's speedwell, is very unusual, with long arching stems along which pairs of waxy grey oval-shaped leaves clasp and encircle the stem. The young foliage is bronze-tipped. Lavender flowers, changing from dark to pale from the outer to inner edges of a petal, are carried in racemes.
DECIDUOUS SUB-SHRUBS   60 CM (24 IN)
FULL SUN   ZONES 8-9

PHLOX

Some of the small trailing early-flowering phlox are very valuable front-of-border plants, subtle colouring and pale leaves making mounds of delicate colours for many weeks.

P. 'Chattahoochee', a hybrid, probably between *P. divaricata* and *P. pilosa*, has dark hairy rather pointed leaves. Flowers of a rich soft blue, with dark centres of purplish tone which fade to light blue, make a lovely blended mixture. Grow it beside the pewter-grey foliage of *Artemisia* 'Powis Castle' and in front of *Parahebe perfoliata*, whose long lax stems

Nepeta 'Six Hills Giant'

Phlox 'Chattahoochee'

with blue speedwell flowers bend over the phlox. I think it prefers some shade. Certainly the blues become even richer and more lustrous if planted under a light canopy, and the length of flowering season is extended.
DECIDUOUS PERENNIAL   23 CM (9 IN)
FULL SUN OR HALF SHADE   ZONES 6-9

SCILLA

S. peruviana, from the Mediterranean seaboard countries, has dense blue flower-heads rising above strap-shaped leaves. It requires a warm spot at the foot of a wall. Except for the flower colour, it hardly resembles more ordinary winter-flowering scilla species (see above).
BULB   30 CM (12 IN)   FULL SUN   ZONES 7-9

Gentiana acaulis

SUMMER

Wisteria floribunda

SYRINGA LILAC

Common lilac, *S. vulgaris*, needs little description. Large greedy bushes with an invasive root system have erect panicles of richly scented dark pinkish-violet-blue flowers, which as 'lilac' have given the language a colour term much used to describe rather variable shades.

There are innumerable hybrids and cultivars; colours, too, are innumerable, and change from hour to hour as the flower-buds open and wither. Lilac-red, lilac-blue, lilac-pink are all descriptions given to specific named cultivars, but choose one in a colour that relates to a specific scheme.
LARGE DECIDUOUS SHRUB
FULL SUN OR HALF SHADE   ZONES 6-9

VERONICA SPEEDWELL

Most veronicas are sun-lovers for any well-drained soil. They quickly form clumps and are ideal for the fronts of borders, strong and reliable flowerers. *V. austriaca teucrium* 'Crater Lake Blue' is one of the best, with very bright blue flowers and a hummock-forming habit. Plant with purple and bronze foliage shrubs behind, and with any flower in the blue-violet-crimson range of the spectral wheel.
DECIDUOUS PERENNIAL   30 CM (12 IN)
FULL SUN OR HALF SHADE   ZONES 6-9

WISTERIA

There is no more beautiful climbing plant, or it may be trained as a standard specimen – when skill and patience are needed. Twining through old trees, as often seen in hot climates, draping an arbour or pergola, or pruned back to get maximum benefit from a brick or stone wall, wisterias have a multitude of scented white, blue-mauve or dark mauve pea-flowers which hang in long dangling racemes. Plant with other flowers in a blue-violet-mauve range or, if space permits, plant to flower alone.

W. floribunda, Japanese wisteria, has slender white, lilac-blue or violet-blue racemes. Emerging pinnate leaves are pale green. The best form may be *W.f.* 'Macrobotrys', with racemes hanging to 90 cm (36 in), more or less, and lilac tinged with violet-purple. It will reach 11 m (36 ft). Grow on an arbour or against grey stone, perhaps twining in and out of balustrading.
DECIDUOUS CLIMBER   FULL SUN   ZONES 6-9
W. sinensis, Chinese wisteria, will climb and twine to 18-20 m (60-67 ft) – exceptionally, more. Mauve or deep lilac scented racemes hang to 30 cm (12 in) and flowers all open together while the branches are leafless. Prune after flowering, and again in winter.
DECIDUOUS CLIMBER   FULL SUN   ZONES 6-9

CAMPANULA BELLFLOWER

In gardens campanulas cover a wide range of strong tall border perennials and little creeping or clump-forming rock or edging plants, and include the well-loved biennial and annual Canterbury bell, forms of *C. medium*. The colours of the typically bell- or star-shaped flowers similarly cover a wide spectrum from pure to violet-blue, lavender, deep purple, pale pink and milky-white, and the sophisticated grey-white of the earlier-flowering *C.* 'Burghaltii'. Herbaceous perennial campanulas love rich well-worked soil, rock-garden types need sun and good drainage; others, such as the tender *C. isophylla*, lovely for pots and hanging baskets, should overwinter in a greenhouse. Alternatively, take cuttings in autumn and keep them frost-free.

C. carpatica, a little clump-forming species, has a wide colour range; choose from plants in flower or from a well-illustrated catalogue. Bright green leaves are covered with masses of large cup-shaped flowers in shades of blue. Grow it at the front of a border or in drifts on a rock garden.
DECIDUOUS PERENNIAL   30 CM (12 IN)
FULL SUN   ZONES 6-9
C. cochleariifolia (syn. *C. pusilla*) is tiny and has minute bell-flowers on wiry stems. Best in a trough, where its clumps grow and spread.
DECIDUOUS PERENNIAL   10 CM (4 IN)
FULL SUN   ZONES 5-9
C. garganica, a dwarf form for dry walls, has star-shaped blue flowers.
DECIDUOUS PERENNIAL   15 CM (6 IN)
FULL SUN   ZONES 8-10
C. glomerata is a coarse plant, invasive in borders, but has the deepest purple-violet flowers of the taller types. Some of the garden cultivars are less vigorous. *C.g.* 'Superba' has particularly rich dark bell-shaped flowers and will thrive in light shade.
DECIDUOUS PERENNIAL   90 CM (36 IN)
FULL SUN OR HALF SHADE   ZONES 6-9
C. isophylla, a tender trailer, has pale blue starry flowers, larger than most and very freely carried. It makes a superb houseplant in the flowering season.
SEMI-EVERGREEN PERENNIAL   23 CM (9 IN)
FULL SUN   ZONES 8-10
C. lactiflora, a tall border plant, has flowers described as lilac- or lavender-blue. I think of them as a pale washed-out blue, and perhaps this is one of the original 'type' colours. Plant anywhere with anything; it sounds dull, but the bell-shaped flowers on open branching stems go with every colour, and they make a misty haze in a border.
DECIDUOUS PERENNIAL   1.5 M (5 FT)
FULL SUN OR HALF SHADE   ZONES 6-9

C. latifolia has rounded basal leaves which get narrower as the stem rises. Flowers of named cultivars can be violet-blue or white.
DECIDUOUS PERENNIAL   1.2 M (4 FT)
FULL SUN OR HALF SHADE   ZONES 4-9
C. latiloba (syn. *C. grandis*) has lilac or lavender-blue flowers as well as a white form, *C.l.* 'Alba'. The stalkless cup-shaped flowers are carried in profusion along the stems.
EVERGREEN PERENNIAL   90 CM (36 IN)
FULL SUN OR HALF SHADE   ZONES 4-9
C. medium, from which garden forms of the biennial Canterbury bell come, should be sown the previous June for current summer flowering. Large cup-and-saucer flowers of *C.m. calycanthema* type have bell-shaped petals surrounded by similar-coloured conspicuous calyx. Ideal showy plants in blues and white, they are useful for filling bare patches, especially in a new garden.
BIENNIAL   60-90 CM (24-36 IN)
FULL SUN OR HALF SHADE   ZONES 7-9
C. persicifolia has the narrow peach-like leaves its name denotes. Blue flowers stud the stems and a white form, *C.p.* 'Alba', is useful in a white garden. Double forms in blue and white exist but are difficult to obtain.
EVERGREEN PERENNIAL   90 CM (36 IN)
FULL SUN   ZONES 6-9
C. portenschlagiana (syn. *C. muralis*) is an invasive creeper, most useful for growing next to stone steps. It is covered for much of the summer with deep blue-purple flowers.
DECIDUOUS PERENNIAL   15 CM (6 IN)
FULL SUN   ZONES 6-9
C. poscharskyana is even more rampant, and taller-growing. The flowers are stars of clear lavender blue.
EVERGREEN PERENNIAL   23-30 CM (9-12 IN)
FULL SUN   ZONES 6-9
C. pyramidalis, chimney bellflower or steeple bells, has tall spires, pyramid-shaped and covered in clear blue or pure white flowers. Generally treated as a biennial, flowering from seed planted the previous summer, I find that often old woody plants survive the winter in favoured sites and may flower a little later than young stock overwintered in frames or greenhouse. Use it as a spectacular houseplant; once in flower it needs little attention and survives in a dark corner. Do not feed richly.
BIENNIAL OR PERENNIAL   1.8 M (6 FT)
FULL SUN   ZONES 6-9
See also The whites: early summer.

CODONOPSIS

C. ovata has pale blue campanula-like bell-flowers which hang down, hiding orange and purple markings on the insides of the petals. There is some confusion between this and the later-flowering *C. clematidea*, but the latter flowers in late summer and has brown and black markings. Grow codonopsis on a bank to see the insides of the petals.
DECIDUOUS PERENNIAL   30 CM (12 IN)
FULL SUN   ZONES 6-8

DELPHINIUM

The large-flowered delphinium hybrids, although commonly seen, are seldom really well grown. Slugs love emergent green shoots in spring, the brittle long stalks are difficult to stake adequately, and storms quickly damage the heavy flower-heads. They need full sun and rich feeding, but the soil should not become waterlogged in winter. They dislike being moved, so take cuttings in spring.

If this is discouraging, remember the beauty of blues and purples and even pale pink and pinkish-white, planted in mixed borders next to clumps of pale yellow thalictrum, white, yellow or orange lilies – this for the pure blue shades, and decide to overcome the difficulties.

Breeding has been directed not only towards creating new shades of red, orange and yellow, but towards sturdy smaller plants. However, much beauty is lost when thick flower-heads sit on stunted stems; delphiniums should be tall and of graceful habit.

Choose from named colour forms: *D. elatum* hybrids can be up to 195 cm (80 in) tall; *D. belladonna* hybrids are smaller with branching heads. Grow the dark blues with purple-leaved berberis and even crimson-flowered *Geranium psilostemon* or lychnis. Grow bright blues with contrasting complementary yellow. Grow paler blues with glaucous-leaved *Hosta sieboldiana*, near *Melianthus major* and *Ruta graveolens* 'Jackman's Blue'.
DECIDUOUS PERENNIALS
60-195 CM (24-80 IN)   FULL SUN   ZONES 6-9

Campanula portenschlagiana

Delphinium 'Blue Dawn'

Felicia amelloides

Lithospermum diffusum 'Heavenly Blue'

ERYNGIUM

The silvery or grey-blue foliage of many eryngiums (see also Foliage framework) makes an attractive foil for the steel-blue or lavender flowers.

E. giganteum 'Miss Willmott's Ghost' has silvery metallic leaves and pale shimmering blue-grey thistle-heads. It is a biennial, but allow it to seed *in situ*, arranging the tiny seedlings in groups as desired before the long tap roots grow too much. Clumps in borders or in gravel look ghostly, appearing at their most effective as daylight fades. Grow next to strong glossy-leaved acanthus for foliage contrast, or in a 'silver' border with tinted white and pastel colours. Dark lavenders and purples also harmonize; try near the violet-purple *Heliotropium × hybridum* 'Marina'.
BIENNIAL   1 M (3 FT)   FULL SUN   ZONES 7-9
E. × oliveranum has blue-green very deeply cut leaves and vivid steel-blue flower-heads, carried for many weeks.
DECIDUOUS PERENNIAL   60 CM (24 IN)
FULL SUN   ZONES 7-10
E. tripartitum, a garden hybrid, has wide branching stems crowded with deep lavender-blue cones, surrounded by thistle-like blue

spiny bracts. Give it a prime position to get good results; too often it is grown in poor soil and gives a correspondingly poor performance. Plant with yellow achilleas as contrasting neighbours, bright *Achillea filipendulina* 'Coronation Gold' for impact, *A. ×* 'Moonshine' for a more restful, soft picture.
DECIDUOUS PERENNIAL   75 CM (30 IN)
FULL SUN   ZONES 7-9
E. × zabelii is among the best, with blue flowers above bristly green leaves. There are several named cultivars, all good.
DECIDUOUS PERENNIAL   60 CM (24 IN)
FULL SUN   ZONES 7-10

FELICIA

F. amelloides, blue daisy, is a half-hardy semi-woody plant with pale blue flowers. Sometimes also called blue marguerite, its mid-green leaves are oval-shaped and smooth. Take cuttings each summer and plant out after the last frost in pots or in clumps in sunny borders.

F. pappei (syn. *Aster pappei*, as used by botanists) is a small bushy plant, which will not survive any frost. Take cuttings in summer and use as bedding or pot plants the following spring, putting outside only after the last frost.

The daisy flowers are bright china-blue, the leaves narrow, fresh green, and healthy.
EVERGREEN SUB-SHRUBS
25-45 CM (10-18 IN)   FULL SUN   ZONES 7-10

GERANIUM CRANE'S BILL

G. himalayense (syn. *G. grandiflorum*) makes a dense clump of dissected green leaves which colour brilliantly in autumn. The violet-blue flowers have rich dark veins. Grow with pale yellow shrub roses or with *Rosa × alba* 'Celestial' with shell-pink semi-double flowers and soft green leaves. Sword-like iris leaves give excellent foliage contrast, so put clumps of geranium in front of an iris bed, in rich soil separate from the irises.
DECIDUOUS PERENNIAL
30-45 CM (12-18 IN)   FULL SUN   ZONES 7-9
G. × magnificum has violet-blue flowers, darkly veined, soft hairy leaves and flopping stems. A vigorous clump-forming plant, it is best with pale yellows and pinks. (See also Foliage framework: silver and grey.)
DECIDUOUS PERENNIAL   45-60 CM (18-24 IN)
FULL SUN OR HALF SHADE   ZONES 7-9
G. pratense, meadow crane's bill, has pale blue or violet flowers, petals crimson-veined and almost transparent. The form *G.p.* 'Plenum Violaceum' has the deepest violet-blue flowers, and 'Johnson's Blue' is a paler version of it.
DECIDUOUS PERENNIAL   75 CM (30 IN)
FULL SUN OR HALF SHADE   ZONES 5-9
G. wallichianum 'Buxton's Blue' has pale blue flowers, white-centred with dark stamens. A first-class plant with silky light green leaves and hairy stems, slow to increase but worth a place in even the smallest garden.
DECIDUOUS PERENNIAL   30 CM (12 IN)
FULL SUN OR HALF SHADE   ZONES 6-9

IPOMOEA MORNING GLORY

I. rubro-coerulea is a twining climber generally grown as an annual for a warm sunny situation or to ramp through the branches of conservatory plants. The sky-blue wide-open flowers are 10 cm (4 in) across. Sow under glass in early spring and plant out after the last frosts.
ANNUAL CLIMBER   FULL SUN   ZONES 8-10

LAVANDULA LAVENDER

Soft misty-coloured lavender spikes above grey foliage (see Foliage framework) are the essence of an English summer garden, where pink China roses and silver-leaved *Stachys olympica* undercarpet rose-beds lined with lavender hedges. Humming bees cover the pale lavender to violet flowers. Old English lavender, *L. angustifolia*, gives its name to lavender colour; *L.a.* 'Hidcote' has violet

spikes. For drying, cut the flower-heads before they fade. Lavender dislikes rich well-manured soil, so do not mix with herbaceous perennials.
SMALL TO MEDIUM EVERGREEN SHRUBS
FULL SUN   ZONES 7-10

LINUM FLAX
L. narbonense, beautiful flax, has panicles of rich blue saucer-shaped flowers and narrow grey-green leaves. It makes slender growth, suitable for planting among roses and lavender. It does not live long but seeds itself very freely. Grow with white lilies, allowing haphazard seeding and informal drifts.

L. perenne, perennial flax, has sky-blue flowers, fading in one day to papery pastel-blue. Grow with white and pale yellow flowers.
DECIDUOUS PERENNIALS
45-60 CM (18-24 IN)   FULL SUN   ZONES 7-9

LITHOSPERMUM GROMWELL
L. diffusum (now called *Lithodora diffusa*) is hardly lime-tolerant, happiest in sandy peat soil in an open bed. Plant in groups to make a bright blue carpet on a bank or rock garden. *L.d.* 'Grace Ward' is prostrate-growing, with larger flowers than the species, while 'Heavenly Blue' is the deepest blue of a blue sky.
PROSTRATE EVERGREEN SHRUB
FULL SUN   ZONES 7-9

LOBELIA
The little bedding lobelia, *L. erinus*, loves sun and heat. A half-hardy perennial, grown as an annual; the garden varieties are grouped under those which maintain a compact sturdy form of growth, and the Pendula cultivars which love to trail, spilling over the edges of window boxes, tubs and hanging baskets. Grow from seed sown in the spring; plant out after the last frost. Of the bush forms *L.e.* 'Cambridge Blue' has pale flowers, 'Crystal Palace' has dark blue flowers and bronze foliage. Trailing lobelias are 'Light Blue Basket' and 'Pendula Sapphire' with bright flowers, white-eyed. They are very drought-resistant and dislike being overwatered.
ANNUAL   15 CM (6 IN)
FULL SUN   ZONES 9-10

MAHONIA
M. aquifolium bears decorative blue-black berries by midsummer after early-spring flowering of rich yellow. Grow it in shade for leaf, flower and fruit.
SMALL EVERGREEN SHRUB
SHADE   ZONES 6-9
See also Foliage framework: green.

Mahonia aquifolium

NIGELLA
N. damascena, love-in-a-mist, has grassy delicate foliage and cornflower-like blue flowers, surrounded by thread-like bracts. Ornamental brown seed-pods follow. Sow outdoors in spring for summer flowering; it will self-seed freely. Allow to spread through iris rhizomes where its filmy foliage will do no damage. *N.d.* 'Miss Jekyll' is a clear blue.
ANNUAL   45-60 CM (18-24 IN)
FULL SUN   ZONES 4-9

PHACELIA
P. campanularia, California bluebell, is another bedding annual with bright blue upturned bell-flowers. It makes a sturdy plant and can be successfully grown for the house. September-sown plants should be covered with a cloche during the winter.
ANNUAL   23 CM (9 IN)
FULL SUN   ZONES 6-9

SALVIA SAGE
S. farinacea 'Victoria' is best grown as an annual in most gardens. With intense violet-blue flower-spikes, it can make bright clumps in mixed borders. It is lovely with the sober grey of *Senecio* 'Sunshine' or deep enough to be exciting clashing with strong velvet reds.
ANNUAL   45-60 CM (18-24 IN)
FULL SUN   ZONES 8-10
S. patens, a tuberous-rooted half-hardy perennial, is often most easily kept in a garden by sowing each spring, but sow each seed in a separate small pot. Bright, bright blue hooded flowers are carried on branching stems for many weeks. In a warm climate it remains evergreen and becomes woody with age; in cold areas it will often survive if the crowns are given protection. A pale blue form is lovely. Planted together in a container, they could make a stunning picture.
ANNUAL OR PERENNIAL   60-90 CM (24-36 IN)
FULL SUN OR HALF SHADE   ZONES 8-10
One of the annual salvias, *S. viridis*, usually listed as *S. horminum*, produces coloured bracts of different shades of purple-blue, pink and white. A mixture of all these planted together is attractive. The flowers may be dried for winter ornament. Sow seed in spring and plant out after the last frosts. Lovely near purple-flowering lavender, especially *S.v.* 'Blue Bouquet', with purple-blue bracts.
ANNUAL   45 CM (18 IN)   FULL SUN   ZONES 9-10

LATE SUMMER

Solanum crispum 'Glasnevin'

SOLANUM
S. crispum, the Chilean potato tree, has slightly scented purple-blue potato flowers with yellow centres. A form *S.c.* 'Glasnevin' is a richer colour with a long flowering season. Stems scramble over stumps, up walls or, with help, hide unsightly buildings with semi-evergreen leaves. Grow it between yellow climbing roses or close to the pineapple-scented Moroccan broom, *Cytisus battandieri* with pale yellow flowers and silvery foliage, and above *Penstemon × gloxinoides* 'Alice Hindley' with blue-purple white-lipped flowers.
SEMI-EVERGREEN SHRUB
FULL SUN   ZONES 7-10

TEUCRIUM GERMANDER
T. fruticans, tree germander, recommended for its silvery-grey leaves (see Foliage framework), has a long flowering period, pale blue flowers studding the bush with soft colour. The deeper blue of *T.f.* 'Azureum' makes the grey foliage seem paler and gleaming.
MEDIUM EVERGREEN SHRUB
FULL SUN   ZONES 7-9

VIOLA
PANSY, VIOLET, HEART'S EASE
V. cornuta, the horned violet, makes a spreading carpet with very neat fresh green leaves covered in tall stems bearing flowers in lilac-blue or white. Keep cutting back as flowers fade to encourage new buds. Grow in drifts between white roses or between spring bulbs. This violet likes a cool moist position, not one where drying winds and sharp drainage encourage early dormancy.
DECIDUOUS PERENNIAL   15-23 CM (6-9 IN)
HALF SHADE   ZONES 5-9

ACONITUM
MONKSHOOD, WOLF'S BANE
A. × cammarum (syn. *A. × bicolor*) has the typical hooded flowers of *A. napellus*: deep violet-blue spikes held above stiff or branching stems and deeply cut dark green leaves which emerge in late winter. Divide and move the poisonous roots in autumn. They like moist rich soil. Several named varieties can be grown for specific colour effects. *A. × c.* 'Bressingham Spire' has strong violet-blue flowers early, while the true *A. napellus* flowers into the autumn, making an excellent companion to late-flowering white *Chrysanthemum uliginosum*.
DECIDUOUS PERENNIAL   90 CM (36 IN)
FULL SUN OR HALF SHADE   ZONES 6-9

AGAPANTHUS BLUE AFRICAN LILY
Sun-loving plants, mainly with blue flowers, the names of many grown in gardens are confused. They all need a fertile soil, moist rather than dry, yet well-drained, particularly during winter months. They contribute good pure blues to the garden in late summer, besides having some beautiful creamy-white forms (see The whites: late summer).
   A. africanus (syn. *A. umbellatus*) has deep blue umbels of tightly crowded flowers and usually keeps its leaves in winter. In many gardens it benefits from wintering under glass.
DECIDUOUS OR SEMI-EVERGREEN PERENNIAL
60-75 CM (24-30 IN)   FULL SUN   ZONES 8-10
A. campanulatus and its various forms have pale and lilac-blue flowers as well as white. Almost completely hardy, especially if given a protective winter mulch, it can be grown in beds or containers. It does best when tightly packed, flat heads of soft blues rising above grey-green leaves for many weeks. The grassy leaves become straw-coloured in autumn.
DECIDUOUS PERENNIAL   75-100 CM (30-40 IN)
FULL SUN   ZONES 8-10
A. Headbourne Hybrids are the hardiest of all. Spherical umbels are dark blue, violet-blue, pale blue and white. To get the exact shade required choose plants when in flower. Grow in containers or at the base of a wall, where plants can get plenty of moisture early in the season. Fortunately they finish flowering before bright pink nerines and *Amaryllis belladonna* start. Interplant clumps with pale grey foliage of lavender and artemisia.
DECIDUOUS PERENNIAL   60-120 CM (24-48 IN)
FULL SUN   ZONES 8-10

AGERATUM
A. houstonianum has long-lasting flowers which, if given sufficient moisture, or if in pots watered daily, will continue in bloom all summer. Sow in spring and plant out when the last frost is over. Usually grown as attractive edging, several good flower forms exist with colours between a soft lavender, almost misty-blue, and a brighter blue-mauve.
ANNUAL   15-60 CM (6-24 IN)
FULL SUN   ZONES 9-10

ASTER MICHAELMAS DAISY
Most of the tall perennial asters are listed, in gardens, as Michaelmas daisies. Some old species are just as good as the garden forms, which are very numerous and often prone to disease, particularly mildew. Most like good rich deep soil; taller varieties may need staking.
   A. amellus is low-growing with rough, coarse leaves bearing clusters of large lavender-to-violet daisies. One of the best of its garden forms is *A.a.* 'King George', but others, such as 'Moorheim Gem', have even more pronounced violet-blue flowers.
DECIDUOUS PERENNIAL   38-60 CM (15-24 IN)
FULL SUN OR HALF SHADE   ZONES 5-8
A. × frikartii 'Mönch', a named hybrid, is certainly one of the best late-flowering plants. Warm lavender-blue flowers with yellowish centres last for many weeks. Plant this softly coloured aster near to silver-grey *Artemisia* 'Powis Castle', mix it with pastel pink and pale powder-blue flowers and edge the bed with grey felted leaves of *Stachys olympica* 'Silver Carpet'. It needs no staking, branching stems carrying many flower-heads to make a shapely bush.
DECIDUOUS PERENNIAL   90 CM (36 IN)
FULL SUN   ZONES 5-8
A. thomsonii 'Nanus' is a smaller version of *A. × frikartii* 'Mönch', and is in fact one of the parents. It has the same starry lavender flowers and may be easier to fit into a small garden. The leaves are valuable through the season, grey-green and neatly stem-clasping.
DECIDUOUS PERENNIAL   38-45 CM (15-18 IN)
FULL SUN   ZONES 4-8
The tall *A. novi-belgii* species has been superseded by very numerous garden hybrids. Look for the particular blue to fit a colour scheme. An old one, *A.n-b.* 'Climax', tall and vigorous with huge pyramidal panicles of light lavender-blue daisies, might be a good choice. I do not plant the smaller forms; they seem artificial, all flower and no stalk, looking as if stunted – which they are.
DECIDUOUS PERENNIAL
38-180 CM (15-72 IN)   FULL SUN   ZONES 4-8

BUDDLEIA
The deciduous forms of these bushes, beloved by butterflies in late summer, are well known. Generally hardy, they bear sweet scented

terminal trusses of slender tubular flowers, basically of lilac-purple in the species *B. davidii*, but many new garden forms extend the colour range through a rich red-purple to violet, lilac and pale blue. Varieties of *B. davidii* and of the less hardy grey-leaved *B. fallowiana* should be pruned hard in winter to encourage new growth on which the current year's flowers are borne. Over the years bushes become ungainly; nevertheless the soft-coloured flowers are a boon at a time when few shrubs flower.

B. davidii 'Empire Blue' has powder-blue racemes with a prominent yellow eye. *B.* × 'Lochinch', a hybrid of *B. davidii* and *B. fallowiana*, has dense conical panicles of violet-blue, each flower with an orange eye. Grey pubescent leaves have conspicuous grey undersides. A plant with a more graceful arching habit than most buddleias, fit it into a mixed border of pale flowers.

MEDIUM DECIDUOUS SHRUBS
FULL SUN   ZONES 7-9

CALLICARPA
C. bodinieri is grown for its deep lilac fruit carried among rose-tinted autumn foliage. Plant a group together (both male and female are necessary) to make an impact with purple and yellow neighbouring autumn leaves.
MEDIUM DECIDUOUS SHRUB
FULL SUN   ZONE 5

CARYOPTERIS
C. × *clandonensis* has lavender-blue flower clusters held on aromatic grey-green-foliaged branches, which arch prettily to make a rounded bush when successfully pruned in late spring. The cultivar *C.* × *c.* 'Ferndown' is of deeper blue with a mauvish touch. Grow next to the strong green foliage of *Acanthus mollis*.
SMALL DECIDUOUS SHRUB
FULL SUN   ZONES 7-9

CEANOTHUS CALIFORNIA LILAC
The group of deciduous ceanothus which flowers at the end of the season has either pale powder-blue or dark blue flowers. They should be pruned hard in spring. In most gardens they can be grown in open borders, becoming part of a carefully planned colour scheme, just at the time when flowering shrubs seldom give much colour. Ceanothus and buddleia at this time cover a range of blue, lavender, violet and purplish-blue.

C. 'Gloire de Versailles' has pale blue flowers fitting well into misty pastel schemes, while 'Topaz' and 'Henry Desfosse' are much brighter and darker in tone, best perhaps with other strong blues such as *Salvia ambigens*.

Caryopteris × *clandonensis*

C. × 'Autumnal Blue' is evergreen, and needs a sheltered site. Dark blue flowers and rich green leaves thickly clothe a warm wall. Grow next to yellow-flowering *Clematis orientalis* forms.
LARGE EVERGREEN OR DECIDUOUS SHRUBS
FULL SUN   ZONES 7-9

CERATOSTIGMA HARDY PLUMBAGO
Shrubby and herbaceous species all have bright deep blue flowers, and the small leaves have purplish tints. They thrive in well-drained soil, even the woody forms often dying to the ground each winter.

C. plumbaginoides, perennial leadwort, will succeed in poor soil as long as it is in full sun; roots push through paving cracks, each stem bearing bristling heads of dark blue.
DECIDUOUS PERENNIAL   45 CM (18 IN)
FULL SUN   ZONES 7-9
C. willmottianum is a shrub that is woody, but dies to the ground in most winters except in favoured warm microclimates. Wiry stems bear bright blue flowers for many weeks.
SMALL DECIDUOUS SHRUB
FULL SUN   ZONES 7-9

CLEMATIS
Clematis flowers often open with bright vivid colours but fade to paler shades. Among the many hybrids the choice is vast. A large-flowered hybrid, *C.* 'Daniel Deronda', has violet-blue flowers, paler at the centre.
DECIDUOUS CLIMBER
FULL SUN, ROOTS IN SHADE   ZONES 7-9
C. heracleifolia davidiana makes a mound suitable for covering a tree stump, or can sprawl or climb to suit the situation. It is very vigorous, herbaceous in habit, bearing rich

Decaisnea fargesii

pale blue flowers among the leafy growth. There are several forms with variable flower colour; *C.h.d.* 'Wyevale' is a brighter lilac-blue.
DECIDUOUS PERENNIAL
90-150 CM (36-60 IN)
FULL SUN, ROOTS IN SHADE   ZONES 6-9
C. × *jouiniana* 'Praecox' bears scented pale lavender-blue flower trusses, each small flower with a creamy stamen. It will make a woody climber in favoured areas, reaching high into tall shrubs or up small trees. In other areas treat as an herbaceous plant, cutting down to the base each winter.
DECIDUOUS CLIMBER OR PERENNIAL
FULL SUN, ROOTS IN SHADE   ZONES 6-9
See also The whites: spring.

DECAISNEA
D. fargesii has elegant pinnate green leaves, between which dangle racemes of yellowish-green in summer. Pods of metallic-blue, shaped like those of broad beans, make a spectacular show after the leaves fall, especially after a hot summer, but the plant is subject to injury by late spring frosts.
LARGE DECIDUOUS SHRUB
FULL SUN OR HALF SHADE   ZONE 5

DIANELLA
D. tasmanica is a plant for a warm sheltered garden. Preferring acid soil, it bears beautiful turquoise-blue berries, carried in arching sprays above bronze-green broad grass-like leaves. If it will grow for you, try it next to clumps of *Crocosmia* × *crocosmiiflora* 'Solfatare': its berries should coincide with the smoky apricot-yellow flowers.
EVERGREEN PERENNIAL   1 M (3 FT)
FULL SUN OR HALF SHADE   ZONES 8-10

Gentiana × macaulayi

Hibiscus syriacus 'Blue Bird'

ECHINOPS GLOBE THISTLE

These are plants with handsome metallic thistle-heads of grey-blue. *E. ritro* has jagged green leaves, grey on the undersides; grey stems bear steel-blue spherical heads. Miss Jekyll loved to plant it behind earlier-flowering herbaceous plants and to draw the globe thistle's stems forward over dying leaves. Plant in full sun and do not feed richly, or growth becomes lank.

DECIDUOUS PERENNIAL
60-120 CM (24-48 IN)   FULL SUN   ZONES 6-9

ECHIUM VIPER'S BUGLOSS

The little annual echium, *E. lycopsis* (syn. *E. plantagineum*) is useful for bedding out and the form *E.l.* 'Blue Bedder' makes a sheet of quiet blue, with spikes of tubular flowers held above hairy leaves. Sow in the spring for summer flowering.

ANNUAL   30-90 CM (12-36 IN)
FULL SUN   ZONES 6-9

GENTIANA GENTIAN

G. asclepiadea, willow gentian, has slender arching stems and there are many good colour forms of blue, ranging from the very bright *G.a.* 'Knightshayes' to the pale Cambridge-blue 'Phaeina'. They all love deep moist humus-rich soil, preferably acid (but do surprisingly well where the pH is high) and some shade. Clumps of different 'blues' could look lovely together. Usually one form is present and this will seed happily to increase each year. Grow near glaucous-leaved *Hosta sieboldiana* or the 'blue'-leaved hybrid *H. × tardiana*, both of which like the same conditions.

DECIDUOUS PERENNIAL   45-60 CM (18-24 IN)
HALF SHADE OR SHADE   ZONES 6-9

G. farreri is lime-tolerant (although preferring acid soil) and has bright luminous Cambridge-blue upturned trumpets above mats of green leaves.

DECIDUOUS PERENNIAL   10 CM (4 IN)
FULL SUN   ZONES 6-9

G. × macaulayi is very similar to *G. farreri*, one of its parents, but has deeper blue trumpets and will tolerate partial shade.

DECIDUOUS PERENNIAL   10 CM (4 IN)
FULL SUN OR HALF SHADE   ZONES 6-9

G. septemfida is variable, flowers of different shades of blue being produced in tight clusters on slightly arching stems above fresh green tufts. It is one of the easiest gentians to grow.

DECIDUOUS PERENNIAL   15-30 CM (6-12 IN)
HALF SHADE   ZONES 6-9

G. sino-ornata is acid-loving – totally lime-intolerant – and perhaps the most exciting, the flowers in a glorious glowing blue shade

Gentiana asclepiadea

streaked with green. Wide spreading mats of green foliage need a place where no other plants can interfere with growth.
DECIDUOUS PERENNIAL   10 CM (4 IN)
FULL SUN   ZONES 6-9

HIBISCUS

H. syriacus, often used for hedging in warm climates, and a good motorway plant, since it survives pollution, is a much-branched shrub with mallow-like flowers. *H.s.* 'Coelestis' has mauvish-blue 7.5 cm (3 in) wide blooms and is one of the best. *H.s.* 'Blue Bird' is similar, and is perhaps easier to find.
MEDIUM DECIDUOUS SHRUB
FULL SUN   ZONES 7-10

HYDRANGEA

H. macrophylla 'Blue Wave' is one of the most attractive lacecap hydrangeas. Central violet-blue fertile flowers are surrounded by infertile florets in pinkish-blues. In acid soil the colour tends to a purer blue. Plant in rich soil in woodland conditions.
MEDIUM DECIDUOUS SHRUB
SHADE   ZONES 7-9
H. macrophylla serrata 'Bluebird' has dome-shaped corymbs of pale blue surrounded by ray florets, reddish-blue in alkaline soil, a deep sea-blue in acid.
SMALL DECIDUOUS SHRUB
HALF SHADE   ZONES 7-9
See also The whites: late summer.

PEROVSKIA RUSSIAN SAGE

Like fuchsias and ceratostigma, this semi-woody plant is generally cut to the ground (or nearly so) each winter. There are two species grown in gardens, one of which, *P. atriplicifolia*, has blue forms, *P.a.* 'Blue Spire' and 'Blue Haze', rather than the pale lavender-blue of the type. The other, *P. abrotanoides*, has more deeply incised leaves and pale flowers. Plant in groups to thicken up rather leggy growth; pruning to shape during the summer will be at the expense of flowers.
DECIDUOUS SEMI-WOODY SHRUBS
90-120 CM (36-48 IN)   FULL SUN
ZONES 7-9

PLATYCODON BALLOON FLOWER

This is a genus with but one species, with white, pink and blue forms.
P. grandiflorum has light blue flowers. The flower-buds give it the name balloon flower, as they are strangely inflated just before popping open. It is late coming into leaf in spring, so mark its position with a stick in autumn.
DECIDUOUS PERENNIAL   45 CM (18 IN)
FULL SUN   ZONES 7-9

P.g. 'Mariesii' is a shorter form with bluer flowers. Find it in flower at a nursery to make certain of the exact colour.
DECIDUOUS PERENNIAL   23 CM (9 IN)
FULL SUN   ZONES 7-9

PLUMBAGO

P. capensis with lovely ice-blue flowers is a greenhouse shrub which benefits from having its untidy growth tied back to a wall. It can be successfully grown in a container if overwintered with temperatures just above freezing. Prune after flowering and water very sparingly through cold months.
LARGE EVERGREEN SHRUB OR CLIMBER
FULL SUN   ZONES 9-10

SALVIA SAGE

S. guaranitica (syn. *S. ambigens*) has rough dark green leaves and intense royal-blue sage flowers. It is not reliably hardy, so root cuttings in autumn. It generally succeeds if covered with a protective mulch.
DECIDUOUS PERENNIAL   100-150 CM (40-60 IN)
FULL SUN OR HALF SHADE   ZONES 8-10
S. uliginosa, bog sage, needs the same treatment; it does not survive the winter if waterlogged as its name suggests it might, but obviously, like all salvias, it needs plenty of moisture during the growing season. Bright azure-blue flowers are carried on waving arching stems. There is no other plant like it.
DECIDUOUS PERENNIAL   1.5 M (5 FT)
FULL SUN   ZONES 8-10

STOKESIA STOKES' ASTER

S. laevis 'Blue Star' has cornflower-like flowers above strap-shaped green leaves. It flowers well into autumn. Grow clumps in the front of a border, preferably next to grey-leaved plants.
DECIDUOUS PERENNIAL   45 CM (18 IN)
FULL SUN   ZONES 5-8

Hydrangea macrophylla 'Blue Wave'

FOLIAGE

'Blue' leaf colouring, like grey, is largely a matter of surface texture affecting the appearance of a green-pigmented leaf. The glaucous blue-grey colouring of the leaves in this section may vary considerably during a season as hot sun encourages the waxy bloom which protects the surface of a normally green leaf. Most plants with this leaf colouring need full sun and good drainage, but a valued few thrive in some shade and tolerate or even enjoy moist conditions.

The range of colours in this section overlaps with both the green and the silver and grey divisions of the Foliage framework chapter. See also information on leaf surface texture in Appendix I: 'Colour in plants'.

Elymus arenarius

Festuca glauca

ABIES SILVER FIR
A. concolor 'Glauca Compacta', a dwarf shrub, is very slow-growing and has leaves of an intense grey-blue, which when crushed smell of tangerines. It acts as a focus in any planting scheme.
DWARF EVERGREEN CONIFER
FULL SUN   ZONES 3-8

ACAENA NEW ZEALAND BURR
Acaenas make lovely ground cover with foliage from pale buff-green to an intense grey-blue. In *A. magellanica*, which is often confusingly called *A. adscendens*, the pinnate leaves are borne on scrambling stems to 30 cm (12 in).

A. 'Blue Haze' is larger in all its parts and even more glaucous in leaf, the stalks red and glowing in winter.
EVERGREEN PERENNIAL   5 CM (2 IN)
FULL SUN   ZONES 6-9

CEDRUS CEDAR
C. atlantica glauca, the 'blue' cedar, has intensely bright leaves, perhaps the bluest in tone of all glaucous foliage plants: certainly it is the only one which becomes, in time, a large forest tree. For this reason, use it carefully: it tends to dominate a landscape, becoming a focal point among green leaves in woodland or inappropriately eye-catching on a garden lawn. Plant it in a hidden glade or deliberately make it the basis of a contrived colour scheme, undercarpeting it with plants of bronze or purple foliage.
LARGE EVERGREEN TREE
FULL SUN   ZONES 6-8
See also Foliage framework: green.

CUPRESSUS CYPRESS
C. glabra, the smooth-barked Arizona cypress, has blue-green textured foliage, the arrangement of scale leaves reflecting variable light and shade. For small gardens there is a dwarf form, *C.g.* 'Compacta', or a medium-sized small tree, 'Pyramidalis'. The latter is perhaps the best of all 'blue' conifers.
SMALL TO MEDIUM EVERGREEN CONIFERS
FULL SUN   ZONES 7-9

DIANTHUS PINKS AND CARNATIONS
In full sun pinks make useful and attractive edging and ground cover, their mainly glaucous leaves maintaining colour throughout the winter months. Most pinks get woody, especially, perhaps, if grown as edging in beds where other plants have been given rich feeding. In late summer take little 'slip' cuttings, which root easily and can be planted out in the following spring. They dislike wet soil; give them plenty of gritty compost.

D. 'Mrs Sinkins' has fringed double white flowers, very fragrant, making a lovely carpet of associated flower and leaf. *D.* 'Excelsior', pink-flowered, is equally satisfactory. There are many other old cottage-garden pinks as well as modern hybrids, best chosen individually for good, silvery-blue foliage and for appropriate flower colour. Besides white, flowers are pink, red and crimson and often a combination of two pink tones.
SEMI-EVERGREEN PERENNIAL
23-30 CM (9-12 IN)   FULL SUN   ZONES 6-9

DICENTRA
D. eximia, *D.* 'Boothman's' and *D.* 'Langtrees' have fretted glaucous leaves which retain their cool grey even in semi-shade. They look pretty under a light canopy of shrub roses, their mauve-pink flowers blending with many old rose colours.
DECIDUOUS PERENNIAL   30-45 CM (12-18 IN)
FULL SUN OR HALF SHADE   ZONES 6-9

ELYMUS
E. arenarius, lyme grass, has graceful broad blue-grey leaves, topped in summer by wheat-like spikes of blue-grey flowers. Beloved by Gertrude Jekyll and often used in her grey foliage schemes, it makes a waving sea of glaucous colour, an ideal foliage plant if only it were less of a colonizer. Poor soil keeps the colour cool and pure.
DECIDUOUS PERENNIAL   I M (3 FT)
FULL SUN   ZONES 5-9

EUCALYPTUS GUM TREE
Very variable between species for general hardiness, these trees have valuable glaucous leaves, the juvenile shapes often differing markedly from those on mature specimens, sparsely branched broad-headed crowns and striking mottled bark. Growing rapidly from seed, eucalyptus may be pruned or coppiced to produce only juvenile foliage. More radically they can be used as 'bedding', cut back ruthlessly to make low carpets of glaucous-grey leaves for one summer season, as exotic in a colour scheme as any foliage 'bedder'. Choose your gum carefully for the garden: they vary in hardiness and ability to adapt to foreign climates. As with other 'exotics' try to get seed from gum trees growing in high mountains.

E. coccifera, the Tasmanian snow gum, is wind-resistant and fairly hardy. *E. gunnii*, the cider gum, generally considered one of the hardiest, has round silvery-white young leaves, changing when adult to lance-shaped grey-green. The sparse foliage is beautiful against a bright blue sky.
TALL EVERGREEN TREE   FULL SUN   ZONES 8-10

EUPHORBIA SPURGE
E. myrsinites, a trailing species from southern Europe, has fleshy blue-green leaves on 40 cm (16 in) stems, perfect all through the winter, and pale lime-green flowers in early spring (see Clear yellows: spring).
EVERGREEN PERENNIAL   15 CM (6 IN)
FULL SUN   ZONES 7-9

FESTUCA
F. glauca, blue fescue, is a small tufted grass with grey-blue leaves suitable for edging or for frontal groups. Flowers and dead foliage are straw-coloured, softening the solid glaucous colouring. Easily divided in spring, festuca looks untidy in winter, but blue and luminous under the summer sun.
EVERGREEN PERENNIAL   30 CM (12 IN)
FULL SUN   ZONES 5-10

HEBE
SHRUBBY VERONICA, SHRUBBY SPEEDWELL
H. glaucophylla, with blue-green leaves, has a neat bushy habit and bears white flowers towards late summer.
SMALL EVERGREEN SHRUB
FULL SUN   ZONES 8-10
H. pimelioides 'Glaucocaerulea' is semi-prostrate and one of the hardiest, with pale lavender flowers above steely grey-blue leaves.
DWARF EVERGREEN SHRUB
FULL SUN   ZONES 7-9

HELICTOTRICHON
H. sempervirens (*Avena candida* of gardens) makes a dense non-spreading clump of narrow erect steel-blue leaves, in midsummer overtopped by slender waving buff flower-heads. Ideal in a white garden and beautiful with purple-tinted ground cover. It needs tidying in spring.
EVERGREEN PERENNIAL   1.2 M (4 FT)
FULL SUN   ZONES 7-9

HOSTA PLANTAIN LILY
Hostas, with splendid architectural leaves of varying green shades, grey-green, glowing glaucous-blue and innumerable different patterns of variegation, are mainly shade- and moisture-loving, thriving in open situations only if frequently watered. The grey-blue forms glow handsomely next to glossy green foliage or light up, by contrast, the heavy tones of purple leaves. A dull *Prunus cerasifera* 'Pissardii' underplanted with *H. sieboldiana* or the much smaller *H.* × *tardiana* assumes a new importance in a garden.
Foliage appears late in spring, and dies down, brown and unsightly, before most other perennial leaves. Useful also in containers, hostas bear white or lavender-tinged flowers on tall stems. The greatest hazards to hosta growing are slugs and snails, which make unsightly patterns of holes in the leaves.
H. sieboldiana has the largest leaves, to 1 m (3 ft), and lilac-white trumpet-flowers.
DECIDUOUS PERENNIAL   1 M (3 FT)
HALF SHADE OR SHADE   ZONES 5-10
H. × *tardiana* hybrids with cultivar names such as *H.* × *t.* 'Buckshaw Blue', 'Hadspen Blue' and 'Halcyon' are much smaller, perhaps 30 cm (12 in), and more intensely blue, keeping their colour even in woodland, where these plants are happiest.
DECIDUOUS PERENNIAL   30 CM (12 IN)
HALF SHADE   ZONES 5-10

OTHONNOPSIS
O. cheirifolia, hardy if in a well-drained site, preferably in a raised bed or hanging over a container edge, has paddle-shaped very glaucous leaves on sprawling stems, and bears harsh orange-yellow daisy-flowers in summer.
EVERGREEN PERENNIAL   30 CM (12 IN)
FULL SUN   ZONES 9-10

PARAHEBE
P. perfoliata, sometimes called *Veronica perfoliata* (see early summer, above), and known in its native Australia as digger's speedwell, has long arching sprays set with pairs of waxy grey-blue leaves which clasp and encircle the stem. Violet-blue flowers are held in racemes in summer.
DECIDUOUS SUB-SHRUB   60 CM (24 IN)
FULL SUN   ZONES 8-9

PICEA SPRUCE
Spruces are hardy evergreen conifers of variable height and leaf colour, all conical in shape when young. The dwarf forms make staccato focal points in foreground planting.
P. pungens, the medium-sized Colorado spruce, has a blue-needled cultivar, *P. pungens glauca* 'Koster' which has an attractive conical habit. A prostrate form, *P.p.g.* 'Procumbens', makes a weedproof glaucous mat, useful for a corner or for covering conspicuous manholes.
SMALL EVERGREEN CONIFER
FULL SUN   ZONES 4-8

RUTA RUE
R. graveolens has blue-green leaves, which are ornamental as well as culinarily useful in salads. The cultivar *R.g.* 'Jackman's Blue' is small and compact, with deeply divided brighter blue leaves.
SMALL EVERGREEN SHRUB
FULL SUN   ZONES 8-10

Hosta sieboldiana

Picea pungens glauca 'Koster'

Ruta graveolens 'Jackman's Blue'

CHAPTER VI

PINKS AND MAUVES

The pinks and mauves traditional in the cottage garden blend and weave, mixing and paling as distance increases into a soft unregimented blur. We think of these 'pastel' colours as the tinted and 'greyed' versions of stronger hues, the reds and blue-reds; linked by their lightness and undisturbed by the presence of discordant spectral hues, they combine in gentle, pleasing pictures. But there is a fine line between the subtle and the insipid: fierce sunlight can bleach these delicate tints to washed-out paleness, unless deeper tones of pink are introduced to add strength. In the evening light, however, these pale pastels, like white flowers, appear most luminous as other non-reflecting deeper hues darken and fade from sight.

A bed of mixed Chinese peonies, pale and darker pinks and mauves with strong green leaves, expresses the spirit of such an unsophisticated colour mix; pink and mauve old roses, some with flower-petals striped in mauve and white, evoke old-fashioned garden ideas of the time before roses were bred in tints and shades of vermilion and yellow. A Michaelmas daisy border in late summer will be filled with clouds of small-flowered daisy heads in pastel pinks and mauves, perfect when given structure and emphasis with groups of strong white flowers and grey- and silver-foliage edging plants.

Pinks and mauves show up against a background of grey stone, and marry well with the mellow tints of old brick. They become rich and telling against cottage whitewash and richer-tinted 'red' when contrasted with dark green hedges or emerald lawns.

Pinks and mauves are easily influenced by neighbouring colours, but seldom exert an influence in their turn, and are thus safe and neutral in most situations. Pinks look darker beside white and silver, brighter with grey, redder with green. Through all the seasons flowers in these colours form a gentle restful background to or interlude between more

definite areas where strong complementary blues and yellows or violets and oranges paint distinct pictures, or where schemes of related colours such as vivid warm red, orange and yellow focus the eye and demand attention.

Less telling, these quieter tints reassure the viewer of the essential restfulness of garden scenes, evoking a peaceful atmosphere absent from the bright lively contrasting yellows and blues of spring, and the deep reds and oranges of high summer which are often accompanied by heavy green foliage. Pale pink, warm when other pastel tints become cool and distant, is with white the colour of fruit blossom in kitchen gardens and the massed froth of an apple orchard. Pinks and mauves do not seek to impress, rather, they are self-effacing and undemanding of attention, part of nature's background flower colour rather than exclamation marks to emphasize garden features.

Pink, whether in soft rose or sharper salmon, clearly retains its red derivation, and its essential qualities of warmth and welcome. Pinks are soft, gentle and luxurious, colours which are difficult to grasp and to define. Pinks can be shell, blush, shrimp, flesh-coloured, of seemingly infinite gradation, tints which appear to change as you look at them. Pink can be tinged white and yellow-flushed. Aretino described the colour of flesh as like snow mixed with vermilion. These soft flower colours can express the essence of garden delight, pale and restful by day, luminous and beckoning at dusk. A bowl of pink roses blends with any scheme of interior decoration, harming no adjacent colours, evocative of garden scent and tradition.

Mauve is more complicated. As a colour description it is derived from the French name for 'mallow'. By definition, it is a delicate tint of purple-violet, a pink with bluish-violet in it, less a colour in its own right than a link between the paler violet tints and the richer crimson-reds. Purple is impressive, the colour of emperors and kings; mauve, its poor relation, is often used in a somewhat derogatory sense; somehow it is

PREVIOUS PAGE **Pinks and mauves are always quiet and restful, needing no adjustment by the eye. With some of red's warmth, yet more influenced by cool paled blue pigment, a combination cannot appear discordant. Here mauve geranium is the deepest colour, adding substance to the planting scheme in a sheltered border, but it is the paler pink daisies of osteospermum and the white *Libertia formosa* that glow as evening falls – while blue salvia melts into the twilight.**

Pinks and mauves are tinted versions of adjacent red and violet segments on the spectral wheel, and their colour values can range from very pale to medium-toned. The gardener can choose to keep a pastel planting pale, light and delicate, as in the spring picture, TOP RIGHT, where all the flowers in sunlight appear as closely related pale purplish pinks, separated by quiet foliage greens. The froth of prunus blossom dominates, but is balanced by foreground flowers of rhododendron and bergenia. The darker, more vivid red rhododendron in the middle distance fades into shadow, and isolated clumps of eye-catching yellow tulips add interest without becoming part of an integrated or self-conscious colour scheme.

Alternatively, dramatize a pastel planting by accentuating one of the colours on the palette, choosing a magenta or violet as the stronger and more intense relation of the predominant mauves and lilacs. The rich magenta flowers of the *Geranium psilostemon*, BOTTOM RIGHT, dominate a planting where paler pinks share the same red and blue pigments. The colour in the shadows of the foxglove trumpets and in the folds of the Bourbon rose link these palest pinks with the strong magenta; blue pigment is distinct in the mauve petals of the climbing *Rosa* 'Veilchenblau' and in the starry *Allium christophii* flowerheads in the foreground. Individual flower-petals may contain their own gradations into deeper colour, or be marked with distinct veining, suggesting the colour to use to contribute this stronger note to the planting composition.

Subtle, low-toned colours of moisture-loving plants, LEFT, thriving happily together reveal the hand of an expert. Feathery pink meadowsweet, *Hosta fortunei* 'Albomarginata' with flowers of palest mauve, and elegant grasses are stabilized by low foreground planting of purple ajuga. Distant effects are enhanced by pale creamy-white and green variegated foliage and by the pale pink *Filipendula palmata* and deeper *F. purpurea* at the back. Even when seasonal flowers are not present, the choice of textured foliage plants will make this an interesting garden picture.

ABOVE **Even the most succinct planting association has a colour message. A pink convolvulus grows in a stone pot in the entrance yard at Tintinhull House. This invasive Mediterranean plant with attractive greyish-green leaves and a twining, trailing habit benefits from the company of grey foliage plants, which help to make the pale pink petals more brilliant. The tender** *Helichrysum petiolatum*, **with its more substantial velvet-textured grey leaves, makes a** **perfect companion plant, similarly thriving in poor well-drained soil and enjoying hot sunshine.**

OPPOSITE **A summer border with a foreground planting of pale mauve verbena, clouds of white gypsophila, violet-blue** *Salvia pratensis* **and pink and white spires of** *Acanthus spinosus* **expresses the spirit of traditional English gardening, where misty colours blend in a border of free natural planting. These pale colours and indistinct flower shapes quickly lose definition as they merge in a distant view, but here the plants are massed into well-balanced drifts.**

In contrast to the lower-growing plants in front, the bold acanthus spires stand out clearly and give height and emphasis. A barely defined pathway seems to beckon and invite exploration.

associated in the mind with mourning and middle-aged widows, and, perhaps for this reason, is seldom used in a plant catalogue colour description. Instead, a flower may be described as a tint of purple or magenta, or a variation of lilac. Mauve depends greatly on its textural quality, whether dull or light-reflecting, and when dull can indeed look muddy and greyed. It becomes more attractive and positive when its sheen recalls that of faded satins and velvets, themselves redolent of past riches.

Although pale light colours in broad masses tend to lose architectural distinction, they can be stabilized by patches of dark rich colour. Choose plants with leaves of strong architectural structure and flowers with firm outlines to contrast with the blending and blurred effects of pale mingling colours. The shining green of bergenia links a lawn with beds filled with pale pink flowers. A background hedge of dark yew unites a border of these indefinite blending colours, holding it together by the finite shape of clipped hard lines which contrast with the absence of definition in the pastels. Deep red or violet flower groups and bushes with dark purple foliage can give formality and purpose when symmetrically

set at intervals between flowing, interweaving patterns of pale colour. Dark reds are warm beside pinks and mauves, while violet or darkest blue will make pinks seem nearer and warmer in contrast. Pale, soft, gentle tints become swamped and further desaturated by neighbouring bright hues, however, so use grey leaves to separate, brighten and link, and white flowers to make the pale colours seem deeper.

A blending bed of shadowy mauves and pinks can be given structure by interposed repetitive blocks of grey foliage plants. Felted leaves of *Stachys olympica*, *Senecio* 'Sunshine', or hairy dorycnium, white silvery-leaved *Senecio leuchostachys* and feathery artemisias and santolinas, and satin-foliaged *Atriplex halimus* will brighten insipid pale colours and give a firm architectural cohesion to borders of indefinite colour shapes. Statuesque artichokes, yucca and giant thistle make splendid corner plants in full sun, while in shade conditions undulating elaeagnus leaves and grey-green hosta foliage continue the achromatic link.

Examined in detail, the pink and mauve-tinted flowers attract by subtle differences of texture and gentle gradations of colouring. Lacking eye-catching quality, they compensate with close-up delicacy and sophistication that merit detailed observation. An almost-white rose can be just flushed with pink; a pale yellow rose may be flushed with pink to reveal apricot tints; a mallow flower examined closely reveals dark mauve veining in each triangular petal. Papery-thin cistus flowers are translucent, while camellia blooms are as tempting as confectionery. Pink-tinted penstemons have markings of scarlet on their inner tubes, mauve foxgloves have brown and purple bee-marks to guide pollinators. Look closely at these pale flowers; do not leave it to the botanist or botanical painter to notice the infinte gradations of colour. A dierama flower opening to give a pinkish colouring has petals moving through violet shades to mauve, pale pink and almost white in the frilled edge of overlapping petals. These subtle differences help the garden artist to make balanced pictures using pastel flowers next to those, brighter and darker, which are closely linked to the brightest and darkest hints of colouring in the paler petals. A darker violet flower is telling beside a pale pink flower, just tinged with violet. A pale mauve flower is enhanced and given body by having neighbouring flower colour which matches its darkest shading.

Nor, even when arranging these pale tints, should complementary colour effects be neglected. Pale mauves and 'blued' pinks find their complements in lime and yellowish-green flowers and foliage. Try growing lime-green alchemilla, nicotiana and angelica to make neighbouring mauve and pinkish-mauve flowers more glowing and rich. Such arrangements demonstrate the value of understanding colour language.

Take these soft colours through the season in the garden, placing them where a visitor may linger to find rest from more dominating hues. At each period of the year there are appropriate flowers for every type of soil and aspect. In winter and early spring, flowering cherries, leafless, contrast with the perfect symmetry of camellia flowers which thrive in deep shade and peaty soil and are borne between shining evergreen leaves. In spring pink montana-type clematis and delicate Japanese cherries are matched by pink and mauve rhododendrons and kalmias in woodland glades. Later, deutzias, kolkwitzias and weigelas are companions to pink-flowered hardy crane's bill geraniums which carpet the ground and flower again in late summer, if carefully cut back after their early flush.

Rose species and purple-mauve globular-headed alliums can be grouped with tree peony species whose elegant foliage enhances any planting scheme through all the seasons. Feathery-headed mauve thalictrums and pale pink creeping phlox in sunny borders are matched in damp acid soil by drifts of mauve and rosy-pink candelabra primula with bronze and purple foliage of rheum and rodgersia.

Grow a pink and white striped *Clematis* 'Nelly Moser' through or over the leaves of a dark *Cotinus coggygria* 'Royal Purple' or a purple berberis. Pink-flowered *Rosa glauca* and its own intensely blue-grey leaves make a picture together. Match mauve flowers with lime-green *Alchemilla mollis* or the pale yellow umbels of tall angelica.

By midsummer grey- and silver-leaved plants are at their peak, having recovered from the ravaged looks produced by hard wet winters. Plan a whole border of 'silvers' to complement pink flowers, allowing shrubby mallows to give height and background. Clumps of white flowers make the glowing pinks seem darker and more impressive. Miss Jekyll had an August border of these colours, where her pinks and mauves were threaded with clumps of silvery thistles and white lilies and backed with grey-leaved sea buckthorn, *Hippophae rhamnoides*. Clouds of white and pink gypsophila gave feathery silhouettes to contrast with angular hollyhock and round purple heads of globe thistle, *Echinops nivalis* or *E. ritro*. She used dahlias and pink godetias to give extra colour, where hardy penstemons and phlox might be used in a labour-saving garden today. Yellowish pinks were separated from blue-tinted rose flowers by grey leaves; today use the lacy pewter-grey foliage of *Artemisia* 'Powis Castle' to prevent any pink or mauve flower from looking drab and 'muddy', as they may when neighbouring flowers are in pure spectral hues.

By late summer borders with other seasonal colour schemes earlier could switch to the pink of nerines and amaryllis. These sun-lovers thrive under a hot wall, while pink or white Japanese anemones spread in damper conditions and thrive in shade. In woodland mauve and pink lacecap hydrangeas make elegant clumps and autumn-flowering cyclamen carpet the ground under deciduous trees and shrubs. Mauve colchicums and crocus make drifts in grass, preparing the way for later winter-flowering crocus in shades of mauve, purple and violet. Michaelmas daisies and old cottage-garden sprays of hardy pink chrysanthemums continue flowering in early winter, hardly leaving a significant interval before the first spring cyclamen and mauvy-blue *Iris unguicularis*. A small garden will expand in dimension with these gentle, undemanding colours taken through all the year. In a larger garden, restful areas of pale colour will give sharp contrast to bright seasonal effects in strong hues and give the mind peace after the exertions of focusing and adjusting to harsh contrasts or to colourful rainbow schemes.

Keyline drawing

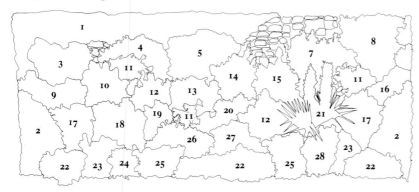

Planting plan. Figures in parentheses indicate the number of plants in a group.

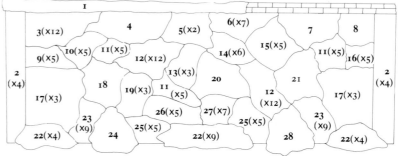

In high summer when hot colours and strong reds predominate in gardens, the wide choice among pinks, mauves and whites offers alternative plantings in softer pastel tints. The silver and grey foliage which complements these subtle colours is in its prime at this season, and the pale colours and whites glow throughout the long midsummer twilight.

This artist's impression depicts the border in full bloom: for most of the summer more linking foliage is visible between the ephemeral flower colours.

The border measures about 10 × 3.5 m (33 × 11 ft) and needs a well-drained site in full sun. Not indicated on the planting plan are the bulbs that announced the pastel theme earlier in the year: groups of pink and Lily-flowered white tulips, and drifts of mauve alliums. For the end of summer, clumps of white *Galtonia candicans* interplanted with the *Lilium regale* sustain the theme.

Plant key
1. *Polygonum baldschuanicum*
2. *Lavandula angustifolia* 'Hidcote'
3. *Anemone × hybrida* 'Honorine Jobert'
4. *Rosa glauca*
5. *Gypsophila paniculata*
6. *Anemone × hybrida* 'Prinz Heinrich'
7. *Lavatera olbia*
8. *Lathyrus latifolius* 'Albus'
9. *Geranium sanguineum* 'Glenluce'
10. *Phlox maculata* 'Alpha'
11. *Lilium regale*
12. *Cleome hasslerana*
13. *Fuchsia magellanica molinae*
14. *Artemisia lactiflora*
15. *Phlox maculata* 'Omega'
16. *Geranium endressii*
17. *Rosa* 'Natalie Nypels'
18. *Escallonia* 'Apple Blossom'
19. *Fuchsia* 'Margaret Brown'
20. *Abelia × grandiflora*
21. *Yucca recurvifolia*
22. *Stachys olympica*
23. *Nicotiana alata* 'Grandiflora'
24. *Artemisia absinthium* 'Lambrook Silver'
25. *Sedum spectabile*
26. *Penstemon × gloxinoides* 'Alice Hindley'
27. *Anaphalis triplinervis*
28. *Artemisia* 'Powis Castle'

WINTER

ANEMONE WINDFLOWER
A. blanda is a little spreading plant, suitable for growing in grass, but perhaps most effective under deciduous shrubs. Normally blue (see The blues: spring), it has pink and white forms of great charm.
DECIDUOUS TUBER   10-15 CM (4-6 IN)
HALF SHADE   ZONES 7-9

CAMELLIA
The clear pink of the attractive flowers makes a fine contrast with the dark green glossy leaves (see Foliage framework: green).
   C. × williamsii 'Caerhays' has a somewhat pendulous habit. Its buds, resistant to frost, open to a pale lilac-rose. *C. × w.* 'Donation' has semi-double very pretty pink flowers.
LARGE EVERGREEN SHRUBS
HALF SHADE OR SHADE   ZONES 8-9

CROCUS
C. chrysanthus 'Ladykiller' has mauvish flowers which can be planted in drifts in grass. There are many other *C. chrysanthus* hybrids covering a wide range of colours (see Clear yellows: spring). The very pale mauve *C. sieberi* from Greece flowers early and has yellow at the base of the petals and rich red stigmas. *C.s.* 'Violet Queen' is a darker form.
CORMS   7.5 CM (3 IN)
FULL SUN   ZONES 5-9

DAPHNE
Deciduous and evergreen shrubs of great garden merit, daphnes need a well-drained soil and partial shade. The European mezereon, *D. mezereum*, bears its sweetly scented mauve-pink flowers before the leaves unfurl. One of the least fussy daphnes, birds distribute its red fruits, which germinate easily. A white form, *D.m.* 'Album', has considerable charm.
SMALL DECIDUOUS SHRUB
HALF SHADE   ZONES 6-9

ERICA HEATH
E. herbacea (syn. *E. carnea*) has many different flower colour forms (see also The whites: winter). One of the best is *E.h.* 'Praecox Rubra' which flowers from midwinter for two or three months, the prostrate plants covered in rich deep pink bloom. The well-known *E.h.* 'King George' is compact, with rich pink flowers.
SMALL EVERGREEN SHRUB
FULL SUN OR HALF SHADE   ZONES 5-8

PRUNUS FLOWERING CHERRY
Among the earliest flowering cherries (see also The whites: spring) are pink varieties that glow against bare trees and clear blue skies.
   P. 'Accolade' and one of its parents, *P. sargentii*, have pink flowers; in the former semi-double and drooping, in the parent single and clear pink. This latter has pale bronze young leaves and splendid autumn crimson and orange tints (see Foliage framework).
   P. conradinea has pinkish-white flowers carried early if given a sheltered position. A semi-double form is most striking. The well known *P. subhirtella* produces its pink-tinted flowers in early spring, while the form *P.s.* 'Autumnalis' has semi-double flowers intermittently from late autumn to spring.
SMALL DECIDUOUS TREES
FULL SUN OR HALF SHADE   ZONES 6-9
P. mume, the Japanese apricot, can be grown against a warm wall where it bears almond-scented pale pink flowers at the end of winter. Place it near a frequently used doorway to have the benefit of fragrance, and prune after flowering.
SMALL DECIDUOUS TREE OR WALL SHRUB
FULL SUN   ZONES 6-9

VIBURNUM
V. farreri (previously known as *V. fragrans*) and the hybrid *V. × bodnantense* flower from late autumn through most of the winter months. The former has pink buds opening white if not caught by frost, the hybrid has rose-pink bloom and buds which are especially frost-resistant. In both plants the flowers are very sweetly scented. The cultivar *V. × b.* 'Dawn' is worth obtaining. The leaves also colour well in autumn. One of these should be in every garden, not least because the fragrant flowers are excellent for bringing into the house.
LARGE DECIDUOUS SHRUBS
FULL SUN OR HALF SHADE   ZONES 5-9
See also Foliage framework: green.

Camellia × williamsii 'Donation'

Viburnum × bodnantense

Erica herbacea 'Praecox Rubra'

SPRING

ANDROSACE ROCK JASMINE

A. sarmentosa (now correctly *A. primuloides*) is a Himalayan alpine, represented in gardens by various developed clones of which *A.s.* 'Chumbyi' is one, with larger flowers on a smaller plant. Grow in open situations in well-drained gritty soil. Dome-shaped pink heads rise above attractive green rosettes, which are greyish in winter.
EVERGREEN PERENNIAL   5-10 CM (2-4 IN)
FULL SUN   ZONES 6-9

BERGENIA

B. cordifolia, with rounded bullate leaves, and *B. crassifolia* have mauvish-magenta flowers. *B.* 'Morgenrote' has carmine-pink flowers and carries the bloom again in summer. Plant these as strong drifts, or use as edging; the evergreen leaves give splendid winter interest, many forms having bronze colouring in spring.
EVERGREEN PERENNIALS   30-45 CM (12-18 IN)
FULL SUN OR SHADE   ZONES 6-9
See also Foliage framework: green.

CHAENOMELES

JAPANESE QUINCE, JAPONICA
Closely related to the true quince, *Cydonia oblonga*, forms of chaenomeles have saucer-shaped flowers in various colours from a deep crimson, almost scarlet, to pale pinks and whites. Choose the right one to suit your spring colour scheme. One of the most charming is *C. speciosa* 'Moerloosii', with pink and white clustered flowers which will look lovely with pink or white tulips. These hardy shrubs can be grown in borders to make large hummock shapes, but are more usually given a sheltered wall to encourage early blooming. Cut them back hard after flowering.
LARGE DECIDUOUS SHRUB
FULL SUN   ZONES 6-9

CLEMATIS

C. armandii 'Apple Blossom', the pretty pink-tinged form of the white species, has long leathery glossy green leaves and loves to trail through low tree branches or over a wall. Feed it generously to get it to flower freely; it is one of the best spring-flowering climbers, but not a hundred per cent hardy.
EVERGREEN CLIMBER
FULL SUN OR HALF SHADE, ROOTS IN SHADE
ZONES 7-9
C. macropetala 'Markham's Pink' has strawberries-and-cream flowers, lovely if allowed to trail through grey foliage, or over grey stonework. *C. montana* 'Elizabeth' and *C.m.* 'Tetrarose' have scented flowers of soft pink and lilac-rose respectively. Perhaps neither clematis is quite so vigorous as the

Clematis montana 'Elizabeth'

white species: this characteristic may be an advantage in a small garden, where a rampant climber very soon becomes a problem. Grow either clematis over a low wall, and keep it firmly trained.
DECIDUOUS CLIMBERS
FULL SUN OR HALF SHADE, ROOTS IN SHADE
ZONES 4-9
See also The whites: spring.

DAPHNE

D. odora 'Aureomarginata' has variegated glossy leaves (it is more vigorous and hardier than the plain-leaved species) and fragrant pink flowers. Reserve a sheltered corner for this charming plant, valuable for leaf all year and lovely with other pinks in flower.
SMALL EVERGREEN SHRUB
FULL SUN   ZONES 8-10

DICENTRA

D. formosa has pretty lacy grey-green leaves and bears drooping flowers of pinky-mauve. With especially glaucous foliage, both *D.* 'Langtrees' and 'Boothman's' are desirable. Grow them in half shade as a ground cover below shrub roses; the colouring is good with the pinks and mauves typical of these roses.
DECIDUOUS PERENNIAL   30-45 CM (12-18 IN)
HALF SHADE   ZONES 6-9

ERYTHRONIUM DOGTOOTH VIOLET

E. dens-canis has rosy-pink to mauve cyclamen-like small flowers above leaves blotched in brown and green. Grow in patches in light woodland where their small corms, like the canine teeth of a dog, will quickly spread.
CORM   15 CM (6 IN)
HALF SHADE OR SHADE   ZONES 5-9

FRITILLARIA FRITILLARY

F. meleagris, the snake's head fritillary, grows wild in damp meadows, but thrives in quite dry flower-beds or in rough grass. The type has drooping bell-flowers, white or with a whitish-purple base and purple chequered markings.
BULB   30 CM (12 IN)
FULL SUN OR HALF SHADE   ZONES 6-9

Rhododendron desquamatum

MAGNOLIA

M. × *soulangiana* 'Lennei' has large goblet-shaped flowers, rose-purple outside and white stained pink inside. It makes a wide spreading many-stemmed shrub, lovely as a lawn specimen. Grow spring bulbs under its canopy, or carpeting autumn-flowering *Cyclamen hederifolium*. Like all magnolias it will flower more freely if richly fed, especially in alkaline soil where the leaves easily become pale and chloritic.

M. × *loebneri* 'Leonard Messel', like its parents, *M. kobus* and *M. stellata rosea*, has star-like flowers. The flowers are lilac-pink opening from mauve buds.
LARGE DECIDUOUS SHRUBS
FULL SUN   ZONES 6-9
See also Foliage framework: green.

PELTIPHYLLUM

P. peltatum, umbrella plant, has round heads of starry pink flowers, carried on tall stems before the shield-shaped leaves emerge. Plant beside a stream with drifts of primulas and other moisture-loving perennials. A dwarf form, *P.p.* 'Nana', is on a more appropriate scale for a small garden.
DECIDUOUS PERENNIAL
30-150 CM (12-60 IN)
FULL SUN OR SHADE   ZONES 6-9

PRIMULA

For gardens with moist acid soil primulas provide pink and red drifts of colour in spring and early summer. Most will seed prolifically and those that prefer no lime often live only one season in alkaline soil, flowering, seeding and then dying. The earlier primulas are followed by taller, more exotic species, the candelabra, which carry their flowers in whorls around the sturdy stems.

One of the best early primulas is *P. rosea*, with bright rose-pink flowers; make sure it is not overwhelmed by later-flowering primula thugs.
DECIDUOUS PERENNIAL   15-20 CM (6-8 IN)
HALF SHADE   ZONES 6-9

PRUNUS FLOWERING CHERRY

P. cerasifera 'Pissardii' has metallic coppery-coloured leaves and rose-pink flowers. The leaf and flower-colour combination sets an example of harmonious pairing, which can be matched with other plants through the seasons. *P.* 'Hokusai' has wide spreading branches, bronze emergent leaves and semi-double pale pink flowers; a suitable tree for a larger garden.
MEDIUM DECIDUOUS TREES
FULL SUN OR HALF SHADE   ZONES 6-9

P. tenella, the dwarf Russian almond, is a charming suckering shrub, with freely borne pink flowers.
SMALL DECIDUOUS SHRUB
FULL SUN   ZONES 6-9
See also The whites: spring.

RHODODENDRON
Too often the planter of rhododendrons becomes a collector and forgets the harmonious arrangement of groups by colour which makes or mars a garden. Appropriately grown in the deep acid woodland soil in which they thrive, this genus can make unforgettable garden pictures, but colours placed at random without thought to true harmonies simply become bright and even garish mounds, red flowers vivid with complementary green leaves, betraying a lack of true colour education.

Many rhododendrons have excellent green foliage, which is discussed in Foliage framework, but it is the flowering period that concerns us here, when brilliant scarlet-crimsons, dark clarets and rose pinks, lighter salmon and rose and dark crimson to magenta flowers can be arranged in sunlight, leaving the paler purples and pinks and yellows to glow under the shade of tall forest trees. In her own garden Gertrude Jekyll arranged groups to please her in three distinct colour ranges. Fine crimson-reds together, light scarlet rose colours and, in shade, the cooler clear purples with neighbours of lilac-white. There is no point in quoting her named choices, since so many new species and hybrids have been introduced in this century, but perhaps her sure colour sense may still guide us. Here we consider the pinks, mauves and paler purples.

R. calophytum has large trusses of white or pink bell-shaped flowers, each with a maroon basal blotch. It grows to tree proportions, has large leaves and is hardy. *R. desquamatum* has aromatic foliage and funnel-shaped pinkish-mauve flowers, very freely borne.
LARGE EVERGREEN SHRUBS
HALF SHADE   ZONES 6-8
R. hippophaeoides is small, suitable even for a town garden, grey leaves looking attractive all year. The funnel-shaped flowers can be in tints of lavender, rose, or even lilac-pink.
SMALL EVERGREEN SHRUB
HALF SHADE   ZONES 6-8
R. 'King George', in the Loderi group, has soft pink buds which open to pure white. One of the most beautiful in the genus. If you prefer pinker flowers, choose the similar 'Pink Diamond', which holds the pink and has a basal flash of carmine.
LARGE EVERGREEN SHRUBS
HALF SHADE   ZONES 7-9

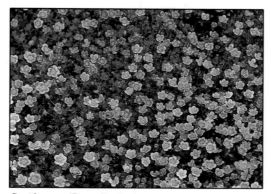

Saxifraga × 'Peter Pan'

R. pentaphyllum is deciduous, the leaves delightfully tinted before falling. The flowers, appearing before the leaves, are shallow bells, almost saucer-shaped and a rich peach-pink.
MEDIUM DECIDUOUS SHRUB
HALF SHADE   ZONES 6-8
R. vaseyi is another deciduous shrub with good autumnal tints. The flowers, earlier than the leaves, are wide funnel shapes, pale or rose-pink, or white, usually spotted with orange.
MEDIUM DECIDUOUS SHRUB
HALF SHADE   ZONES 5-8
R. williamsianum has attractive bronze young growth and lovely bell-shaped shell-pink flowers. Spreading and almost prostrate in habit, it is for the small garden.
DWARF EVERGREEN SHRUB
HALF SHADE   ZONES 7-9

SAXIFRAGA SAXIFRAGE
S. moschata makes a mossy cushion, suitable for an edging, creeping happily over stone or gravel, and making drifts in well-drained rock gardens. There are pink- and white-flowered forms and even one with golden leaves, replacing the bright fresh attractive green of the type. A mossy hybrid *S.* × 'Peter Pan' has a profusion of pink flowers prettily veined with mauve.
EVERGREEN PERENNIAL   7.5-15 CM (3-6 IN)
FULL SUN   ZONES 6-9
S. × *urbium*, London pride, has dark green leaf rosettes and spreads quickly to make a weed-smothering carpet, or a dense edging mat. Rich pink flowers flutter on tall stems above the leaves.
EVERGREEN PERENNIAL   30 CM (12 IN)
FULL SUN OR HALF SHADE   ZONES 5-9

TULIPA TULIP
Pink tulips need careful choosing: descriptions and colour names in catalogues can mislead. Look for clean colours which do not distract with flecks of white and pale frilled edges, and which seem quiet and solid with background grey-greens.

Double early *T.* 'Garanza' has very large flowers of rich pink, 30 cm (12 in) tall.
Triumph *T.* 'Emmy Peck' is a deep lilac-rose, at 40 cm (16 in) tall.
BULBS   FULL SUN   ZONES 5-9
See also Clear yellows: spring.

Erythronium dens-canis

EARLY SUMMER

ALLIUM ONION
Most useful bulbs, different allium species flower all through the summer months. Most flowers are pinkish-mauve, but white and yellow extend the colour range.

A. aflatuense has spherical heads of tiny deep lilac flowers carried on tall strong stems. Grow it between later-flowering perennials; it bridges the gap left by spring bulbs.
BULBS   75-150 CM (30-60 IN)
FULL SUN   ZONES 7-10

A. rosenbachianum also has tall stems and the flower-heads are deeper, almost maroon.
BULB   60-120 CM (24-48 IN)
FULL SUN   ZONES 7-10

A. siculum is unusual and very handsome. Papery envelopes open to reveal greenish striped plum-coloured dangling bells. Another form, *A.s. dioscoridis*, has creamy-green waxen bells. This is the one more frequently seen. Later, seed-heads are straw-coloured and decorative.
BULBS   60-90 CM (24-36 IN)
FULL SUN   ZONES 7-10

ALSTROEMERIA PERUVIAN LILY
Quickly spreading and almost invasive, alstroemerias are difficult to first establish. Grow them from seed and plant them straight from pots in the required position. The grey-leaved *A.* Ligtu Hybrids have lax stems and flowers in shades of pale pink and even pastel yellows. These hybrids and the old yellow Peruvian lily, *A. aurantiaca* (see Hot colours: summer), have an informal habit which make them appropriate for cottage-type gardening.
DECIDUOUS PERENNIAL   1.2 M (4 FT)
FULL SUN   ZONES 7-10

ARMERIA THRIFT
A. maritima has grey-green leaves and makes a charming hummock in a well-drained border. Pink flower-heads cover it for many weeks. The form *A.m.* 'Merlin' is an improved version with darker more vivid pink flowers.
EVERGREEN PERENNIAL   15-30 CM (6-12 IN)
FULL SUN   ZONES 7-9

CENTAUREA KNAPWEED
C. dealbata, the perennial cornflower, has deeply cut grey-green pinnate leaves with silvery undersides. The lilac-pink flowers are carried again in late summer. *C.d.* 'Steenbergii' has dark pink flowers, while those of *C. hypoleuca* are rose-coloured.
DECIDUOUS PERENNIALS   60 CM (24 IN)
FULL SUN   ZONES 6-10

CENTRANTHUS RED VALERIAN
C. ruber has panicles of rosy-red tiny flowers held on long stems above grey-green leaves. It naturalizes in old limestone walls and can become a nuisance, but adds considerable charm. Plant it in a new garden to give an aura of maturity. Pull out ungainly plants after seeding.
DECIDUOUS PERENNIAL   60-90 CM (24-36 IN)
FULL SUN   ZONES 7-10

CERCIS
C. siliquastrum, Judas tree, flowers best in warm climates but will perform well the season following a hot summer. Rosy-lilac flowers wreathe the leafless branches, so profusely carried as to give the effect from a distance of a rosy mist. The leaves are unusually roundish with heart-shaped bases and a smooth texture.

Grow as a specimen in a lawn, or to cast light shade in a mixed border. A white form, *C.s.* 'Alba', and a darker purple-flowered form, 'Bodnant', can be found.
SMALL DECIDUOUS TREE
FULL SUN   ZONES 7-10

CISTUS SUN ROSE
C. 'Peggy Sannons' has very good felted grey leaves and delicate pink flowers. It is one of the best for a grey and pink border. *C.* × *purpureus* has green leaves and rosy-crimson papery flowers with chocolate basal splashes. *C.* 'Silver Pink' is deservedly popular for its hardiness and clusters of freely carried flowers. *C.* × *skanbergii* is more difficult, but rewarding with small clear pink flowers.
SMALL TO MEDIUM EVERGREEN SHRUBS
FULL SUN   ZONES 8-10
See also Foliage framework: green.

CLEMATIS
C. 'Nelly Moser' is large-flowered and robust, thriving happily on a north wall and giving a second display in late summer. It is essential not to prune in the winter, common practice for the large-flowered hybrids, since it produces its bloom on the previous season's wood. Cut back after flowering. The bloom is wheel-like, each pinkish-mauve sepal round-tipped and striped down the centre with carmine spokes. *C.* 'Bees Jubilee' is brighter in both colours. Grow through the purple foliage of *Cotinus coggygria* 'Royal Purple'.
DECIDUOUS CLIMBER
FULL SUN OR SHADE, ROOTS IN SHADE
ZONES 7-9
See also The whites: spring.

Cistus × purpureus

Dictamnus albus purpureus

DAPHNE

D. × *burkwoodii* 'Somerset' is one of the faster-growing daphnes. Very fragrant pink flowers cover the bush in season.

SMALL SEMI-EVERGREEN SHRUB
FULL SUN   ZONES 6-9

D. cneorum 'Eximia', a form of the garland flower, is low-growing, its crimson buds opening to rich rose-pink. Reputedly difficult to establish, it is worth a struggle.

DWARF DECIDUOUS SHRUB
FULL SUN   ZONES 6-9

See also winter, above.

DEUTZIA

D. chunii has pink buds which open into flowers which are almost white, exposing yellow anthers, borne in panicles among grey-green leaves. It is one of the best of this genus, but needs plenty of moisture just before flowering, and rich feeding. *D.* × *rosea* has arching gracefully held branches with wide bell-shaped pink flowers. There are several different forms, all good; *D.* × 'Carminea' is darker pink.

MEDIUM DECIDUOUS SHRUBS
FULL SUN   ZONES 5-9

DICTAMNUS

D. albus purpureus, burning bush, has soft mauve-veined flowers carried lily-like on upright spikes. The whole plant smells of citrus oil, and a lighted match will ignite the volatile oil when held next to seed-pods; hence the name of burning bush. It and its white form (see The whites: early summer) take time to develop but are valuable early-flowering border plants.

DECIDUOUS PERENNIAL   45-90 CM (18-36 IN)
FULL SUN   ZONES 8-10

ERYSIMUM

E. 'Bowles' Mauve' (perhaps now correctly *Cheiranthus* 'Bowles' Mauve') is the name usually given this plant in gardens; in catalogues it is sometimes *E. linifolium* 'E.A. Bowles'. Clear pale lilac wallflower spikes are carried above green-grey leaves for many weeks. Plant it in front of mauvy-blue *Abutilon* × *suntense* and behind pale blue early-flowering *Iris pallida dalmatica*. Mounds of silvery-grey foliage make it glow. Take cuttings each spring and plant out in late summer.

EVERGREEN WOODY PERENNIAL   60 CM (24 IN)
FULL SUN   ZONES 5-9

GERANIUM CRANE'S BILL

The paler mauve- and pink-flowered geraniums make their own colour scheme against soft grey-green leaves.

G. cinereum 'Ballerina' is low-growing, very charming with pink flowers veined in a deeper shade. Grow it with mats of silvery-leaved *Artemisia schmidtii* 'Nana'.

DECIDUOUS PERENNIAL   15 CM (6 IN)
FULL SUN   ZONES 7-10

G. 'Claridge Druce' is very vigorous and taller. A hybrid of *G. endressii*, it has mauve-pink flowers carried above mounds of grey-green evergreen leaves.

EVERGREEN PERENNIAL   45 CM (18 IN)
FULL SUN   ZONES 7-10

G. endressii, with mid-green fresh foliage, bears pale pink flowers. In *G.e.* 'A.T. Johnson' the flowers are more silvery. All *G. endressii* cultivars look lovely under the early-flowering shrub roses, invasive and ground-covering without a tendency to overpower.

DECIDUOUS PERENNIAL   45 CM (18 IN)
FULL SUN   ZONES 7-10

G. palmatum (syn. *G. anemonifolium*), a most striking plant from Madeira, and almost indistinguishable from *G. maderense*, is not quite hardy, but once it flowers it should seed prolifically. Place a few seedlings in a cold frame each winter to ensure keeping your stock. Beautiful pink flowers are carried all summer above attractively tinted deeply divided leaves. Grow it with pale 'yellows' or deep magenta-flowered roses.

EVERGREEN BIENNIAL   60 CM (24 IN)
FULL SUN   ZONES 8-9

G. sanguineum 'Glenluce' has dark green hairy leaves and soft pink flowers. One of the best.

DECIDUOUS PERENNIAL   30 CM (12 IN)
FULL SUN   ZONES 7-10

See also Foliage framework: silver and grey.

HELIANTHEMUM ROCK ROSE

H. 'Wisley Pink' has pale grey-green leaves with pale undersides. Pale pink saucer-shaped flowers are carried on sunny days all through the summer. Keep in shape by regular trimming to encourage flowering.

DWARF EVERGREEN SHRUB
FULL SUN   ZONES 7-9

See also Foliage framework: silver and grey.

HESPERIS

H. matrionalis, sweet rocket, has dark narrow leaves above which white, pink and mauve flowers are freely carried. A true cottage-garden plant, sweet rocket is deliciously scented in the cool of evening. Grow it as a biennial, sowing seed in midsummer for flowering the following year. A desirable double form is very attractive but rarely available in commerce.

EVERGREEN BIENNIAL OR PERENNIAL
75-120 CM (30-48 IN)   FULL SUN   ZONES 6-9

Geranium endressii 'A.T. Johnson'

Hesperis matrionalis

HEUCHERA

Most named garden forms of heuchera are *Heuchera* × *brizoides* hybrids. Woody roots produce large clumps of rounded hairy leaves, marbled grey and green. Wiry stems hold tiny bell-shaped flowers of pinky-buff, coral and brighter pinks. Choose a suitable colour to harmonize with neighbouring flowers and foliage. *H.* × *b.* 'Freedom' has warm pink sprays and 'Apple Blossom' is paler, as the name denotes.

DECIDUOUS PERENNIAL   60 CM (24 IN)
FULL SUN   ZONES 5-9

H. sanguinea, the American coral bells, has shorter stems, and subtly coloured dark grey and green leaves. It and the evergreen satin leaf *H. americana* are often grown for foliage interest alone; pink and red shades of flower bells are just a bonus.

DECIDUOUS PERENNIAL   30 CM (12 IN)
FULL SUN   ZONES 5-9

Nymphaea × marliacea 'Rosea'

Rosa 'Ballerina'

HIPPEASTRUM

Although requiring winter protection, hippeastrums, usually known as amaryllis, are easy to grow effectively and make splendid flowering plants for containers outside or in the drawing-room. One of the most charming is summer-flowering *H.* 'Candy Cane', white flushed and striped with pinkish-crimson. Feed and water when in leaf and flower, allowing tightly packed pots to dry out when bulbs are dormant. The minimum temperature should be 13°C (55°F), but they survive temperatures below this for some of the winter.

BULB   45 CM (18 IN)   FULL SUN   ZONES 9-10

KALMIA AMERICAN LAUREL

K. latifolia, the tender mountain laurel or calico bush from North America, needs acid soil and likes warm humid climates. Very beautiful bright pink saucer-shaped flowers open from silvery buds. In cold gardens try growing it in a pot and protecting it in winter.

LARGE EVERGREEN SHRUB

FULL SUN   ZONES 7-9

KOLKWITZIA

K. amabilis, beauty bush, is one of the best early summer shrubs and thrives even in chalky soils. Drooping branches are draped with soft pink bell-shaped flowers. *K.a.* 'Pink Cloud' has dark pink buds opening pale pink, almost white. This gentle colouring makes it a feature shrub in any garden, and it can be planted next to the most strident yellows. Alternatively, mix with shrub roses and underplant with pink *Geranium endressii*.

LARGE DECIDUOUS SHRUB

FULL SUN OR HALF SHADE   ZONES 7-9

LILIUM LILY

L. cernuum is a Turk's cap lily from the Far East. Graceful nodding heads of pink with pale reddish-purple spots distinguish it from other lime-tolerant Turk's cap lilies, usually with muddy mauve flowers. Plant in any rich soil in borders or in woodland.

BULB   30-90 CM (12-36 IN)

FULL SUN OR HALF SHADE   ZONES 7-9

See also The whites: summer.

MALUS FLOWERING CRAB

M. floribunda, Japanese crab, has arching branches wreathed in flowers with crimson buds opening to a pale blush-pink, almost white. The cloud-like haze of pink is quite outstanding; grow near to bronze- or purple-leaved *Prunus cerasifera* 'Pissardii' or make it a focal point in the garden.

M. tschonoskii has a strong conical shape, grey incised leaves attractively bronze-tinted in autumn and pale pink, almost white flowers. Yellowish fruits are tinged purple.

SMALL DECIDUOUS TREES

FULL SUN   ZONES 5-9

NYMPHAEA WATER LILY

N. × laydekeri 'Lilacea' is suitable for water depth of as much as 60 cm (24 in). Fresh green leaves show off fragrant pale pink and deep rose flat flowers. *N. × marliacea* 'Rosea' is a reliable flowerer for a water depth of up to 60 cm (24 in). Vigorous leaf spread, to 1 m (3 ft), necessitates frequent division, but is well worth the trouble. Large flowers are of a glowing pink.

DECIDUOUS WATER PERENNIAL

FULL SUN   ZONES 7-9

PAEONIA PEONY

P. mascula arietina has grey-green foliage and light magenta-pink flowers. It is suitable for a main border or a shrubbery edge, leaves remaining handsome most of the summer.

DECIDUOUS PERENNIAL   75 CM (30 IN)

FULL SUN   ZONES 7-9

P. officinalis, the old cottage peony in many shades from deep crimson through mauves and pale pink to white, is mainly seen now in double forms. Choose your own colour, or look for a lovely clear rose-coloured single *P.o.* 'China Rose'. Plant under shrub roses or make clumps in a summer border, where the leaves are always decorative beside later-flowering perennials.

DECIDUOUS PERENNIAL   60 CM (24 IN)

FULL SUN OR HALF SHADE   ZONES 6-9

P. lactiflora, the later-flowering Chinese peony, has many superb named cultivars. Pale pink flower petals surround central creamy ribbon-like petaloids in *P.l.* 'Bowl of Beauty'. 'Lady Alexandra Duff' is pale pink and double. 'Globe of Light' is rose with a yellow centre. If you have the space, line a path with these beautiful peonies with catmint cascading out in front. A foaming mass of grey leaves and pale misty-blue flowers make a perfect foreground to pink peonies behind.

DECIDUOUS PERENNIAL   1 M (3 FT)

FULL SUN   ZONES 7-9

See also Foliage framework: green.

PHLOX

The little alpine phloxes are dense carpeters for the front of sunny borders.

P. amoena is rarely cultivated and garden plants with this name are usually *P. × procumbens*; *P. × p.* 'Rosea' has matted leathery leaves and rose-pink flowers. *P. douglasii* of gardens has many cultivars, including *P.d.* 'Boothman's Variety' with awl-shaped leaves and pale mauve blooms. The mossy phlox, *P. subulata*, is the most attractive, thin leaves making a low-growing wavy mass. Several good colour forms are pink: *P.s.* 'Apple Blossom' is one of the best.

SEMI-EVERGREEN PERENNIALS

10-15 CM (4-6 IN)   FULL SUN   ZONES 6-9

PRIMULA

P. pulverulenta, a candelabra type, has green wrinkled leaves and yellow-eyed, red or pink flowers carried on stems covered in floury meal. Flower colour of garden cultivars varies between almost scarlet and brick-red to softer tints of pink. *P.p.* 'Bartley Strain' is pink with a darker eye. Plant in drifts at a pond's edge; bronze rodgersia or giant gunnera leaves make a backcloth to these beautiful tiered plants. They prefer acid soil.

DECIDUOUS PERENNIAL   90 CM (36 IN)

FULL SUN OR HALF SHADE   ZONES 6-9

P. sieboldii makes creeping tufts of crinkled fresh green leaves and has umbels of freely carried rosy-purple flowers. Different garden cultivars have flowers in a range from white,

pink to a deeper purple. It prefers rich moist soil, but should have adequate drainage.
DECIDUOUS PERENNIAL   15-25 CM (6-10 IN)
FULL SUN OR HALF SHADE   ZONES 6-9
See also spring, above.

ROSA ROSE

Modest-sized shrub roses, ramblers and climbers have elegant foliage, graceful shapes and often hips in season as well as contributing a very wide range of flower colour. Roses need good soil, annually enriched with fertilizers, and plenty of sunlight to ripen and harden the wood. Bush roses of the hybrid tea type also need very strict pruning and are best when massed together in appropriate colour drifts in specially prepared and formal rose-bed settings, where their graceless winter appearance, although to be regretted, has an accepted presence. We leave the reader to choose the best from the catalogue of reliable rose nurserymen; the range is vast.

The roses described here are plants for mixed beds, with shrub-like qualities rather than perfection of individual bloom, and climbing or rambling roses which drape against garden walls or climb through old fruit trees to become part of garden colour associations.

Among the alba roses distinguished by their graceful grey-green leaves (see Foliage framework), *R. × alba* 'Celestial' has soft pink loosely folded blooms. A Bourbon rose, 'Madame Pierre Oger' flowers early and again later, and is exquisite with blush-pink cupped and rounded individual heads. Among the Damasks, the fragrant mauve-pink flowers of the somewhat ungainly grower 'Ispahan' are appropriate in schemes of pastel mixtures, where grey-leaved catmints and lavenders combine with palest blush tints of pink to deeper mauve and almost velvety maroons.

Hybrid Musks are 'Penelope' and 'Ballerina', the former making a vigorous fan-shaped bush and bearing scented semi-double flowers of creamy-apricot, and the latter with large clusters of small single pink roses with white centres. Both these will flower twice if carefully dead-headed, their later-summer flowering coinciding with a period when pink-flowering shrubs are scarce.

The size of these roses depends very much on the degree of winter pruning.
MEDIUM TO LARGE DECIDUOUS SHRUBS
FULL SUN   ZONES 6-9
R. 'Complicata' is a tall straggling rose ready to scramble through the lower branches of trees. Its huge, wide single pink flowers carried once only, are quickly followed by hips.
TALL DECIDUOUS SHRUB
FULL SUN   ZONES 6-9

Rosa 'Madame Pierre Oger'

A *rugosa* rose, 'Frau Dagmar Hastrup' has single papery clear pink flowers with creamy stamens, followed by large crimson hips. Flowering continues through the summer, flower and fruit often coinciding. The disease-free fresh green foliage and compact habit make this a useful and desirable shrub.
MEDIUM DECIDUOUS SHRUB
FULL SUN OR HALF SHADE   ZONES 6-9
R. 'Natalie Nypels' (sometimes spelled 'Nathalie') is a polyantha-type bush rose of China rose origin. Semi-double rose-pink flowers are held in airy clusters, above excellent glossy foliage. It closely resembles the old floribunda 'Else Poulsen', but is healthier and not prone to mildew.
SMALL DECIDUOUS BUSH ROSE
FULL SUN   ZONES 6-9
Two Modern Shrub roses are well worth having if there is space. *R.* 'Constance Spry' is large and grows untidily, benefiting from some sort of support. Its very heavy heads are double and a beautiful rose-pink. *R.* 'Fritz Nobis', a *rubiginosa* hybrid, holds its scented double soft

pink flowers in clusters. It flowers only once, but for four weeks.
LARGE DECIDUOUS SHRUBS
FULL SUN   ZONES 6-9
Among climbers, *R.* 'Aloha' will grow to 3 m (10 ft), has scented very tightly double dark pink flowers and glossy green leaves, and flowers twice. 'Climbing Cecile Brunner' is a sport of a bush rose. Very vigorous, growing to 6 m (20 ft), it has thimble-sized blushed-pink flowers which are shaped like miniature hybrid teas.
DECIDUOUS CLIMBERS   FULL SUN   ZONES 6-9
R. 'Madame Gregoire Staechlin' flowers early; magnificent loosely formed double pink flowers are freely carried, but once only. More adaptable than many roses, it will flower quite well on a north wall. On a south wall grow silvery-leaved plants at its feet. It grows to at least 6 m (20 ft).
DECIDUOUS CLIMBER
FULL SUN OR HALF SHADE   ZONES 6-9
Rambler *R.* 'Albertine' is almost coppery-pink in colour, but the very double flowers are many

Weigela florida 'Variegata'

Thymus serpyllum

gradations of pale and dark pink when examined closely. It is much healthier if allowed to ramble freely through trellis, over a pergola or into a host tree: when tied against a wall it is prone to mildew. It is vigorous, trailing to 6 m (20 ft), but benefits from hard pruning. Do this after flowering, and again in the autumn.
DECIDUOUS RAMBLER
FULL SUN OR HALF SHADE   ZONES 6-9
R. × *paulii* has very fiercely armed stems which arch and trail. It and the more vigorous white *R.* × *paulii* (see The whites: early summer) are among the few roses which naturally trail horizontally or downwards. Its pink white-eyed flowers are single and the petals are silky. Use it for rough ground cover; it will flower in half shade.
DECIDUOUS SHRUB   TRAILS TO 3.7 M (12 FT)
FULL SUN OR HALF SHADE   ZONES 6-9

R. 'Max Graf' is a hybrid *rugosa*, but does not share the characteristics. It trails flat, its clusters of bright pink single flowers freely carried among the glossy foliage.
DECIDUOUS SHRUB   TRAILS TO 1.5 M (5 FT)
FULL SUN   ZONES 6-9

SAPONARIA
S. × 'Bressingham', a garden relation of the invasive soapwort, *S. officinalis* and of the later-flowering *S. ocymoides*, makes a low green hummock, covered in season with rosy-pink white-eyed flowers, with pale chocolate-brown calyces. Plant in drifts on a rock garden or use for edging.
DECIDUOUS PERENNIAL   5 CM (2 IN)
FULL SUN   ZONES 6-9

STACHYS
S. macrantha (syn. *S. grandiflora* and *Betonica grandiflora*) has distinctive green triangular leaves and the flowers are carried in whorls. In the type they are deep purple but in *S.m.* 'Rosea' they are rich pink, in 'Violacea' a dusky violet. Plant in good clumps between peonies or to accompany shrub roses, especially hybrid musk types with bare fan-shaped stems.
DECIDUOUS PERENNIAL   60 CM (24 IN)
FULL SUN   ZONES 7-9

SYRINGA LILAC
S. microphylla has pretty rose-lilac flowers and small leaves; quite a different type of shrub to the large *S. vulgaris* hybrids (see The blues: early summer). The scented flowers are carried again in late summer.
S. × *persica*, Persian lilac, has pale lilac-scented flowers which are carried in great profusion. Among syringas, perhaps, this should be a first choice for a garden of limited size, its graceful rounded shape fitting easily into any border scheme.
MEDIUM DECIDUOUS SHRUBS
FULL SUN   ZONES 6-9
S. × *prestoniae* 'Isabella', a Canadian hybrid, has large erect panicles of pale purple, and is strong-growing.
S. × *josiflexa* 'Bellicent', another Canadian hybrid, has deep green leaves and carries plumes of very fragrant clear rose-pink flowers. Plant on the edge of woodland or at the garden boundary; the roots are too greedy for a border of mixed planting.
LARGE DECIDUOUS SHRUBS
FULL SUN OR HALF SHADE   ZONES 6-9

TAMARIX TAMARISK
T. ramosissima (syn. *T. pentandra*) with delightful airy green-grey foliage (see Foliage framework: grey) is covered with a cloud of

pink for several weeks. Its brown branches, light-coloured leaves and flower colour are a perfect example of colour blending: from a distance the bush becomes a subtle low-toned haze of brownish-pink.
LARGE DECIDUOUS SHRUB
FULL SUN   ZONES 7-9

THALICTRUM MEADOW RUE
T. aquilegifolium has clouds of fluffy mauve flowers held in panicles above the greyish pinnate leaves. It is a first-class plant, ideal in a formal colour scheme or blending into freer cottage-garden planting.
T. delavayi (syn. *T. dipterocarpum*) has more open loose sprays of tiny pinkish-mauve flowers, conspicuous yellow anthers giving extra colour interest.
DECIDUOUS PERENNIALS
60-150 CM (24-60 IN)   FULL SUN   ZONES 6-9

THYMUS THYME
T. serpyllum, creeping wild thyme, with deliciously aromatic small leaves, carries clusters of pink or white flowers.
T. pseudolanuginosus (the *T. lanuginosus* of gardens) has grey hairy foliage and lilac-coloured flowers. Grow this mat-forming plant in paving cracks where feet and hands can easily touch it to release its scent.
EVERGREEN PERENNIALS   5-7.5 CM (2-3 IN)
FULL SUN   ZONES 7-9

TULIPA TULIP
Darwin *T.* 'Peerless Pink' is a satin-textured pink, 40 cm (16 in). 'Queen of the Bartigons' is a pure salmon-pink, 65 cm (26 in). Lily-flowered *T.* 'Mariette' is rose-pink, with small very reflexed petals, 50 cm (20 in).
BULBS   FULL SUN   ZONES 5-9
See also spring, above.

WEIGELA
Decorative and easily grown shrubs, weigelas have clusters of small foxglove-shaped flowers in a range of colours from white to pink and red. One of the best, *W. florida* 'Foliis Purpureis', has purplish leaves and pale pink flowers and remains quite compact.
SMALL DECIDUOUS SHRUB
FULL SUN   ZONES 5-9
Another weigela, *W.f.* 'Variegata' of gardens, has green leaves margined with cream and delicately pale flushed pink flowers. Among other vigorous hybrids, *W.* 'Conquete' has large tubular flowers of deep pink, and 'Heroine', with a more upright habit, has pale rose flowers.
LARGE DECIDUOUS SHRUBS
FULL SUN   ZONES 5-9

SUMMER

ALLIUM ONION
A. cernuum is small, with drooping heads of rich lilac-pink, ideal for growing under shrub roses, and a rapid colonizer.
BULB 45 CM (18 IN) FULL SUN ZONES 7-9
A. christophii (syn. *A. albopilosum*) has huge spherical heads of pale violet stars, held on strong stems above untidy leaves. Grow it behind or through later-season flowerers, or as at Sissinghurst between bearded iris rhizomes: the alliums begin to flower just as the iris flowers fade, and the grey-green sword-like leaves will look splendid with the allium heads.
BULB 60 CM (24 IN)
FULL SUN OR HALF SHADE ZONES 7-9
A. pulchellum has grassy thin leaves and seeds prolifically. Dangling bells in dusky purple (there is also a good white form) look lovely with grey- and silver-foliaged plants. It should be seen more often.
BULB 30-60 CM (12-24 IN)
FULL SUN ZONES 7-9
See also early summer, above.

ASTILBE
Astilbes prefer deep moist loamy soil and most prefer some shade. Plumes of white, pink, rose-pink, red and magenta are carried on graceful arching deeply divided stems above often bronze- or mahogany-tinted leaves.
The *A.* × *arendsii* hybrids cover a large number of named varieties, giving a wide choice of colour and size to the gardener. *A.* × *a.* 'Bressingham Beauty' has clear pink flowers, and 'Hyacinth' is rose-pink. Plant them in groups beside water or to contrast with solid architectural hosta leaves.
DECIDUOUS PERENNIAL 30-150 CM (12-60 IN)
HALF SHADE ZONES 7-9

BESCHORNERIA
B. yuccoides is for a favoured warm microclimate, or can be grown in pots as long as temperatures do not drop below freezing. The great arching spikes held high above sword-like grey-green leaves have coral-pink and red bracts surrounding green hanging bells. This is not an easy plant, and flowering is not assured even in the perfect site. In flower it gives any garden an exotic aura, besides the colour effects – which are stunning.
EVERGREEN PERENNIAL 2.5 M (8 FT)
FULL SUN ZONES 8-10

BUDDLEIA
B. crispa needs a warm wall and plenty of hot sun. It has deeply toothed felted grey leaves and fragrant lilac-pink flowers, each with an orange throat, held in terminal panicles. After a mild winter it flowers early; after a severe one it makes late growth and will flower at the end of summer. Give it a prime site. It is a first-class plant.
MEDIUM SEMI-EVERGREEN WALL SHRUB
FULL SUN ZONES 8-9
See also The blues: late summer.

CAMPANULA BELLFLOWER
C. lactiflora 'Loddon Anna' is a pale pink flowering form of the tall perennial which is so useful in summer borders (see The blues: summer). Traditional soft tints of pink, blue, and mauve are background colours for many conventional planting schemes.
DECIDUOUS PERENNIAL 1.2 M (4 FT)
FULL SUN ZONES 6-9

CISTUS SUN ROSE
C. creticus is rather variable but has pale grey shaggy leaves and flowers in mauve and pink shades. Plant it in a pink, white and grey border: its flowers and leaves in soft gentle colours are exactly right.
SMALL EVERGREEN SHRUB
FULL SUN ZONES 8-10
See also The whites: early summer.

CONVOLVULUS
C. althaeoides has dissected pale grey, almost silver leaves (these are green in early spring and can be mistaken for weeds) and shell-pink flowers. A sun-lover from southern Europe, it seems surprisingly hardy and running roots spread rapidly. Don't be put off. Its perfect leaf and flower are worth moments spent in disentangling plants round which it twines. Grow it over a wall or in a raised bed where root run is contained, and allow it to rampage.
DECIDUOUS PERENNIAL 60 CM (24 IN)
FULL SUN ZONES 8-10

DIANTHUS PINKS AND CARNATIONS
There are so many charming border pinks from which to choose that a gardener will do best to see them in flower at a local nursery. Fortunately many old cottage favourites are now again available, so choose for colour, fragrance and good glaucous foliage. Old clove carnations grow taller and tend to have more vivid darker reddish flowers and belong in other chapters, but the familiar blue-grey foliage has a definite emotional association with pastel-pink border schemes rather than with stronger summer colours. Fringed and laced flower petals, often two-coloured, and evocative heavy scent give pinks their charm, but they are also useful for their good foliage.
EVERGREEN PERENNIALS 15-60 CM (6-24 IN)
FULL SUN ZONES 6-9
See also The blues: foliage.

Allium cernuum

Erigeron mucronatus

ERIGERON
E. mucronatus from Mexico becomes a weed if it likes you, seeding in paving cracks and walls. All good gardens should have it. Flowering all summer the daisy-petals are pink and white, the pink varying considerably in colour. Woody branching stems develop in a border site.
DECIDUOUS PERENNIAL 30 CM (12 IN)
FULL SUN ZONES 8-10

ESCALLONIA
E. 'Apple Blossom', one of the smaller hybrids, can be planted as part of a general border scheme or in a shrubbery bed. Cup-shaped pink and white petals are set among glowing green leaves. Use it with misty colours; its definite shape and habit gives form to blending colours which can lose their firm outlines.
MEDIUM EVERGREEN SHRUB
FULL SUN ZONES 7-9

Filipendula palmata

E. 'Donard Seedling' has an attractive weeping habit, pink and white flowers making a veil of gentle colour. Plant it as a cascading hedge. Prune hard after flowering.
LARGE EVERGREEN SHRUB
FULL SUN   ZONES 7-9
See also Foliage framework: green.

FILIPENDULA MEADOWSWEET
F. palmata has broad pink heads composed of minute flowers, carried above elegant foliage. Various forms with more or less purplish flowers can be found. Plant in large groups in moist soil, letting it contrast with more massive solid foliage plants such as hostas.
DECIDUOUS PERENNIAL   90 CM (36 IN)
FULL SUN   ZONES 6-9

FRANCOA
Francoas have hairy leaves and attractive wands of whitish-pink flowers. Grown in containers in cold gardens and wintered under glass, they look quite exotic; in warmer climates they are a useful evergreen ground cover. *F. sonchifolia*, bridal wreath, has deep pink flowers with darker red at the inside base of the individual petal.
EVERGREEN PERENNIAL   60-90 CM (24-36 IN)
FULL SUN   ZONES 7-9

FUCHSIA
Hardy and half-hardy evergreen and deciduous shrubs (some semi-woody in gardens), fuchsias are very useful summer flowerers, continuing to bloom for a long season, right into the autumn. Where climate allows, fuchsias make tall colourful hedges; elsewhere small plants are useful for hanging baskets and in the front of borders. Many have two-toned flowers; pendulous bell-shaped flowers have tubular spreading sepals

overlapped by petals in another colour. Reds, pinks, mauves, violet and white can make garish combinations. I prefer those where shades of one colour firmly predominate. *F. magellanica molinae* (still sometimes known as *F. magellanica*) 'Alba', has slender flowers of pale pink, not showy. A variegated form, 'Sharpitor', has the same pale flowers, but the leaves are grey-green with creamy margins. A very hardy hybrid is *F.* 'Margaret Brown', a medium-sized shrub for a mixed border.
SMALL TO LARGE DECIDUOUS SHRUBS
FULL SUN OR HALF SHADE   ZONES 7-9

GALEGA GOAT'S RUE
G. officinalis, basically with pale, washed-out blue or white flowers, has several good garden forms of lilac, lavender or pinky-mauve. These pea-flowers are carried over green pinnate leaves, and they make attractive clumps for the back of a border. An old cottage-garden plant, galega is now quite difficult to get. *G. × hartlandii* 'Lady Wilson' is mauve and cream.
DECIDUOUS PERENNIAL   90-150 CM (36-60 IN)
FULL SUN OR HALF SHADE   ZONES 6-9

GERANIUM CRANE'S BILL
G. × 'Russell Prichard' starts flowering in summer and continues into the autumn. Pink-red flowers and stalks trail above pale grey palmate leaves.
DECIDUOUS PERENNIAL   15 CM (6 IN)
FULL SUN   ZONES 6-9

HEMEROCALLIS DAY LILY
H. 'Pink Damask' has warm pink flowers with brownish-yellow throats. Plant next to bronze or purple foliage, or under pink-flowered shrub roses: I first grew it beside a purple-leaved cotinus.
DECIDUOUS PERENNIAL   75 CM (30 IN)
FULL SUN OR HALF SHADE   ZONES 6-9
See also Foliage framework: green.

LILIUM LILY
L. martagon, martagon or Turk's cap lily, is a most useful member of its genus, thriving in shade and not at all fussy about soil. Scattered seed will germinate under trees and flower after four or five years; a mature garden usually has plenty of self-sown seedlings in unexpected places. Like most lilies, groups are more effective than single specimens. Its petals are pinkish-purple with darker spotting, not showy or colourful but effective, stems rising above low ground-cover plants. Named forms include the white *L.m. album*.
BULBS   100-200 CM (40-80 IN)
SHADE   ZONES 5-9
See also The whites: summer.

LINUM FLAX
L. grandiflorum is a hardy annual flax with saucer-shaped pink flowers. Sow seeds in flowering site in September and thin out as required. There are several good forms including a brighter red *L.g.* 'Rubrum'. This flax can also be pot-grown and overwintered under glass for early flowering.
ANNUAL   30-50 CM (12-20 IN)
FULL SUN   ZONES 8-10

LYCHNIS CAMPION
L. flos-jovis, flower of Jove, has silvery leaves and stems and small pink to purple flowers. A rather sprawling habit makes it essential to grow this plant in groups beside later taller-flowering perennials, but for flower and leaf colour alone it deserves a place in a summer border. Plant it next to bushes of pewter-grey *Artemisia* 'Powis Castle'.
DECIDUOUS PERENNIAL   30 CM (12 IN)
FULL SUN   ZONES 5-9

PELARGONIUM 'GERANIUM'
Confusedly called geraniums, but not to be mistaken for the hardy crane's bills, these tender sub-shrubs are most useful and colourful in the summer garden. Carefully chosen for good effect, banks and drifts of subtle colouring mix with neighbouring bedding-out plants. But, as Gertrude Jekyll once said, it is not the fault of the geranium that it is so often badly used. The most showy are perhaps the ivy-leaved trailers, *P. peltatum*, with mainly pinkish-mauve flowers; ideal for window boxes and containers. *P.p.* 'Madame Crousse' has double bright pink flowers, 'Santa Paula' has semi-double mauve flowers.

Zonal pelargoniums, *P. × hortorum*, make branching shrubs, and carry dense rounded flower clusters of white, pink, red and scarlet-orange. Dead-heading ensures bloom all through the summer. Grow named forms from seed or make a careful choice of colour. An old one, *P. × h.* 'The Boar', has pretty salmon-pink flowers and dark foliage.

I find it easiest to overwinter one plant of each form or colour and take spring cuttings which root quickly, but if space is limited strike tip cuttings in late summer and keep frost-free through severe weather.
SMALL EVERGREEN SUB-SHRUBS
FULL SUN   ZONES 9-10
P. crispum 'Variegatum' has pale pink flowers but is grown mainly for its wedge-shaped scented leaves, margined with creamy-white. *P. graveolens*, rose geranium, is an upright grower with rough aromatic green leaves.
SMALL EVERGREEN SHRUBS
FULL SUN   ZONES 9-10

LATE SUMMER

PETUNIA
P. 'Pink Joy' is salmon-pink and comes into flower early. Have young plants ready for bedding out as soon as frosts in your area are finished. 'Chiffon Magic' has soft lilac flowers with paler creamy throats.
ANNUAL   30 CM (12 IN)
FULL SUN   ZONES 9-10
See also The whites: summer.

PHLOMIS
The phlomis best suited to the pink-and-pastel coloured scheme is *P. italica*, which has silvery-grey felted leaves and very pale pink flowers. It is a little tender, so give it a prime site (of which it is worthy), sheltered from severe winds, and make certain the roots do not stand in waterlogged soil in winter. Prune hard in early summer to make a shapely bush.
MEDIUM EVERGREEN SHRUB
FULL SUN   ZONES 7-9
See also Foliage framework: silver and grey.

PHYGELIUS
P. aequalis needs rich soil but a sheltered warm situation. Coral-red flowers with yellow throats are held at the tip of long woody stems. It needs spraying with an insecticide just before flowering begins. Cut off dead-heads and another crop of bloom will follow in late summer. A plant with subtle colouring; place at eye level, close enough for details to be seen.
MEDIUM DECIDUOUS SUB-SHRUB
FULL SUN   ZONES 8-9

POLYGONUM KNOTWEED
Ranging from climbers, large bamboo-like canes to little mat-forming creepers, as well as including the climbing Russian vine, *P. baldschuanicum*, many polygonums are useful garden plants, the foliage often with attractive veining and flowers shades of white, delicate pink and red. Most prefer a damp moisture-retentive soil, and some are invasive.

P. affine is a carpeter, green leaves becoming bronze in winter. In *P.a.* 'Donald Lowndes' the upright poker-flowers are semi-double and salmon-pink. By nature a rock plant, grow it over the edge of paving to make a dense mat.
SEMI-EVERGREEN PERENNIAL
23-30 CM (9-12 IN)   HALF SHADE   ZONES 6-9

RODGERSIA
R. pinnata has astilbe-like fluffy pink flowers held above its attractive foliage (see Foliage framework: green). *R.p.* 'Superba' is more striking, taller, the flowers brilliantly pink and leaves bronze.
DECIDUOUS PERENNIAL   100-120 CM (40-48 IN)
HALF SHADE   ZONES 6-9

ABELIA
A. × *grandiflora* is one of the best late-flowering shrubs (see also Foliage framework: green). Glossy evergreen leaves have bronze-pink tints all year, and the pink and white honeysuckle-like flowers are carried freely, wafting scent through the garden. Give this bush a prime site near a doorway or path where it contributes beauty all year.
MEDIUM EVERGREEN SHRUB
FULL SUN   ZONES 8-10
A. schumannii has less glossy foliage, which it loses in winter, and pale mauve flowers. Perhaps not such a good all-rounder as the former, but useful where its pale flowers will complement bronze or purple foliage.
MEDIUM DECIDUOUS SHRUB
FULL SUN   ZONES 8-10

ACANTHUS BEAR'S BREECHES
A. mollis and its form *A.m. latifolius* have such beautiful leaves (see Foliage framework: green) that the tall flower-spikes of white and purple (crinkly flower petals and overlapping bracts) are a bonus. Freely carried if in full sun – the leaves are effective and roots less invasive if planted in shade – they give strong vertical emphasis and fit into any colour scheme.
DECIDUOUS PERENNIAL
90-120 CM (36-48 IN)   FULL SUN   ZONES 6-9

ALTHAEA HOLLYHOCK
Usually grown as biennials or even annuals, hollyhocks, now classified as *Alcea*, are traditional cottage-garden plants with single or double flowers in all sorts of gentle colours, ranging from dark to pale pink, pale yellow and white. The green hairy leaves are prone to rust if the plants are retained into a second year. Unfortunately they do not seed true to a colour. *A. rosea* (*Alcea rosea*) has many named varieties but seeds most readily available are usually in mixed packets which confuse a colour plan. What a pity; they are lovely plants for the back of a late border.
BIENNIAL OR ANNUAL
1.2 M (4 FT) OR 2.4-3 M (8-10 FT)
FULL SUN   ZONES 6-9

AMARYLLIS
A. belladonna, the belladonna lily, likes well-drained soil at the base of a sunny wall. Pale pink trumpet-shaped scented flowers are borne on sturdy stems after the strap-shaped untidy leaves have died away. Water and feed while leaves show plant is in growth. There are some listed varieties or hybrids. Try not to allow foreground plants to shade the bulbs. Split up when dormant in midsummer.
BULB   75 CM (30 IN)   FULL SUN   ZONES 8-10

Abelia × *grandiflora*

ANEMONE WINDFLOWER
A. × *hybrida* 'Prinz Heinrich' is the best of the pink forms, but make your own choice between double and single, and notice variation in petal shapes. At Tintinhull, *A.* × *h.* 'Prinz Heinrich' flowers with nerine and belladonna lilies. It is very invasive, but worth the effort of frequent curbing for superlative display for many weeks.
DECIDUOUS PERENNIAL   1.2 M (4 FT)
FULL SUN OR HALF SHADE   ZONES 6-9

ASTER MICHAELMAS DAISY
A. lateriflorus 'Horizontalis' has only one fault: although needing plenty of warm sun, it wilts quickly in a drying breeze and has to be watered if you want successful flowering. The tiny foliage, coppery-purple in autumn, is borne on horizontal branching side stems and the lilac and rose flowers give a misty effect of brownish rosy-mauve. Plant to flower near *Sedum spectabile*, whose fleshy pale leaves and flat heads of pink make a complete contrast of form.
DECIDUOUS PERENNIAL   90 CM (36 IN)
FULL SUN   ZONES 5-9

Amaryllis belladonna

Nerine bowdenii

Cleome hasslerana

CLEOME
C. hasslerana (*C. spinosa* of gardens), spider flower, is an annual for late-summer flowering. Strange white and flushed-pink flowers appear at the tip of spiny stalks. *C.h.* 'Pink Queen' is a free-flowering form. Seeds of 'Colour Fountain' are in mixed colours, all shades of purple and pink; one of the few packets of mixtures to be recommended, as colours weave and blend charmingly.
ANNUAL   1 M (3 FT)   FULL SUN   ZONES 9-10

CRINUM
Bulbous plants from warm climates, crinums need heat, and greenhouse cultivation in cold areas. *C. × powellii* is a hybrid with pink and white flowers; some a mixture, others one colour or the other. Leaves, unfortunately, often get frost-marked in early spring, and remain disfigured all season.
BULB   45 CM (18 IN)
FULL SUN   ZONES 8-10

CYCLAMEN
C. hederifolium (syn. *C. neapolitanum*) is hardy, with variable marbled leaves attractive in winter and early spring, after which they die

down. Flowers are mauve to pale pink, and white, very freely carried, especially in a wet season. Mulch with peat to conserve moisture during the summer.
CORM   15 CM (6 IN)
HALF SHADE OR SHADE   ZONES 6-9
See also The whites: foliage.

DIERAMA WANDFLOWER
D. pulcherrimum has a very elegant habit when in flower, arching stems fluttering in the wind with silvery calyces opening to hanging bells of pale to deep rose. The stems are grassy and evergreen, a bit untidy. Grow these plants to hang over water, the constant movement reflected in the surface. A few plants will give plenty of self-sown seedlings. They seem to thrive in any soil, but do not like to be waterlogged in winter.
EVERGREEN PERENNIAL   1.5 M (5 FT)
FULL SUN   ZONES 8-10

EUPATORIUM HEMP AGRIMONY
E. purpureum has whorls of pointed green leaves. Its flat flower-heads held on branching stems are rosy-purple. The form *E.p.* 'Atropurpureum' has purple leaves and stems and darker flowers. Plant groups of this valuable, but little-seen, plant at the back of a border.
DECIDUOUS PERENNIAL   1.8 M (6 FT)
FULL SUN OR HALF SHADE   ZONES 7-9

HYDRANGEA
H. macrophylla serrata 'Preziosa' has purplish stems, bronze leaves and globular heads of pinkish-red, deepening in colour after opening. One of the more interesting hydrangeas for the smaller garden, and flowers remain perfect as leaves begin to assume autumnal tints.
MEDIUM DECIDUOUS SHRUB
HALF SHADE   ZONES 7-9
H. aspera (syn. *H. villosa*) can be lilac-blue or mauvish-pink, depending on the alkalinity of the soil, but it thrives in almost any conditions. Recommended for shade, I have found it flowers more freely in full sun. Hairy leaves, dull green above, soft and grey below, are handsome; flat corymbs of lacecap type are held horizontally.
LARGE DECIDUOUS SHRUB
FULL SUN OR HALF SHADE   ZONES 7-9
See also The whites: late summer.

LAVATERA TREE MALLOW
L. olbia has large wide-open flowers of mallow-pink, sometimes darker. Grey-green, three- to five-lobed leaves set them off. A quick grower, useful in a new border, and with flowers

carried very freely over a long period. Plant in a grey and pink colour scheme; there are few pink-flowering shrubs so late in the season.
MEDIUM DECIDUOUS SHRUB
FULL SUN   ZONES 7-9

LYTHRUM LOOSESTRIFE
Lythrum will grow in any reasonable soil, and flower freely in shady conditions. Two perennial species have given rise to some good garden forms. From *L. salicaria*, purple loosestrife, we have the slender flower spikes of red-purple in an old favourite *L.s.* 'Brightness' or rosy-red 'Robert' and 'The Beacon'. Seedlings will revert, so dead-head and increase by division.
DECIDUOUS PERENNIAL   1.2 M (4 FT)
HALF SHADE   ZONES 6-9
L. virgatum is more elegant and slender, flowers and leaves smaller and less coarse. Good forms are *L.v.* 'Rose Queen' in rose-pink, and 'The Rocket', which is similar but a deeper tone.
DECIDUOUS PERENNIAL   75 CM (30 IN)
HALF SHADE   ZONES 6-9

MONARDA BERGAMOT
M. didyma, bee balm, with dense whorled flower-heads of bright scarlet (see Hot colours: late summer) has several good garden forms in paler tints. *M.d.* 'Croftway Pink' is rosy and 'Melissa' is a pale pink. Plant in enriched moisture-retaining soil; all bergamots dislike drought.
DECIDUOUS PERENNIAL
90-120 CM (36-48 IN)
HALF SHADE   ZONES 7-9

NERINE
N. bowdenii is hardy and an invaluable flowerer for the end of the season. In a warm border, pink umbels on strong stems are borne just before leaves emerge (those in most species die down in early summer). Nerines increase quickly and are lovely in groups at the front of borders and for picking. More tender forms of *N. sarniensis*, Guernsey lily, need greenhouse protection in winter and a hot summer to flower well.
BULBS   30-45 CM (12-18 IN)
FULL SUN   ZONES 8-10

PENSTEMON
Garden penstemons are confusing, dividing themselves into low-growing alpine species, and taller border plants, some half-hardy and some woody sub-shrubs. Many will survive quite severe winters to succumb to cold drying winds in spring. The best policy is to take cuttings (easily rooted in late summer) and

replant in late spring. Border penstemons cover a range of colours from bright scarlet hybrids of *P. × gloxinoides*, a name for hybrids between *P. hartwegii* and *P. cobaea*, to paler pinks and mauves of *P. campanulatus* hybrids such as *P.c.* 'Evelyn' (pink), 'Garnet' (wine: see Strong reds: summer), and 'Hidcote Pink' (pink with a pale throat and scarlet streaks). *P. × gloxinoides* 'Alice Hindley' has tubular flowers of pale bluish-purple and *P. × g.* 'Sour Grapes' is a bit darker, almost pale wine-coloured. Plant in groups for colour in a late border, although in a favourable season flowering will begin much earlier and be almost continuous, if dead-heading is regular.
EVERGREEN PERENNIAL   45-100 CM (18-36 IN)
FULL SUN   ZONES 8-10

PERNETTYA
P. mucronata, an acid-loving small shrub, is grown mainly for its lovely coloured fruits, which cover a wide range between white, pinks, reds and purples. The fruits are like hanging marbles between small glossy evergreen leaves, and thickets in one colour or mixed drifts are lovely as massed ground cover under taller woodland shrubs or trees. Plant a proven male form among groups of females to ensure fruiting, although the plants are not strictly dioecious. Plant in full sun for the best display, but moist soil in light shade is adequate. A sheltered winter garden, with rich acid soil, should be made beautiful with plantings of this lovely shrub.
SMALL EVERGREEN SHRUB
FULL SUN OR HALF SHADE   ZONES 4-9

PHLOX
P. maculata has tall cylindrical spikes of mauvish flowers and the cultivar *P.m.* 'Alpha' is soft pink.
DECIDUOUS PERENNIAL   I M (3 FT)
FULL SUN OR HALF SHADE   ZONES 6-9
P. paniculata now has many good named varieties between violet-blue, purples and pinks. To obtain a particular shade ideally choose from a plant in flower rather than a catalogue description, but *P.p.* 'Sandringham' is cyclamen-pink with a dark centre and 'Fairy's Petticoat' is pale mauve with a darker centre.
DECIDUOUS PERENNIAL   I.2 M (4 FT)
FULL SUN OR HALF SHADE   ZONES 6-9
See also The whites: late summer.

POLYGONUM KNOTWEED
P. campanulatum has the most attractive veined and bronze-marked leaves, which appear in early spring. The wide heads are shell-pink and it flowers for many weeks. Plant it in a good group, but beware the invasive habits typical of the genus.
DECIDUOUS PERENNIAL   I M (3 FT)
FULL SUN   ZONES 7-9
See also summer, above.

ROSA ROSE
R. virginiana is a suckering species with glossy green leaves which turn rich shades of crimson and yellow in autumn. It is the last rose to flower, doing so when other repeat-flowerers are almost starting their second flush. Cerise-pink single flowers are fragrant.
MEDIUM DECIDUOUS SHRUB
FULL SUN OR HALF SHADE   ZONES 6-9
R.v. 'Rose d'Amour', the St Mark's rose, has paler pink double flowers, the centre darker than the outer petals. Grow it in a shrubbery which tends to have little flower at this time of the year, or include it in a mixed border for flower and foliage.
SMALL DECIDUOUS SHRUB
FULL SUN   ZONES 6-9
See also early summer, above.

SAPONARIA SOAPWORT
S. officinalis, bouncing Bet, the leaves of which can be distilled for making soap (still used today for washing old fabrics) is very invasive, but if space can be found where running roots are contained, plant it or its charming double form, *S.o.* 'Roseo-plena'. Grow it in the herb or kitchen garden where its flowers are welcome when many aromatic-foliaged plants have become unsightly by the end of summer.
DECIDUOUS PERENNIAL   60-90 CM (24-36 IN)
FULL SUN   ZONES 7-9

SCHIZOSTYLIS KAFFIR LILY
Thriving in damp soil, groups of *S. coccinea* are effective for splashes of strong colour. Grassy foliage above quickly spreading roots is inconspicuous in early summer but cup-shaped shining flower-petals of rich crimson, warm rose or pale pink later make up for it. Not altogether hardy, plants should not stand in wet soil in winter; they flower well if there is plenty of moisture during the growing period. Best known among the pink cultivars is *S.c.* 'Mrs Hegarty', but 'Sunrise' has larger flowers, and 'Viscountess Byng' is pale pink.
DECIDUOUS RHIZOME   60 CM (24 IN)
FULL SUN   ZONES 7-9

SEDUM
S. × 'Ruby Glow' has wide, flat heads of tiny pinkish flowers, beloved by butterflies.
S. spectabile has fleshy white and green leaves and pink flower-heads, with a mauvish tint. *S.s.* 'Brilliant' is of a deeper rose colour. Grow at the edge of a border.
DECIDUOUS PERENNIAL   25-30 CM (10-12 IN)
FULL SUN   ZONES 6-9
See also Foliage framework: green.

Dierama pulcherrimum

CHAPTER VII

STRONG REDS

Red, the most bold and provocative of spectral hues, in the garden becomes a key colour, an exclamation mark seen from afar, deep and mysterious close to. Commanding and eye-catching in all its moods, it appears most vibrant where it is enriched by the complementary mid-greens of trees, plants and grass. In the tropics bright reds, easily spotted among the luxurious foliage by predatory birds, ensure flower pollination, while in more temperate climates red berries guarantee seed dispersal. Except in the extravagance of autumn foliage, nature uses the brightest reds in moderation, sometimes merely as spots of vivid colour set amidst a low-toned background of greens and greys; a touch of warm, advancing colour giving perspective to other tonal shades and tints which emphasize distance and depth. The artist is inspired by the red poppies in a golden cornfield or the wild red anemones in an Italian spring landscape, which sparkle and shimmer like precious stones and bring the landscape closer.

Bossy, warm, advancing and eye-catching red deepens its interest and subtlety when toned with blue or brown. The colour range in this chapter is the shadow-counterpart of Chapter VI, which deals with pinks and mauves – reds and blue-reds paled with white. Here the reds are full-strength, or are darkened or 'shaded' with an element of blue or brown, towards purple, maroon and almost black itself. Like the pastels in the previous chapter, they belong to the 'cold' side of the reds, and contain no warming yellow: the 'hotter' scarlets will be discussed in Chapter VIII. It is never easy to mix the 'blued' reds and pinks with the 'sunset' colours of yellowed reds and oranges, and so they are considered quite separately in this book.

The touchstone among the 'strong' reds of this chapter is crimson, by definition a deep red tinged with blue. Magenta, a brilliant crimson, is named after the battle of 1859 between the French and Austrians which coincided with its invention. An aniline dye obtained from coal-tar, its glowing intensity makes the dark, deep red of crimson itself appear quite dull. Carmine, the crimson pigment obtained from cochineal, is used as an adjective more or less synonymously with crimson, while cerise, the French for cherry, is a strong blue-red.

All reds seem to retain their characteristic redness however the colour dimensions change. A very pale pink, almost white, still clearly has red pigment; a very dark shade of almost black or brown is still recognizably red. Red in greyish tones becomes smoky and mysterious, but plant dull red flowers next to grey foliage and they become rich and compelling (although the grey leaves will become noticeably greenish).

The colour we associate with earth (but, of course, in soils enormously variable) is a sombre red-brown, a red with black added. Bronze is a metallic brown, closely linked with deep crimson-reds. Maroon is a brownish-crimson, perhaps the colour of claret. These low-toned colours are more common in foliage than in flowers; the comparatively few flowers such as the mysterious *Cosmos atrosanguineus*, which has deliciously chocolate-scented velvety maroon petals, and the thistle-heads of *Cirsium rivulare* are much prized for this deep, subtle colouring. Claret and burgundy are deep purple wine-reds, and purple itself a rich red-violet, the colour used by emperors and ecclesiastics and, until synthetic dyes could be substituted, obtained in minute quantities from shellfish since history began. Amethyst is a clear purple, at its palest belonging in the blue-violet range, but translucent and with close links to the hotter reddish-purples we call fuchsia. Some of these definitions, while we continue to use colour words which are associated with variable substances, will always remain subjective.

Any objective judgement, too, is further clouded by the effects 'blued' reds have upon each other when placed together. Their common 'blueness' will become less obvious as juxtaposition makes them appear more different, but if the dimensions of value and intensity are widely apart there will

PREVIOUS PAGE In a red border, bright red dahlias ('Bishop of Llandaff', 'Blaisdon Red' and 'Doris Day'), *Penstemon* 'Firebird' and annual nicotiana are linked by the deep-toned purple foliage of *Lobelia cardinalis* 'Dark Crusader', *Iresine herbstii* and Swiss chard. Through the combined influence of yellow evening sunlight and the camera, many of the reds have warmed to a mellow scarlet: examined in a northern light, their 'true' colour would be nearer crimson. Green foliage, and particularly the near-by lawn, intensify the redness. Individual colours and plant forms mix optically to give an impressionistic effect of glowing textured patterns. In this choice of warm rich colours, we are reminded of Monet's approach to gardening, and of his juxtaposing colours which would reassemble at a distance to create a picture. The effects of light on these plant shapes and colours recall the vigorous brush strokes drawn in oils on an artist's canvas. In a colour scheme where, as here, the basic framework of reds and purples is strong enough, the flower colours could extend their range towards the blues to include intense crimson, magenta and even dark violet, or could move in the opposite direction towards yellow, and encompass rich orange-reds.

RIGHT The low tones of the deep purple lupin flowers are echoed in the foliage of purple-leaved sage in a wall border. Although contrast in lightness and darkness between the lupins and the pale pink papery-textured petals of the oriental poppy is extreme, nevertheless they both share characteristic redness, which remains distinguishable to the eye in the palest tints of pink, the darkest almost black reds, and the low smoky tones of textured foliage. Here we see two separate garden pictures. Sculptured grey leaves of artichoke *(Cynara scolymus* 'Glauca') prevent the dark lupins from seeming dull by enriching their colour; at the same time the silver-grey leaves help to make the pale pink of the poppy flowers more brilliant, thus increasing the effects of contrast with lupin and sage.

This dramatic contrast of flower forms and colours – between the slender white *Lilium* 'Black Dragon' and the clump of deep red sweet William (*Dianthus barbatus*) – also demonstrates one of the qualities of colour that is perhaps the most difficult to describe: its relative 'weight'. The lily is light in colour, smooth-textured, and its fine elegant lines give the illusion of its also being light in weight. The sweet William seems heavier in every respect. Its deep rich colour is derived from a velvety petal texture and the concentric ring of deeper colour that marks each flower; the flower-heads are held in solid clusters whose bulk is emphasized by the play of light and shade. This combination of colour and texture creates an effect like a sumptuous red velvet cushion. Its mass anchors and stabilizes the soaring lily, without whose presence the picture might become too sombre and weighty.

Foliage contrasts are seen on a large scale, RIGHT. In a well-balanced spring composition, the wine-coloured *Acer palmatum* contrasts with the pale sophora beyond and harmonizes with the two red mollis azaleas, paler and darker reds echoing paler and darker greens. Notice how many colours the maple alone displays: shiny upper leaf surfaces reflecting an almost bluish light, black shadows, and warm red tones where the leaves are translucent.

OPPOSITE This close-up of the red border seen on page 153 shows how surface texture affects colours. The dark leaves in this picture are intrinsically the same purple shade. The matt perilla leaves, furrowed with deep veining, are low-toned and mysterious, contrasting with the dramatic shiny leaves of *Beta vulgaris*. In a predominantly single-colour composition, such textural contrasts maintain background interest. Here flowers and leaves of *Sedum maximum* 'Atropurpureum' subtly continue the muted purple theme, while scarlet *Phlox drummondii* adds vital warmth.

be less obvious alteration, although one or other of the 'blued' colours will become less rich. Bright pure spectral red quickly darkens as it moves towards a pure violet, and this natural progression from lighter to darker hues indicates a natural harmony which will never appear unpleasing. A full red side by side with deep purple will appear rich and good; place it next to a lighter purple and it appears harsh and unpleasant. In flowers such as clematis, fuchsias and petunias, where there are obvious gradations of colour, purples are always darker than crimsons; in roses and carnations, crimsons will be darker than reds.

The texture of a red petal, calyx or leaf surface affects the 'redness' we see; shining satiny tulips appear much lighter and brighter than the velvet of some rose petals, although the colours of the two may well match on a chart. One flower-petal in rain might become richer and more shining, another becomes sodden and dull. From a distance red flowers retain their strong eye-catching and advancing quality and do not blend quickly with their own complementary green leaves to look pale yellow at a distance.

Place red flowers among leaves of 'linked' purple and bronze, and their redness becomes less isolated, their presence less dominating, the whole picture becoming a harmony of shades linked by their mutual red and blue pigment. Foliage colour, in fact – except when the fiery tones of autumn – is seldom bright red (although some young growth is scarlet, as in pieris and photinia); it is more often deep and matt, giving an impression of depth and weight. It is often richest when the sun's rays are longest and reddest in the evening, especially glowing when light shines through a leaf towards the observer. A monochrome garden scheme in deep reds seems mysterious, as purple and bronze foliage in low tones absorb the vivid colours, flowers and leaves linked by common pigment, the opposite effect to the 'rejection' and brightening of red by a complementary green-leaved background. Blue-reds are linked with blue-green leaves by the mutual blue pigment, and their colour is less vivid with blue-green than it is with bright almost spectral green leaf colour. Pure bright green finds its opposite and complementary red in a shade of magenta, while leaves of bluish-green find their complement in reds which reach towards vermilion and orange; though – as we have said – foliage tones are seldom as pure in hue as flower colours can be.

Just as nature uses bright pure reds to focus the eye, the

courageous gardener may also introduce touches of scarlet and even orange into a predominantly blue-red border. A scheme of reds, crimsons and purples may be improved by such an addition, the designer drawing inspiration from the vividness of autumn colour, where purples, crimsons, reds, scarlets and yellows weave patterns that recall oriental carpets. Similarly, among the hottest and harshest colours discussed in the next chapter, the addition of a purple leaf or flower may add the required mellowness of tone. In gardening as in any decorative art, a splash of contrasting or complementary pigment will balance a 'cool' scheme with a touch of 'warmth', giving the eye and brain the necessary contrast to provoke interest. Place a drift of luminous yellow flowers among dark colours, or use cool glaucous leaves to make pools of light. Take a foliage border of deep red and purple leaves: cotinus, berberis and plum, with summer foliage of ricinus, canna and bronze-leaved *Dahlia* 'Bishop of Llandaff', can be brought alive by a golden-leaved dogwood such as *Cornus alba* 'Spaethii', mellowed and darkened by contrast with groups of blue-green hosta leaves or silver-grey santolina, and quietened and enriched by the related deep violet flowers of *Clematis* × *jackmanii*.

In spring, reds are mainly represented in the flower garden by tulips and by wallflowers in bronze and crimson. Blue-reds and purples of honesty, *Lathyrus vernus*, pleiones and pale dogtooth violet (*Erythronium dens-canis*) are more seasonal than the brighter hot scarlets, and plenty of leaves have strong purple tones. Evergreen bergenia, the backs of satin-leaved *Heuchera americana* and the rarer *Saxifraga fortunei*, and the young foliage of many prunus have purplish-pink tints matching the dull, almost black, flowers of some of the Lenten hellebores (*Helleborus orientalis*). Low-growing pulsatillas and sun-loving *Erysimum* 'Bowles' Mauve' are matched in shade by darker honesty. Try growing honesty with lime-green euphorbias, or magenta- and crimson-flowered rhododendrons undercarpeted with weed-smothering *Euphorbia robbiae*. Yellowish-green flowers and foliage complement the dark purples of flower or leaf, but put together the colour tones in the sequence in which their relative 'weight' seems to suit them best – pale yellow with dark purple: the reverse, a light purple with a darkened yellow shade, will injure both.

In acid woodland flowers transform the heavy green foliage of rhododendrons; overhead shade deepens the strong reds

This 14 × 4 m (45 × 13 ft) border in front of a hedge which divides its colour theme from the rest of the garden has been planned to contribute colour through most of a summer season. Foliage plants with wine-coloured or glaucous leaves make a low-toned background to predominantly blue flowers in the earlier months; later crimson roses, dark violet clematis, crimson phlox and lythrum weave drifts of strong colour to link their blue pigment to the heavy foliage. Facing east, the border is bright in sunlight, but becomes dark and mysterious in twilight, with only the blue salvia remaining luminous until complete darkness falls.

Anemone apennina makes a sheet of blue in early spring, and ajuga and shade-tolerant *Lamium* 'Beacon Silver' have been encouraged to make weedproof ground cover beneath the canopies of cotinus and prunus. Most of the herbaceous plants flower best if divided every few seasons, and the roses chosen for this border flower almost all summer if carefully dead-headed and kept free of disease.

Keyline drawing

which – to conserve their strength – are best grouped in closely related gradations of colour. In moist soil, plant drifts of crimson and purple primula beside the emergent foliage of bronze-leaved rodgersia or translucent dark rheum, using the paler rose-coloured *Peltiphyllum peltatum*, which flowers early before shield-shaped leaves unfurl, to lighten a dark scheme.

As spring moves to early summer, peonies and dark oriental poppies mix with paler purple and pink flowers in open borders, while the darkest-flowered purple lilac gives depth and mystery. Experiment with violet and brighter blue flowers set among banks of purple foliage, related blue pigment giving a beautiful harmony. In summer, among fresh green leaves, the glowing velvet-reds and crimsons of roses weave an oriental pattern with herbaceous geraniums; choose the dark warm colours and place them together to give the depth and richness of colour not reached by pale pastel pinks and mauves. Use these glowing colours with assurance and confidence, remembering how nature makes red flowers bright as 'eye-catchers' among green leaves. The distance and dimension of blue and greens may make gardens seem larger, but by carrying the eye into the distance destroy a sense of security and containment. Arrange planting schemes so that an area of strong red creates the most vivid impression, after the observer has moved through a quiet planting of restful green. Best of all, emerge from a shady covered arbour or the deep shade of woodland, into a sunlit area where strong reds backed by reddish-shadowed foliage glow.

Planting plan. Figures in parentheses indicate the number of plants in a group.

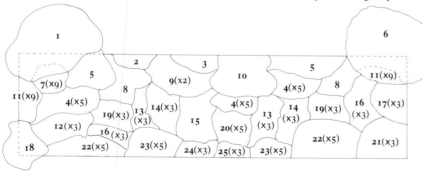

Miss Jekyll arranged her great summer border at Munstead Wood in such a way that when viewed from a distance the eye travelled from the cool colours of grey leaves and pastel flower at the extreme ends to the complementary warmth of vivid hues in a central panel, where she used orange and vermilion as well as dark purple shades. In a small garden, dramatic, rich reds and purples are too dominating and reduce not only space but the feeling of restfulness. In a larger area, however, the mind and eye crave distraction and stimulation from the 'safe' low tones and pale colours which are more easily focused upon. A riot of colour, brash and clashing when extremes of contrast mingle in a small front garden, becomes enriching and satisfying when kept as a hidden feature to be approached through quiet planting. The emotional qualities of red make their strongest impact if they come as a surprise.

In high summer there are plenty of border reds, and purple leaves tend to get heavier and even greener. Fuchsias with flowers in two tones of crimson and rich dark purple, dark red tobacco plants with rich evening fragrance, magenta-flowered *Salvia involucrata* 'Bethelli' with bronze-tinted foliage, hollyhocks, dahlias and penstemons which flower until the first frosts, all give garden colour, while purple-leaved cotinus, subtly enriched by smoky-bronze panicles, makes a background to bright red *Lobelia* 'Dark Crusader' or crimson and magenta phlox. Crimson Kaffir lily, *Schizostylis coccinea*, flowers late, its colour linked with the crimsons and scarlets of autumn foliage.

WINTER

Camellia japonica 'Mathiotiana Rubra'

Helleborus orientalis hybrids

BERGENIA

The reddish tinges of the leaves of many bergenias in winter provide a colour theme in miniature which the deep red flowers emphasize.

One of the earliest to flower is named after the Somerset plantswoman: *B.* 'Margery Fish' has broad glossy leaves and branching heads of rich red-purple. It should be given a sheltered site.

EVERGREEN PERENNIAL   45 CM (18 IN)
FULL SUN OR HALF SHADE   ZONES 6-9
See also Foliage framework: green.

CAMELLIA

Rarely part of a specific colour scheme, camellias are almost floral 'exotics', visually dominated by the symmetrical perfection of each glowing flower set among the strong glossy leaves. The *C. japonica* cultivars have perhaps the more brilliant and richer reds, colours with almost the same purity and value as the deep green of the leaves. Flowering time covers a long season, but can last from late winter to early summer, depending much on site, growing conditions and the season.

C.j. 'Adolphe Audusson' has deep blood-red semi-double flowers; 'Anemoniflora' is dark crimson, and 'Mathiotiana Rubra' is crimson and double.

LARGE EVERGREEN SHRUBS
HALF SHADE OR SHADE   ZONES 7-9
See also Foliage framework: green.

CROCUS

Among crocus the deeper colours ranging between dark purple and deep violet are much affected by the light conditions. A purple shade appears more violet in dull weather, or when grown under a canopy of trees, or – as colour theory tells – when grown next to deeper reds. The cultivar *C.* 'Purpureus Grandiflorus' can therefore fit into this chapter and might also find its place in The blues. Place it next to bright blue scilla and its colour becomes more red; place it beside a drift of carmine cyclamen and it becomes distinctly 'blued'.

C. vernus is a name used to cover many large-flowered garden hybrids which come into flower just as aconites fade.

C. 'Negro Boy' has glossy deep purple petals, and 'Purpureus Grandiflorus' has large purple flowers.

CORMS   7.5-10 CM (3-4 IN)
FULL SUN OR HALF SHADE   ZONES 6-9
See also Clear yellows: spring.

CYCLAMEN

C. coum, a hardy winter-flowering species, has distinctive rounded small leaves with lovely silvery centres and reddish undersides. The flowers are variable in colour and include bright carmine, pink and white. The pointed buds open to broad rounded petals with a deeper spot at the base.

CORM   7.5 CM (3 IN)   HALF SHADE
ZONES 6-9

HELLEBORUS HELLEBORE

Some hellebores have dramatic dusky colours somewhere between a deep rich plum with a blue bloom and almost black. Place these treasures where the subtle colours can be seen easily.

H. atrorubens, a garden hellebore, is with *H. niger* one of the first to flower, heralding a new season. Deciduous leaves die down in autumn and the flowers of rich plum-purple are conspicuous.

DECIDUOUS PERENNIAL   30 CM (12 IN)
HALF SHADE   ZONES 6-10

H. orientalis covers a large group of hybrids with variable colours from plum, rich and spotted, to creamy-white spotted with plum and maroon. The evergreen leaves keep down weeds and make a handsome base for sheaves of tall stems carrying beautiful flowers for many weeks. Seedlings are self-sown and very numerous, and if grown on often produce new and exciting flower colours in all sorts of cream and purple tints.

H. abchasicus is purplish with maroon spots.

EVERGREEN PERENNIALS   45 CM (18 IN)
SHADE   ZONES 6-9

H. purpurascens has a hybrid, *H. torquatus* (of gardens), which is dusky-maroon and glaucous, almost transparent. A new hybrid, 'Pluto', is even darker.

DECIDUOUS PERENNIAL   30 CM (12 IN)
HALF SHADE   ZONES 6-9
See also Foliage framework: green.

SPRING

CHAENOMELES
JAPANESE QUINCE, JAPONICA
C. speciosa 'Cardinalis' has crimson flowers.
Plant against a wall or in a shrubbery beside
dark purple or white tulips, but keep away from
the deeper yellow daffodils. I prefer such
strong contrasts later in the year.
   C. × superba 'Crimson and Gold' has deep
crimson petals and central golden anthers, and
is a smaller plant.
MEDIUM DECIDUOUS SHRUBS
FULL SUN   ZONES 6-9
See also Pinks and mauves: spring.

CHEIRANTHUS WALLFLOWER
C. cheiri 'Carmine King' is deep carmine. Plant
with pink or dark purple tulips, not mingling as
in illustrated lists, but in large drifts or clumps
– separate but adjacent. *C.c.* 'Blood Red' and
'Vulcan' are also deep crimson. Sow in
previous summer for spring flowering.
BIENNIAL   37 CM (15 IN)
FULL SUN   ZONES 6-9
See also Clear yellows: spring.

CYCLAMEN
C. repandum is one of the most charming
cyclamen: the scented bright flowers have
twisted petals. Flowers vary from pale pink to
white but are most often deep carmine. The
leaves are mottled and splashed with silver (see
also The whites: foliage).
CORM   15 CM (6 IN)   HALF SHADE   ZONES 6-9

LATHYRUS
L. vernus, spring vetch, has dissected ferny
leaves and carries small pea-flowers of intense
purplish-crimson. Plant in drifts with dwarf
willows, which like the same moist soil.
DECIDUOUS PERENNIAL   35-45 CM (14-18 IN)
HALF SHADE   ZONES 6-9

MAGNOLIA
M. liliiflora 'Nigra' has dark red-purple
chalice-shaped flowers, opening before the
shining broad elliptical leaves. An acid-lover,
this magnolia will not thrive in alkaline soil. In
suitable conditions, this is a dramatic medium-
sized magnolia.
MEDIUM DECIDUOUS SHRUB
FULL SUN   ZONES 7-9
See also Foliage framework: green.

MALUS FLOWERING CRAB
M. × eleyi has purple-tinged leaves and dark
crimson flowers, followed by purplish-red
fruits in autumn. In *M.* 'Lemoinei' the flowers
are wine-red and the habit is more erect.
SMALL DECIDUOUS TREES
FULL SUN   ZONES 5-9

Malus × eleyi

Magnolia liliiflora 'Nigra'

Cheiranthus cheiri 'Vulcan'

EARLY SUMMER

Pulsatilla vulgaris 'Rubra'

PULSATILLA

Pulsatillas thrive in chalky soils in full sun. Their attractive flowers are followed by copper-brown seed-heads which, with the leaves, give interest all summer.

P. vulgaris, the pasque flower, has delicate finely cut foliage developing as the purple flowers fade. The silky buds appear first, cup-shaped and nodding. Plant in a choice spot with perfect drainage. The form *P.v.* 'Rubra' is a dark red.

DECIDUOUS PERENNIAL   30 CM (12 IN)
FULL SUN   ZONES 6-9

RIBES FLOWERING CURRANT

R. speciosum, the fuchsia-flowered currant, is a very superior member of this genus. Bright red fuchsia-like flowers are held on stems with red bristles. Hanging in clusters, the bush looks most impressive if trained back against a wall and if lateral branches are pruned fan-shaped. It suits the plant, too, since the heat encourages flowering and protects it from frosts.

MEDIUM SEMI-EVERGREEN SHRUB
FULL SUN   ZONES 5-9

SCHISANDRA

A lovely early-flowering twining climber, *S. grandiflora* has pink flowers, but the dark red *S.g. rubriflora* is even more desirable. The female will bear scarlet berries if a male is planted near by for fertilization.

DECIDUOUS CLIMBER
FULL SUN   ZONES 7-10

TULIPA TULIP

Some of the strong red tulip shades are deep mysterious colours. Look for those in deep maroon and use them in planting schemes with blocks of brighter crimsons. Single Early *T.* 'Colour Cardinal' is a rich crimson to plum shade of red.

BULB   30 CM (12 IN)   FULL SUN   ZONES 5-9
See also Clear yellows: spring.

CYTISUS BROOM

C. scoparius 'Burkwoodii' has rich crimson broom-flowers on arching branches. It is spectacular and deserves a prominent place; a shrub with unusually vivid colour so early in the season. Plant at the back of a border where perennials will grow tall in front for later colour contributions.

MEDIUM DECIDUOUS SHRUB
FULL SUN   ZONES 6-9
See also Clear yellows: spring.

DIANTHUS PINKS AND CARNATIONS

D. deltoides 'Wisley Variety', a clone of the maiden pink, has dark carmine flowers and fresh green leaves. Seedlings are often quite a good colour. Plant in paving.

EVERGREEN PERENNIAL   23 CM (9 IN)
FULL SUN   ZONES 7-10
D. × allwoodii 'Ian', a modern garden pink, has large dark crimson flowers and good healthy grey foliage.

EVERGREEN PERENNIAL   30 CM (12 IN)
FULL SUN   ZONES 7-10

DIGITALIS FOXGLOVE

D. purpurea, the European woodland species, seeds very freely in gardens. It is difficult to be certain of having a very dark colour to complement a scheme, but if you gradually eliminate all lighter ones, it is possible. Plant in drifts with the darker *Gladiolus byzantinus* or allow to flower freely among early shrubs. The foxglove flower needs no description, but look closely at the beautiful markings which attract the pollinators.

BIENNIAL   100-150 CM (40-60 IN)
FULL SUN OR SHADE   ZONES 6-9

GERANIUM CRANE'S BILL

Many of these hardy geraniums have pink, blue or violet flowers, but some of the darker and richer 'reds' make splashes of strong colour, especially effective when placed next to foliage plants with leaves in related purple shades.

G. phaeum, the mourning widow, a European native, has maroon, almost black, silky flowers. A plant for detail rather than stunning colour effects, as the foliage tends to predominate. Plant in a shady corner.

DECIDUOUS PERENNIAL   60-75 CM (24-30 IN)
HALF SHADE OR SHADE   ZONES 5-9
G. pratense 'Kashmir Purple' has saucer-shaped flowers 4 cm (1½ in) across. The foliage is upright and branching, deeply dissected. The purple petals are veined with thin red.

DECIDUOUS PERENNIAL   45 CM (18 IN)
FULL SUN   ZONES 6-9

G. sanguineum, the bloody crane's bill, has almost woody stems, its divided green leaves forming a hummock. The flowers are a vivid magenta and are produced again in late summer.

DECIDUOUS PERENNIAL   30 CM (12 IN)
FULL SUN   ZONES 5-9
G. wlassovianum has dark velvety leaves and deep violet flowers, the latter veined with rich purple.

DECIDUOUS PERENNIAL   60 CM (24 IN)
FULL SUN OR HALF SHADE   ZONES 5-9

GLADIOLUS CORN FLAG

Among the early-flowering species, *G. byzantinus*, with the typical sword-like untidy leaves of the genus, has the brightest of dark vivid purple flowers. Grow it in large clumps and try not to let it spread. It makes an important impact if seen once or twice in a garden, but loses its effect if odd flowers are dotted through beds. Plant next to *Geranium psilostemon*; in most years their flowering will just overlap, and *Rosa rugosa* 'Roseraie de l'Hay'. Purple-leaved cotinus makes a glowing background to the gladiolus.

BULB   75-90 CM (30-36 IN)
FULL SUN OR HALF SHADE   ZONES 7-9

IRIS

I. graminea, plum tart iris, is one of the beardless iris with grassy foliage which almost hides the charming dark purple flowers with blue-purple veining. The strong scent is delicious, like ripe plums. Plant in moist soil.

DECIDUOUS RHIZOME   45 CM (18 IN)
FULL SUN OR HALF SHADE   ZONES 6-9
I. kaempferi, Japanese iris, usually with a yellow streak on the broad fall, makes a perfect and exotic flower. Colours range from rich blue and red-purple to more delicate pink, lavender and white. Try to obtain a named form that you have seen in bloom to fit into a colour sequence. Grow with the rhizomes in water, or in a very moist rich acid soil.

DECIDUOUS RHIZOME   90 CM (36 IN)
FULL SUN   ZONES 7-9
Bearded iris with petals and falls of different colours are not useful in colour schemes. They seem merely curiosities. Go for the hybrids with an overall colour and texture. Tall *I.* 'Sable Knight' is dense black-violet, and 'Gay Trip' is a rich mahogany-red.

DECIDUOUS RHIZOMES   45-150 CM (18-60 IN)
FULL SUN   ZONES 6-9

LAVANDULA LAVENDER

L. stoechas, French lavender, is a delightful small bush. Strongly aromatic foliage is good all winter. The flower-heads are terminal

clusters, not long spikes as in ordinary English lavender (see The blues), of rich dark purple. Plants flower all summer and need well-drained warm soil.
SMALL EVERGREEN SHRUB
FULL SUN   ZONES 7-9

LEPTOSPERMUM
Leptospermums are tender evergreens related to myrtles. They prefer a well-drained acid or neutral soil. Many have silver-grey leaves, but *L. scoparium* 'Nichollsii' has small glossy leaves of dark bronze (see foliage, below) and bright carmine flowers. *L.s.* 'Red Damask' is similar, but with double red flowers.
MEDIUM EVERGREEN SHRUB
FULL SUN   ZONES 8-10

LUNARIA HONESTY
The deep purple or mauve flowers of the biennial honesty look most telling in shade, where they flower later than if planted in an open sunny site.

L. annua has coarse green heart-shaped leaves, seeds very freely in odd corners, but also makes a splendid massed effect of deep purple colour. Try it with drifts of *Euphorbia robbiae*: in shade this 'works'; in full sun it is daring and perhaps garish, although like so many schemes where strong contrasts are tried, it becomes rich and mellow in evening light.
EVERGREEN BIENNIAL   75 CM (30 IN)
FULL SUN OR SHADE   ZONES 5-9

PAEONIA PEONY
P. daurica from south-east Europe and *P. broteroi* from Spain and Portugal are very similar. Leaves are greyish-green and flowers vivid cerise-magenta with bright yellow stamens. If it is happy in a garden, it will self-seed.
DECIDUOUS PERENNIALS   60 CM (24 IN)
FULL SUN OR HALF SHADE   ZONES 7-9
P. potaninii is a suckering peony with small flowers of maroon-red, almost mahogany.
DECIDUOUS PERENNIAL   60-90 CM (24-36 IN)
FULL SUN   ZONES 6-9
P. tenuifolia has finely divided leaves and single crimson flowers with bright yellow stamens. It is choice, but unfortunately difficult to get.
DECIDUOUS PERENNIAL   45 CM (18 IN)
FULL SUN   ZONES 7-9

PAPAVER POPPY
P. orientale, oriental poppy, is a magnificent sun-loving species, with huge papery flowers on sprawling stems. The hairy grey or green foliage dies away after flowering; grow other plants to hide it with later flowers and leaves.

The type is of bright vermilion with a maroon centre; *P.o.* 'Goliath' is darker, glowing rather than brilliant. Grow it with dark tulips to open the season for a border of vivid deep reds and purples.
DECIDUOUS PERENNIAL   60 CM (24 IN)
FULL SUN   ZONES 6-9

PHLOX
P. subulata, the moss phlox, makes a spreading mat of soft foliage, covered in early summer with purple or pink flowers (see Pinks and mauves: early summer). *P.s.* 'Temiscaming' is a brilliant magenta-red. Grow it to scramble over paving at the front of a bed.
DECIDUOUS PERENNIAL   10 CM (4 IN)
FULL SUN   ZONES 6-9

PRIMULA
P. japonica 'Miller's Crimson' is a candelabra type, with whorls of bright red flowers above grey-green rosettes. It thrives in acid soil beside streams, flowers sparkling against neighbouring green foliage.
DECIDUOUS PERENNIAL   75 CM (30 IN)
FULL SUN OR HALF SHADE   ZONES 6-9

RHODODENDRON
R. 'Bagshot Ruby' has rounded trusses of funnel-shaped ruby-red flowers.
LARGE EVERGREEN SHRUB
HALF SHADE   ZONES 6-8
R. 'General Eisenhower', a hybrid of the tender *R. griffithianum* but itself quite hardy,

Rosa 'Tuscany'

has large trusses of deep carmine, a good rich positive colour for woodland accent.
MEDIUM EVERGREEN SHRUB
HALF SHADE   ZONES 6-8
R. 'Grenadier', an Exbury hybrid, has deep blood-red flowers.
LARGE EVERGREEN SHRUB
HALF SHADE   ZONES 8-9
See also Pinks and mauves: spring.

ROSA ROSE
Among the Gallica shrubs, *R.* 'Charles de Mills' has tightly packed petals with rich and sumptuous colouring of deep crimson and purple. It needs plenty of moisture early, and hot sun for flowering, otherwise buds remain half-closed. *R.* 'Tuscany' has semi-double flat velvety maroon flowers with yellow stamens;

Primula japonica

Rosa 'Parkdirektor Riggers'

Trillium sessile

R. 'Tuscany Superb' is similar but has larger flower-heads. *R. gallica officinalis*, apothecary's rose, is a bit smaller and needs vigorous pruning. Flowers are semi-double and a bright light crimson. It looks lovely when several plants are grown massed together. It needs little feeding, suckering freely, so spring bulbs can be grown at the base. The red rose of Lancaster, it is deservedly an old favourite. All Gallicas should be sprayed with fungicides to prevent mildew and blackspot.
SMALL DECIDUOUS SHRUBS
FULL SUN OR HALF SHADE   ZONES 6-9
R. californica 'Plena' is a species with wiry arching branches and pale carmine-crimson double flowers. Not too large, it should be in every garden. Plant near lime-green umbels of angelica, and underplant with *Alchemilla mollis* and *Geranium sanguineum* which will flower twining through the rose stems.
MEDIUM DECIDUOUS SHRUB
FULL SUN   ZONES 5-9
R. pimpinellifolia (syn. *R. spinosissima*) 'William III' is a dwarf suckering shrub of great charm. It is not so invasive as most of the other burnet

or Scotch roses and is lovely under bronze or purple foliage. Semi-double magenta-crimson petals change to a darker colour as flowers fade.
SMALL DECIDUOUS SHRUB
FULL SUN OR HALF SHADE   ZONES 6-9
R. 'Fellemberg' is a crimson China rose with clusters of medium-sized cupped crimson flowers. An adaptable bush, it seems to flower freely in quite deep shade.
MEDIUM DECIDUOUS SHRUB
FULL SUN OR SHADE   ZONES 6-9
R. 'Zéphirine Drouhin' has cerise blooms fading to pink. It is thornless, and a fine repeat-flowerer with foliage copper-tinted when young. Like most Bourbons, it is inclined to get black spot and mildew.
DECIDUOUS SHRUB   4 M (13 FT)
FULL SUN   ZONES 6-9
R. rugosa 'Roseraie de l'Hay' has double velvet-textured wine-red flowers, very sweetly scented. Like all the double rugosas, it seldom bears hips, but continues spasmodic flowering into the autumn.
DECIDUOUS SHRUB   1.8 M (6 FT)
FULL SUN OR HALF SHADE   ZONES 6-9

R. 'Rosemary Rose' is a bush rose of the floribunda type. Large flat camellia-shaped blooms are bright carmine, carried above distinctly bronze-purple leaves (see foliage, below). It flowers twice and will produce the attractive tinted leaves whenever cut back through the summer months.
DECIDUOUS SHRUB   1 M (3 FT)
FULL SUN   ZONES 6-9
R. 'Cerise Bouquet' is a very large arching modern shrub, with extremely thorny branches. The leaves are grey-green and massed clusters of semi-double cerise-crimson scented flowers are carried for many weeks. Plant only where space allows.
DECIDUOUS SHRUB   1.8 M (6 FT)
FULL SUN   ZONES 6-9
R. 'Guinée' is a climber, not very vigorous but of subtle colouring: the very dark maroon flowers are sophisticated, but not eye-catching. Grow it for this quality of elusiveness, and for its strong sweet fragrance.
    R. 'Parkdirektor Riggers' has medium-sized double flowers of glowing crimson. Flowering freely with large trusses carried among the

SUMMER

healthy glossy leaves, it grows to 4.5 m (15 ft) and is an excellent climbing rose.

R. 'Crimson Glory' is a climbing sport of a spreading hybrid tea type bush, with cupped double flowers of deep velvety-crimson. It will flower well twice in a season and has healthy glossy leaves. Some of the attractions of these 'formal' climbers lie in the skill of excellent pruning, branches carefully trained parallel, vertical and symmetrical, creating a green framework to 3 m (9 ft).
DECIDUOUS CLIMBERS   FULL SUN   ZONES 6-9
See also Pinks and mauves: early summer.

SYRINGA LILAC
S. vulgaris 'Souvenir de Louis Spaeth' has the darkest flowers of all the lilacs. The blooms are wine-red; it is a reliable and consistent flowerer, performing best the season after a very hot summer. Grow it in a bed of mixed planting, where its dark flowers give strength to neighbouring pale pink and mauve shrub roses and an underplanting of herbaceous geraniums.
LARGE DECIDUOUS SHRUB
FULL SUN   ZONES 5-9
See also The blues: early summer.

TRILLIUM WAKE ROBIN
T. sessile, toadshade, has three leaves marbled in brown and green; the dark maroon flowers, also composed of three calyces and three petals, are held upright. A choice plant for a woodland corner.
DECIDUOUS PERENNIAL   20-30 CM (8-12 IN)
SHADE   ZONES 4-9

TULIPA TULIP
Among the Darwin tulips, T. 'Queen of the Night' is a deep velvety-maroon and 'Demeter' is a bright reddish-purple, both 70 cm (28 in) tall. 'Greuze' is a dark violet-purple, 65 cm (26 in). Triumph T. 'Negrita' is dark purple, veined in beetroot-red, 45 cm (18 in). Lily-flowered T. 'Red Shine' is violet-carmine, 65 cm (26 in) tall. T. 'Black Parrot' is a glossy maroon-black, a texture you almost wish to touch, and 67 cm (27 in) tall.
BULBS   FULL SUN   ZONES 5-9
See also spring, above.

VINCA PERIWINKLE
V. minor, with blue, white or purple single flowers, has a lovely double purple-flowered cultivar, V.m. 'Multiplex'. It flowers most freely in half shade, but performs quite well in a dark corner.
DWARF EVERGREEN SHRUB
HALF SHADE OR SHADE   ZONES 5-9
See also Foliage framework: green.

CIRSIUM
C. rivulare (sometimes, in gardens, Cnicus atropurpureus) is a thistle-like plant which thrives in damp soil and full sun. The flower-heads, especially in C.r. 'Atropurpureus', are deep crimson, like pincushions, held on branching stems. The leaves are deeply dissected.
DECIDUOUS PERENNIAL
60-100 CM (24-40 IN)   FULL SUN   ZONES 5-9

CLEMATIS
C. × jackmanii has large blue-purple flowers; C. 'Jackmanii Superba' is dark violet-purple. Both flower for many weeks. Plant to clamber through bronze-coloured foliage such as that of the claret vine, Vitis vinifera 'Purpurea'. Prune in late winter and constantly train and tie in neatly all through the early summer. It is less effective if allowed to become bunched up, with flowering heads at the end of long stalks.
DECIDUOUS CLIMBER
FULL SUN, ROOTS IN SHADE   ZONES 7-9
C. viticella has charming nodding heads of dark purple. Grow it through a shrub such as early-flowering viburnum, where it will rise through the branches to flower in the light. C.v. 'Abundance' is typical, but has softer purple petals. C.v. 'Purpurea Plena Elegans' is paler in colour, almost rose-purple, the sepals packed densely together in a rosette. 'Rubra', often misnamed 'Kermesina', is deep reddish-purple with a brownish-black centre. All need hard pruning in early spring.
DECIDUOUS CLIMBER
FULL SUN, ROOTS IN SHADE   ZONES 6-9
C. texensis 'Sir Trevor Lawrence' is semi-herbaceous with flowers like upright bells of cherry-red, almost crimson. C.t. 'Gravetye Beauty' is paler, almost pink enough to be in Pinks and mauves. Prune in early spring.
DECIDUOUS CLIMBER
FULL SUN, ROOTS IN SHADE   ZONES 8-9
See also The whites: spring.

COSMOS
C. atrosanguineus is a most desirable perennial, very different from the annual cosmos. This rare and difficult plant has velvet-textured maroon-crimson dahlia-like flowers, richly chocolate-scented. It needs moisture-retentive soil and some protection for the crowns in a severe winter.
DECIDUOUS PERENNIAL   75-90 CM (30-36 IN)
FULL SUN   ZONES 8-10

FUCHSIA
F. 'Mrs Popple', a hardy fuchsia, has large flowers, scarlet sepals and deep violet petals, with long protruding crimson stamens and

Clematis viticella 'Abundance'

style. The combination of colours creates an impression of strong red. Plant in groups at the front of a border; it flowers from summer to the first frosts.
SMALL DECIDUOUS SHRUB   FULL SUN
ZONES 8-10
See also Pinks and mauves: summer.

GERANIUM CRANE'S BILL
G. nodosum has evergreen glossy lobed leaves, and thrives in almost complete shade. It has lilac-red flowers.
DECIDUOUS PERENNIAL   20-50 CM (8-20 IN)
SHADE   ZONES 6-9
G. psilostemon has very elegant leaves and bright magenta flowers with black centres. Grow near Gladiolus byzantinus and tall shrub roses with similar flower colours. It is slow to establish after a move, so divide only when absolutely necessary. Lovely in woodland planting with contrasting colour groups of white philadelphus and pink deutzias.
DECIDUOUS PERENNIAL
75-120 CM (30-48 IN)
FULL SUN OR HALF SHADE   ZONES 7-9

HEMEROCALLIS DAY LILY

H. 'Morocco Red' is a subtle maroon-red colour, not very showy but useful in a colour scheme, linking paler with more vivid reds. *H.* 'Stafford' is a mahogany-red, blending with the strong 'blued' reds of this chapter or with the flame-coloured scarlets of Hot colours.
DECIDUOUS PERENNIAL   1.2 M (4 FT)
FULL SUN OR HALF SHADE   ZONES 6-9
See also Foliage framework: green.

LAVANDULA LAVENDER

One or two cultivars of the traditional old English lavender, *L. angustifolia* (see The blues: summer), are strong enough in colour to merit the description 'purple' rather than the eponymous lavender-violet shades. *L.a.* 'Twickel Purple' has broad grey-green leaves and slender purple flower-spikes. It makes a substantial thick low hedge and its darker flower colour is welcome among pastel blues.
SMALL EVERGREEN SHRUB
FULL SUN   ZONES 7-9

LILIUM LILY

L. martagon, martagon or Turk's cap lily, has various forms with deep wine or maroon colouring. The Backhouse Hybrids, derived from *L. martagon* × *L. hansonii*, have good wine-red forms and are free-flowering.
BULBS   100-200 CM (40-80 IN)
HALF SHADE   ZONES 5-9
See also The whites: summer.

NICOTIANA TOBACCO PLANT

N. alata (syn. *N. affinis*), flowering tobacco, with loose clusters of flowers – especially fragrant in the evening – has several good colour forms. As in the case of many annually raised plants, it is not always easy to get packets of one colour only. Hybridization has produced many red-flowered cultivars under the name *N.* × *sanderae*. Look for a deep maroon, although the mixed colours are well worth having and give a touch of informality. Sow in early spring and bed out after the nights get warmer.
ANNUAL OR DECIDUOUS PERENNIAL
60-90 CM (24-36 IN)   FULL SUN   ZONES 8-10

NYMPHAEA WATER LILY

N. 'Escarboucle' needs a depth of water around 45-60 cm (18-24 in) and has brilliant crimson petals, the outer ones paling. The centre is pale yellow.

N. 'William Falconer', which needs shallower 25-45 cm (10-18 in) water, is a very deep shade, almost beetroot-red, with lots of overlapping petals and the stamens glistening golden-yellow.
MEDIUM WATER PERENNIALS
FULL SUN   ZONES 7-10

PELARGONIUM 'GERANIUM'

The red geraniums of window-boxes and summer bedding schemes are traditionally scarlet, but here we consider those with distinctly 'blue' tinges in the red hues, colours which are less warm and advancing and easier to fit into dark colour schemes, and also more appropriate with bright blue bedders such as lobelia. But remember that placing a pure crimson red next to a pure violet of equal value ensures that the crimson becomes more nearly scarlet. Remember, too, that these reds are difficult to reproduce accurately on the printed page: always try to see a flower, especially of these easily distorted reds and blues, before planting.

P. peltatum, the ivy-leaved geranium, has a deep crimson flowering form known as both *P.p.* 'Mexican Beauty' and 'Claret Crousse', with flowers carried very freely over trailing glossy leaves.

P. × *domesticum* 'Aztec', a regal pelargonium, is an upright shrubby plant whose bright red flowers have purple veining. *P.* × *hortorum* 'Electra', a zonal pelargonium, has bright crimson flowers.
SMALL OR TRAILING SUB-SHRUBS
FULL SUN   ZONES 9-10
See also Pinks and mauves: summer.

PENSTEMON

P. campanulatus 'Garnet' is quite hardy and quickly makes a bushy plant once more after severe pruning in early spring. Tubular flowers of deep purple-red are carried from summer to late autumn. Grow it beside alchemillas and under pink shrub roses. By careful dead-

Hemerocallis 'Stafford'

Skimmia japonica

LATE SUMMER

heading, it will continue to flower as a companion to *Hydrangea villosa* in late summer and early autumn.
EVERGREEN PERENNIAL   40-60 CM (16-24 IN)
FULL SUN   ZONES 7-10
See also Pinks and mauves: late summer.

PETUNIA
P. 'Burgundy' is a large-flowered Grandiflora petunia with rich velvet-textured flowers of wine-red with black veining and centres. Grow with neighbouring cream and white variegated leaves. I have put them in a pot with trailing ivy tumbling over the sides (*Hedera canariensis* 'Gloire de Marengo', but a smaller ivy would be in proportion in smaller pots); neither needs a great deal of moisture, but the petunia, to ensure continuous flowering, must have sticky dead-heads continually removed.
ANNUAL   30 CM (12 IN)
FULL SUN   ZONES 4-9
See also The whites: summer.

SKIMMIA
Grown mainly for their excellent fruit colours in summer, these evergreen shrubs are tolerant of shade, seaside winds and industrial pollution. They do prefer a deep acid soil, the leaves becoming pale and sickly in alkaline conditions.
   Most forms of *S. japonica* have good fruits, and those of the type are bright red. *S.j.* 'Foremanii' has rich globular red fruits in larger clusters. Plants of both sexes are required for the production of fruit.
   S. reevesiana, which is not lime-tolerant, is hermaphrodite, and the fruit is matt-textured and vivid dark red.
SMALL EVERGREEN SHRUB
SHADE   ZONES 7-9

VIOLA
PANSY, VIOLET, HEART'S EASE
V. × wittrockiana 'Arkwright Ruby' is summer-flowering, with bright crimson scented flowers. Of the Swiss Giant strain, *V. × w.* 'Alpenglow' is mahogany-red, and 'Crimson Queen' is velvety-red with a dark blotch. In general, sow outside in early summer and transplant in late summer for flowering the following winter and spring. It is equally possible and desirable to sow under glass in early spring for flower displays in summer and autumn. They make good front-of-border plants, some of these deep colours closely relating to the hot oranges and reds of high and late summer. Plant in drifts between perennials and dead-head regularly.
ANNUAL OR BIENNIAL   15-23 CM (6-9 IN)
FULL SUN   ZONES 4-9

Althaea rosea

ALTHAEA HOLLYHOCK
Appropriately placed for height and size at the back of a border, hollyhocks represent spots of bright colour, excellent foils to colour schemes and evocative of the traditional cottage-garden flower-bed. The colour expert and the artist should look more closely: the individual flowers, especially those in deep red shades, deserve detailed attention. Transparent petals allow filtered sunlight to touch inner folds, so that colour seems to be constantly changing, paler and darker hues giving the impression of depth and volume. It is difficult to get seeds of named colours, and the range of *A. rosea (Alcea rosea)* will overlap into the pastel tints of Pinks and mauves; however, the occasional lapse in perfect colour matching can give a garden life and interest.
BIENNIAL OR ANNUAL
1.2 M (4 FT) OR 2.4-3 M (8-10 FT)
FULL SUN   ZONES 6-9

ANTIRRHINUM SNAPDRAGON
Among the Nanum cultivars, *A. majus* 'Black Prince' has deep crimson flowers and bronze leaves. It flowers best in full sun, and a good group can be spectacular. Sow in early spring and bed out as soon as possible. *A.m.* 'Crimson Monarch' is a rust-resistant form, rather similar but with green foliage.
ANNUAL   45 CM (18 IN)
FULL SUN   ZONES 5-9
See also Clear yellows: late summer.

BUDDLEIA
B. davidii 'Black Knight' bears long trusses of intensely deep violet flowers. Grow it daringly behind bright scarlet *Dahlia* 'Bishop of Llandaff' or more soberly with pastel-coloured Michaelmas daisies, giving strength and depth to a late border where grey leaves and gentle colouring predominate. Winter pruning keeps it in scale with lower-growing perennials.
   B.d. 'Royal Red' is much redder, almost purple, and associates with the blues of late-flowering deciduous ceanothus or the white flowers and maroon calyces of *Clerodendron trichotomum* – and occasionally will coincide with its colourful bright blue berries.
MEDIUM DECIDUOUS SHRUBS
FULL SUN   ZONES 7-9
See also The blues: late summer.

CLEMATIS

C. 'Comtesse de Bouchard' has pinky-mauve wide flowers with cream stamens. Grow it into a purple-leaved cotinus or among repeat-flowering climbing rose, *Rosa* 'Crimson Glory'.

C. 'Lady Betty Balfour' is very vigorous, for a large-flowered hybrid, with shining young copper-coloured leaves and rich purple-cupped flowers. Grow with the claret vine, *Vitis vinifera* 'Purpurea'.
DECIDUOUS CLIMBERS
FULL SUN, ROOTS IN SHADE   ZONES 7-9
See also The whites: spring.

COBAEA

C. scandens is a most attractive climber, annual in most gardens but perennial and earlier-flowering in town or warm microclimates. Known as cathedral bell or cup and saucer plant, the purple bell-shaped corolla is enclosed by a green-coloured calyx. Its exotic appearance is exciting.
CLIMBING ANNUAL OR PERENNIAL
FULL SUN   ZONES 8-10

COLCHICUM

C. speciosum 'Atrorubens' has crimson-purple flowers and is lovely at the edge of woodland or shrubbery. Grow next to the more gentle pink drifts of *Cyclamen hederifolium* where mulch is

Schizostylis coccinea

thickly applied as colchicum and cyclamen leaves fade in early summer.
CORM   LEAVES 30-40 CM (12-16 IN),
FLOWERS 15-30 CM (6-12 IN)
HALF SHADE   ZONES 6-9

CROCUS

C. sativus, the saffron crocus, has rich purple flowers and makes a lovely drift of warm colour. It needs a hot climate to ripen corms.
CORM   IO CM (4 IN)   FULL SUN   ZONES 5-9
See also Clear yellows: spring.

DAHLIA

D. 'Comet' is anemone-flowered, double flowers arranged in closely packed petals. The deep maroon colour is subtle, matt rather than glowing, but fitting into a colour scheme of deep reds and pinks.
TUBEROUS PERENNIAL   90 CM (36 IN)
FULL SUN   ZONES 9-10
See also foliage, below, and Hot colours: late summer.

GLADIOLUS CORN FLAG

G. cardinalis is definitely tender, but has bright rich crimson flowers and is lovely in a group: it is much less likely to stray than *G. byzantinus*. Plant it near the front of a warm sun-baked border.
CORM   60 CM (24 IN)
FULL SUN   ZONES 7-10

HEBE
SHRUBBY VERONICA, SHRUBBY SPEEDWELL

Hebes with flowers in strong red shades are rare, and those that exist in gardens are tender. They grow so easily and quickly from cuttings that the following cultivars of *H. speciosa* are worth including for any garden with a cold frame to give winter protection. They need hot sun and plenty of moisture – similar conditions to those for penstemons, and they make good companions to these colourful long-flowering plants. *H.s.* 'La Seduisante' is a tender hybrid cultivar with bright crimson racemes. Take cuttings annually and expect to use as an annual. 'Simon Deleaux' makes a neat rounded bush, covered in season with rich crimson flowers.
SMALL EVERGREEN SHRUBS
FULL SUN   ZONES 8-10
See also Foliage framework: grey.

HELIOTROPIUM
CHERRY PIE, HELIOTROPE

H. × *hybridum* 'Marina' has very fragrant violet-purple flowers and wrinkled bronze-tinted leaves. Sow seed under glass in early

spring and bed out after the last frost, or use in containers. It is lovely when used as embroidery with intertwining silver-foliaged plants. I have grown it under the claret vine with great success, the leaf of the grape blending perfectly with the violet-shaded flowers.
ANNUAL   38 CM (15 IN)
FULL SUN   ZONES 9-10

IPOMOEA MORNING GLORY

I. purpurea is a twining annual with dark purple convolvulus-like flowers which fade to almost pale violet after opening. After soaking it, sow seed in individual pots during early spring. Plant out in summer in rich soil and give plants a very warm wall to climb on, or encourage them to clamber through wall-shrubs. Less common than the blue morning glory, it is a very worthwhile climbing annual and a perfect flowering foil to bronze- or purple-tinted foliage.
ANNUAL CLIMBER   TO 3 M (10 FT)
FULL SUN   ZONES 8-10

LYTHRUM LOOSESTRIFE

L. salicaria, purple loosestrife, is a useful border perennial, thriving in any soil in sun or shade. Use it with coloured foliage plants: bronze and purple leaves blend harmoniously; creamy-variegated and grey and silver leaves create contrast, but keep away from strong yellows and golden foliage.
DECIDUOUS PERENNIAL
FULL SUN OR SHADE   ZONES 5-8

ORIGANUM MARJORAM

O. laevigatum, with leaves untypically not fragrant, has attractive purple flowers held in tall spikes above grey-green leaves. A very good late flowerer for the front of a border, especially valuable with grey-foliaged plants. It adds depth to a colour scheme based on grey iris leaves, lavenders and misty mauve flower colour.
DECIDUOUS PERENNIAL   30-45 CM (12-18 IN)
FULL SUN   ZONES 7-9

PHLOX

P. paniculata 'Russian Violet' has violet-purple flower-trusses and *P.p.* 'July Glow' has heads of carmine-crimson. 'San Antonio' is even darker, with purple-red flowers. All should be planted in generous-sized groups. They give colour to companion plantings of more sombre purple foliage.
DECIDUOUS PERENNIALS
90-120 CM (36-48 IN)
FULL SUN OR HALF SHADE   ZONES 6-9
See also The whites: late summer.

FOLIAGE

SALVIA SAGE
S. involucrata, itself with rather blunted flowers of reddish-mauve, has a more brilliant-flowered form, *S.i.* 'Bethellii', where the flowers in long spikes are in shades of magenta and crimson. The soft hairy bronze leaves are veined with pink and the stalks are reddish-tinted. It is a spectacular plant but stems are brittle, so find it a sheltered position.
DECIDUOUS SHRUBBY PERENNIAL
FULL SUN   ZONES 8-10

SANGUISORBA BURNET
S. officinalis, great burnet, has red bottle-brush flowers held above pinnate foliage. It makes a graceful arching plant for the back of a richly fed border.
DECIDUOUS PERENNIAL   1.2 M (4 FT)
FULL SUN   ZONES 6-9

SCHIZOSTYLIS KAFFIR LILY
S. coccinea thrives in rich moist soil and has bright crimson cup-shaped flowers held in slender spikes above grassy leaves. Various good strong reds exist: one of the best is *S.c.* 'Major', with large flowers of deep crimson.
DECIDUOUS RHIZOME   60 CM (24 IN)
FULL SUN   ZONES 7-9
See also Pinks and mauves: late summer.

SEDUM STONECROP
Herbaceous sedums with thick fleshy leaves are useful at this season. Their flat heads of tiny stars, beloved by butterflies which congregate in large numbers when the sun is shining, can be pinkish, yellow or dull red in colour. These 'reds' are low-toned gentle colours, very different from warm crimsons.
    S. telephium 'Munstead Red' is an herbaceous stonecrop, suitable for edging borders and valuable for the fleshy green leaves and flat flowers in low-toned dusky red held neatly on strong stems. Its compact habit makes it more useful in a border than the purple-leaved *S. maximum atropurpureum* (see foliage, below), which is beautiful but untidy in growth.
DECIDUOUS PERENNIAL   45-80 CM (18-32 IN)
FULL SUN   ZONES 7-9

TRICYRTIS TOAD LILY
T. formosana likes rich moist soil, partly shaded but not overhung too densely with other plants. The strange orchid-like spotted flowers are mauvish, dark spots on a paler ground, with yellow throats. *T.f. stolonifera* is of a richer purple and spreads rapidly. Plant where the close detail of the flowers can be seen clearly.
DECIDUOUS PERENNIAL   60-90 CM (24-36 IN)
HALF SHADE   ZONES 7-9

'Strong red' foliage encompasses a range from bright crimson through muted metallic bronze and coppery tinges to deep purples and the 'black' shades often designated by 'nigrum', 'nigrescens' or 'atro-' as elements in the name. Translucent pink tints and young scarlet growth which later mature to rich summer greens belong here, as do subtle burnished or rich crimson overtones in a green leaf. This section also includes leaves with conspicuous red tinges at any time; they may contribute colour for a whole season or – like flowers – make colour incidents for a shorter period. Unless illuminated from behind by the sun's rays, these lighter reds are seldom brilliant, but more often subtle and mysterious. Surface texture and the angle of the light may make the weightier purple foliage matt and sombre or glossy and glowing.
    Few evergreens have strong red foliage, although some assume purplish tones with winter frosts. For deciduous autumn reds, see the Foliage framework.

ACER MAPLE
A. palmatum 'Atropurpureum' and *A.p.* 'Dissectum Atropurpureum' have distinct lobed leaves and make rounded bushy shapes, the latter having leaves so divided and cut as to be like lacework, strongly mitigating the strength and solidity of the heavy purple colour. Other 'dissectum' forms have leaves of a more muted colour, somewhere between purple and green, more or less bronze. They prefer a deep rich soil tending towards acid.
LARGE DECIDUOUS SHRUB
FULL SUN OR HALF SHADE   ZONES 7-9

AJUGA BUGLE
A. reptans 'Atropurpurea' has dark purple leaves, perfect with the strong blue colour of the flower in early summer. Even in winter the leaf is dark, especially if grown in full sun, whereas *A.r.* 'Multicolor' develops its fascinating blotches of pink and purple only during the summer. Try either round the base of the magnificent *Melianthus major* or under the light canopy of *Cornus controversa* 'Variegata'.
EVERGREEN PERENNIAL   10 CM (4 IN)
FULL SUN   ZONES 5-9
See also The whites: foliage.

ASTILBE
A. × arendsii garden hybrids have deeply divided feathery leaves, pinkish to purple-tinted when young, though by flowering time in summer the leaves are usually green. Grow them with early-flowering pink primulas and with moisture-loving grasses.
DECIDUOUS PERENNIAL   60-120 CM (24-48 IN)
HALF SHADE   ZONES 7-9
See also Foliage framework: green.

Acer palmatum 'Dissectum Atropurpureum'

Berberis thunbergii 'Atropurpurea'

BERBERIS BARBERRY
B. thunbergii 'Atropurpurea' and its dwarf form, *B.t.* 'Atropurpurea Nana', have rich reddish-purple leaves, which glow in sunlight.
    B. × ottawensis 'Purpurea' is a graceful bush, the arching branches carrying purplish leaves shading to green. Related flower colours of violet-blue or purple-crimson bring the heavy dullness of purple foliage to life.
DWARF TO MEDIUM DECIDUOUS SHRUBS
FULL SUN OR HALF SHADE   ZONES 5-9

BERGENIA
B. cordifolia 'Purpurea', one of Gertrude Jekyll's favourites, has purple-flushed rounded green leaves which take stronger purplish tones in winter. Tall stems bear magenta flowers in early spring. Plant groups in front of Lenten hellebores.
EVERGREEN PERENNIAL   60 CM (24 IN)
FULL SUN OR SHADE   ZONES 6-9
B. purpurascens has narrow leaves, dark green in summer but rich beetroot-colour in winter, the undersides mahogany-red. The flower-stalks are pink, a little darker than the early-spring flowers.
EVERGREEN PERENNIAL   30 CM (12 IN)
FULL SUN OR SHADE   ZONES 6-9
See also Foliage framework: green.

BETA SPINACH BEET

B. vulgaris, beetroot as well as Swiss chard or spinach beet, is generally grown as an annual or biennial in the kitchen garden. The highly ornamental form *B.v.* 'Ruby Chard' has glowing red stalks and mid-ribs which attract all eyes in a strict vegetable garden formation, or when grouped as a splash of scarlet and green in a border.

ANNUAL OR PERENNIAL   90 CM (36 IN)
FULL SUN   ZONES 6-9

Cotinus coggygria 'Royal Purple'

Ophiopogon planiscapus 'Nigrescens'

CANNA

C. × generalis, a semi-tropical perennial, usually planted as annual bedding-out, has two particularly good purple-leaved forms. *C. × g.* 'Egandale' has erect banana-like leaves of rich deep bronze, and small scarlet flowers. In *C. × g.* 'Purpurea' the leaves are only shaded with purple and are therefore much less dark, blending rather than contrasting with other foliage. Use both leaf forms in striking flower-colour schemes of scarlet, red and orange: the hot strident colours linked by bronze-tinted canna leaves.

DECIDUOUS RHIZOME   1.2 M (4 FT)
FULL SUN   ZONES 9-10

CLEMATIS

C. recta 'Purpurea' is herbaceous, with small white scented flowers. The purple leaves are modest but give colour and interest in a border planned primarily for flowers, and look particularly effective with a pink-flowered theme. The lax stems need some support.

DECIDUOUS PERENNIAL   1.2 M (4 FT)
FULL SUN, ROOTS IN SHADE   ZONES 6-9
See also The whites: spring.

CORDYLINE CABBAGE PALM

C. australis 'Atropurpurea', more tender than the green type (see Foliage framework), is for mild climates only. Its leaves are bronze-purple, not too harsh.

LARGE EVERGREEN SHRUB OR SMALL TREE
FULL SUN   ZONES 8-10

CORYLUS HAZEL

C. maxima 'Purpurea', the purple-leaved filbert, has rounded coarsely toothed and rough-textured leaves. The dark matt colouring gives this upright growing bush a solid appearance. Contrast it with light airy plants, small-leaved and pale, to accentuate differences. Cut it to the ground every few years; this is less trouble and more effective than annual thinning of the branches.

LARGE DECIDUOUS SHRUB
FULL SUN OR HALF SHADE   ZONES 6-9

COTINUS SMOKE BUSH

C. coggygria 'Foliis Purpureis' and *C.c.* 'Royal Purple' have plum-purple and richer wine-purple leaves respectively. The latter keeps its translucent quality all through the summer and turns fiery-red in autumn. Plant it so that the sun's rays light the leaves from behind. The fawn flower-plumes are enhanced by the rich foliage of these coloured bushes.

LARGE DECIDUOUS SHRUBS
FULL SUN   ZONES 7-9
See also Foliage framework: green.

DAHLIA

In mild areas treated as hardy perennials, but more generally grown as summer bedding plants, dahlias are very free late-summer flowerers, colours ranging in warm hues of yellow and scarlet- and crimson-reds as well as pale pinks and whites. The elegant metallic bronze-purple leaves of the peony-flowered *D.* 'Bishop of Llandaff' set off the fierce scarlet blooms (see Hot colours: late summer). The pinnate leaves, resembling those of a cut-leaf elder, *Sambucus racemosa*, are unlike the more normal coarse pinnate structure in both texture and shape, and make it invaluable in mixed planting. Mass this dahlia with vivid red spikes of *Salvia fulgens*, behind clumps of bright two-toned fuchsias, to add substance and bulk to a late-summer 'hot' border, or use toned-down reds for subtle effects.

EVERGREEN TUBER   1.2 M (4 FT)
FULL SUN   ZONES 9-10

EPIMEDIUM

E. grandiflorum has almost browny-beige young spring leaves, above which flower-stems carry mauve-pink sprays.

E. × rubrum has pale green-pink young leaves which rapidly deepen from pink to almost brick-red. Crimson flowers with white spurs are held above the leaves in early spring.

E. × versicolor 'Sulphureum' has primrose flowers above bronze-tinted leaves.

DECIDUOUS PERENNIALS   23-30 CM (9-12 IN)
FULL SUN OR HALF SHADE   ZONES 5-9
See also Foliage framework: green.

EUPHORBIA SPURGE

E. sikkimensis, in spring, has bright foliage, emerging as pink rosettes, from which tall translucent red stems bear leaves with veins etched in white. As the season proceeds the leaves turn to a quiet green before the greenish-yellow bracts give colour in late summer. It thrives in damp soil, roots running for quite a distance.

DECIDUOUS PERENNIAL   90 CM (36 IN)
FULL SUN OR HALF SHADE   ZONES 7-9
See also Foliage framework: green.

FAGUS BEECH

F. sylvatica 'Riversii', purple beech, is the best of the purple-leaved clones. Beautiful in the spring when leaves unfurl almost translucent and shining pale purple. By midsummer the leaf darkens and the colour looks solid and heavy. It should be grown as a specimen to make a shapely tree in lawn or parkland.

LARGE DECIDUOUS TREE
FULL SUN   ZONES 5-9
See also Foliage framework: green.

FOENICULUM FENNEL

F. vulgare 'Purpureum' has thread-like feathery leaves on tough shining stalks; and, in this bronze-tinted form, is useful for clumping in mixed borders. Normally grown for its aromatic leaves, used for flavouring fish and salad dishes, it is ornamental in kitchen or flower garden.

DECIDUOUS PERENNIAL HERB   1.8 M (6 FT)
FULL SUN   ZONES 7-9

HEUCHERA CORAL FLOWER

H. americana, satin leaf, has marbled young leaves of soft browns and coppery-green, glistening with a satin sheen. New leaves appear all through the summer, making this a most desirable foliage plant for the front of a border. The flowers, in early summer, are pale flesh-coloured (see Pinks and mauves: early summer); other heucheras are brighter. One of Miss Jekyll's favourite plants, it mixes well with small spring bulbs, and gives colour and interest through the summer.

DECIDUOUS PERENNIAL   23 CM (9 IN)
FULL SUN OR SHADE   ZONES 6-9

HOUTTUYNIA

H. cordata is a small invasive plant for moist shade. The bronze-tipped leaves are green, blotched brownish-purple, and smell of Seville oranges. Single or double white flowers (see The whites: summer) have cone-shaped centres. Plant it under deciduous shrubs where spreading roots can do no damage.

DECIDUOUS PERENNIAL   30 CM (12 IN)
SHADE   ZONES 6-9

IRESINE

I. herbstii 'Brilliantissima' has long almost cordate leaves of beetroot or blood-red. It is a tender bedding plant, best massed in formal patterns with contrasting greys or silvers, its dense habit smothering annual weeds. Treat like a pelargonium and take cuttings for overwintering.

DECIDUOUS SUB-SHRUB   30-45 CM (12-18 IN)
FULL SUN   ZONES 9-10

LIGULARIA

These are hardy perennials thriving in shade and moist soil. The daisy-flowers are shades of orange and yellow.
    L. dentata (syn. *Senecio clivorum*) 'Desdemona' has large heart-shaped leaves, beetroot-red when young, gradually turning metallic-green. Blackish branching stems support orange daisy-flowers in late summer (see Hot colours).

DECIDUOUS PERENNIAL   1.2 M (4 FT)
FULL SUN OR SHADE   ZONES 6-9

LOBELIA

Some species of perennial lobelia are invaluable plants in the herbaceous border. *L. cardinalis*, the cardinal flower, has glowing beetroot-coloured foliage. Emerging in spring as bright rosettes, the leaves are topped in late summer by scarlet or dark red flower-spikes (see Hot colours). Not reliable hardy, so protect crowns with bracken in winter.

DECIDUOUS PERENNIAL   60-90 CM (24-36 IN)
FULL SUN   ZONES 8-10

Heuchera americana

OPHIOPOGON LILYTURF

O. planiscapus 'Nigrescens' has black grassy leaves and spreads in tufted clumps, making a dark carpet at the edge or front of sunny beds. (The ordinary green form is used as 'lawn' in suitable climates.) Plant in generous-sized clumps at first, as plants increase only slowly. The colour is difficult to place in a garden, exotic and unusual but drawing the eye as firmly as a bright patch of red. Make a feature of it by emphasizing its dramatic potential with yet more deep purple foliage. *Cotinus coggygria* 'Foliis Purpureis' underplanted with black glistening ophiopogon could be exciting.

EVERGREEN PERENNIAL   23 CM (9 IN)
FULL SUN   ZONES 7-9

PHORMIUM

P. tenax 'Purpureum' has grey-green leaves overlaid with a purplish sheen. Some of the dwarf forms of *P. cookianum*, such as *P.c.* 'Bronze Baby' and 'Dazzler', have coppery and reddish-brown leaves. All individually good foliage plants, yet difficult to use in a garden. Try them in containers and place them where an emphatic point is needed. They are not very hardy but will thrive, and look appropriate, in a town microclimate with other exotic foliage plants.

SMALL TO MEDIUM EVERGREEN SHRUB
FULL SUN   ZONES 8-10
See also Foliage framework: green.

Iresine herbstii 'Brilliantissima'

Photinia × fraseri 'Birmingham'

Saxifraga fortunei 'Wada's Variety'

Vitis vinifera 'Purpurea'

PHOTINIA

A genus of mainly evergreen shrubs from Asia. The young leaves, as they unfold, rival *Pieris formosa forrestii*, with brilliant copper-red translucent tints. *P. × fraseri* 'Birmingham' and 'Red Robin' have sharply toothed glossy green leaves with bright bronze-red and brilliant red young growth respectively. Grow them against a wall where extra heat will protect young leaves from frosts and encourage flowering. Allow a late-flowering clematis, not too vigorous, such as *C. flammula*, to twine among the glossy leaves.

LARGE EVERGREEN SHRUB
FULL SUN   ZONES 7-10

PIERIS

Pieris are acid-loving shrubs for damp woodland, needing conditions similar to those favoured by rhododendrons. Many of them are grown for their often startling red young leaf growth in early spring. It is so bright that from a distance the bush looks as if covered in scarlet flowers. New growth is easily damaged by spring frosts, so plant where a light canopy of overhead branches will give some protection.

Among the best pieris for coloured young growth are cultivars of *P. formosa forrestii*, *P.f.f.* 'Jermyn's' and 'Wakehurst'. A hybrid with the hardier *P. japonica, P.* 'Forest Flame', produces the most brilliant coloured foliage.

TALL OR MEDIUM EVERGREEN SHRUBS
HALF SHADE OR SHADE   ZONES 7-9

PITTOSPORUM

P. tenuifolium 'Purpureum' has young green growth which turns rapidly to shining purple. In spring the two-colour effect is bizarre, but later in the season it becomes one of the most attractive purple-foliaged shrubs, the undulating leaf edges reflecting light and shade.

TALL EVERGREEN SHRUB
FULL SUN   ZONES 8-10
See also Foliage framework: green.

PRUNUS FLOWERING CHERRY

P. cerasifera 'Pissardii' has leaves that are dark red when young, turning to a deep purple. In early spring, pink buds open to a profusion of white flowers. The cultivar *P.c.* 'Nigra' has even deeper purple foliage. Heavy and rather lifeless in tone, these small trees give a quiet sober background to flower colour. Crimson roses and dark blue-purple *jackmanii* clematis, underplanted with violet-blue *Geranium × magnificum*, light up the blue tones in the solid dark purple.

SMALL DECIDUOUS TREE
FULL SUN OR HALF SHADE   ZONES 6-9

P. 'Cistena', the purple sand cherry, has rich red leaves, translucent and glowing with the sun behind them. A small shrub, it can be used for hedging, or in clumps to make attractive foliage impact. Grow pink and white autumn-flowering cyclamen at its feet.

SMALL DECIDUOUS SHRUB
FULL SUN OR HALF SHADE   ZONES 5-9
See also The whites: spring.

RHEUM ORNAMENTAL RHUBARB

R. palmatum 'Atrosanguineum' has vivid red young foliage, later deep wine-purple, the leaves more deeply dissected than in the green type. The flowers are dark cerise-crimson, carried early in summer when many perennials have tinted pastel or bright pure blue colours.

DECIDUOUS PERENNIAL   1.5 M (5 FT)
FULL SUN   ZONES 7-9
See also Foliage framework: green.

RICINUS

R. communis 'Gibsonii' is the purple-leaved castor oil plant. Its large palmate leaves and upright habit make it a valuable plant for foliage borders. The colour, a deep bronzy-purple, lasts through the season. Grow it from seed sown the previous summer and overwintered free from frost.

EVERGREEN SHRUB   1.5 M (5 FT)
FULL SUN   ZONES 9-10

ROSA ROSE

R. 'Climbing Lady Hillingdon' has lovely coppery-coloured foliage and pale lemon-buff flowers. Long pointed buds are typical of hybrid tea roses, perfect for picking and lasting well in water. The original bush form, now rare, with long lax branches, may be grown in a border of mixed shrubs and perennials.

EVERGREEN SHRUB OR CLIMBER
FULL SUN   ZONES 6-9

R. 'Rosemary Rose' has dark purple-tinted young foliage, later turning dark green. The flowers are flat and double, camellia-shaped, of bright currant-red, carried in a first glorious flush in midsummer, and again later, if pruned back and new purple foliage encouraged.

MEDIUM SHRUB   FULL SUN   ZONES 6-9

SALVIA SAGE

S. officinalis 'Purpurascens' has rough-textured leaves, grey washed over in purple, the tints more prominent after pruning. A more gaudy plant is *S.o.* 'Tricolor', where pink, purple and cream are splashed over the grey foundation.

SMALL EVERGREEN SHRUB
FULL SUN   ZONES 7-9
See also Clear yellows: foliage.

SAXIFRAGA SAXIFRAGE

S. fortunei 'Wada's Variety' is clump-forming, with rounded leaves, rich bronze on the top and with the undersides bright purple-red. Grow it in a raised bed to get full value from the leaf-back. Foaming white flowers are carried in late summer. It likes a cool place, rich moist soil and half shade.

DECIDUOUS PERENNIAL   30-40 CM (12-16 IN)
HALF SHADE   ZONES 6-9

SEDUM STONECROP
S. maximum atropurpureum, sometimes considered a sub-species of *S. telephium*, is herbaceous, just losing its fleshy leaves in winter. The leaf colour is subtle, a delicate purplish-grey early but deepening to a dark purple at flowering time in late summer. This dull colouring makes a foil for bright neighbouring flowers. Its own flat flower-heads, composed of tiny stars, are pinkish-brown and are carried on lax stems.
DECIDUOUS PERENNIAL   45-80 CM (18-32 IN)
FULL SUN   ZONES 7-9

STRANVAESIA
S. davidiana, a cotoneaster-like shrub, has dark green leaves, some of which turn bright scarlet in autumn. This gives a two-colour effect different from usual autumn shading, almost spring-like in freshness and impact. Sometimes grown as a wall-shrub, specimens may be grown as trees with a single trunk and bushy head. Hardier than bay or holly, stranvaesia may then be used quite formally to line a path or frame a view or gateway.
LARGE EVERGREEN SHRUB OR SMALL TREE
FULL SUN OR HALF SHADE   ZONES 6-9

TELLIMA
T. grandiflora 'Purpurea' is dense and clump-forming. It also seeds freely but unfortunately seedlings are generally green-leaved. It has hairy purplish leaves, the colour much more pronounced in winter; the undersides of the leaves are pinkish. It is a ground-cover plant for massing in shady garden areas, the warm, glowing colour welcome in winter. Pinkish-white bells are carried on tall stems in summer.
EVERGREEN PERENNIAL   25-50 CM (10-20 IN)
SHADE   ZONES 7-9

VIOLA
PANSY, VIOLET, HEART'S EASE
V. labradorica 'Purpurea' has dark purple, almost mauve, leaves and charming violet-blue flowers in early summer (see The blues). It seeds very freely and is surface-rooting. Leaves become dark green by the end of the season. A lovely sight at the edge of a rose-bed, occasional seedlings spreading into gravel or germinating in cracks between paving stones. The silver-leaved *Stachys lanata* may be planted in alternating groups with this little viola, since both thrive in hot sun. *Veronica teucrium* makes a companion group in a blue-toned colour scheme, the viola's dark foliage making a foil to the flowers of both.
DECIDUOUS PERENNIAL   15 CM (6 IN)
FULL SUN OR SHADE   ZONES 2-8
See also Foliage framework: green.

Pieris formosa forrestii 'Wakehurst'

VITIS GRAPEVINE
V. vinifera 'Purpurea', the claret vine, has young leaves of claret-red, later deepening to heavy dark purple. One of the few climbers with purple tints, it is attractive twined on pergolas or trellis. The blue-purple flowers of *Clematis × jackmanii* or lemon-peel flowers of *C. orientalis* enrich its sombre shades.
DECIDUOUS CLIMBER   FULL SUN   ZONES 7-9
See also Foliage framework: green.

WEIGELA
W. florida 'Foliis Purpureis' has subtle bronze-purple leaves. Plant silver-variegated ajuga or variegated astrantia at its feet for spring interest, and both will appear brighter. Surround it with pink and red flowers and the colours become less garish.
MEDIUM DECIDUOUS SHRUB
FULL SUN OR HALF SHADE   ZONES 5-9
See also The whites: foliage.

CHAPTER VIII

HOT COLOURS

The craving for bright colour is like that of a child reaching for a scarlet crayon. Impulsive and primitive, advancing and positive, distorting distance and reducing dimension, the vermilion-reds, oranges and harshest egg-yolk yellows can produce a confused glare on the retina, the eye blinking and adjusting its focus to cope with a new wavelength of light. The more perfectly restful and pleasing are the textured greens and greys of assorted foliage, the more the eye might long for such bright contrast which will jolt and disturb tranquility, giving a welcome stimulus and overruling and dominating neighbouring colours that are easier to combine.

In colour symbolism these sunset colours represent the warmth of fire and flame (in spite of the fact that flame turns blue when most intensely hot). In a garden, assemble these warm and most immediately eye-catching hues against a mass of relatively low-toned foliage or flower colour. As in nature, a small amount of vivid colour is most telling and rewarding when glimpsed through a tracery of green leaves, an incidental splash of colour in a green vista. In spring, when green foliage is young and pale, these colours need careful placing to glow like precious stones, valuable for rarity rather than quantity. As summer advances heavy greens of hedging background and smooth velvet lawns make more appropriate settings. These spectral reds, oranges and yellows are not only the warmest colours but are also light and bright, lacking the mystery and depth of 'blued' reds or deepest violets. Darken their purity by using colours with shaded pigment, or plant them in shade where violet light links and darkens and the glare is reduced. As the long red rays of the evening sun mellow and enrich, these bright hues become deeper and more sombre.

'Hot colours' follow the spectrum through from red to yellow, taking a segment from pure red through scarlet, vermilion and cinnabar round to the richer orange-yellow.

These reds contain no blue – such stronger crimsons are considered in Chapter VII – but are increasingly influenced by yellow. The limit of the segment is reached as the deep yellows lose their orange tinge. Pure yellow is not a hot colour: it gleams with light rather than glowing with warmth, and is outside the sunset range. In this book it is covered in Chapter IV. Orange itself is bright, yet dark, lacking the luminosity and clarity of yellow, yet in flower petal colour it is often translucent and appealing – a foil to neighbouring yellows and reds. In shade it becomes bronzed, tinged with brown to sienna. Harsh, hot yellows are the hard colours of forsythia and double kerria, the fierce orange-yellow of *Berberis darwinii* and the glowing colour of the brightest of golden daffodils and deep yellow tulips.

A spring garden could be planned with drifts of these plants, enlivened and extended by appropriate wallflowers of golden-bronze. In a large garden treat this bright area like a brilliantly coloured painting on the wall in a room where other shades are muted; do not make it the principal area of the garden, or the eye and mind will too quickly tire. Bright colours are for emphasis, contrast and warmth; their impact depends on skilful and rare planning. Consider the effect of a glade of scarlet or orange azaleas in a wood, a drift of bright daffodils glimpsed through dark shade like a patch of sunlight, red tulip flower petals complementing their smooth green leaves, the double orange kerria glowing against the foil of green holly leaves. Scarlet stems of willow, *Salix alba* 'Chermesina', and dogwood, *Cornus alba* 'Sibirica', close to evergreen photinias, which have translucent scarlet leaves among darker foliage colour, make one picture in an open vista. If the soil is acid, add groups of *Pieris formosa* or *P.* 'Forest Flame', with startling young scarlet-bronze tinted leaves and clustered white lily-of-the-valley flowers in late spring. The Chilean fire bush, *Embothrium coccineum*, glows with flame flowers in sheltered woodland, a most spectacular shrub where conditions suit it.

PREVIOUS PAGE **In a shaft of late-summer sunlight orange-flowered** *Crocosmia masonorum* **and golden rudbeckias rise above the textured foliage of a prostrate juniper to warm a dark corner. Silhouetted against glossy evergreens, the flowers glow and seem to advance towards the spectator. Golden leaves of** *Juniperus communis* **'Depressa Aurea' lit by sunshine become as bright as flowers, and are linked by yellow pigment to the hot colours in the picture. With colour values so equally balanced between the contrasting orange tones and the greens, variety in plant and flower shapes and rhythmic leaf patterns become important sources of interest.**

ABOVE **Tulips rising through a carpet of lower-growing wallflowers make an exciting colour picture that successfully challenges my normal antipathy towards the 'dotting about' of mixed and multi-coloured plants. (My preference is almost invariably for distinct blocks of a single colour or for drifts of blending colours.) Such an intense blaze of colour needs thoughtful handling in a moderate-sized garden: a substantial frame of low box hedging would contain it, or it could be discovered in a hidden area, with surrounding low-toned greens to balance its intensity. A bright image like this certainly needs to be kept well separate from any other colour planting, and also needs to be viewed from a sufficient** distance to allow reds and yellows to mingle in the eye and give the impression of a lively orange. Interestingly, the colour blending is repeated in close-up in each individual tulip petal, where the gradations between red and yellow show nature's own ordering of colour harmonies.

On a more domestic scale, RIGHT, the corner of a small town garden is warmed by a group of *Tulipa* 'General de Wet'. Orange and red flowers make the most impact, necessitating a conscious refocusing of the eye's lens when viewed in association with strong bright complementary greens from the opposite side of the spectral wheel. Here the background foliage of *Hydrangea petiolaris* and the greyer leaves of the tulips themselves above the brick edging make a low-toned setting, reducing the glare of pure contrast and 'hotness' of the tulip flowers. These tulips, at first brighter and more solid in colour, have opened to reveal a gradation towards paler yellow in the centre and some yellow patterning throughout the petals.

By early summer scarlet oriental poppies, scarlet trumpet honeysuckle (*Lonicera* × *brownii* 'Fuchsioides'), single-flowered scarlet *Paeonia lobata* and scarlet *Rosa moyesii* will make isolated splashes of colour. Later many flowers in these vivid colours impress in high summer: *Alstroemeria aurantiaca*, with golden-orange flowers, *Anthemis sancti-johannis*, with purest orange and forms of *Anthemis tinctoria* with glowing yellow daisies build up towards darker verbascums and coreopsis.

Keep to a natural order of colour 'weight' or strength with the tones of these strong spectral colours: a pale yellow looks best with a dark orange, which itself demands a strong ver-milion, which in its turn looks best with darker crimson. Scarlet roses with velvet petals, bergamot (*Monarda didyma* 'Cambridge Scarlet'), *Lychnis chalcedonica* and bronze-red hemerocallis are effective planted in drifts where three or four closely related colours touch and shimmer together. In damp soil both *Mimulus guttatus* and the pale orange *M. aurantiacus* make foreground planting to drifts of orange-red *Primula* 'Red Hugh'. The famous 'red' borders at Hidcote have dark green hedging of yew as a frame for flowers and foliage of reds, orange and purple. Dark red and scarlet dahlias, canna with red flowers and dark purple leaves, ricinus, crocosmia and curtonus in strongly outlined clumps,

Hot colours are not invariably brash and bright. Here two borders create totally diverse moods and demonstrate different planting philosophies.

OPPOSITE Each interlocking plant clump has a distinct shape and colour, and no attempt has been made to merge or weave them together. The drama of the bold composition is heightened by the long red rays of the evening sun and by the pronounced shadows that they generate. Strong colour contrasts are often most effective when the pure hues are firmly placed among flowers and leaves in deeper and lower colour tones which are allowed to occupy a greater proportion of the visual field. The purplish foliage and smoky flowers of *Cotinus coggygria* 'Foliis Purpureis' are a foil to the golden-yellow achilleas. The rusty-red helianthus is a warm colour, containing yellow pigment, but its brownish centres links it firmly to the murky colour of the cotinus. The sharply defined forms of the spiky iris leaves contrast with solid plate-like achillea flower-heads, and with the shadowy blurred shape of the cotinus.

In a more subtle border of subdued misty tones, LEFT, even the most graphic and clear-cut leaf shapes are present in greyed or variegated forms which diminish their architectural impact and allow them to weave together in a low-toned mingling of impressionistic lines and patterns. Spikes of *Phormium tenax* 'Variegatum' rise above glaucous *Euphorbia wulfenii* to link it with the smoky grey cloud of *Hippophae rhamnoides* in the background. These pale colours which recede increase the sense of perspective and exaggerate the distance from the *Tritonia* × *crocosmiiflora* in the front of the bed. Since hot colours advance, they are generally best when planted in the foreground, tending to distort dimension when placed in the middle or far distance. In this tapestry of blending foliage, seed-heads, fruits and even the glowing orange flowers are incidental embroidery. The quality of diffused daylight from a cloudy sky does not disrupt the soft weaving patterns with highlights and shadows.

benefit from annual marigolds and gazanias which make eye-catching foreground drifts, establishing a rhythm of planting along the edge of green lawn.

Miss Jekyll suggests an orange garden leading to one of predominantly grey foliage, the latter 'seen at its best by reaching it through the orange borders. Here the eye becomes saturated and filled with the strong red and yellow colouring . . . making the eye eagerly desirous for the complementary colour, so that . . . turning to look into the grey garden, the effect is surprisingly – quite astonishingly – luminous and refreshing.' In her 'orange' garden Miss Jekyll grew scarlet dahlias and yellow heleniums, orange marigolds and golden coreopsis, orange kniphofia and *Rudbeckia fulgida* and the large-flowered yellow daisy *Buphthalmum salicifolia*, a rich and stimulating mixture.

These border schemes retain their bright colours into autumn, and individual plants contribute interesting bright colour as leaves and flowers fade in the garden. Orange trumpet *Campsis radicans* bears its flowers sparsely among healthy green foliage, scarlet-flowered pomegranate flowers against a sunny wall and the scarlet nasturtium *Tropaeolum speciosum* clambers through yew or shrubs in cold north-facing borders, each cluster of scarlet bright and shimmering among the pale fresh green leaves. The velvet flowers of *Salvia fulgens*, of rich scarlet, make clumps of colour in an enriched border.

Deep yellows and orange are represented by helianthus and heleniums and are useful in strong groups in a border, carefully graded colours of each leading up to the darker shades of red.

The scarlet flowers of California fuchsia (*Zauschneria californica*) are almost translucent and enriched by its silvery leaves. Grey artemisias, particularly pewter-coloured *A.* 'Powis Castle', which makes a shapely bush, separate and link these colours, making them almost too bright but keeping the colours pure and brilliant. Any red, orange or hard yellow planted close to a sea of grey leaves will make a telling picture, but remember that grey makes pure rich hues as brilliant as is possible, and therefore the use of low-toned grey plants increases the dazzling effects. Similarly blocks of white-flowering plants add to the brightness of the scene, making the reds, oranges and even the yellows, by contrast, deep and glowing.

Cream plumes of plants such as *Aruncus dioicus* and the later-flowering *Artemisia lactiflora* (with green foliage) quieten the whole effect. Feathery billows of gypsophila and *Clematis recta* do not have the 'solid' white effects of white

phlox, and blend in the eye to reduce the glare. In a hot climate with fierce sun these bright hues appear paler, but under grey skies the shimmering colours become almost garish, although by evening light the brightness is gradually mellowed.

Bright reds, oranges and yellows can be placed against a background of low-toned complementary or contrasting colour. Bright orange flowers can be coloured incidents in a sea of pale blue catmint; scarlet tulips make exclamation marks in a bed of pale blue forget-me-not, and violet-coloured lavender flowers can soften a bed of the harshest bright yellow roses. It is all a question of getting the balance right. When pale and low-toned colour is spread over a relatively larger area, acting as a foil so that the stronger and brighter colour is seen as isolated splashes, eye-catching among more sober background, the normally unsettling effects of such determined contrasts in hue and relative strength are avoided. Alternatively, use bright pairs of complementaries deliberately, to make smaller separate pictures, taken in at a glance but not part of a whole garden theme. Try spring blues and yellows in neighbouring drifts, orange lily and blue delphinium, yellow verbascum and violet campanula, blue late-flowering *Gentiana septemfida* growing under self-seeding biennial oenothera, and clumps of stately blue-flowered *Aster × frikartii* 'Mönch' with orange-flowered coreopsis.

For many gardeners large expanses of such strong related colours are too bright and exhausting. Instead, experiment with these colours in pairs of different relative strength. A bright harsh orange-yellow is pleasing with a magenta pink, though it injures a yellowish pink. Yellow is effective with a dark mauve but tends to make a pale light purple look 'dirty'. A scarlet-vermilion injures a dark yellow, but a pale yellow makes the bright colour deeper and more jewel-like.

With these strong colours brick walls of warm orange, red-toned or buff, will be better than stark red brick, and garden furniture should be of plain low-toned or dark colours. Terracotta pots need to be weathered and aged or the garden becomes a sea of bright muddled rainbow colours.

Gardening with muted colours and textures appeals to many, and it is surely true that a green and silvery-grey area is emotionally the most restful. Some gardeners even cut off discordant coloured flower-heads, incidentally also probably improving the glow and richness of foliage texture. However, bright cheerful warm colour provides an outlet for strong impulsive feelings and for the adventurous gardener to experiment, to introduce some element of startling colour and to jar the mind from complacency.

Keyline drawing

Planting plan
Figures in parentheses indicate the number of plants in a group.

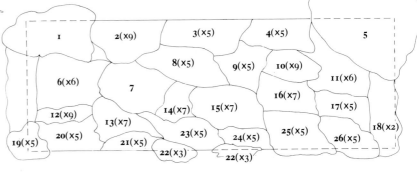

The vivid colours of the late-summer border illustrated show how linked pigments flow together harmoniously once the eye has adjusted to the section of the spectrum from which they come. Harsh yellow flowers make drifts joining wine-coloured leaves with scarlet and crimson flowers and fruit. The carefully planned colour sequences follow a natural order of darkness and lightness value and the succession of hues in the spectral wheel. The heavy purple leaves of berberis contain blue pigment which, with crimson flowers, extends the colour range beyond the narrower segment that we define as 'hot'.

To the left of the picture the greenish-grey leaves of elaeagnus give solidity to the border structure while brightening near-by reds. It is balanced at the opposite end of the border by bushy senecio, often grown for its grey leaves alone, but here contributing its bright orange-yellow daisies.

Make this planting area the climax to a garden tour, allowing the eye and the mind to be prepared for maximum impact by an approach through a planting of restful and shady green, indicated to the left. In evening light, as the sun's rays lengthen and become first red and then violet, mellowing and enriching these bright hues, the effect of the border becomes more sober.

Plant key
1 *Rosa moyesii*
2 *Phlox paniculata* 'Signal'
3 *Thalictrum speciosissimum*
4 *Ligularia dentata* 'Desdemona'
5 *Malus* × 'John Downie'
6 *Elaeagnus macrophylla*
7 *Berberis thunbergii* 'Atropurpurea'
8 *Achillea filipendula* 'Coronation Gold'
9 *Kniphofia rooperi*
10 *Lilium* 'Enchantment'
11 *Dahlia* 'Bishop of Llandaff'
12 *Lilium bulbiferum croceum*
13 *Lythrum salicaria*
14 *Lilium* 'Cinnabar'
15 *Lobelia cardinalis* 'Dark Crusader'
16 *Coreopsis verticillata*
17 *Helianthus salicifolius*
18 *Senecio* 'Sunshine'
19 *Bergenia purpurascens*
20 *Monarda didyma* 'Cambridge Scarlet'
21 *Potentilla* 'Gibson's Scarlet'
22 *Helianthemum nummularium* 'Beech Park Scarlet'
23 *Salvia fulgens*
24 *Anthemis sancti-johannis*
25 *Lobelia cardinalis*
26 *Rudbeckia hirta*

SPRING

Rhododendron: Knap Hill hybrid azaleas

ANEMONE WINDFLOWER
In Mediterranean countries bright red anémones shimmer in green fields. In less favoured climates, grow under a warm wall, where a group makes a splash of early colour.

A. × *fulgens* has brilliant scarlet petals; those of *A.* × *f.* 'Annulata Grandiflora' are scarlet with yellowish-black centres.
BULB   30 CM (12 IN)   FULL SUN   ZONES 6-9

CAMELLIA
Most camellias are soft pink, white or crimson, and the more fiery scarlet tints are rare. *C. japonica* 'James Allan' has bright, almost scarlet, variably formed double or semi-double (sometimes even single) flowers, and has a good habit. The scarlet *C.j.* 'Jupiter', sometimes blotched white, is smaller and suitable for planting in groups, as well as making a splendid pot plant.
LARGE EVERGREEN SHRUBS
HALF SHADE OR SHADE   ZONES 7-9
See also Foliage framework: green.

CHAENOMELES
JAPANESE QUINCE, JAPONICA
The early-flowering forms of *C. speciosa* include some with scarlet and orange-red petals. *C.s.* 'Kermesina Semiplena' is semi-double and scarlet, and 'Eximia' is deep brick-red. The hybrid forms of *C.* × *superba* make compact mounded shrubs and are not quite so vigorous. *C.* × *s.* 'Knap Hill Scarlet' is bright orange-red and 'Fire Dance' is a glowing scarlet, with prostrate habit suitable for growing as a specimen in a bed.
LARGE DECIDUOUS SHRUBS
FULL SUN   ZONES 6-9
See also Pinks and mauves: spring.

Fritillaria imperialis

CHEIRANTHUS WALLFLOWER
C. cheiri has many good colour forms from which to choose for containers or for drifts of colour in early borders. *C.c.* 'Fire King' is a vivid orange-red, 'Orange Bedder' is smaller and deep orange. Sow seed in summer and put in permanent flowering position in autumn.
BIENNIALS   20-45 CM (8-18 IN)
FULL SUN   ZONES 6-9
C. 'Harpur Crewe', an old wallflower, is a perennial with golden double flowers suitable for some dry cranny in a stone wall. Grow it from cuttings and be prepared to replace leggy plants every few years. Put it near the bright-coloured biennials or with pure white double arabis, *Arabis caucasica* 'Flore Pleno'. Try this perennial wallflower with the scarlet dwarf tulip, *Tulipa praestans* 'Fusilier'.
EVERGREEN PERENNIAL   25 CM (10 IN)
FULL SUN   ZONES 6-9
See also Clear yellows: spring.

CLIANTHUS
C. puniceus, parrot's bill or lobster claw, is a vigorous but tender scandent shrub, needing support to show off its scarlet claw-like racemes. Elegant pinnate leaves are carried on lax stems. Not very hardy, it makes a good conservatory plant, but will often succeed against a hot sunny wall.
SEMI-EVERGREEN CLIMBER
FULL SUN   ZONES 8-10

FRITILLARIA FRITILLARY
F. imperialis 'Aurora' is a deep, harsh golden-yellow, *F.i.* 'Orange Brilliant' is a brownish-orange, and 'Rubra Maxima' is dark dusky-red. Plant these strong-coloured fritillaries behind bronze and scarlet wallflowers for colour association, or behind emerging leaves of a perennial foliage plant, such as hosta or rodgersia, where good leaves will hide the fritillaries' untidy dying stems.
BULB   90 CM (36 IN)   FULL SUN   ZONES 7-9
See also Clear yellows: spring.

NARCISSUS DAFFODIL
Daffodils look their best when grown in drifts of one species and one colour. Personally I much prefer those where perianth and cup are similar shades, and these are obviously most useful for creating colour effects in association with other plants. Many narcissi are paler light yellows. Among the more strongly coloured for a 'hot' scheme are the Trumpet *N.* 'Golden Harvest', with deep yellow slightly twisted petals; a large-cupped deep yellow is *N.* 'Galway', the central cup just a little brighter than surrounding petals.
BULB   45 CM (18 IN)   FULL SUN   ZONES 6-9

EARLY SUMMER

RHODODENDRON

R. cinnabarinum is a (mainly) compact shrub (see also Foliage framework: green), with attractive leaves and pendent, bell-shaped tubular flowers, bright orange cinnabar-red in the type. *R. thomsonii*, with glaucous small leaves, has trusses of cup-shaped flowers which are crimson to scarlet. It is a parent of many fine hybrids, named forms of which can be chosen for specific colours.

MEDIUM EVERGREEN SHRUBS
HALF SHADE   ZONES 7-9

Many types of azalea, derived from different *Rhododendron* species, have bright orange and scarlet flower colours. It is best to see which are readily available, and plan carefully for progression of colour over the spring weeks. The dwarf evergreen Kurumes love deep woodland soil and make jewelled patterns in woodland glades.

SMALL EVERGREEN OR DECIDUOUS SHRUBS
HALF SUN   ZONES 6-8
See also Pinks and mauves: spring.

TULIPA TULIP

This is an opportunity to be dramatic. Plant tulips with mixed flame and red colours in their petals in spring and early-summer gardens. But use these rich colours sparingly, as they attract and dominate the eye. Pockets of these colours should be discovered in a garden walk and not shout at you across a quiet lawn. Municipal planting fulfils a different need: since people linger only for short visits in parks, bright patches of these eye-catching colours on a large scale are invigorating rather than exhausting.

T. greigi 'Red Riding Hood' has scarlet flowers 23-30 cm (9-12 in) held high above marbled and striped grey-green leaves. Flowering very early, it coincides with or precedes the species scarlet tulip *T. praestans*.

T. praestans 'Fusilier' has brilliant orange-scarlet flowers, 25 cm (10 in) high, four to six held on each stem. Plant on a rockery to complement vivid dwarf azaleas.

T. kaufmanniana 'Winner' has outer petals of cardinal-red, inner scarlet with yellow at base, 22 cm (8 in) high. A very early flowerer, it has attractive mottled leaves.

T. fosterana 'Madame Lefeber' (syn. *T.f.* 'Red Emperor') is bright scarlet, very large-flowered, and 38 cm (15 in) tall. It is hard to beat for sheer vulgarity of colour and size, yet can be daring and exciting in a carefully contrived colour scheme of red and orange. Of similar height, 'Orange Emperor' is orange with yellow inside petals.

BULBS   FULL SUN   ZONES 5-9
See also Clear yellows: spring.

ALYSSUM

There are good garden species which are grown as annuals, perennials and sub-shrubs, some (usually annuals) with white flowers, but most with pale or dark yellow flowers.

A. saxatile (sometimes *Aurinia saxatilis*), gold dust, carries corymbs of harsh yellow bloom above attractive grey-green leaves. It is useful for edging.

EVERGREEN SHRUBBY PERENNIAL
FULL SUN   ZONES 6-9
See also Clear yellows: early summer.

EMBOTHRIUM

E. coccineum, the Chilean fire bush, needs well-drained lime-free soil which can be enriched with annual mulches. Plant it in sheltered woodland in favoured gardens, where it remains almost evergreen. Brilliant orange-scarlet racemes are very freely carried in the best forms; the whole effect vivid and startlingly bright. Of upright habit, the type will sucker if conditions suit it, but *E.c. lanceolatum* makes a slender and graceful fastigiate shrub; *E.c.l.* 'Norquinco Valley' is particularly free in flower and the hardiest. Glowing among complementary green foliage, this shrub must have carefully chosen neighbours, avoiding rhododendrons with mauvish or pink tinges in the flower. Choose scarlet-flowered rhododendron hybrid 'Adder', or pure whites.

LARGE SEMI-EVERGREEN SHRUB
HALF SHADE   ZONES 8-10

EUPHORBIA SPURGE

E. griffithii 'Fireglow' has tomato-red flower-heads and foliage veined with red and orange. It looks lovely with pale yellows and spreads quickly with a running root system. Plant near the Chilean fire bush *Embothrium coccineum*, if the soil is acid, or next to pale fragrant *Rhododendron luteum* (the old *Azalea pontica*) in a neutral soil, with tangerine-flowered *Potentilla fruticosa* 'Tangerine' if the conditions are alkaline. The bronze- to orange-tinted leaves enhance a 'hot' border through the season.

DECIDUOUS PERENNIAL   90 CM (36 IN)
HALF SHADE OR SHADE   ZONES 6-9
See also Foliage framework: silver and grey.

GENISTA BROOM

G. lydia has slender pendulous branches smothered through early summer weeks in intensely yellow pea-flowers. Seldom growing beyond 90 cm (36 in) in height, but spreading to double that distance, it can find a place in even quite a modest-sized garden.

DWARF DECIDUOUS SHRUB
FULL SUN   ZONES 7-9

KNIPHOFIA RED HOT POKER

Kniphofias are variable in colour, some with flowers of orange and yellow, often scarlet-tipped, others plain pale single yellow. Different species and hybrids can be found to flower from early summer to autumn; many have good architectural leaves which are yucca-like in quality. Much hybridization has produced good named forms. *K.* 'Atlanta' produces orange-red pokers very early. Cut off dead flower-spikes and more flowers will follow in late summer.

EVERGREEN PERENNIAL   1.2 M (4 FT)
FULL SUN   ZONES 7-9

PAEONIA PEONY

P. peregrina (syn. *P. lobata*) has glossy leaves and single flowers of fiery scarlet, opening from a globular bud. The form *P.p.* 'Sunshine' is more salmon in tone, with an orange gleam, very desirable. Plant with bronze- and purple-leaved plants or with dark red and pink oriental poppies.

DECIDUOUS PERENNIAL   60 CM (24 IN)
FULL SUN   ZONES 7-9
See also Foliage framework: green.

Euphorbia griffithii 'Fireglow'

183

Papaver orientale

PAPAVER POPPY

P. orientale, the oriental poppy, has flat transparent papery flower-heads in exciting colours: pink, white with a black eye, bright scarlet, and rich glowing dark red. Leaves in early spring are attractive, greyish and hairy, but after flowering look most untidy. Arrange your colour scheme so that later-flowering perennials can be trained forward over poppy leaves and stalks. Miss Jekyll used the white-flowered perennial pea, *Lathyrus latifolius* 'Albus' for this purpose, yellow-flowered heleniums, or cloud-like blooms of gypsophila. It is worth taking trouble as the poppy flowers are glorious in season. Plant *P.o.* 'Marcus Perry', which is rich red, or try a 'hotter' shade of salmon such as 'Salmon Glow'. 'May Queen' is double and orange-vermilion. All these are worth looking for, taking their place as early flowerers in a border of hot bright summer colour.
DECIDUOUS PERENNIAL   75-90 CM (30-36 IN)
FULL SUN   ZONES 6-9

POTENTILLA

P. fruticosa forms are earlier in flower than most of the perennials. *P.f.* 'Tangerine' has bright copper-orange flowers, perhaps a little inconspicuous among the fresh green foliage, but worth having in a suitable colour arrangement, where the regular mound-like habit gives useful formality with plants of freer growth. Grow next to scarlet-flowered *Salvia fulgens* for later-season effects.
SMALL DECIDUOUS SHRUB
FULL SUN OR HALF SHADE   ZONES 6-9
See also Foliage framework: silver and grey.

PRIMULA

Among the candelabra primulas, the cultivar *P.* 'Red Hugh' has outstanding vivid orange-red flowers; flowers which seed more or less to a true colour. A colour as bright as this viewed on a chart seems hard and almost abrasive, but carefully placed with closely related bright oranges and reds makes a valuable link between the two neighbouring colours. Keep a separate garden area, perhaps in part shade where colours become duller, for this sort of colour scheme, and prepare the eye for it by planning a quiet approach through sober greens.
DECIDUOUS PERENNIAL   60-90 CM (24-36 IN)
FULL SUN OR HALF SHADE   ZONES 6-9

RHODODENDRON

R. haematodes makes a compact bush and, flowering later than many of the genus, extends the woodland season. Its bell-shaped brilliant scarlet-crimson flowers are eye-catching, and

it needs careful placing with early-summer colours. Perhaps it should have a site to flower alone, in shade, among greens of a woodland glade.
SMALL EVERGREEN SHRUB
HALF SHADE OR SHADE   ZONES 6-8
See also Pinks and mauves: spring.

ROSA ROSE
R. chinensis 'Mutabilis' has strange flowers, the petals changing from flame to buff, pink and coppery-red. Make a feature of it rather than using it in a colour scheme. The foliage has attractive bronze tints. It can grow high, but is most satisfactory when pruned annually into a compact shape.
MEDIUM TO LARGE DECIDUOUS SHRUB
FULL SUN   ZONES 5-9
R. foetida, the Austrian yellow briar, has arching stems bearing flowers of bright clear yellow; the sport *R.f.* 'Bicolor', Austrian copper, has flame-red inner petals, the outsides orange-yellow. It is one of the most vivid flower colours for this early season, and could be startling behind drifts of late-flowering scarlet tulips.
MEDIUM DECIDUOUS SHRUB
FULL SUN   ZONES 6-9
R. 'Maigold' has semi-double bronze-yellow flat flowers, fragrant and long-lasting even in a period of continuous hot sun, when other roses quickly fade. It flowers only once, but is very showy.
DECIDUOUS CLIMBER OR LARGE SHRUB
FULL SUN   ZONES 5-9
R. moyesii, a species rose and parent to many good seedlings, with erect branching very spiny stems and frond-like leaves, has scarlet-red single flowers. Later it carries flagon-shaped crimson fruits.
TALL DECIDUOUS SHRUB
FULL SUN   ZONES 6-9
R. 'Scarlet Fire' is a Gallica rose, but not at all like in habit. It throws out long arching canes bearing single flowers of bright blazing scarlet. Try growing it into shrubs with purple leaves.
LARGE DECIDUOUS SHRUB
FULL SUN   ZONES 6-9
R. 'Frensham' is a floribunda bush rose prone to mildew; if sprayed consistently it provides rich crimson-scarlet velvet-textured flowers held above glossy leaves. It is a good repeat-flowerer if regularly dead-headed. Grow next to bright reds or combine with the fierce yellow flowers of *Achillea* 'Coronation Gold'. Dark blue and purple flowers, too, will make an impact, but stick to deep shades: pastels and tints make the rose look garish.
MEDIUM DECIDUOUS SHRUB
FULL SUN   ZONES 5-9

R. 'Paul Crampel', a bush rose formerly classified as *polyantha*, has bright orange-scarlet double flowers and is vigorous enough to be part of a mixed border scheme of bright hot colours.
SMALL DECIDUOUS SHRUB
FULL SUN   ZONES 5-9
R. 'Danse du Feu', a large double-flowered climber, has fragrant blooms which open flat. They are bright scarlet at first, fading to a duller darkish purple. It has glossy leaves and flowers again in late summer.
DECIDUOUS CLIMBER   FULL SUN   ZONES 6-9
R. 'Longleat' is a vigorous miniature rose with flame-coloured flowers. Plant it in containers or in a raised bed.
DECIDUOUS SHRUB   30 CM (12 IN)
FULL SUN   ZONES 5-9
See also Pinks and mauves: early summer.

TULIPA TULIP
The larger and later-flowering tulips have a very wide range of colours. Deep yellows and scarlets can be found among most types, but look increasingly garish with size. They are

Rosa foetida 'Bicolor'

best in large-scale schemes in parks, and difficult to harmonize in small gardens.
 T. 'Orange Favourite' is a very bright orange-scarlet Parrot tulip, the petals tinged dark rose. Lily-flowered *T.* 'Queen of Sheba' has brownish-red flowers with broad margins of bright yellow.
BULBS   60 CM (24 IN)
FULL SUN   ZONES 5-9
See also Clear yellows: spring.

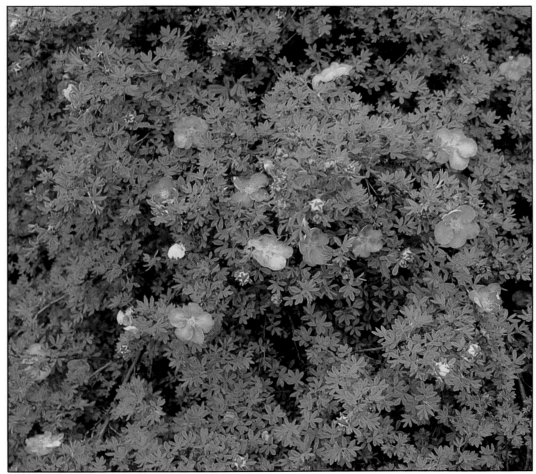

Potentilla fruticosa 'Tangerine'

SUMMER

ACHILLEA YARROW
A. filipendulina 'Gold Plate' has green feathery leaves above which flat flower-heads rise to make a symmetrical shape. Tiny daisy-flowers are a bright yellow. *A.f.* 'Coronation Gold' is very similar but the leaves are greyer and it has shorter flower-stems. Both are lovely with mauvish-violet, or suitable to enhance closely related red and orange flower colours. Grow next to scarlet *Potentilla* 'Gibson's Scarlet' or bronze-leaved *Dahlia* 'Bishop of Llandaff'.
DECIDUOUS PERENNIAL   1-1.2 M (3-4 FT)
FULL SUN   ZONES 5-9

ALSTROEMERIA PERUVIAN LILY
A. aurantiaca is useful and has flowers of variable light and dark orange. Very invasive, it needs careful placing but is invaluable for its colour range. *A.a.* 'Dover Orange' is deep and rich; it is striking with hot scarlets but is also strangely successful with pale pinks.
DECIDUOUS PERENNIAL   90 CM (36 IN)
FULL SUN   ZONES 7-9
See also Pinks and mauves: early summer.

ANTHEMIS
A. sancti-johannis has rich orange daisy flowers, a perfect pure colour rare in gardens, where orange is often harsh or muddied. Look for the true species and reject hybrid substitutes. Cut down immediately after flowering and water in a dry summer.
DECIDUOUS PERENNIAL   60 CM (24 IN)
FULL SUN   ZONES 6-9

Calendula officinalis 'Geisha Girl'

A. tinctoria 'Grallagh Gold' is a strong yellow. Parsley-like green leaves make feathery hummocks above which stems hold upturned yellow daisies.
DECIDUOUS PERENNIAL   60-90 CM (24-36 IN)
FULL SUN   ZONES 6-9

ASTILBE
A. × arendsii is a group with many named hybrids among which flowers with vivid scarlet colouring can be found. One of the best is *A. × a.* 'Red Sentinel', deep crimson-scarlet open flowers held above typical feathery foliage, which is mahogany-tinted in spring.

Alstroemeria aurantiaca

Grow in moist soil. It flowers early, will coincide with pale sulphur-yellow *Alchemilla mollis* and looks rich with green hosta leaves.
DECIDUOUS PERENNIAL   75-90 CM (30-36 IN)
FULL SUN OR HALF SHADE   ZONES 7-9
See also Pinks and mauves: summer.

CALCEOLARIA
Calceolarias have strange pouch-like flowers in yellow colouring, often marked brown and orange. Many forms are developed for growing as pot plants in glasshouses and these tend to have the more spectacular flowers, shades of yellow, orange and red, spotted and blotched with crimson. Look for named varieties of *C. × herbeohybrida*, or F₁ seedlings of the plain bright yellow *C. integrifolia* (see Clear yellows: late summer). Both types can be grown as greenhouse pot plants or bedding annuals.
SHRUBBY PERENNIAL   45 CM (18 IN)
FULL SUN   ZONES 8-10

CALENDULA MARIGOLD
C. officinalis, pot marigold, has daisy-flowers in shades of pale to dark yellow, orange and pinkish. A short-lived perennial grown as an annual, sow in the previous autumn – possibly with cloche protection – for early flowering. They thrive in the poorest soil, and being undemanding, groups can make splendid splashes of colour in the front of a border or in dry corners. *C.o.* 'Geisha Girl' is a reddish-orange and 'Orange King' is deep orange. Grow these with pale yellow-flowered neighbours or with scarlet roses for sunset effects.
ANNUAL   30 CM (12 IN)   FULL SUN   ZONES 5-9

CESTRUM
C. aurantiacum has long tubular flowers of deep orange-yellow. Not very hardy, it thrives in a conservatory or in a pot in full sun. Grow it next to orange lilies and bright blue *Salvia patens*. Soft and hairy bronze-tinted leaves make the plant attractive even when not in flower, but in a cold winter it can be cut to the ground.
MEDIUM SEMI-EVERGREEN WALL SHRUB
FULL SUN   ZONES 9-10

DESFONTAINEA
D. spinosa is a tender slow-growing shrub for sheltered woodland and deep acid loam. The leaves are small and spiny like those of holly, and the tubular flowers are scarlet with yellow throats. A rare form, *D.s.* 'Harold Comber', has vermilion to scarlet flowers, longer than the type.
MEDIUM EVERGREEN SHRUB
HALF SHADE   ZONES 8-10

ECCREMOCARPUS
CHILEAN GLORY FLOWER
E. scaber, although not reliably hardy, always seeds freely so needs little attention, plants reaching to 3 m (10 ft) in a season. A climber, it loves to clamber through wall shrubs, its tubular orange-scarlet flowers startling among dark green-foliaged plants. It is not successful with pinks and mauves but can be rich and vivid with scarlet and crimson climbing roses. Crimson-red seedlings are desirable and easier to use with the other blue-pigmented reds. Surprisingly they tend to come true from seed.
EVERGREEN SEMI-HERBACEOUS CLIMBER
FULL SUN   ZONES 8-10

ESCHSCHOLZIA   CALIFORNIA POPPY
Usually grown as brightly coloured annuals, the cultivars of *E. californica* have papery transparent poppy-like flowers in orange-yellow colours. Plant a whole bed in mixed colours of yellows and oranges. Sow in the ground in early spring and thin out as required. The soil should be poor or growth will be lax and lush.
ANNUAL   20-40 CM (8-16 IN)
FULL SUN   ZONES 6-9

FREMONTODENDRON
Petalless flowers with conspicuous bright yellow calyces are carried over a very long season. A plant of the tender *F. californicum*, grown well against a hot sunny wall, is spectacular. Plant white-flowering *Solanum jasminoides* beside it, or even the tougher blue-mauve potato-flowered *Solanum crispum* – but keep away from pink and mauve flowering roses. Ceanothus and violet-blue *Abutilon ×suntense* also make good complementary companions, the long flowering season of the fremontodendron making it the dominant partner in a yellow-blue planting scheme.
EVERGREEN WALL SHRUB
FULL SUN   ZONES 8-10

GAZANIA
Gazanias are tender and usually grown as annuals; cuttings should be taken at the end of each summer. The daisy-flowers, which close in the evening, are mainly orange, but are centrally zoned with brown and even pinkish shades. *G.* 'Bridget' is orange-yellow with maroon zone. 'Silver Beauty' has intensely grey, almost white, leaves and yellow-orange black-centred daisy-flowers. Grow them as colour groups at the front of a border or in pots, where both foliage and flowers are clearly visible.
EVERGREEN PERENNIAL   23 CM (9 IN)
FULL SUN   ZONES 8-10

Eschscholzia californica

GENISTA   BROOM
G. cinerea has arching branches covered in the flowering season in scented bright yellow pea-flowers. A very strong eye-catching colour, this bush can relate to a definite colour scheme of oranges and reds, or remain a focal point among green leaves.
LARGE DECIDUOUS SHRUB
FULL SUN   ZONES 7-9

GEUM
G. chiloense is usually grown in gardens as named forms. A useful perennial border plant, geums have yellow and red bowl-shaped flowers held above pinnate green leaves. *G.c.* 'Lady Stratheden' is a warm yellow, and 'Mrs Bradshaw' a flaming brick-red. Grow them at the front of a border; copper-coloured foliage of plants such as *Crocosmia × crocosmiiflora* 'Solfatare' give contrast.
DECIDUOUS PERENNIAL   60 CM (24 IN)
FULL SUN   ZONES 6-9

HELIANTHEMUM   ROCK ROSE
Rock roses opening their flowers with the sun have a wide colour range equally effective if planted in a mass of one definite hue or grown as if from a packet of mixed seeds. The strong hot colours are well represented in named forms. *H. nummularium* 'Ben Heckla' is a deep orange-bronze, *H.n.* 'Beech Park Scarlet' a vivid crimson-scarlet. A popular double red is 'Mrs C.W. Earle' (syn. 'Fireball'), and 'Red Orient' is a single scarlet. The leaves are valuable at the front of a border all year, but an open site is essential for a fine colour display, and the flowers remain closed unless in full sunshine.
DWARF EVERGREEN SHRUB
FULL SUN   ZONES 7-9

Geum chiloense 'Mrs Bradshaw'

HEMEROCALLIS   DAY LILY
The old favourite *H. fulva* 'Kwanso Flore-pleno' (syn. *H. disticha* 'Flore Pleno'), with richly scented double orange-buff flowers and spreading root system, is desirable. The emergent spring foliage can be as bright as a flower colour. *H.* 'Cartwheels' is a bolder, brighter orange than *H. fulva*. There are several modern hybrids listed as having orange or golden flowers, but colour descriptions seem far from accurate: it is best to see them in flower before choosing.
DECIDUOUS PERENNIAL   60-120 CM (24-48 IN)
FULL SUN OR SHADE   ZONES 6-9

Helianthemum nummularium 'Ben Heckla'

IMPATIENS

I. wallerana, busy Lizzie, usually grown as a floriferous house plant and very easy to cultivate, has five-petalled bright scarlet flowers. Some of the small bedding cultivars are useful, making bright splashes of colour in a sunny border and flowering all season. Choose a colour in a garden centre or obtain unmixed seed.

PERENNIAL OR ANNUAL   20-60 CM (8-24 IN)
FULL SUN   ZONES 8-9

KNIPHOFIA RED HOT POKER

Some of the named hybrids can be chosen for a 'hot' scheme, dwarf forms fitting into the scale of a small garden. It is probably best to get named types from a reputable nursery as available.

Summer-flowering bright scarlet *K. uvaria nobilis* (syn. *K. praecox*) has very long bright flower-spikes and continues flowering into late summer. *K. rooperi* (syn. *K. uvaria*) 'C.M.

Prichard' also has a long flowering period, continuing well into autumn. Tall orange spikes rear above lax green leaves.

DECIDUOUS PERENNIALS   1.2-1.8 M (4-6 FT)
FULL SUN   ZONES 7-9

LIGULARIA

Herbaceous daisy-flowers (sometimes classified in the genus *Senecio*), these are useful perennials for moist soil. *L. dentata* (*Senecio clivorum*) 'Desdemona' and 'Othello' have large deep orange daisy-flowers held on branched stems above mahogany-backed metallic-green leaves. Plant with quiet green- or grey-leaved hostas.

DECIDUOUS PERENNIAL   1.2 M (4 FT)
FULL SUN OR HALF SHADE   ZONES 6-9

LILIUM LILY

L. 'Enchantment', an Asiatic hybrid of the Mid-Century group, has erect flowers of orange with brown speckles, and is sturdy, easy

and reliable. 'Cinnabar', another lily of the Mid-Century group, is redder, very vivid and makes a splendid cluster in a prominent border position.

L. hansonii has stems up to 1.5 m (5 ft) tall, each bearing a dozen or so orange-yellow flowers, conspicuously brown-spotted.

L. bulbiferum croceum, the old herring lily – so described because flowering time coincided with the return of the Dutch herring-fishing fleets – coincides with blue-flowered delphiniums. This was a combination recommended by Gertrude Jekyll: blue and orange glowing and intense beside each other in a border. This could, using different plants flowering in season, be the basis for a whole scheme, shades of blue and orange in blocks and drifts giving constant contrast.

BULBS   1-1.5 M (3-5 FT)
FULL SUN OR SHADE   ZONES 6-9

LONICERA HONEYSUCKLE

L. × *brownii* 'Fuchsioides', the scarlet trumpet honeysuckle, is always an eye-catcher, its long orange-scarlet trumpets vivid and glowing at a distance. I prefer it isolated among dark green foliage, perhaps to be followed in seasonal sequence by the more vigorous orange trumpet vine, *Campsis radicans*. The semi-evergreen trumpet honeysuckle *L. sempervirens* needs a warm wall, where it will bear rich orange-scarlet tubular flowers with yellow colouring within. It seems a shy flowerer, or perhaps takes many seasons to get well established.

DECIDUOUS CLIMBERS   FULL SUN   ZONES 7-9
See also Clear yellows: summer.

LYCHNIS CAMPION

L. chalcedonica, Maltese or Jerusalem cross, has heads of very clear scarlet flowers, unfortunately although flat not quite broad enough in proportion to the plant's general size. Nevertheless it is invaluable for its pure bright colour, and can be used in daring colour schemes. Grow next to deeper reds, or experiment with neighbouring bronze and purple leaves which absorb some of the 'hot' colour. Grey and silver leaves make it seem even brighter without destroying the purity.

DECIDUOUS PERENNIAL   90 CM (36 IN)
FULL SUN   ZONES 6-9

MIMULUS

MONKEY FLOWER, MONKEY MUSK
M. aurantiacus (syn. *Diplacus glutinosus*) has pale orange flowers and a sprawling habit. Grow it in an urn to trail downwards or at the edge of paving, but not near too narrow a path since it is brittle and resents being trodden on. It rarely lasts through a winter except in the

Lilium 'Enchantment'

mildest climates, but cuttings are easily struck in late summer.
DWARF EVERGREEN SHRUB
FULL SUN   ZONES 9-10
M. guttatus, monkey flower or musk, is a larger version of the yellow *M. luteus*, its bright flowers splashed with dots and blotches of mahogany-brown. Plant in moist soil and allow to ramp and make drifts with astilbe and rodgersia. It can grow with its roots covered in water to a depth of 5-7 cm (2-3 in).
DECIDUOUS PERENNIAL   60 CM (24 IN)
FULL SUN OR HALF SHADE   ZONES 5-9

PAPAVER POPPY
P. nudicaule, the Iceland poppy, and the hairy grey-leaved *P. rupifragum*, with orange-red flowers, from Spain, are effective if grown in substantial clumps. Shades and tints of orange and yellow in the former associate with grey foliage in a well-drained hot border, while *P. rupifragum* (with *P. pilosum* and *P. atlanticum*) are more delicate and silky. They seldom survive for long, but seed prolifically – sometimes where not wanted.
DECIDUOUS PERENNIALS OR ANNUALS
60 CM (24 IN)   FULL SUN   ZONES 7-9

PELARGONIUM 'GERANIUM'
P. × hortorum 'Ringo', a zonal pelargonium, is bright scarlet, best in municipal bedding schemes or for emphatic eye-catching planting. *P. × h.* 'Scarlet' is a little less glaring.
EVERGREEN SUB-SHRUB
FULL SUN   ZONES 9-10
See also Pinks and mauves: summer.

PENSTEMON
P. × 'Schoenholzeri' is scarlet and very free-flowering, an ideal plant for a border of reds, continuing until late autumn. It is reasonably hardy, but cuttings taken the previous autumn tend to make bushier, more compact plants; if kept under glass they will start to flower earlier; the plants outside need pruning to the ground in spring.
EVERGREEN PERENNIAL SUB-SHRUB
90 CM (36 IN)   FULL SUN   ZONES 8-10
See also Pinks and mauves: summer.

POTENTILLA CINQUEFOIL
Among the herbaceous potentillas *P.* 'Flamenco', with bright red single flowers, and 'Gibson's Scarlet', correspondingly more scarlet, are strong growers for a mixed or perennial border. Notice the texture of the petals of each flower and the darker veining.
DECIDUOUS PERENNIAL   45 CM (18 IN)
FULL SUN   ZONES 6-9
See also Foliage framework: silver and grey.

SALVIA SAGE
S. fulgens, the cardinal sage, has bright red-hooded, velvet-textured flowers, held above green bronze-tinted leaves. Not very hardy, and tending to become woody and ungainly, it is best grown annually from cuttings. Keep one plant under glass and strike cuttings in early spring; those already rooted the previous autumn are less satisfactory. Grow as a specimen in a container, since it is sufficiently exotic to attract attention. In a border its hot colour matches bright red roses, dahlias and the continuous-flowering *Potentilla* 'Gibson's Scarlet', to which it is a perfect companion.
SMALL TO MEDIUM EVERGREEN SHRUB
FULL SUN   ZONES 8-10
S. neurepia has fresh green leaves and grows quite large in warm areas. Elsewhere it can be cut to the ground in winter, but may well recover, perhaps flowering rather later. The small flowers are a brilliant scarlet.
MEDIUM SEMI-EVERGREEN SHRUB
FULL SUN   ZONES 8-10
See also Foliage framework: silver and grey.

TAGETES MARIGOLD
T. erecta, the African marigold, is a fiery-flowered annual with single or double daisy-flowers of yellow, gold and orange. Useful infillers for summer colour in new borders, and with deeply cut scented and glossy leaves. Choose suitable colours from good F_1 hybrid named seed, sow early and plant out after the last frost.

Lonicera sempervirens

T. patula, French marigold – but from Mexico – makes bushy floriferous plants for sunny borders and for containers. Flower colours range from yellow and gold to browns and crimson. Often used as edging to rose-beds, reputedly helping to prevent blackspot. Hybrids of African and French marigolds cover a large number of named plants.
ANNUALS   20-75 CM (8-30 IN)
FULL SUN   ZONES 9-10
See also Clear yellows: late summer.

Potentilla 'Gibson's Scarlet'

LATE SUMMER

Crocosmia × crocosmiiflora

Lilium tigrinum

ANTIRRHINUM SNAPDRAGON
A. majus 'Monarch Orange' is low-growing and rust-resistant. Plant it and *A.m.* Nanum 'Scarlet Monarch' in thick clumps between grey-leaved shrubs or other closely related flower colours.
ANNUAL 45 CM (18 IN) FULL SUN ZONES 6-9
See also Clear yellows: late summer.

CAMPSIS
C. radicans, trumpet vine, has brilliant orange and scarlet flowers held in terminal clusters. Prune hard in winter for prolific flowering on the current year's wood; even so, a good summer is essential, and a warm site against a heat-reflecting wall. Pinnate leaves are no real compensation if flowering is meagre. The colouring of its flowers is a prelude to autumn.
DECIDUOUS CLIMBER FULL SUN ZONES 6-10

CANNA
C. indica, Indian shot, usually kept under glass but surviving in a warm microclimate, has red and yellow flowers with brown calyces. *C. × generalis* hybrids with other species, give a wider colour range where bright flowers combine with shades of bronze or green foliage for exotic colour. Among these hybrids *C. × g.*

'Le Roi Humbert', with copper leaves and red blooms, compares with *Dahlia* 'Bishop of Llandaff' for use as bedding in a strong hot colour scheme. It is used effectively in the red border at Hidcote in Gloucestershire. 'Wyoming' has apricot-orange flowers and purplish leaves.
DECIDUOUS RHIZOME 1.5 M (5 FT)
FULL SUN ZONES 9-10
See also Strong reds: foliage.

COREOPSIS
C. verticillata has hair-like fine foliage and very bright brassy-yellow daisy-flowers. For bright pure colour a group of this fine daisy is hard to beat. Grow it next to dark reds, bright orange curtonus or crocosmia with sword-like leaf contrast, or associate it with pale yellow × *Solidaster luteus*.
DECIDUOUS PERENNIAL 60 CM (24 IN)
FULL SUN ZONES 6-9

CROCOSMIA MONTBRETIA
The old favourite *C. × crocosmiiflora* (syn. *Tritonia × crocosmiiflora*) is not to be despised, and is a weedproof colonizer for rough corners – but some of its hybrid seedlings (with *C. aurea*) are much less invasive and cover a range of 'hot' colours: the pale yellow *C. × c.* 'Solfatare' is in Clear yellows.
   C. masonorum, with flowers turned upwards at the tip of long stems among green sword-like leaves, adds dimension to a hot border, harmonizing with closely related darker oranges and reds as well as with the paler cool yellow colours. You need space for this plant, a rapid colonizer, and should plant at least two strong clumps in any scheme: one alone draws the eye as a dominating focal point. Try its orange-vermilion flowers next to the pale blue *Buddleia ×* 'Lochinch' or the darker blue *Ceanothus* 'Topaz'. Crocosmia and the numerous hybrids – many named forms have flower-colour variation – thrive in rich soil.
DECIDUOUS PERENNIAL 60-100 CM (24-36 IN)
FULL SUN OR SHADE ZONES 7-9

CURTONUS
C. paniculatus (syn. *Antholyza paniculata*) has long ridged sword-like leaves and arching flower-sprays of orange-red trumpets. Where space is limited the hybrids with the genus crocosmia have the best colour forms, combining the strong vibrant flower colour of the former with the larger more architectural leaves of the curtonus. Fiery reds, flame and orange make these hybrids invaluable. *C.p.* 'Bressingham Blaze' is an intense orange.
CORM 75-120 CM (30-48 IN)
FULL SUN OR SHADE ZONES 7-9

DAHLIA
Flowering over a long period, well-grown and carefully staked dahlias contribute reliable blocks of late-summer colour. The most vivid hues are difficult to find in other flowering plants. The many hybrids are best obtained from a specialist dahlia nursery, since flower colour and form as well as leaf colour should be taken into account. Avoid artificial shapes and look for simple flower-heads. Enriched soil and regular dead-heading ensure success. In mild areas the tubers can be left in the ground all winter.
   D. 'Bishop of Llandaff' is an old favourite, now seldom available in commerce but often obtainable from a friendly private garden. (See also Strong reds: foliage.) Other old varieties are *D.* 'Ella Britten', a bright gold, and 'Madame S. Stappers', bright orange-red, neither of them growing too tall, and both with green-bronze leaves.
DECIDUOUS TUBERS 60-120 CM (24-48 IN)
FULL SUN ZONES 9-10

FUCHSIA
F. fulgens is tender but has such lovely colouring that it is well worth considering for containers and for ornamental use in the house. Soft pinkish-red stems bear bronze leaves and the terminal clusters of tubular flowers are scarlet, tipped with green. Keep at temperatures above freezing during the winter and repot in spring, frequently giving liquid fertilizer before and during the long flowering period. Tip cuttings taken in spring are easily rooted.
SMALL DECIDUOUS SHRUB
FULL SUN ZONES 9-10
See also Pinks and mauves: summer.

HELENIUM SNEEZEWEED
H. bigelovii 'Aurantiacum' is bright yellow with darker yellow centres. Grow it with strong reds and related orange, with pale yellows and with nearby plants providing striking foliage through the earlier months of summer; helenium foliage and habit are not distinguished, and it is grown for fleeting flower colour. See also Clear yellows.
DECIDUOUS PERENNIAL 1.2 M (4 FT)
FULL SUN ZONES 6-9

HELIANTHUS SUNFLOWER
The late-flowering *H. salicifolius* (syn. *H. orgyalis*) has willow-like leaves of mid-green and bears elegant sprays of yellow daisy-flowers, with a purple-brown disc.
DECIDUOUS PERENNIAL 1.8 M (6 FT)
FULL SUN ZONES 6-9
H. annuus, the annual sunflower, has coarse

heart-shaped leaves and huge cartwheel heads of yellow florets with central discs of brown or purple. A double form, *H.a.* 'Flore Pleno', is vigorous. Growing very tall, these annuals are fun to have for a season but probably too coarse for inclusion in a garden every year. Grow them in a clump, to shock in a garden where much of the planting is carefully planned in conventional muted greys and misty colours.
ANNUAL   TO 3 M (IO FT)
FULL SUN   ZONES 6-9
The *H. × multiflorus* hybrids (*H. annuus × H. decapetalus*) start to flower earlier but continue into late summer. *H. × m.* 'Loddon Gold' is a rich golden yellow and 'Miss Mellish' is deep yellow.
DECIDUOUS PERENNIAL
90-150 CM (36-60 IN)   FULL SUN   ZONES 6-9

KNIPHOFIA RED HOT POKER
Low-growing pokers with grass-like leaves and smaller flower-spikes are useful in modest-sized borders. *K. macowanii* is a deep orange-red and *K. nelsonii* 'Major' is flame-red.
DECIDUOUS PERENNIALS   75 CM (30 IN)
FULL SUN   ZONES 7-9

LIGULARIA
L. przewalski has tall black stems carrying uncharacteristic spires of daisy-flowers, of deep yellow. The leaves are deeply cut. Tough and invasive, this elegant plant would be ideal in a real wild garden, but it is difficult to keep within bounds in a mixed border. Try this bright yellow with 'blued' crimsons of phlox or lythrums, but not with pale rose tints, which it will injure.
DECIDUOUS PERENNIAL   1.8 M (6 FT)
FULL SUN OR HALF SHADE   ZONES 6-9

LILIUM LILY
L. tigrinum, tiger lily, is usually grown in the vigorous forms of the more floriferous *L.t. fortunei* and *L.t.f.* 'Giganteum', which is an excellent tall-growing lily for a mixed border. Orange-red petals are spotted and flecked with black and purple. Tiger lilies are not fussy about situation but prefer acid soil, and can easily be increased by potting up freely produced stem bulbils.
BULBS   90-180 CM (36-72 IN)
FULL SUN   ZONES 7-9

LOBELIA
L. cardinalis, the North American cardinal flower, has a basal rosette of bronze leaves above which spikes of lipped scarlet flowers make a splendid and exciting show. Not reliably hardy, they need rich damp soil during the summer but should be covered with

bracken in winter. They survive consistently cold winter conditions; it is warm spells in winter that, by encouraging premature growth, destroy them. Hybrid *L.c.* 'Queen Victoria' has deep red flowers, and 'Dark Crusader' is even deeper – perhaps the best. *L. fulgens* from Mexico has purplish leaves and scarlet flower-spikes, but is more tender.
DECIDUOUS PERENNIALS
30-90 CM (12-36 IN)   FULL SUN   ZONES 8-10

MONARDA BERGAMOT
M. didyma, bee balm, needs moisture to survive, quickly dying in even short periods of drought, but is worth growing well. Bright rich red flowers have purple calyces and make a splendid group among neighbouring bronze-leaved plants.
DECIDUOUS PERENNIAL
90-120 CM (36-48 IN)   FULL SUN   ZONES 7-9

PHLOX
P. paniculata 'Signal' has scarlet flowers; *P.p.* 'Starfire' is brilliant red, deeper and more glowing. Grow them next to bright orange crocosmias and curtonus as part of a planned 'hot' scheme. They need rich soil.
DECIDUOUS PERENNIAL
90-120 CM (36-48 IN)   FULL SUN   ZONES 6-9
See also The whites: late summer.

RUDBECKIA CONEFLOWER
Rudbeckias are grown in gardens as relatively short-lived perennials and as annuals, many with lighter flower colour (see Clear yellows: late summer). The best late-flowering species is perennial *R. hirta*, black-eyed Susan, with a branching habit and golden ray petals with deep brown central cone. *R.h. pulcherrima* 'Gloriosa' comes in shades of yellow and brownish-red. Annual forms of *R. hirta* are useful for infilling gaps in newly planted borders. Bristly branching stems carry bright gold black-centred daisies. Sow in spring for summer and late-summer show.
DECIDUOUS ANNUALS AND PERENNIALS
30-90 CM (12-36 IN)   FULL SUN   ZONES 7-10

TROPAEOLUM
T. majus, nasturtium, is a climbing or trailing annual with wavy-edged green leaves and yellow, orange or red flowers. There are many good garden strains, all easily grown in pots and hanging baskets, or allowed to clamber over a trellis or fence.
ANNUAL   TO 1.8 M (6 FT)   FULL SUN   ZONES 6-9
T. speciosum, flame nasturtium, is a startling scarlet-flowered climber loving to trail through deciduous shrubs in cool north-facing borders in acid or neutral soil. A difficult plant to

Zauschneria californica

establish, wayward and temperamental, it grows in some gardens and refuses others. Pale light green delicate leaves are lobed and stems clamber up any available support. Plant among spring-flowering azaleas and summer-flowering roses. It is jewel-like twining into the north side of yew hedges. After a mild winter flowering is early and plenty of seed may ripen. Sow at once, and pot on into compost before planting out, never disturbing the fleshy roots. It is worth every effort.
DECIDUOUS HERBACEOUS CLIMBER
SHADE   ZONES 7-10

ZAUSCHNERIA
CALIFORNIA FUCHSIA
To succeed *Z. californica* needs a well-drained site and hot sun. Pale grey hairy leaves make attractive mounds above which slender erect stems bear scarlet trumpets. Best as a border edging or on a rock garden. Divide in spring or take basal cuttings as material appears in early summer. The pale foliage and scarlet flowers are an uncommon combination, so a mass of this little plant flowering prolifically, as it will if circumstances suit it, is particularly desirable.
DWARF WOODY-BASED PERENNIAL
FULL SUN   ZONES 8-10

AUTUMN FRUITS AND BERRIES

This section is concerned not with botanical definitions of fruit and berries but with their colour contribution. Blue, yellow and white fruits are treated in this book as incidental colour much in the same way as flowers, but as bright red tends to be the dominant fruit colour of late summer and autumn, the plants on which this is found are grouped here in a section of their own. Unfortunately, since birds' eyesight is particularly adapted to seeing reds, seed dispersal is assured at the expense of appearance: the red fruits seldom play a part in garden colour for more than a few weeks.

ACTAEA BANEBERRY
Actaea, with ferny astilbe-like leaves of fresh green, has species with both red and white berries. *A. rubra*, red baneberry, carries its clusters of glistening scarlet berries in spikes above the fern-like leaves. Grow it in colourful clumps between drifts of hostas: both plants thrive in cool shade and moist soil.
DECIDUOUS PERENNIAL   45 CM (18 IN)
HALF SHADE OR SHADE   ZONES 4-8

Euonymus europaeus

Iris foetidissima

ARBUTUS STRAWBERRY TREE
A. unedo, the Killarney strawberry tree, produces its red fruits in late autumn, sometimes simultaneously with its white pitcher-like flowers. Unusual among *Ericaceae* for being lime-tolerant, these small trees with attractive deep brown gnarled bark cheer the winter landscape.
LARGE EVERGREEN SHRUB
FULL SUN OR HALF SHADE   ZONES 7-9
See also Foliage framework: green.

AUCUBA
Grow female clones of the evergreen *A. japonica* and its many variegated forms to get clusters of bright scarlet berries from late summer to spring: male plants are also needed for fruit. Thriving in poor soil and deep shade, these shrubs are useful foliage and fruiting specimens when there are few seasonal flowers to give colour.
LARGE EVERGREEN SHRUB
SHADE   ZONES 7-9

BERBERIS BARBERRY
B. prattii, *B. × rubrostilla* and *B. wilsoniae* forms all have coral-red berries. *B. prattii* is the largest, for open woodland, and has pinker fruit, while *B. × rubrostilla* and *B. wilsoniae* are useful shrubs in a mixed flower border. The latter has sea-green leaves which, before they fall, assume autumn tints to coincide with the salmon- to coral-red fruits.
SMALL TO LARGE DECIDUOUS SHRUBS
FULL SUN OR HALF SHADE   ZONES 6-9
See also Foliage framework: green.

COTONEASTER
C. bullatus has attractive bullate leaves, richly coloured in autumn, among which its large bright red fruits are conspicuous.
MEDIUM DECIDUOUS SHRUB
FULL SUN OR HALF SHADE   ZONES 6-8
C. × watereri 'Cornubia', almost a tree in dimension, and almost evergreen, carries large red fruits through the winter months. It might well be the important winter tree in any garden, rich and glowing in colour for such a long period; it is also distinguished in summer with foliage clothing it to the ground.
LARGE SEMI-EVERGREEN SHRUB
FULL SUN OR HALF SHADE   ZONES 6-8
C. horizontalis, with its herringbone pattern of horizontal branches, is well known for its architectural quality. In autumn the foliage becomes pinkish-bronze, a foil for the rich scarlet fruits.
MEDIUM DECIDUOUS SHRUB
FULL SUN OR SHADE   ZONES 6-10
See also Foliage framework: green.

CRATAEGUS THORN
C. × lavallei is a dense-headed small tree. The bright orange-red fruits persist almost all winter, giving vivid contrast among rich green leaves, which are generally held until late autumn. This valuable tree links the solely ornamental with more domestic fruiting trees and is a useful bridge between garden and landscape, or arboretum and orchard.
SMALL DECIDUOUS TREE
FULL SUN   ZONES 5-8

EUONYMUS SPINDLE TREE
The most striking spindles have orange-yellow fruits; these later split to reveal seed which ripens to scarlet. Others have large scarlet and rose-pink fruits.
    E. europaeus, the common spindle, has attractive scarlet fruits for a hedgerow or woodland corner. *E. myrianthus* has flat-topped square-sided yellowish fruits, which split by midwinter to make a glowing picture of yellow and red among the evergreen leaves.
LARGE EVERGREEN SHRUBS
FULL SUN OR HALF SHADE   ZONES 6-9
E. oxyphyllus has carmine fruits which, in late summer, split to reveal scarlet seeds, and which hang on long slender stalks among richly purple-tinted foliage.
SMALL DECIDUOUS TREE
FULL SUN OR HALF SHADE   ZONES 5-8
E. planipes (syn. *E. sachalinensis*) has scarlet fruits and brilliant autumn foliage tints.
LARGE DECIDUOUS SHRUB
FULL SUN   ZONES 7-9
See also The whites: foliage.

HYPERICUM
H. × inodorum has pale yellow flowers, followed by attractive red fruits. Its form *H. × i.* 'Elstead' is the best, the fruits ripening to orange-scarlet. Grow it in a clump on the edge of woodland, where it links the flower garden with mellow autumn colours beyond.
MEDIUM DECIDUOUS SHRUB
FULL SUN OR HALF SHADE   ZONES 6-9

ILEX HOLLY
The many holly species, hybrids and cultivars are grown for their glossy leaves, architectural form and suitability as hedging plants, and for their glowing red berries for garden and Christmas decoration. Look for good female clones which berry freely. There is plenty of choice between those with plain green leaves and those with gold or silver variegation. I prefer the scarlet berries among variegated leaves: the glossy surface makes plain green almost too bright and complementary to the scarlet fruit. Others love the Christmas effects

and brilliance of the combination of almost saturated green and scarlet.

I. × altaclarensis 'Hendersonii' has dull matt leaves and may bear heavy crops of large fruit. *I. aquifolium* has attractive free-fruiting forms with variegated leaves, but beware some which bear female names such as 'Golden Queen' and 'Silver Queen' and are male. Choose your plant from a good list and then make certain you get just the leaf form and colour appropriate.

LARGE EVERGREEN SHRUBS
FULL SUN OR SHADE   ZONES 6-9

IRIS
I. foetidissima, the European stinking gladdon, gladwin or roast beef plant, has dark green grass-like leaves and rather insignificant greenish or buff flowers. However, in the late summer, pods burst to reveal startling scarlet-orange seeds which persist for some time. It makes lovely (self-seeding) natural groups under deciduous trees and is beautiful and effective when used indoors as flower decoration. The form *I.f.* 'Citrina' has pale yellow or mauvish flowers and bears exceptionally large seed pods.

EVERGREEN PERENNIAL   45 CM (18 IN)
HALF SHADE   ZONES 6-9

MALUS FLOWERING CRAB
M. × 'John Downie' is one of the best fruiting crab apples, lovely to look at and culinarily useful for jelly preserve. The large conical bright orange and red fruits are one of the sights in orchard and garden in late summer. A regular-shaped tree beautiful in flower and fruiting season, grow it formally in pairs to frame a vista or gateway.

SMALL DECIDUOUS TREE
FULL SUN   ZONES 6-9

PYRACANTHA FIRETHORN
Pyracanthas are vigorous evergreens with feathery white flowers in summer, in general followed by fruits of vivid red, orange and yellow. One of the best is *P. coccinea* 'Lalandèi', which can be planted to make a tall dome. A specimen plant needs little attention and care. Alternatively it responds well to formal pruning against a wall, where the skilful gardener can time his pruning to allow free fruiting. Large orange-red fruits last well into winter.

LARGE EVERGREEN SHRUB
FULL SUN OR SHADE   ZONES 6-8

ROSA ROSE
Roses are grown for their splendid coloured hips as well as for flower, leaf colour and fragrance. Roses have been fully described in their appropriate colour sections, but this list indicates fruit colours. Shrub roses with one season of flowering should be chosen for good colourful hips.

Rosa glauca (syn. *R. rubrifolia*), one of the best fruiting roses, has clusters of orange-red berries, very freely carried especially after a warm summer. The greyish-green, almost glaucous, leaves make a perfect setting to the rich fruit and enhance schemes with strong purple neighbouring foliage.

MEDIUM DECIDUOUS SHRUB
FULL SUN OR HALF SHADE   ZONES 6-9
R. 'Highdownensis' has magnificent flagon-shaped orange-scarlet fruit, carried sparsely on tall erect branches. *R. moyesii*, one of the latter's parents, has bright flagon-shaped dark red fruits, fitting well into a colour scheme of 'blued' reds and dark colours.

TALL DECIDUOUS SHRUBS
FULL SUN   ZONES 6-9
R. rugosa and cultivars in general have bright red tomato-shaped fruit, most freely borne on single-flowered types. Often carried simultaneously with the second crop of flowers in late summer.

MEDIUM DECIDUOUS SHRUBS
FULL SUN   ZONES 6-9
R. longicuspis, a vigorous semi-evergreen rambler with terminal panicles of small creamy flowers, bears clusters of small ovoid scarlet and red fruits.

SEMI-EVERGREEN CLIMBER
FULL SUN   ZONES 6-9
R. villosa, apple rose, has grey gentle-coloured foliage, pink flowers and bears large bristle-clad red apple-like fruits in late summer.

MEDIUM DECIDUOUS SHRUB
FULL SUN   ZONES 6-9
See also Pinks and mauves: early summer.

SORBUS
S. aucuparia, the mountain ash or rowan, has beautiful pinnate foliage, colouring to delicate tints in late summer. Attractive clusters of bright red fruits look lovely among the leaves; unfortunately very tempting to birds, they are quickly devoured.

MEDIUM DECIDUOUS TREE
FULL SUN OR HALF SHADE   ZONES 5-8

STRANVAESIA
S. davidiana bears globular brilliant crimson fruits in pendent clusters among its green and red foliage. The smaller *S.d.* 'Undulata' has wide spreading branches and is useful for clothing a bank.

MEDIUM OR LARGE EVERGREEN SHRUB
FULL SUN OR HALF SHADE   ZONES 6-9
See also Strong reds: foliage.

VIBURNUM
Viburnums are among the best shrubs for subtle fruit and leaf interest in early autumn. Deciduous species colour well, bronze and red leaves harmonizing with bright fruits.

V. betulifolium is one of the best fruiting shrubs. Mature plants grouped at the edge of woodland have heavy bunches of glistening redcurrant-like fruit carried along the elegant swaying branches. *V. dilatatum* is equally beautiful when covered with bunches of deep vivid-red berries. It has a yellow-fruiting form, *V.d.* 'Xanthocarpum', which is also spectacular.

LARGE DECIDUOUS SHRUBS
FULL SUN OR HALF SHADE   ZONES 5-8
V. opulus, guelder rose or water elder, common in Europe and western Asia, has copious clusters of glistening redcurrant-like fruits, which it carries through many months from early autumn. A form, *V.o.* 'Notcutt Variety', has particularly large fruits.

LARGE DECIDUOUS SHRUB
HALF SHADE   ZONES 4-8

Stranvaesia davidiana 'Undulata'

Rosa rugosa 'Frau Dagmar Hastrup'

CHAPTER IX

—FOLIAGE FRAMEWORK—

Throughout all the seasons the green, grey and coloured leaves of living plants form the background and fabric of a garden. In summer the leaf colours are brightest, young growth in shades of green, grey, gold, patterns of cream and yellow, and tones of bronze, purple and even scarlet mix with the generally more muted shades of evergreens and with ephemeral flowers. In winter the garden is more sombre; low-toned greens, brown and buff fallen leaves, browny-green moss, dark earth and green grass predominate, and deciduous trees become sculptured frameworks of grey and brown. The few evergreen plants with coloured foliage, and trees and shrubs with coloured bark and stems, then become garden features.

Foliage plants shape a garden and establish its structure. Hedges make boundaries at garden limits and compartments within a garden, and are the sober background for grouped flower colours. At every level, tree shapes are silhouettes against the sky or the distant landscape and form backdrops to nearer planting. Climbing plants also give vertical emphasis, and are particularly valuable in town gardens, to clothe the walls of adjacent buildings and form a congenial background to flower display.

Individual plants make varying contributions according to their size, shape and habit. Those with leaves densely set together make solid shapes, heavy and dull when the leaves are matt-surfaced, or brighter with glossy textures, undulating leaf edges and the ever-changing tones of young growth. Plants of open habit have branches and leaves set well apart, allowing interplay of light, shade and movement. Vertical or conical forms create staccato points, while rounded, fan-shaped or pendulous shapes contrast with the ordered lines of hedges and walls. All, by emphasis and by repetition of architectural shape, can link and unify a garden scheme. Plants with large sculptured leaves of intricate design or arresting colour similarly provide a focus for the eye: a single one can dominate a corner, and a pair can frame a path or doorway. At lower levels, shrubs and perennials can hug the ground to form impenetrable carpets. Some, like grass of single- or two-toned green, make quiet underplanting for striking plants grouped above; others, with rich and subtle tonal variations, make a feature in their own right.

New labour-saving garden styles have developed with hardy foliage plants massed in contrasting colour groups for all-year-round effects. Even the average-sized garden may find inspiration in the designs of the South American Roberto Burle-Marx. In his schemes curving beds follow the broad outlines of housing estate and motorway banks and match the contours of the landscape beyond. Branching and arching shrubs grow like billowing waves and give movement and vigour to static scenes. These bands and sweeps of interlocking colour are deliberately contrived pictorial images; strong harmonious colour associations leading to the natural groupings of the native countryside, whether forest, moorland, green fields or pale desert sands or rock.

Shapes of individual leaves vary as much as size, colour and texture. The needle-like leaves of most conifers are attached to small branching stems giving an impression of density quite different from the small leaves of a typical evergreen shrub; both give a bush a sort of architectural solidity. Large glossy palmate leaves of shrubs such as fatsia, steely grey pinnate leaves of melianthus or smooth simple leaves of magnolia species create an exotic semi-tropical atmosphere, casting shadows and creating a feeling of space and distance, quite different from the effect of tightly knit small-leaved bushes such as box, rhamnus or phillyrea. The latter lack inner shadow and depth, although young growth makes changing colour effects. Shrubs and herbaceous plants with deeply cut and dissected leaves lighten a planting scheme with their filmy elegance. Light-coloured pinnate leaves of small trees such as gleditsias or robinias make feathery billows against the sky.

The leaves of two plants examined together in isolation may have surface colour identical in both shade and texture, definable in a precise colour term. However, their respective parent plants may grow in such different ways that the impression is of two different colour masses. Their colour will be further modified by the effects of neighbouring garden colours.

Besides flower and fruit in their seasons, some individual specimen plants have qualities of foliage colour and shape and habit of growth which make them as decorative and useful in the garden as sculpture. The eye will focus naturally on an architectural plant – a plant of such definite colour or form that neighbouring plants fade to comparative unimportance in a design. Symmetry of shape or colour, too, makes it possible to use these plants to frame views or doorways, to line a pathway or simply unify a border by repetition.

Evergreen shrubs such as bay, green and pale variegated box, green and grey junipers and dark green or gold yew change colour in every season, and as they are clipped into solid or sculptural forms. Conical and dome-shaped conifers make strong accents, but their more feathery foliage of green, grey and golden variegated shades, excellent when young, is often resentful of regular pruning. Indeed, many conifers have defined outlines only when immature, turning later into romantic broad-headed trees, dominating and architectural in any garden but impossible in a small one. Broad-leaved evergreens such as camellias, elaeagnus, escallonia, holly and osmanthus can make regular mounds or pyramids of either shining green or brightly variegated patterns of green, and cream and white. Magnolias with very large leaves always look exotic.

Deciduous trees and shrubs with pinnate or deeply dissected leaves in green, gold, variegated and purple tones catch the light and make airy shapes against the sky or are silhouetted against darker, denser foliage. In open countryside grey-leaved poplars and willows glisten in sunlight against a sky which seems more intensely blue behind their outlines. In southern Europe the cloudy grey of olive trees deepens and accentuates the green of pencil-slim cypresses. Some trees and shrubs have distinctive habits which make them architectural links in a garden. Weeping pendulous shapes contrast with sweeps of lawn and the horizontal surface of water; tiered horizontal branches make corner features or, on a bank, unite upper and lower levels. Their forms or cultivars with coloured foliage make even greater impact and are beautiful as specimens, but may disturb a quiet garden scheme.

Deeply lobed glossy-leaved acanthus, silvery-grey artichokes, archangelica and heracleum with huge dissected leaves, and the glaucous pinnate-leaved *Melianthus major* are as important as sculpture. Although herbaceous (perennial or biennial), they make fine features in a summer season. Moisture-loving gunnera, rheum and rodgersia are superb foliage plants, their leaves rough-textured and bronze or purple-tinted. Groups of astilbes, with feathery green or red-toned foliage and plume-like flowers, make admirable foils to more solid, dense plants.

At border edges strong contrasting shapes are provided by alchemillas with pale palmate leaves, sword-like iris, sisyrinchium and the larger phormium (forms of *P. tenax* and *P. cookianum*) and grassy-leaved hemerocallis, kniphofia and yucca. Even low-growing bergenias, London pride (*Saxifraga × urbium*) and *Chiastophyllum oppositifolium* make evergreen feature plants for border fronts, anchoring the design firmly in its place through all the seasons.

Boundaries of a garden can be rigidly defined by hedges of coloured foliage, or can be concealed informally by mixed groups of plants in deep beds inside the perimeter. In either case the colour and texture of the leaves affect the definition of the enclosed space as well as providing the background framework for colour within the garden. Dark-surfaced leaves such as yew (although through much of the summer its young leaf shoots give a tapestry effect) tend to make space close in; the bright, cheerful green of young beech or pale, crinkled leaves of rugosa roses have the opposite tendency.

In countryside gardens the foliage colour and texture of perimeter plants should merge into fields or landscape beyond; brightly coloured leaves will often strike a discordant note. If the garden leads to woodland, plant some of the trees or undergrowth from it as garden and wood merge, making a visual and physical link as important for the garden owner looking out as for the ecologist looking in. Around a rural cottage garden plant local field-hedge plants. A tall boundary line of conifer plants with feathery evergreen leaves, green, grey or gold-toned, stands out like a sore thumb against the softer rounder shapes and green-grey-toned colours of broad-leaved trees.

In an urban environment the garden barrier is for seclusion as well as for screening unsightly neighbourhood buildings. The garden and gardener are inward-looking, creating a private haven of peaceful colour. Just as a green-toned hedge is a perfect foil to most flower colours, so also is green the most restful contrast to city buildings. In a small backyard garden high walls or openwork trellis draped with coloured

PAGE 195 A woodland picture of texture and mass demonstrates the variety of interest which 'monochrome' green is capable of generating. The eye falls first upon a pool of light made up of the lacy leaves of ferns which contrast with the solid rough-textured palmate foliage of gunnera behind. The ferns themselves make a repeating pattern of light-reflecting upper surfaces and bright translucent yellow-green undersides. Deciduous shrubs and feathery chamaecyparis make an intricate tapestry backdrop. The surface smoothness of luminous grey and golden bark is the single element of colour contrast in the picture, enriching the tones of the many greens.

RIGHT Under a willow, foreground plants with strong foliage shapes are grouped informally beside a pond. Behind, blocks of clipped hedging and an entrance of yew topiary contrast abruptly with the natural planting and provide a structured framework to unite the wilder outer garden with the more disciplined gardening beyond. The spectator is invited to walk from shade to sunlight, his steps directed by the mown grass and the defined entrance. The smooth empty planes of sky and reflecting still water make a balanced composition of space and massed planting, united by the expanses of lawn. The contrasting density of light ethereal laburnum above heavy clipped foliage is echoed on a smaller scale by the contrast between the leaf patterns among the foliage groups at the waterside.

Although disguised by free-flowing plant shapes and by flower and fruit colour, this garden has strongly defined structural lines and a basic symmetry. Geometric yew hedging establishes vertical and horizontal direction and a central path gives axial perspective. Above the blocks of yew soar twin pairs of crab-apples (*Malus* × 'John Downie') and liquidambars. In the foreground clumps of silvery santolina, *Rosa* 'Iceberg' and a pair of emphatic stone pots underline the symmetry. Within this frame a nepeta-lined gravel path leads from the central group of white agapanthus towards a distant cider orchard.

leaves and trees in neighbouring gardens will take the place of vertical hedging plants, forming together the walls of an outer room, where planning garden colour schemes is nearer to interior decoration.

Dense-growing hedges of yew, holly, beech and hornbeam can be straight-sided and flat-topped giving a plain all-over colour, especially when just clipped. Sloping sides, and tops clipped into points or curves, change the reflection of light, shape, density and texture giving a patterned colour effect of dark and light. (Even yew and beech species, if grown from seed rather than vegetatively, show great individual colour variation.) Beech leaves, buff-coloured in winter, give a hedge distinctive seasonal variation and the twiggy growth of the smaller-leaved hornbeam is like trelliswork in winter, with light showing between the small stems. Because a complete hedge of bright variegated hollies could be too emphatic, intersperse plain green plants between variegated specimens to make a tapestry effect; similarly, purple beeches can enrich the summer dullness of a line of the green 'type' hedging.

Escallonias make dark flowering hedges but, like berberis and roses, they cannot be cut into rigid shapes or into topiary patterns. Pyracantha can be trained on wires or on a wall to make symmetrical vertical and horizontal branches as firmly

as any fruiting apple or pear. Such a hedge usefully casts little shade on beds to the northern side.

Tall inner hedges, arranged geometrically, make inner 'rooms' in a large garden, living foliage backgrounds to separate colour schemes or seasonal displays. Traditional yew, box, rosemary and lavender can be clipped to make formal edging lines; dwarf box, *Euonymus fortunei radicans*, and santolina, at lower levels, enclose beds of bulbs, annuals and low-growing foliage plants. Smaller prostrate grey-leaved hebes or even saxifrages make equally appropriate edging where the scale is in proportion.

Trees within a garden or near the perimeter give weight and scale, their different shapes and leaf density balancing with the architecture of the house and neighbouring buildings. Long-lived and slow to mature, a large specimen tree dominates the structure of a garden and yet links it to the country or to the urban landscape beyond. In Italian renaissance gardens shades of green composed pictures quietly receding into a landscape, the dark green of vertical cypresses becoming the focal point among green textures of massive evergreen oak, rounded grey-green olives and patterns of bay and box hedges. Interest and atmosphere were achieved by contrast of pale and dark leaves, light and shade. Similarly an eighteenth-century English park was a composition in the

Architectural topiary echoing the geometry of an oast-house roof creates an atmosphere and a logic of its own in a separate garden area. The severe clipped shapes are softened by foliage, and the different faces of the solids make patterns of light and shade. In the quiet stillness of this dramatic tableau subtleties of colour that are normally overlooked can be studied: the difference between the shiny ilex hedges and the duller yew topiary; the mossy roof tiles; the mowing stripes on the lawn, and the beckoning stone path. Glimpses of free-growing plants here and there demonstrate the balance of firm structures and natural shapes – the basis of successful garden planting.

greens of trees and grass against a skyline or receding into the distant blues and the purple tones of woodland.

Coloured trees in the distance come closer and those in the foreground dominate, especially in the misty light of temperate climates where colours become garish without the 'fading' influence of bright sunlight.

Where there is space compositions of tree foliage and underplanting can be as vivid as a flower border. Glaucous-leaved conifers or silvery eucalyptus give contrast with purple-leaved cotinus and berberis and ground cover of blue-flowered bronze-leaved ajuga. Purple-leaved plum associated with the golden foliage of *Cornus alba* 'Spaethii', and *Philadelphus coronarius* 'Aureus' make a startling picture, which may be softened and harmonized by foreground planting of greys and bronze. Golden leaves, especially of evergreens in winter, link winter colours of brown and russet with fresh green leaves of spring, the different textures of conifers, holly and golden privet giving patterned light and shade against dark evergreens.

Smaller ornamental trees such as the gold *Robinia pseudo-acacia* 'Frisia', variegated *Cornus controversa*, purple-leaved *Prunus pissardii* and textured grey, glaucous and golden conifers need quiet architectural or green-leaved backgrounds. A glade in a wood or an arboretum such as Westonbirt can be

a patterned scheme of coloured leaves of small trees and shrubs, anticipating the orange, crimson and reds of autumn. In a small garden a single specimen or group of brightly hued trees become a dominating design feature. Pale gold leaves in a northern aspect are as bright as sunshine; creamy-white variegation gives a feeling of lightness and movement, and purple leaves, especially as they darken in summer, become heavy and dull enough to anchor the garden to its site.

Climbing plants are simply plants with long, lax shoots looking upwards for support, reaching towards the light where they can carry flowers. Some, like ivy, anchor themselves with aerial roots; others, such as Virginia creeper (and other forms of parthenocissus), have suction pads. Clematis have leaf tendrils which fasten round trellis, wire or other plant stems. Honeysuckle has twining stems, and vines have stem tendrils curling tightly round any support. Even climbing and rambling roses have thorns especially recurved which hook over neighbouring plant stalks or supports.

The leaves of climbers on wall, trellis and fence make background colour to other planting, solid and textured against a wall, but filtering light when on open frames. Pergolas, arbours and verandahs become shady refuges with heavy foliage 'ceilings' making enclosed rooms and passages. The house can have architectural style or detail enhanced or hidden by appropriate climbers, coloured leaves perhaps harmonizing with brick, stone or paintwork. Ivy and many other plants can be pruned and trained symmetrically to surround windows or to make buttress or pyramid shapes against a wall, where their usefulness as design features is equivalent to more solid masonry. Pyracantha and coton-easter are trained in horizontal and vertical lines, making a pattern of leaf, stem, flower and fruit as regular as trelliswork. The traditional cottage porch is wreathed in casually inter-twined leaf and flower.

Wall plants, often tender genera with evergreen and exotic leaves which benefit from the shelter and from the reflected wall heat, are useful in the small enclosed yard and against dividing walls in larger gardens. Ceanothus, escallonias and pittosporum have evergreen leaves of differing texture whose restful patterns on a sunny wall make an ideal complement to bright flower colour. The purple claret vine, *Vitis vinifera* 'Purpurea' might twine between grey-leaved coronilla, *Cytisus battandieri* and the tender white-flowered evergreen *Solanum jasminoides*. In another colour scheme the strange pink, green and white leaves of *Actinidia kolomikta* could be mixed with pink and white *Clematis* 'Nelly Moser' with fore-ground planting of purple foliage. On north-facing walls and in heavy shade the climbing *Hydrangea petiolaris* and ivies frame wall shrubs such as garrya, *Pilostegia viburnoides* and fatsia.

Individual climbing plants such as roses, clematis and honeysuckle can clamber into trees and large shrubs, ming-ling foliage and flower colour and aping nature's tangled growth in woodland or hedgerow. Each separate plant com-bination makes a planned garden picture that fits into the whole design. Old orchard trees blossoming in spring are hosts to glossy-leaved roses with a later flowering season. Grey-green *Elaeagnus* × *reflexa* will clamber slowly into dark green yew, and a purple-leaved vine into the silver weeping pear (*Pyrus salicifolia* 'Pendula'). In the shade of northern gardens, the fresh bright foliage of *Tropaeolum speciosum*, the Chilean flame creeper, rambles into darker-leaved plants, lighting up a dark corner even before bearing its brilliant scarlet flowers in late summer.

The horizontal surface on which the garden is built up may be patterns of stone or brick, coloured gravel or a carpet of plants. Directional paths not only provide access to different parts of the garden but visually link areas and themes. Grass, cut as smooth emerald lawn, or longer-textured with pale buff stems giving a yellowish effect, is the most restful of ground covers.

Mown grass changes colour a hundred times a day. It glistens with dew at dawn, makes a pool of light in strong sunshine, its surface almost reflecting like still water, and in evening long shadows cast patterns on its surface. The strange grey-purple light just before a storm and the grey light of a winter's day both make lawns a vibrant, intense green. Grass is one of the few plants which survives having its growing tips cut, sometimes as often as twice a week, but to keep it healthy it needs frequent nourishment.

Shapes and heights of trees in a landscape and ornamental plants in a garden disguise natural contours. Smooth grass has the opposite effect, emphasizing subtle curves and mounds on sloping surfaces as well as the flatness of a carefully levelled area. Lawns mown in longitudinal stripes, with light reflected in opposite ways on the short stems, making bands of darker and lighter green, increase the feel-ing of length. Diagonal stripes can make the lawn seem larger, accentuating the dramatic effect if enclosing hedges or walls are high and cast strong shadows. As well as being restful to look at and preparing the eye for bright flower colours, lawn is soft to walk on, and the scent of newly mown grass is an evocative reminder of traditional garden delights.

Where lawns will not grow, because it is too hot, too dry, too wet or too shady, other plants will hug the ground and can be walked on. Camomile, thyme and creeping mints make tight-textured carpets of greens and greys, sweetly fragrant when crushed by the foot. In damp shade the little green *Helxine soleirolii* can make a pattern round a pool, growing between and over stones and even spreading on flat vertical surfaces. In hot dry climates plants such as sagina will make a soft spongy surface (but needs irrigation) and mixes of sub-tropical grasses and ophiopogon (lily-turf) give green colour in summer.

Other plants which grow close to the ground, spreading by underground or surface roots, make flat beds which form design features on their own, offer labour-saving alternatives to grass, and sometimes cover the soil as underplanting to taller plants above – a mass of one species harmonizing with and enhancing the colour of the plants overhead. The best effects are always obtained where planting areas are linked by these broad sweeps. Ivy and periwinkle in shade, flowering ajugas massed in one leaf colour, grey stachys and acaenas in sun make the lowest cover. Sheets of epimedium, *Vinca major*, coarser large-leaved Irish ivy, creeping cotoneasters and prostrate junipers give additional height, carefully adjusted in scale to plants above. Grey leaves under pink roses, blue-flowered brunnera with coarse dark-green leaves

Details from two gardens in quite different styles show how foliage plants can be combined to make totally different effects. A three-dimensional composition of subtle contrasts of texture and colour can be built up from a number of well-arranged plants which weave together but retain individual identity. Alternatively, plants can be deployed in blocks to create defined and artificial images dependent on contrast. In the first case success depends on juxtaposition of harmonious leaf shapes, and in the second on maximizing contrast with neighbouring shapes and colours.

Pale grey felted leaves of prostrate *Stachys olympica*, LEFT, contrast in shape with clipped mounds of feathery pewter-grey santolina in a cool monochrome planting which is dramatic in its simplicity. When such plants take the centre stage, the spotlight will reveal the least flaw, and careful manicuring and maintenance is required. Each plant needs to be kept in perfect health and confined within its allotted space. Behind, a juniper sends out its textured branches in wedding-cake layers, and links the planting with the green of the lawn.

In a small town garden, BELOW, walls and paving are linked and richly clothed with leafy plants which blend together. *Cornus alba* 'Elegantissima' margined with white, feathery *Thujopsis dolabrata*, golden-hued *Lamium maculatum* 'Aureum' and glaucous hostas give sufficient interest to sustain the gardening year without the aid of ephemeral seasonal flowers, but variety and contrast is not present in excess: all the plants are firmly linked together by their shared green pigment.

under large purple-leaved shrubs, alchemilla under pale variegated foliage are examples of appropriate associations of colours and textures.

At higher levels, evergreen and deciduous shrubs make dense cover. In modern building complexes massed trees or shrubs soften hard lines and link ground with masonry; often they are landscaped into patterns and contours that might have been established by nature before the buildings took shape. Some foliage plants with horizontal branches and pendulous tips give the feeling of movement when they cover steep banks and link different ground levels.

All plants, but especially those with attractive leaves and spreading habits, cover the ground as alternatives to bare earth or hard surfaces, but it is their specific use in broad groups which give them artistic value in a garden. Their colours and patterns contribute to the design composition, linking vertical and horizontal planes, sometimes providing shades of restful green as settings to bright flower and foliage colours, and sometimes emphasizing the ground patterns with attractive, strongly coloured leaves.

The colour of the plant pigment chlorophyll, green – in different tones and shades – predominates in most gardening landscapes, and usually prevails in the garden itself. Probably because we associate it with nature – as well as for the physiological fact that the eye receives green light rays almost exactly on the retina, and so has no need to focus and adjust – green represents tranquillity and restfulness. It is the colour we yearn for in our man-made surroundings: we make cool patches of soothing green in the city's concrete jungle, or re-create the hidden garden of the Italian renaissance in a search for privacy and quiet in the centre of town.

Many of the greatest garden scenes have been composed entirely of different-textured greens and greys, interspersed with fine grey statues and stonework and with water reflecting their interlocking patterns. These gardens are architectural compositions, and Louis XIV once wrote an exhaustive description of the manner in which the garden at Versailles was to be viewed without specifying a single plant or colour. In other gardens, foliage greens and greys are the harmonizing settings that show off by contrast the bright flower hues from the opposite side of the colour wheel.

Green as a colour in the visible spectrum lies between blue and yellow. In plants greens have high or low tones according to variations in the leaf pigment which adapts to light, and to textural differences. Polished leaf surfaces which reflect light deepen the greenness; other leaves have dull matt upper or undersurfaces; others seem grey as small hairy projections deflect light rays. These 'grey' plants have developed hairs to protect themselves from hot sun, and their leaf surfaces become smoother and 'greener' when they are grown in shade. Blue-green leaves have developed a waxy layer of molecules which scatter blue and violet light rays; these mix with the green of chlorophyll, making it appear distinctly bluish. In a dark forest, where conifers growing closely together thrive, a higher concentration of chlorophyll is necessary to capture the filtered rays; so the leaves are an intense green. Deciduous leaves can be pale and thinner, their green much less intense, since they get the maximum of sunlight through the summer months. All green foliage colour will tend to 'redden' neighbouring flowers or leaves, but how much effect each green has depends on its other dimensions.

Grey in pure colour terms – as opposed to 'gardening grey' – lies between black and white, and is neutral and achromatic: mid-grey absorbs and reflects all light rays in equal

ABOVE One of the essential foliage plants, grass has an almost infinite range of colour from fresh bright green to buff, depending on the season and the method of upkeep. The contrast between a mown lawn and an area where the grass is uncut can help to define a garden's structure, just as a mown path here leads through the meadow flowers and longer grass towards the circular steps linking the lawn areas with the terraces above.

RIGHT Stonework and architecture combine with foliage shape and textures to create the garden framework and to give an atmosphere of maturity and romantic profusion. Fan-shaped cotoneasters drape themselves diagonally over Victorian-style white iron seats and lawn, while climbers clothe the vertical grey stone of supporting terrace and house walls.

amounts. It is the colour perceived when a pair of complementary colours is mixed together in paints and dyes. Greys include the tones of ash, lead or pewter, and in a garden may be represented by the gradated greys of York stone, gravel chippings, and the grey tones of bare winter branches – as well as the 'greys' of leaves. Covered to a greater or lesser degree in hairy projections, grey leaves are more or less silvery or dull, furry or velvety. Greys cannot clash, and grey has no power to alter an adjacent hue, only to make it more intense and brilliant. Grey can cause fully saturated hues to appear almost too bright, especially in a humid atmosphere where there is no fierce sun to fade them. But greys make more insipid washed-out colours glow.

Grey itself is easily affected by neighbouring hues: it becomes suffused with the 'haze' of a colour's complementary. Next to orange flowers, grey leaves become distinctly bluish in tone; next to red the greys become greenish; next to violet shades grey leaves become distinctly yellow. The more silvery and 'whitish' these leaves are, the less they will assume these hints of complementary tints; nor are they so affected by changes in the light itself. Grey leaves will assume violet tints in shade, and become distinctly yellowed in sun. Evening light can tinge grey leaves with pink.

Green and grey leaves work together in a garden, their various shades and tints making close harmonies and giving no disturbing contrasts. Toned-down, they associate with the natural colours of wood and stone and with most man-made neutral-coloured materials. In winter, evergreens of contrasting texture such as grass, yew, ilex or ivy contribute a wide range of green colour, to harmonize with the buff and brownish tones of dying stems and leaves and the greyness of bare branches and occasional patches of brown warm earth. Hoar frost on thick green or grey leaves reflects patterns of sparkling light. Storm clouds of intense grey make the green of trees and grass intensely emerald, while the red complement of the greens gives grey stones and branches a distinctly pinkish aura, accentuated by the mellow reddish rays of evening light, which in their turn make the greens glow.

GREEN

ABELIA

Most abelias are grown for their pinkish flowers (see Pinks and mauves: early summer), but *A.* × *grandiflora* also has glossy almost evergreen leaves with subdued red tints. In a late-flowering border it makes a beautiful arching shrub, interesting through all the year. It looks well next to bare-stemmed nerine or *Amaryllis belladonna* flowers, or falling loosely over fading iris leaves.

MEDIUM EVERGREEN SHRUB
FULL SUN OR HALF SHADE   ZONES 8-10

ACANTHUS BEAR'S BREECHES

A. mollis latifolius has glossy broad green leaves with wavy margins, making dense foliage cover for corner beds. Striking from a distance as light is reflected from the leaves, in late summer tall white and purple flower-spikes tower above. Needing full sun for flowering, it may equally be grown for dense ground cover under deciduous shrubs. A beautiful picture under olive trees in its native Mediterranean habitats.

DECIDUOUS PERENNIAL 90-120 CM (36-48 IN)
FULL SUN OR HALF SHADE   ZONES 6-9

ACER MAPLE

Maples have green, variegated, gold or purple leaves, very variable in shape, and many turning crimson and scarlet in autumn. Several of the smaller trees have interesting peeling or striped bark (see below).

A. saccharinum, the silver maple, has fluttering green leaves, silvery underneath, on long leaf-stems. Movement and colour give the tree unusual airy grace.

MEDIUM DECIDUOUS TREE
FULL SUN OR HALF SHADE   ZONES 5-9

ALCHEMILLA LADY'S MANTLE

No garden, even the very smallest, can be without at least one alchemilla.

A. alpina, the alpine lady's mantle, makes a neat tuft of green, the leaves glistening silver beneath. It will grow in any cranny; the flowers are greenish. *A. erythropoda* is also small, with pinkish-red arching flower-stems. It is unusual and still rare.

DECIDUOUS PERENNIAL   15 CM (6 IN)
FULL SUN   ZONES 3-8

A. mollis has light green hairy leaves, umbrella-shaped, which collect sparkling little drops of

Alchemilla mollis

dew or rain, and is covered in early summer and again later in clouds of lime-yellow flowers. It thrives anywhere and seeds prolifically if permitted. Grow it to fall over steps, or to contrast with purple leaves.

DECIDUOUS PERENNIAL   30 CM (12 IN)
FULL SUN OR HALF SHADE   ZONES 3-8

AMPELOPSIS

Climbing by means of curling tendrils, ampelopsis willingly cover walls, fences, trellis and pergola, and if given initial support will clamber high into trees. Happy in any ordinary soil, in sun or shade, they are particularly useful in town gardens clothing walls in dense curtains, to make a planting background for border plants.

A. aconitifolia has glossy green leaves variable in shape but deeply divided, giving a light, fishnet effect. The three- or five-lobed leaves of *A. brevipendunculata* are more like those of a hop. After a hot summer, masses of small deep blue fruits are borne.

DECIDUOUS CLIMBERS   FULL SUN   ZONES 7-9

ANGELICA

A. archangelica has deeply dissected aromatic leaves; the thick stems are used, when preserved in sugar, for cake decoration. Flowers, large umbels of clustered yellow-green, are carried on 1.8 m (6 ft) stems.

EVERGREEN BIENNIAL OR PERENNIAL
1.5 M (5 FT)   FULL SUN   ZONES 7-9

ARBUTUS STRAWBERRY TREE

Arbutus are evergreen trees or shrubs with handsome foliage and panicles of pitcher-like white flowers followed by fruits looking somewhat like strawberries, but insipid to taste. Although ericaceous, some will tolerate lime, but appreciate the addition of peat at planting time.

A. unedo will grow to tree-like proportions in a mild climate, but is more usually a large branching shrub. Thriving in acid or alkaline soil, it has glowing green leaves in all seasons. The pinkish-tinted white flowers in late summer coincide with ripening strawberry fruits from the previous year. See also Coloured bark, below.

LARGE EVERGREEN SHRUB
FULL SUN OR HALF SHADE   ZONES 7-9

ARUNDINARIA BAMBOO

Bamboos are the most elegant of all evergreens, some growing in clumps, others spreading by creeping underground, and often becoming invasive.

A. murieliae makes a graceful arching clump, canes bright green but turning yellowish, with wide leaves of duller tone, perfect for planting near water, or shapely and form-giving in an ordinary mixed flower-bed. *A. nitida* is similar, but has purple-flushed canes and narrow leaves.

EVERGREEN BAMBOO   3-4 M (10-13 FT)
FULL SUN   ZONES 7-10

ASTILBE
Most astilbes thrive in moist if not boggy soil. The leaves are attractive, deeply divided and often with purple, bronze or mahogany tints. The flowers are white, red and pinkish, in delightful plumes.

A. rivularis is imposing, with striking leaves and arching stems topped by many small greenish-white flowers (see The whites: summer). Later the seed-heads are an attractive brown. Plant to contrast with solid architectural leaves of other moisture-loving plants such as the giant gunnera or rheum, their delicate and filmy foliage giving a light, airy feeling.

DECIDUOUS PERENNIAL   1.8 M (6 FT)
SHADE   ZONES 7-9

AUCUBA
A. japonica was beloved by Victorians for the spotted leaves of the various clones. The plain glossy wide green leaf of the true species is preferable. Clumps of aucubas in deep shade glow with colour and brighten awkward corners. Strange olive-green flowers appear on open panicles in spring, followed by red berries on female plants; male plants are also needed to ensure fruit.

MEDIUM EVERGREEN SHRUB
FULL SUN OR SHADE   ZONES 7-9

BERGENIA
Bergenias have glossy green leathery leaves, some with red tints in winter (see Strong reds). All make good ground-cover plants in shady north-facing beds, although they are equally happy in sun. The green is strong enough for clumps of these plants to make an architectural base to a broad bed, anchoring it to its foreground.

B. cordifolia has heart-shaped leaves with rounded ends and mauvish-magenta flowers on 30 cm (12 in) stems. *B. crassifolia* has flatter, lower-growing leaves and pink flowers in very early spring.

EVERGREEN PERENNIALS   15-30 CM (6-12 IN)
FULL SUN OR SHADE   ZONES 6-9

BUPLEURUM THOROUGHWAX
Summer-flowering relations of the cow-parsley, bupleurum have yellowy-green umbelliferous heads in late summer (see Clear yellows), the brown-yellow seed-heads held above a plant all through the winter.

B. fruticosum, shrubby hare's ear, is the only woody representative in gardens. It is a fine shrub with almost glaucous shining leaves and a gentle flowing shape suitable for breaking the harsh lines of masonry. The perfect complement to grey foliage, and similar in size and habit to the pewter-grey *Artemisia* 'Powis Castle'; both may be used together in formal designs.

MEDIUM EVERGREEN SHRUB
FULL SUN   ZONES 8-9

BUXUS BOX
In a mature garden a venerable box tree of 3 m (10 ft), clipped topiary shapes or a low hedge of its shining textured foliage is indispensable. Beautiful glossy dark leaves and pale young growth make a pattern of light and shade all the year, while in spring the inconspicuous flowers are deliciously honey-scented, as evocative as the scent of new-mown grass.

B. balearica grows to make an erect small tree; very shining leathery leaves are of dark green. It glows in a shady corner.

SMALL EVERGREEN TREE OR LARGE SHRUB
FULL SUN OR HALF SHADE   ZONES 8-9

B. sempervirens, the common European box, has many variants, some growing eventually to small trees. *B.s.* 'Handsworthensis' is erect and vigorous with large leaves and may be clipped into pyramids or domes to line an axial path, or to make architectural focal points in flower-beds. *B.s.* 'Suffruticosa' is the familiar dwarf hedging plant, making formal patterns, geometrically linked, to define a line or to enclose beds of monochrome planting.

SMALL TO MEDIUM EVERGREEN SHRUBS
FULL SUN OR HALF SHADE   ZONES 7-9

CAMELLIA
Camellias are familiar, slightly tender, acid-loving evergreens, grown for their shining leaves as well as for their charming white, pink and red flowers in early spring (see appropriate chapters). Not altogether hardy in severe climates, it is the buds formed in autumn which are likely to suffer in hard frosts unless plants are screened from early-morning sun. They are excellent pot plants, thriving in the shade of small town gardens. For some reason, unless planted in woodland drifts in favoured localities, they have a rich suburban connotation; perhaps because fashionable urban nurserymen sell them ready-prepared in containers.

As regularly shaped large bushes they become architectural features, especially in a winter landscape when planted near groups of

Clipped *Buxus sempervirens* 'Suffruticosa'

Bergenia cordifolia

deciduous shrubs. In summer the quality of the glossy textured green leaves contrasts with soft matt-surfaced foliage plants. Use them to make dark accents in a formal garden or, in favoured localities, plant in woodland drifts.

LARGE EVERGREEN SHRUBS
HALF SHADE OR SHADE   ZONES 7-9

CARPINUS HORNBEAM

C. betulus may be grown as a single specimen, for hedging or to form shady arbours. It responds well to rigorous clipping and makes dense twiggy thickets with rigid outlines. The foliage, superficially resembling that of beech,

Cedrus deodara

Choisya ternata

is pale green in spring, the leaves ribbed and serrated, turning dark greeny-brown by late summer. In autumn the fruit hangs in decorative chains. *C.b.* 'Fastigiata' is an erect pyramidal-shaped tree, useful in formal planting, a grey fluted bark developing with age.

MEDIUM DECIDUOUS TREES OR SHRUBS
FULL SUN OR HALF SHADE   ZONES 7-9

CEANOTHUS CALIFORNIA LILAC

Primarily grown for their spring, summer and autumn blue flowers, these tender shrubs have attractive dark and pale green leaves. They may be shaped and pruned against warm walls, an attractive contrast to the more free-growing shapes of clematis and other twiners.

MEDIUM EVERGREEN SHRUBS
FULL SUN   ZONES 7-9
See also The blues.

CEDRUS CEDAR

A fortunate gardener inherits a majestic dark-leaved cedar of Lebanon, *C. libani*, or the drooping pale-leaved deodar, *C. deodara*, from the Himalayas: it will take a young tree fifty years to develop the broad head. 'Blue'-leaved forms often strike a discordant note in garden or landscape.

TALL EVERGREEN CONIFERS
FULL SUN   ZONES 7-9

CHIASTOPHYLLUM

C. oppositifolium (syn. *Cotyledon simplicifolia*) has small succulent, dark green leaves, bronze-tinted in winter, useful as dense edging at the front of a border. It is like a dwarf and delicate bergenia, happy in sun or shade. Sprays of yellow flowers on 20 cm (8 in) stems are freely borne in late summer (see Clear yellows).

EVERGREEN PERENNIAL   10 CM (4 IN)
FULL SUN OR SHADE   ZONES 6-9

CHOISYA

C. ternata, Mexican orange, is one of the most desirable of garden shrubs, suitable for both formal and informal planting. Architecturally it associates well with massive stonework, and in spring it is covered with fragrant flowers (see The whites). The aromatic glossy leaves are full of changing light and texture, never sober and dull. In most gardens it prefers a warm south-facing wall, but it may thrive in shade.

MEDIUM EVERGREEN SHRUB
FULL SUN OR HALF SHADE   ZONES 7-9

CORDYLINE CABBAGE PALM

C. australis, the cabbage tree, is tender with arresting sword-like leaves grown in palm-like fronds. It seldom flowers in an average garden,

but in favoured areas panicles of fragrant drooping creamy-coloured flowers are borne in spring. It is often grown as a pot plant, giving an exotic tropical atmosphere. (See also Strong reds: foliage.)

MEDIUM EVERGREEN SHRUB OR SMALL TREE
FULL SUN   ZONES 8-9

COTINUS SMOKE TREE

C. coggygria, the Venetian sumach, has rounded green leaves which assume fine autumn tints of orange and pink, and bears fawn-coloured flower-plumes in summer. A hardy shrub, it thrives in any soil, and eventually grows to tree proportions in woodland or border. In a modest-sized garden it may be planted as a lawn specimen, like a magnolia, with small spring and autumn bulbs flowering contentedly under its canopy.

   C. obovatus (syn. *C. americanus*) has leaves of bronze-purple, shading in summer to pale pure green, and vividly coloured in autumn in shades of scarlet, claret and orange.

LARGE DECIDUOUS SHRUBS
FULL SUN OR HALF SHADE   ZONES 4-9

COTONEASTER

Cotoneasters are grown for fruit and autumn colour as well as for their various habits, upright, horizontal-branching or prostrate. The taller species make informal hedges and wind-breaks. All have dark green leaves; some have variegated forms. *C. dammeri* grows at ground level, the long trailing shoots with white flowers, and later sealing-wax-red berries, covering low banks or carpeting soil under shrubs or trees.

SMALL EVERGREEN SHRUB
FULL SUN OR SHADE   ZONES 6-10
C. horizontalis has spreading branches making a herring-bone pattern at medium height. Thriving in northern exposures, and good against walls, it has rich fruit and leaf colours in autumn.

MEDIUM DECIDUOUS SHRUB
FULL SUN OR SHADE   ZONES 6-10
C. lacteus has oval leathery leaves, grey and hairy on the undersides. It grows tall, revealing both surfaces of foliage, giving an overall pale textured effect. At Glasnevin in Dublin it makes a dense hedge 3 m (10 ft) high, but this is exceptional.

TALL EVERGREEN SHRUB
FULL SUN OR SHADE   ZONES 6-10

CUPRESSUS CYPRESS

The Italian cypress, *C. sempervirens*, in its popular form, grows as a narrow column of tightly knit green foliage, dark against the pale leaves of olive and pine in its native

Mediterranean, but grey-green when outlined against dark yews. The foliage is fragrant, evocative of *maquis* undergrowth in hot sunshine. In colder climates, where it is not reliably hardy, the Irish juniper, *Juniperus communis* 'Hibernica' may be used in its place.
MEDIUM EVERGREEN CONIFER
FULL SUN   ZONES 7-9

DANAË ALEXANDRIAN LAUREL
D. racemosa has brightly shining, narrow leaves carried on arching stems. Tiny flowers produce orange-red fruits after hot summers. It is hardy but revels in heat and damp shade. Graceful and bamboo-like, it is now rare in nurseries, being slow to propagate.
SMALL EVERGREEN SHRUB
SHADE   ZONES 7-9

EPIMEDIUM
Epimediums are all ornamental plants with green leaves tinted pink and bronze in autumn and winter. Hardier and smaller epimediums are good garden plants, but *E. perralderanum* is evergreen, so its winter tints are of the greatest value. The leaves are large, glossy and slightly toothed. It will make a dense carpet in sun or shade, best of all when there is space for a number of plants to be massed. It is then weedproof.
EVERGREEN PERENNIAL   30 CM (12 IN)
FULL SUN OR SHADE   ZONES 7-9

ESCALLONIA
Escallonias are glossy-leaved shrubs for sheltered gardens. Some make arching shapes for informal hedges, others have a pyramidal habit and grow tall. The attractive flowers are red, pink or white. *E.* 'Iveyi' makes a regular-shaped buttress against a sunny wall, delightfully covered in late summer with erect panicles of white (see The whites). In small gardens woody branches may be pruned back every few years. If it is damaged by frosts, cut down into the old wood and new shoots will appear.
LARGE EVERGREEN SHRUB
FULL SUN   ZONES 8-9

EUPHORBIA SPURGE
E. robbiae, Mrs Robb's bonnet, is almost the only truly green-leaved spurge, and is a most useful spreader in dry inhospitable shade. The narrow dark green leaf contrasts with the flower bracts of lime-green which cover it for a long period (see Clear yellows: early summer). Spreading by underground stems, it will become a menace if planted in good open soil.
EVERGREEN PERENNIAL   30-60 CM (12-24 IN)
FULL SUN OR HALF SHADE   ZONES 7-9

FAGUS BEECH
The layered canopy of a beech tree admits little light, and greedy surface roots make survival difficult for smaller neighbouring plants. Yet of all landscape trees it is the most noble and graceful; fresh green leaves in spring make a perfect background to any garden planting, and to hedges and ditches filled with wild flowers.

The common European beech, *F. sylvatica*, may, however, be grown as an attractive and dense hedge. Spring greens become heavy and dull in summer, but the buff dead leaves clinging to the branches in winter give a new colour dimension, blending softly with winter-brown flower stems, moss and brown earth. Green beech combines with purple *F.s.* 'Riversii' (see Strong reds) to make a tapestry hedge.
LARGE DECIDUOUS TREE OR TALL HEDGE
FULL SUN OR HALF SHADE   ZONES 4-8

FATSIA
F. japonica, frequently grown as a pot plant, has rich green glossy leaves, palmate with coarsely toothed lobes. It is quite hardy but grows more shapely if against a north wall. The panicles of flowers in late summer are a surprise each year (see The whites).
LARGE EVERGREEN SHRUB
SHADE   ZONES 8-10

GARRYA
G. elliptica has magnificent long grey-green catkins draping the bush like a delicate curtain. A male form, *G.e.* 'James Roof', with very long catkins, is the best. The leaves are dark and shining, with wavy edges, pale and woolly beneath. Unfortunately, although an excellent shade-loving shrub, the foliage is often badly scorched by bitter spring winds.
TALL EVERGREEN SHRUB   SHADE   ZONES 7-9

GRISELINIA
G. littoralis will grow to tree proportions in favoured climates, but is often best used as open hedging material. The apple-green leathery leaves on dark stems are unusual (see also Clear yellows: foliage), and neighbouring flower colours should be related pale yellows, or sharply complementary mauves. In spring the common dogtooth violet, *Erythronium dens-canis*, and purple-flowered periwinkle, *Vinca*, look lovely at its feet; later, mauve and purplish hardy geraniums mass together, and in late summer *Hydrangea aspera*, which flowers for many weeks, contrasts with the fresh smooth green.
MEDIUM EVERGREEN SHRUB OR SMALL TREE
FULL SUN OR SHADE   ZONES 7-9

Garrya elliptica

Cordyline australis

Fatsia japonica

GUNNERA

G. manicata produces the largest leaves to be grown in temperate zones, sometimes up to 3 m (10 ft) across; of brownish-green, they are kidney-shaped, furrowed and puckered. In a small garden the ornamental rhubarb, *Rheum palmatum*, might take its place. The young growth can be caught by frost in spring. Gunnera needs moisture and plenty of feeding. Primulas and astilbes with pink and red flowers, should be massed near by. Plain rough grass similarly makes a good setting for it, sweeping down towards reflections in still water.

DECIDUOUS PERENNIAL   1.8 M (6 FT)
FULL SUN OR SHADE   ZONES 8-10

HEDERA IVY

Generally grown in clinging curtains, since they have aerial roots, or as dense ground cover, ivy leaves come in many shapes and colours: see The whites and Clear yellows: foliage.

H. colchica, Persian ivy, has heart-shaped foliage, the largest in the genus. It and its variegated forms grow freely and swiftly but do not make dense cover. *H. helix*, common English ivy, has variable leaves, sometimes heart-shaped and small, arrow-shaped, and patterned in different colours. Cuttings from shoots which reach upwards to flower make sturdy flowering arborescent shrubs, useful for group plantings. *H.h.* 'Hibernica', Irish ivy, has large dark leaves and is vigorous, thriving in

almost any conditions and making useful ground cover. 'Baltica', Baltic ivy, is much hardier, with small, graceful closely set leaves. 'Conglomerata Erecta' is non-climbing, with crinkled undulate leaves which give a grey-green mottled effect.

EVERGREEN CLIMBERS
HALF SHADE OR SHADE   ZONES 7-9

HELLEBORUS HELLEBORE

The leaves of hellebores, evergreen or deciduous, are all beautiful, deeply divided, and ideal cover for shady beds. The rich green leaves show off the subtle flower colours of green, creamy-white, rich plum, purple and mauve. All hellebores respond to rich feeding. In spite of their beauty of leaf and flower they look best with simple woodland planting; primroses, violets and snowdrops intermingle naturally.

H. corsicus, which needs shelter from searing winds and frosts, has remarkable foliage. The plant makes shrub-like mounds of grey-green leaves, veined and prickly edged, divided into three parts. The flower-heads are pendent cups, upturned in spring, pale creamy-green and long-lasting.

EVERGREEN PERENNIAL   60 CM (24 IN)
SHADE   ZONES 6-9

H. orientalis hybrids, known as Lenten roses, flower over attractive leaves from the end of winter to early summer.

EVERGREEN PERENNIAL   45 CM (18 IN)
SHADE   ZONES 6-9

HELXINE

H. soleirolii, the curse of Corsica or baby's tears, is a creeping half-hardy persistent plant, perfect for covering flat and low vertical stone surfaces. The tiny leaves are densely arranged, little pink stems rooting as they grow. It is ideal for a warm damp dark corner, growing luxuriantly and almost as smoothly as mown grass.

EVERGREEN PERENNIAL   2.5 CM (1 IN)
SHADE   ZONES 8-10

HEMEROCALLIS DAY LILY

Hemerocallis have grassy leaves, pale yellow or golden when emerging in spring (see Clear yellows: foliage), later green and arching, forming large decorative clumps. The lily-like flowers of the modern hybrids come in good colour ranges from clear yellow to orange, apricot, buff and bronze, during the summer.

H. fulva 'Kwanso Flore-pleno' (syn. *H. disticha* 'Flore Pleno') has spring leaves as bright as golden milium, turning grassy-green before the fragrant orange double flowers bloom in summer. An old favourite from cottage gardens, and none the worse for that. Dying leaves look untidy, but give winter protection until growth begins in early spring.

DECIDUOUS PERENNIAL   1.2 M (4 FT)
FULL SUN OR SHADE   ZONES 6-9

HOSTA PLANTAIN LILY

Hostas are invaluable foliage plants, particularly in shade in deep rich soil, although they may be grown in sun and in containers if given enough moisture. The bold leaves are green, glaucous or variegated. Among green-leaved hostas, *H. fortunei* has long pointed wavy-edged leaves of sage-green; lilac-coloured flowers are carried on tall stems. *H. plantaginea* has bright green glossy arching heart-shaped leaves; in late summer fragrant marble-white lily-like flowers are borne on high stems (see The whites). This hosta makes a splendid pot plant and flowering may be hurried on by keeping it well watered and warm; the leaves are beautiful from early spring.

DECIDUOUS PERENNIALS   60 CM (24 IN)
FULL SUN OR SHADE   ZONES 5-10
See also The blues: foliage.

HYDRANGEA

Hydrangeas are a large genus. Most prefer deep rich soil and some shade, although smaller shrub species often thrive in containers.

H. petiolaris, the climbing hydrangea, is one of the best of all plants for draping a shaded wall or thickly covering bare soil when

Gunnera manicata

encouraged to grow horizontally. Finely toothed leaves are held on rough brown stems, and greenish-white flat corymbs turn into attractive winter seed-heads.

DECIDUOUS CLIMBER
HALF SHADE OR SHADE   ZONES 4-9

H. quercifolia, the oak-leaved hydrangea, is more tender, and the lobed green leaves assume bronze and red tints in autumn. The flowers, in late summer, are large white trusses.

MEDIUM DECIDUOUS SHRUB
HALF SHADE OR SHADE   ZONES 4-9
See also The whites: late summer.

HYPERICUM ST JOHN'S WORT

Since the more attractive pale undersides of the leaves are seldom seen, the foliage of most hypericums appears to be a rather dull green, quiet and unassuming, lit up in summer by cup-shaped yellow flowers (see Clear yellows). The ordinariness of the leaves gives them a special value as a quiet foil to brighter colours.

H. calycinum, rose of Sharon, spreads by underground rhizomes, useful for dense cover on steep banks, or in inhospitable soils under trees. The massed planting of uniform height has a rippled effect suitable for free-flowing modern building shapes or roadside edges.

EVERGREEN PERENNIAL   30 CM (12 IN)
SHADE   ZONES 5-9

H. 'Hidcote' is a regular-shaped bush which will give solidity to a north-facing border and is covered, in late summer, with golden-yellow saucer-shaped flowers.

MEDIUM EVERGREEN SHRUB
FULL SUN OR SHADE   ZONES 6-9

IBERIS CANDYTUFT

I. sempervirens is an old cottage-garden plant with dark green leaves, covered in spring with white flowers (see The whites). A group is effective in the front of a border, especially if it forms a colour link with a dark hedge at the back. There are several good garden cultivars with pink-tinted and double flowers.

EVERGREEN PERENNIAL   23 CM (9 IN)
FULL SUN   ZONES 4-8

ILEX HOLLY

Some hollies have smooth or prickly leaves of glowing green, others have leaves patterned in gold or silver. Some grow upright, showing their green, blackish or reddish-purple stems; others weep, forming dense pyramids clothed to the ground in foliage, making interesting architectural features in a garden. As with English yew, holly responds to severe cutting. Holly may be grown into dense hedges, preferably using the spineless variants to make

Hydrangea petiolaris

Hosta plantaginea

tidying under them less painful. Alternatively it may be trained into solid geometrical tower or turret shapes, useful to line a pathway or form a supporting buttress against a wall, almost as imposing as a masonry pilaster.

I. × altaclarensis 'Camelliifolia' has spineless glossy dark green leaves set on purple stems. Grow it where the light shines on the foliage.

I. aquifolium 'J.C. van Tol', with almost spineless leaves, is often grown as a hedge and is best if cut to slope outwards from the top down. As a specimen it carries a fine crop of scarlet berries in winter.

TALL EVERGREEN SHRUBS OR TREES
FULL SUN OR HALF SHADE   ZONES 6-9

ITEA

I. ilicifolia has dark glossy holly-like leaves held on arching branches, the whole effect light and airy, different from the solidity of many evergreens. In late summer catkin-like racemes of fragrant greenish flowers crowd the branches. It benefits from wall protection.

TALL EVERGREEN SHRUB
FULL SUN OR SHADE   ZONES 8-10

Hypericum calycinum

JUNIPERUS JUNIPER

Most conifers prefer deep acid soil and plenty of moisture, but fortunately junipers, and yews also, thrive on shallow alkaline mixtures in sites exposed to wind and sun. The common juniper, *J. communis*, a native of Europe, is described by Gertrude Jekyll: 'Its tenderly mysterious beauty of colouring . . . as delicately subtle in its own way as that of a cloud or mist . . . very little of positive green; a suspicion of warm colour in the shadowy hollows and a blue-grey bloom of the tenderest quality imaginable on the outer masses of foliage.' Junipers have juvenile needle leaves, on some species remaining even on old plants, in others maturing to scale-like cypress-type foliage. They grow slowly – irritatingly so when a desired visual effect is sought, but a valuable quality in modest-sized gardens. Similarly to yew, they bear fruit, not woody cones, and are thus easily distinguished from other conifers.

J. communis 'Hibernica', Irish juniper, makes a tight-knit, almost glaucous, pencil specimen, broadening with age to become more attractive and less artificial, contributing to a real feeling of maturity in a garden.

MEDIUM EVERGREEN CONIFER
FULL SUN   ZONES 3-9

J. chinensis, Chinese juniper, and *J. virginiana*, red cedar, have many variable garden cultivars. Colour and texture of leaf may be chosen for different planting schemes. Perhaps the best known of the latter is *J.v.* 'Skyrocket', slim, tall and with grey-green leaves.

MEDIUM EVERGREEN CONIFERS
FULL SUN   ZONES 4-9

J. × media 'Pfitzerana' is a wide spreading shrub with drooping tips at the ends of almost horizontal, but slightly ascending, branches. These stout arms bear a mixture of mature scale-like leaves lightened in colour by grey-green juvenile needles from new growth. It is

Pachysandra terminalis

Magnolia grandiflora

much planted in landscape designs, and when massed gives a rippling wave effect of varying heights and depths, and soft textured green colour. Plant on steeply sloping banks for good cover.

LARGE EVERGREEN CONIFER

FULL SUN OR HALF SHADE   ZONES 4-9

J. procumbens, creeping juniper, will make a prostrate carpet, hardly more than 30 cm (12 in) in height; an attractive contrast with stone or brick, over which the low branches with sharply pointed leaves of glaucous green will sprawl.

DWARF EVERGREEN CONIFER

FULL SUN OR SHADE   ZONES 4-9

KIRENGESHOMA

K. palmata is a plant of great dignity, superb in a foliage border where the soil is rich, moist and slightly acid. Beautiful vine-like leaves of pale green are set on dark ebony stems, contrasting well with the rough tinted foliage of rodgersias and graceful rippled surfaces of hosta leaves. In late summer, bell-shaped flowers of soft pale yellow, pastel rather than

luminous (see Clear yellows), complete an harmonious picture of plant form, leaf and bloom.

DECIDUOUS PERENNIAL   90 CM (36 IN)

FULL SUN OR HALF SHADE   ZONES 6-9

LAURUS BAY LAUREL, SWEET BAY

L. nobilis, bay, a traditional sun-loving evergreen, thrives in favoured climates and can be clipped into hedges and arbours. In a cold garden wall protection is essential. The aromatic leaves, used for flavouring many dishes, are dark and glossy, held by the dense twigs at different angles to give patterns of light. (See also Clear yellows: foliage.)

TALL EVERGREEN SHRUB

FULL SUN   ZONES 7-10

LIGUSTRUM PRIVET

Not always appreciated in its common hedging forms, privet is striking and attractive when glossy-leaved types from China and Japan are chosen. Some with variegation are particularly colourful in winter scenes (see Clear yellows).

L. lucidum has long pointed leaves, gracefully held and moving in the wind to cast light flickering shade, soothing in a hot garden in which it thrives. Handsome panicles of white flowers are carried in late summer. The fluted bark of a mature tree is attractive.

SMALL EVERGREEN TREE

FULL SUN OR HALF SHADE   ZONES 8-10

LIRIOPE

L. muscari has grassy foliage held in compact clumps, and is useful for front positions in partial shade. The deep purple flowers are borne in late summer. It makes a substantial ground cover at Kew Gardens.

EVERGREEN PERENNIAL   30 CM (12 IN)

FULL SUN OR HALF SHADE   ZONES 7-9

MAGNOLIA

Magnificent flowering trees and shrubs, and generally hardy in temperate regions, magnolias love rich deep soil and shelter from icy winds. Specimen bushes of spring-flowering species bear large goblets of pink, red or white (see appropriate chapters). Most are deciduous, but *M. delavayi* has evergreen leaves as large as those of *Rhododendron sinogrande*, with exotic-looking matt sea-green surfaces, sometimes as much as 30 cm (12 in) long and a bit less in width. It needs wall protection, and heat encourages the fragrant creamy-white flowers to develop towards the summer's end.

M. grandiflora 'Goliath' has glossy shining leaves with rust-coloured undersurfaces. It is the most lime-tolerant of the genus, growing to

tree-like proportions against a warm wall and producing cream flowers at intervals in summer and autumn.

LARGE EVERGREEN SHRUBS

FULL SUN   ZONES 8-10

MAHONIA

Mahonias have large green or grey pinnate leaves, the leaflets leathery with serrated edges, often spiny. This handsome foliage frames racemes of scented lily-of-the-valley flowers mostly in winter and early spring (see Clear yellows). The best species need shelter, but some modern hybrids are hardy and vigorous.

M. aquifolium, the Oregon grape, makes excellent cover in shade, the polished green leaves assuming purple and red tints in winter.

SMALL EVERGREEN SHRUB

SHADE   ZONES 6-9

MISCANTHUS

M. sinensis has graceful erect stems, towering in great clumps at the back of a border, the brownish-silver plumes opening in late summer. Plant in rich soil against a background of dark yew. The form *M.s.* 'Silver Feather' flowers reliably each year, with arching sprays of pinkish-brown.

DECIDUOUS PERENNIAL   1.8 M (6 FT)

FULL SUN   ZONES 6-9

MYRRHIS

M. odorata, sweet Cicely, has lovely cow-parsley leaves and flowers (see The whites: early summer). Leaves are strongly scented like liquorice and should be cut to the ground after flowering, to promote fresh green growth.

DECIDUOUS PERENNIAL   60 CM (24 IN)

FULL SUN OR HALF SHADE   ZONES 5-9

MYRTUS MYRTLE

Myrtles thrive in mild climates and are excellent maritime plants, their waxed shining leaves resisting salt-laden winds. The foliage is aromatic to the touch, and the pretty flowers emerge in late summer (see The whites).

M. communis suffers in a severe winter but the densely growing smooth clear green leaves are so attractive that it is always worth having a pot-grown plant kept in reserve in a cold frame. It is also a good container plant, in a very small garden playing the same architectural role as a bay tree in a larger space.

M.c. tarentina is a form with small narrow hard leaves, less beautiful, but certainly hardier and more free-flowering. Both look appropriate with soft grey foliage plants from similar habitats.

MEDIUM EVERGREEN SHRUBS

FULL SUN   ZONES 8-10

OSMANTHUS

Osmanthus are useful and hardy shrubs for any situation, making dense bushy shapes of dark and shining green. Two only have showy flowers, *O. delavayi* (see The whites: spring) and its hybrid with *O. decorus*, *O. × burkwoodii*, but all are scented.

O. decorus (syn. *Phillyrea decora*) has hard smooth entire leaves making a dense domed bush, extremely useful for formal planning combining solidity and gracefulness with symmetry. It is slow-growing and cuttings are often reluctant to root; hence it is still uncommon.

MEDIUM EVERGREEN SHRUB

FULL SUN OR HALF SHADE   ZONES 7-10

O. heterophyllus has green holly-like leaves. Cultivars have leaves with purple tints and cream or yellow variegation. The young growth is purplish-glaucous and its habit an upright one. It is sometimes planted for hedging, but equally makes a satisfactory specimen bush.

MEDIUM EVERGREEN SHRUB

FULL SUN OR SHADE   ZONES 7-10

PACHYSANDRA

P. terminalis is an acid-lover and may be used to cover ground under deciduous trees or shrubs. It has diamond-shaped green leaves which contrast unobtrusively with the bright green of mown grass. Like St John's wort or periwinkle, pachysandra can be massed in sweeping curved beds beside modern buildings or on steep motorway banks.

DWARF EVERGREEN SHRUB

SHADE   ZONES 4-9

PAEONIA PEONY

This decorative genus covers a whole range of shrubby and herbaceous plants. The tree peonies, usually forms of the white and pink *P. suffruticosa* or the yellow *P. lutea*, have architectural foliage and flowers in the spring; they may need protection from the morning sun after a frost.

P. suffruticosa, the Moutan, a tree peony, has pale green leaves supporting and making a framework for the flowers. Recommended cultivars are *P.s.* 'Duchess of Kent' with pink flowers, and the rare white 'Rock's Variety' (see The whites: spring).

MEDIUM DECIDUOUS SHRUBS

FULL SUN OR HALF SHADE   ZONES 6-9

Herbaceous peonies have good leaves, often pleasantly tinted in autumn, and making excellent ground cover. Flower colours vary from single cream, yellow and scarlet of the species peonies, to dark double and single reds, pinks and whites of the old cottage-garden *P. officinalis*, and the stylish white and pink fragrant garden hybrids of *P. lactiflora*. The latter are elegant, holding high single blooms, often with conspicuous yellow stamens.

DECIDUOUS PERENNIALS   60 CM (24 IN)

FULL SUN   ZONES 6-9

P. tenuifolia has dissected green ferny foliage, on a small scale, very pretty and delicate, and bears red flowers in early summer.

DECIDUOUS PERENNIAL   45 CM (18 IN)

FULL SUN   ZONES 7-9

PARTHENOCISSUS

Using twining tendrils or adhering to surfaces with adhesive pads, these vine-like climbers have attractive, many-lobed leaves which turn rich orange and scarlet in autumn (see below).

P. quinquefolia, Virginia creeper, climbing to the tops of tall trees in its native eastern USA, will quickly cover a house wall, its vivid autumn colours lasting many weeks.

P. tricuspidata, the Boston ivy, usually has three-lobed leaves of deep green, slightly tinted purple, which turn crimson and scarlet in autumn.

DECIDUOUS CLIMBERS

FULL SUN OR HALF SHADE   ZONES 4-9

PHILLYREA

Very slow-growing, phillyreas are much-neglected evergreens of considerable foliage value. The glistening leaves make a dense mass of foliage which may be fiercely clipped into formal shapes; they were used for topiary in the seventeenth century. *P. angustifolia* becomes a compact rounded bush with narrow plain dark green hairless leaves.

SMALL EVERGREEN SHRUB

FULL SUN OR HALF SHADE   ZONES 7-10

P. latifolia is an elegant olive-like tree, perfect in a small garden where a holm oak, *Quercus ilex*, would be too large and dominating, and perhaps too tender. The small leaves shine in sunlight and flutter slightly in a breeze, revealing the paler undersides.

SMALL EVERGREEN TREE

FULL SUN   ZONES 7-10

PHORMIUM

Phormiums have tough sword-like leaves, growing from the ground in a fan. The leaves are as useful as those of yucca, in sharply defining a spot in the garden, framing paths and doorways or providing contrast with rounded bushes and open-growing perennials. They like rich deep soil, as moist as possible in the growing season, but resent freezing wet conditions round the roots in winter. The many forms with coloured and striped leaves are in general less hardy.

P. cookianum, mountain flax, has pleasant leaves. There are many coloured forms, very popular today for making splashes of green and cream or purple and pink colour in small gardens.

P. tenax, New Zealand flax, is huge; from the base among the 1.8 m (6 ft) leaves tall 3 m (10 ft) stems carry clusters of dull red to black

Phormium tenax

Populus balsamifera × *trichocarpa*

flowers in summer. A form with coloured leaves of brownish-green-purple subtly blending with neighbouring greens, is much less eye-catching than the pink-edged purple forms of *P. cookianum*, which are very exotic. See also Strong reds: foliage.

SMALL TO LARGE EVERGREEN SHRUBS
FULL SUN   ZONES 8-10

PITTOSPORUM

P. tenuifolium, with charming chocolate-brown scented flowers in spring, is generally grown for its crinkled foliage, much used in floristry. The shining wavy-edged leaves are pale green but variegated, and purple-leaved forms have attractive foliage for colour schemes. In cold areas this pittosporum needs wall protection; in warmer climates, it is used for tall wind-breaks.

LARGE EVERGREEN SHRUB
FULL SUN   ZONES 8-10

POPULUS POPLAR

Poplars are fast-growing shapely trees with invasive roots, not suitable for a small garden; their easily recognizable outlines are often familiar garden or landscape features.

P. trichocarpa, black cottonwood from North America, is very fast-growing, but *P. balsamifera* × *trichocarpa* is recognized as the best of the balsam-scented poplars. Large glossy leaves, backed in white, waft fragrant scent through a garden when stirred by a breeze.

P. lasiocarpa, the Chinese necklace tree, has beautiful foliage, very large heart-shaped green leaves with red veins held on red leaf-stalks.

MEDIUM TO LARGE DECIDUOUS TREES
FULL SUN OR HALF SHADE   ZONES 4-9

PRUNUS

This large genus covers innumerable small trees and shrubs as well as the flowering cherries. For foliage effects, grow the evergreen cherry laurel and Portugal laurel. The former, *P. laurocerasus*, although tough and invasive, has cheerful, bright and glossy green foliage, and when space permits is delightful in background massed planting.

LARGE EVERGREEN SHRUB
FULL SUN OR SHADE   ZONES 7-10

P.l. 'Otto Luyken' is a low densely packed shrub with narrow dark leaves, very useful in shade, and free-flowering. Groups of three or five make solid blocks of green for winter interest.

SMALL EVERGREEN SHRUB
FULL SUN OR SHADE   ZONES 7-10

P. lusitanica, Portugal laurel, has dark green leaves and red leaf stalks; white hawthorn-scented flowers are held on long racemes in summer. It is an ideal informal hedging plant for the garden boundary and it is very wind-resistant.

TALL EVERGREEN SHRUB
FULL SUN OR SHADE   ZONES 7-10

RHEUM ORNAMENTAL RHUBARB

R. palmatum has deeply toothed broad rough green leaves, slightly tinged with purple, and in *R.p.* 'Atrosanguineum', its purple cultivar (see Strong reds: foliage), a deep wine colour, splendid and glowing with the sun shining behind it. In scale these ornamental rhubarbs lie between the giant gunnera and rodgersia, similar in habit and leaf, and revelling in deep damp soil. Among the best perennial foliage plants, and rivalling hostas in the ornamental garden. Tall plumes of white, pink or red astilbe-like flowers are borne in summer.

DECIDUOUS PERENNIALS   1.5 M (5 FT)
FULL SUN OR HALF SHADE   ZONES 7-10

RHODODENDRON

Most rhododendrons are acid-loving shrubs, lighting up woodland glades with colour in early spring. Innumerable species and hybrids from dwarf to tree size may be grown in suitable situations. Some are specimen foliage plants of interest and beauty, but the majority when not in flower make bulky, heavy bushes of matt green.

R. cinnabarinum has smoky-grey-green leaves, a lovely foil to plain dark greens, and bears scented tubular orange flowers in late spring (see Hot colours).

MEDIUM EVERGREEN SHRUB
HALF SHADE   ZONES 7-9

R. falconeri, R. fictolacteum, R. macabeanum and giant-leaved *R. sinogrande* are all tall shrubs for woodland, their leaves undercoated with matt-textured red-brown, cinnamon, silvery-white and fawn respectively; all have cream to yellow flowers.

TALL EVERGREEN SHRUBS
HALF SHADE   ZONES 8-10

R. scintillans has leathery green leaves with grey undersides and violet, almost blue, clustered flowers in early summer.

SMALL EVERGREEN SHRUB
HALF SHADE   ZONES 5-9

See also Pinks and mauves: spring.

RODGERSIA

Rodgersias love damp boggy conditions and will spread quickly to make weedproof mats, about 45 cm (18 in) high, of thick greeny-bronze foliage, topped in summer by white or pink flower-plumes.

R. pinnata has deep green pinnate leaves,

bronze-tinted in early summer. The cultivar *R.p.* 'Superba' has even darker leaves and tall panicles of pink flowers (see Pinks and mauves).

R. podophylla is the most drought-tolerant, with grooved triangular leaves with flower-shaped jagged lobes and buff-white plumes (see The whites). Beautiful with small grey-leaved willows, primulas and astilbes.

R. tabularis is quite different, with smoother leaves like pale green umbrellas, and creamy flowers. It is slow to establish but worth waiting for when planted massed in drifts for maximum effect.

DECIDUOUS PERENNIALS   90 CM (36 IN)
FULL SUN OR HALF SHADE   ZONES 5-8

ROSA ROSE

Roses – bush, shrub or climbing – are mainly grown for beauty of flower colour and shape (see Pinks and mauves: early summer), but particularly among the shrub types good form and foliage are added attractions.

R. pimpinellifolia (syn. *R. spinosissima*), the Scotch or burnet rose, has deep green leaflets, giving a fern-like effect among which charming white or pink flowers give pale colour in early summer. Similar shrub roses often have arching stems, sometimes reddish or brown, and small yellow flowers, sweetly scented. Perhaps among the best are the species *R. xanthina*, and hybrid *R.* 'Canary Bird'.

R. rugosa has attractive crinkled apple-green leaves held on thorny stems, and will make

Rhododendron fictolacteum

dense impenetrable hedges. The foliage is always fresh and unblemished, more so perhaps than any deciduous shrub. It is not disease-prone or subject to damage from insects, since aphids seem also not to like the flower-buds. The rugosa forms and hybrids have flowers of strong crimson, purple, pink and white, double and single, often highly scented, and some are followed by red tomato-like fruits.

MEDIUM TO LARGE DECIDUOUS SHRUBS
FULL SUN OR HALF SHADE   ZONES 4-9

Rheum palmatum

Saxifraga × urbium

RUBUS BRAMBLE

R. tricolor has trailing stems bearing handsome heart-shaped lustrous green foliage. Purple tints at the edges of the leaves and pale hairy white undersides give added colour. It quickly spreads to make dense ground cover, even in poor dry soil, most suitable for rough woodland but a possible feature under a specimen garden tree, leaves and undulating stems making a shining carpet.

SMALL TRAILING EVERGREEN SHRUB
SHADE   ZONES 5-9

SARCOCOCCA
CHRISTMAS BOX, SWEET BOX

Sarcococcas are little box-like shrubs for shade, their small glossy leaves glowing under dark shrubs. They flower in midwinter, small creamy vanilla-scented anthers (see The whites) wafting fragrance through the garden.

S. confusa is a dense hardy shrub, with cream flowers followed by black berries. *S. hookeriana humilis* is densely branching and suckers to make spreading carpets of glossy foliage. Pink-cream anthers in midwinter are succeeded by black berries.

SMALL EVERGREEN SHRUBS
SHADE   ZONES 7-9

SAXIFRAGA SAXIFRAGE

Basically saxifrages are alpines and prefer to grow snugly in rock crevices. In fact many adapt readily to garden conditions and can be grown as an edging in a warm dry border, pink or white flowers held on long stalks above rosettes of leaves.

S. × urbium, known affectionately as London pride, has fleshy apple-green leaves and thrives in shade, producing a haze of pink starry flowers in early summer. It is suitable for planting on a low wall, needing little soil and appreciating good drainage.

EVERGREEN PERENNIAL   30 CM (12 IN)
SHADE   ZONES 5-9

SEDUM STONECROP

Generally sedums have thick fleshy leaves designed for water storage. Some thrive on rocks in very poor soil conditions, while others may be treated as normal herbaceous perennials for a mixed border.

S. spectabile, the ice plant, has pale green fleshy leaves, emerging in early spring and growing very slowly through the season. Finally at the end of the summer stems carry flat heads of pink starry flowers (see Pinks and mauves), always, on a warm autumn day, covered in butterflies. The hybrid *S. × 'Autumn Joy'* has dark pink-red flowers and makes a neater shape.

S. telephium 'Munstead Red' grows less stiffly. The leaves are dark green and flower-heads dusky chocolate-red (see Strong reds: late summer).

DECIDUOUS PERENNIALS   45 CM (18 IN)
FULL SUN   ZONES 6-9

TAXUS YEW

The English or common yew, with juniper, before importations, was among the few evergreens in an English landscape. Sombre, solid and dark, yews are impressive as well as beautiful. Anciently endowed with magical qualities, yews give an air of permanence to a garden, but they are slow-growing and are seldom planted today as trees.

T. baccata, the English yew, is the best hedging plant; dense and even-textured, making solid green walls defining a garden's structure and providing a perfect background to flower colour. If the ground is well prepared, a trench being better than individual holes, and frequent feeding is given, a yew hedge grows quickly – at least 30 cm (12 in) a year – and needs only annual clipping. In summer young paler foliage makes a tapestry pattern among the darker green leaves. To the sophisticated a garden of yew, box and mown grass provides the ultimate in sensitive colouring. Flowers of vivid eye-catching hue become intruders, disturbing a quiet scene of blending greens.

T.b. 'Dovastoniana' has a distinctive habit, wide spreading branches growing fan-shaped from the base, the ends elegantly drooping. It is a useful architectural plant, contrasting with rounded bushes and softer foliage plants. *T.b.* 'Fastigiata', Irish yew, grows in a column, erect with closely packed branches, the leaves black-green. Familiar in churchyards, it is often used to define and emphasize a pathway, the solid regular shapes casting equal patterns of light and shade.

LARGE EVERGREEN SHRUBS OR TREES
FULL SUN OR HALF SHADE   ZONES 4-9

TRACHELOSPERMUM

These are evergreen twining climbers for mild microclimates. The dark green leaves will cover a wall as densely as any ivy or self-clinging creeper. Fragrant creamy-white flowers appear among the glossy foliage in summer (see The whites).

Taxus baccata 'Fastigiata'

T. asiaticum is one of the hardiest, with small leaves and a compact form of growth.
T. jasminoides in a favourable climate is the most beautiful of wall-coverings. Vigorous, with glowing leaves, both species are wonderful conservatory plants if outside temperatures are too severe.
EVERGREEN CLIMBERS
FULL SUN   ZONES 8-10

VERATRUM FALSE HELLEBORE
V. nigrum, the black false hellebore, is a striking foliage plant. The leaves, folded and pleated like a fan, push through the soil in early spring to make arching mounds of fresh green. They are attractive to slugs and it is essential to put down bait. Later, in established plants, and if given plenty of moisture, tall leafless stems bear maroon plumes composed of small stars (see Strong reds: summer). The foliage of this statuesque plant is a perfect foil to spring bulbs, which are bright in colours but often lack significant leaves. There is a white-flowered species, *V. album*.
BULB   45 CM (18 IN)   HALF SHADE   ZONES 5-9

VIBURNUM
Viburnums have not only beautifully shaped and textured leaves and scented flowers but also good structural habits. Coloured leaves and fruit in autumn extend their season. Some of the evergreen species are useful foliage shrubs, easy to grow successfully and happy in alkaline soils.
V. × burkwoodii is a wall shrub making a dense background of shining green for its pink-budded white flowers in early spring (see The whites). The undersides of the leaves are felted brownish-grey.
MEDIUM EVERGREEN SHRUB
FULL SUN OR HALF SHADE   ZONES 7-9
V. davidii has low spreading branches with leaves leathery, dark green and veined above, paler below. The corymbs of white flowers in early summer are succeeded by bright turquoise berries, but male and female plants should be grown to ensure fruiting.
SMALL EVERGREEN SHRUB
SHADE   ZONES 7-9
V. tinus, laurustinus, has dark healthy-looking leaves and flowers splendidly through most of the winter months. Tolerant of shade, it can also be used to make a dense informal hedge.
MEDIUM EVERGREEN SHRUB
FULL SUN OR SHADE   ZONES 6-9

VINCA PERIWINKLE
All periwinkles make dense ground cover, except perhaps the variegated form of the greater periwinkle, *V. major*, which has an irritating open upright habit, and will grow in poor soil and dense shade. Vincas are usually neglected; however they all perform much better if given an open site, rich feeding and annual trimming after flowering is over. Quite dull foliage becomes glossy and flowers are borne much more freely.
V. difformis, a slightly tender species, has beautiful pale blue flowers all through the winter. It is one of the very best evergreen ground covers in mild areas, thriving in any soil, but do not let it dry out too much.
DWARF DECIDUOUS SHRUB
FULL SUN OR SHADE   ZONES 6-9
V. minor has rich blue, plum or white flowers. The trailing stems grow in rippling waves, like a choppy sea, a contrast to smooth lawn or textured juniper.
DWARF EVERGREEN SHRUB
FULL SUN OR SHADE   ZONES 5-9

VIOLA
VIOLET, PANSY, HEART'S EASE
The wild scented sweet violet, *V. odorata*, and the cultivated pansy, *V. × wittrockiana*, and many other garden species and forms are part of gardening tradition. Scented velvet-textured flowers can be chosen for bloom in almost all the seasons, in sun or shade, and when out of flower rich green or coloured leaves (see also Strong reds: foliage) can make ground cover under shrubs and roses. *V. odorata* is as useful for its leaves, which make weedproof cover through summer months, as for its scented flowers (see The blues: spring), but beware invasive seedlings.
ANNUALS, BIENNIALS OR DECIDUOUS PERENNIALS   10-23 CM (4-9 IN)
FULL SUN OR HALF SHADE   ZONES 6-9

VITIS GRAPEVINE
Vines cling with tendrils to wire or trellis supports, making curtains of fresh green (or grey or purple) leaves over walls and pergolas. They can also be effective allowed to scramble and twine into trees or over tree stumps. Even commercial vines for grapes are grown up into fruit trees in parts of Italy.
V. coignetiae is spectacular, with large broad heart-shaped leaves, smooth above but covered densely with reddish hairs beneath. It is very vigorous, and at its best when turning spectacular colours of rich yellow, orange-red and crimson in autumn (see below).
V. vinifera, the grapevine, besides coloured-leaved cultivars (see Strong reds), has an attractive parsley-leaved cultivar in *V.v.* 'Apiifolia', which gives a light ferny appearance to the whole plant.
DECIDUOUS CLIMBERS   FULL SUN   ZONES 6-9

Veratrum nigrum

Viburnum davidii

Vinca difformis

SILVER AND GREY

Achillea × 'Moonshine'

The degree of greyness depends initially on the density, length and angle of small hairs on the surface of the green leaf, but the division between the plants included here and the greener greys of the preceding section or the glaucous blue-greys in 'The blues' chapter is to some extent subjective. Here grey is interpreted as grey-green, metallic pewter- and steel-grey, and light-reflecting 'silver'; included, too, are leaves of dusty whitish appearance (dealbatus in botanical Latin, translatable as 'whitewashed').

In the ornamental garden greys are at their best by mid- or late summer. Many plants become less grey in shade and in winter as they absorb light rays rather than deflecting them, or towards flowering time when their energy goes into setting seed. Plants dishevelled during winter need severe pruning after the last frosts. Most greys thrive in full sun and good drainage: more are lost by freezing water collected round their root crowns than by extreme low temperature. A few, particularly small willows, thrive in moist conditions.

ACACIA WATTLE

A. dealbata, silver wattle, with feathery silver leaves, is a beautiful sight all year round, and in spring has the extra bonus of pale primrose flowers, the 'mimosa' of florists (see Clear yellows: spring).
LARGE EVERGREEN SHRUB OR SMALL TREE
FULL SUN   ZONES 8-10

A. pravissima, Ovens wattle, has grey leaves which are flattened stalks. Usually triangular in shape, they give quite a dense impression, very different from the ethereal featheriness of many other wattles.
LARGE EVERGREEN SHRUB OR SMALL TREE
FULL SUN   ZONES 8-10

ACHILLEA YARROW

A. × *argentea* makes a spreading silver cushion, shining and cheerful from spring to early winter. Like all 'silvers', it requires excellent drainage and hot sun. Pretty white flowers are borne on short stems in early summer.
DECIDUOUS PERENNIAL   15 CM (6 IN)
FULL SUN   ZONES 6-9
A. × 'Moonshine' has grey filigree foliage and bears corymbs of pale yellow flowers in summer (see Clear yellows).
DECIDUOUS PERENNIAL   60 CM (24 IN)
FULL SUN   ZONES 4-9

ANTHEMIS

A. cupaniana is mat-forming with finely dissected grey leaves, above which white daisy-flowers are carried in early summer (see The whites). On heavy soil it may succumb to excessive moisture in winter, but rooted pieces may be potted during the autumn and overwintered in a cold frame.
SMALL EVERGREEN SHRUB
FULL SUN   ZONES 7-9

ARTEMISIA

A. absinthium 'Lambrook Silver', a silver variant of the common wormwood, is hardy, almost evergreen, with silver-grey dissected leaves. Although looking scruffy in winter, by midsummer plants are covered by wand-like stems bearing pale yellow flowers. The silver foliage is duller at flowering time. It is an attractive and useful plant, sufficiently regular in habit, particularly if 'shaped' in spring, to give architectural form to any scheme. Its dense silvery appearance acts as a foil to bright colours.
SMALL SEMI-EVERGREEN SHRUB
FULL SUN   ZONES 7-9
A. arborescens is best grown as a wall shrub, carefully tied and shaped to make a graceful and pretty background to border plants. In spring it should be pruned after the last frost, new shoots immediately breaking from below. The leaves are delicate and feathery, pale silver and finely cut, woody stems falling forward in an elegant cascade. A more hardy form, *A.a.* 'Faith Raven', is worth looking for, and survives all but the hardest winters.
MEDIUM EVERGREEN SHRUB
FULL SUN   ZONES 7-9

Artemisia 'Powis Castle' with *Buxus sempervirens*

A. ludoviciana 'Latifolia' is a broad-leaved form of the western mugwort or white sage, the leaves startlingly white in early spring and dulling as the season progresses. Cut back rather lax stems in midsummer, and pale new growth will repeat the spring effects.
DECIDUOUS PERENNIAL 45 CM (18 IN)
FULL SUN ZONES 5-9

A. pedemontana (syn. *A. lanata*) makes a foaming cushion of glistening silver, tightly carpeting the ground and making a feathery edging to a border. It shoots very early in the spring, lovely with white tulips growing up behind.
DECIDUOUS SUB-SHRUB 15 CM (6 IN)
FULL SUN ZONES 6-9

A. 'Powis Castle' seems to have the best characteristics of all the shrubby grey artemisias. It is silvery but pewter-toned. It is tough, shapely and compact. It hardly flowers, so the leaves keep their sheen all season.
MEDIUM EVERGREEN SHRUB
FULL SUN ZONES 7-9

A. stellerana, beach wormwood, is very much the odd-man-out among artemisias, the leaves being shaped like those of chrysanthemums and lacking the typical wormwood pungency. The leaf is felted white. Its great merit is its ability to thrive in shade in damp soil, and still maintain pale glowing foliage.
DECIDUOUS PERENNIAL 30 CM (12 IN)
FULL SUN OR SHADE ZONES 6-9

BALLOTA

B. pseudodictamnus is a compact rounded shrub. The leaves are pale apple-green in spring, rapidly getting greyer and more woolly in texture as the sun gets hotter. By midsummer pale green bracts appear in whorls round the stems, but should be carefully cut off before flowers emerge. New growth of leaves begins and the bush remains shapely and clothed to the ground, a blend of pale green and felted grey.
SMALL EVERGREEN SUB-SHRUB
FULL SUN ZONES 8-10

BAPTISIA

B. australis, false indigo, has attractive grey-green leaves and indigo-blue pea-flowers in summer (see The blues). It prefers rich moist lime-free soil.
DECIDUOUS PERENNIAL
60-120 CM (24-48 IN) FULL SUN ZONES 4-9

CERASTIUM

C. tomentosum, snow in summer, has silver woolly leaves, and needs little soil, cascading like a waterfall down a wall or scrambling out over paving to soften hard outlines and surfaces. The flowers in early summer are saucer-shaped and white. Very invasive, it is a good plant for a low-upkeep garden, easily eradicated when necessary (see The whites: early summer).
EVERGREEN PERENNIAL
7.5-15 CM (3-6 IN)
FULL SUN ZONES 5-9

CHAMAECYPARIS FALSE CYPRESS

The various forms of Lawson cypress, *C. lawsoniana*, may grow to be tall conical trees, 12 m (40 ft) and more high, so need careful placing. The slow-growing *C.l.* 'Fletcheri' has soft feathery greyish-blue leaves, and does not broaden out at the base as it grows. The tall 'Triomf van Boskoop' looks magnificent when grouped in threes, or more if space permits. One makes a staccato point, three make a grey cloud blending into a landscape.
SMALL TO MEDIUM EVERGREEN CONIFERS
FULL SUN ZONES 6-9

CHRYSANTHEMUM

C. foeniculaceum is a shrubby Paris marguerite, with feathery dissected silver-grey leaves, carrying white daisy-flowers all summer (see The whites). It is not hardy, but cuttings are easily rooted and can be overwintered. It is a beautiful plant for bedding or for containers.
SMALL EVERGREEN SHRUB
FULL SUN ZONES 8-9

CONVOLVULUS

C. cneorum has leaves covered in fine silky down which shimmers in sunlight; it is one of the best silver-leaved plants. White flowers, pink-tinted in bud, cover the bush in early summer. It needs good drainage and shelter.
SMALL EVERGREEN SHRUB
FULL SUN ZONES 7-9

CYNARA

C. cardunculus, the cardoon, and *C. scolymus*, the globe artichoke, make bold architectural shapes of dull silver, magnificent as corner features. Unlike most greys, these plants need manure and moisture when growing.
DECIDUOUS PERENNIALS
2.1 M (7 FT)
FULL SUN ZONES 7-9

CYTISUS BROOM

Brooms love poor sandy soil, preferably acid or at least neutral. They are excellent garden plants, varying from the prostrate to large open-growing bushes. The Moroccan broom, *C. battandieri*, has silver, trifoliate leaves covered in silky hairs, giving them a satin sheen. Bright yellow flowers are borne in summer (see Clear yellows). It grows quickly and needs support if exposed to strong winds.
TALL SEMI-EVERGREEN SHRUB
FULL SUN ZONES 8-10

Cynara cardunculus

Dorycnium hirsutum

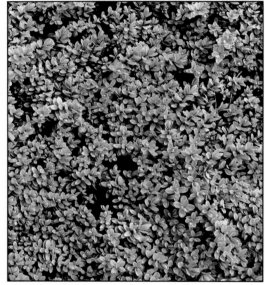

Hebe pinguifolia 'Pagei'

DORYCNIUM

D. hirsutum is a spreading shrub with very hairy grey-green leaves, and pink and white clover-like flowers. The reddish-brown seed-pods are attractive and carried all winter. At least half of the plant's growth should be removed each spring, new shoots quickly replacing the old foliage.
SMALL EVERGREEN SHRUB
FULL SUN   ZONES 7-9

ELAEAGNUS

This is a genus of most decorative and useful evergreen and deciduous shrubs. The former can be used as shapely informal hedging or placed individually to give bulk in a mixed border. Some with grey-green leaves are quiet features, their undulating leaf edge reflecting light and shade; others have startling gold- and green-leaved variegation.

E. angustifolia, Russian olive, is semi-evergreen with thin grey leaves and a pendulous habit, similar to the popular weeping silver pear, *Pyrus salicifolia* 'Pendula', but less dense and more easily fitted in to border planting, and hardier.
TALL SEMI-EVERGREEN SHRUB
FULL SUN   ZONES 2-8

E. commutata, the silverberry, is deciduous but the leaves are broad and intensely silver. Pale yellow flowers are carried in early summer. There are many different local forms of this excellent shrub; try to find a tall-growing one as they seem to flower more freely.
SMALL TO TALL DECIDUOUS SHRUB
FULL SUN OR HALF SHADE   ZONES 3-9

E. macrophylla has silver-backed grey-green leaves with undulating edges. It has a bushy habit, fitting into formal patterns and into woodland planting, a better plant than the more frequently recommended *E.* × *ebbingei*.
LARGE EVERGREEN SHRUB
FULL SUN OR HALF SHADE   ZONES 6-9

ERYNGIUM

Sun-loving eryngiums have spiny leaves and thistle-like flower-heads. In some the foliage is silvery and metallic, in others green, marbled white or deeply cut and blue-green. All seed freely.

E. giganteum is usually biennial with heart-shaped young green leaves which turn aluminium-grey just before the plant flowers in midsummer.
DECIDUOUS PERENNIAL
90-120 CM (36-48 IN)   FULL SUN   ZONES 7-9

EUPHORBIA SPURGE

Good garden plants, many of the spurges are sun-lovers, thriving in poor well-drained soil, and having glaucous fleshy or thin grey-green leaves. Others such as the evergreen *E. robbiae* and the deciduous *E. griffithii* are perennials which spread in light shade. Generally the flowers are insignificant, but are surrounded by attractive petal-like bracts, which vary in colour between harsh orange-red and a delicious gentle lime-green.

E. characias wulfenii is a medium shrub with linear leaves, bluish in summer, grey-green in winter, carrying tall panicles of yellow-green flowers early in the season (see Clear yellows: early summer). Making a symmetrical rounded shape, it is useful in bold designs. *E. characias* is very similar in appearance, but the coloured bracts have dark-centred flowers.
MEDIUM EVERGREEN SHRUBS
FULL SUN   ZONES 7-9

HEBE
SHRUBBY VERONICA, SHRUBBY SPEEDWELL

Generally half-hardy, hebes are grown for their decorative foliage and for their flowers in summer, which are carried in racemes and vary in colour from white to pink and crimson, and shades of lilac to lavender-blue. They make excellent seaside shrubs, the leaves being resistant to salt-laden winds and also to industrial pollution.

H. pinguifolia 'Pagei' makes a wide mat of glaucous-grey, attractive and kempt all year. It is a weed-smothering ground cover, is hardy and has white small flowers in early summer.
SMALL EVERGREEN SHRUB
FULL SUN   ZONES 8-9

HELICHRYSUM
EVERLASTING, IMMORTELLE

Rather variable in hardiness, helichrysums have attractive pale foliage, and are among the most useful for silver and grey gardens and for eye-catching clumps in mixed sunny borders.

H. italicum (syn. *H. angustifolium*), the curry plant, unlike so many grey-leaved plants, retains its silver lustre all through the year. It is one of the hardiest, and in spring the foliage, faintly smelling of curry, may be clipped back to make a tidy shapely bush.
SMALL EVERGREEN SHRUB
FULL SUN   ZONES 7-9

H. petiolatum is best used for temporary summer ground cover, or in containers where good drainage helps it survive until the first severe frosts. In sheltered gardens this helichrysum will live through the winter, growing tightly against a wall, almost climbing, and producing sprays of pale flowers. Individual leaves are heart-shaped, pale green, covered with a short white pile. The branchlets arch, making the whole effect elegant and shapely. It contrasts with other 'silvers' in habit, weaving among neighbouring plants, or looks effective adjacent to glossy-leaved acanthus and twining through the lower branches of ceanothus. In pots, white petunias or trailing blue lobelias combine to make a colour picture and it throws out horizontal spreading branches. *H.p.* 'Variegatum' is a form with variegated leaves, and in 'Limelight' the leaves are a pale gold (see Clear yellows: foliage).
EVERGREEN SUB-SHRUB
30 CM (12 IN)   FULL SUN   ZONES 7-9

HIPPOPHAE

H. rhamnoides, sea buckthorn, has thorny stems with narrow, very silvery leaves and makes a tall straggling background to groups of flower

colour. Clematis and the branching arms of shrub roses may be allowed to wind through its open network, to delightful effect. In winter, if both sexes are grown, pale orange berries are carried on the dark stems (see Hot colours: fruits and berries).
TALL DECIDUOUS SHRUB
FULL SUN   ZONES 4-9

IRIS

The foliage of irises varies between the grassy, untidy tufts of many species to the erect sword-like grey leaves of the bearded irises, which make splendid exclamation marks in borders contrasting with rounded shapes and leaves, or accentuating corners and framing doorways.

The tall flower-stems of the Bearded irises, grown from sun-loving rhizomes, bear blooms of different shades, sometimes with two or three different colours in the individual flower, whose petals and falls are often frilled and shaped. Plain flowers, self-tinted or shaded, are best in simple planting schemes; massed whites, palely tinged with lavender or cream, yellow, bronze and blue, with the strong accented foliage, make a garden picture in early summer. Unfortunately, these irises need beds to themselves; they like poor soil and uncovered rhizomes to get maximum baking. Herbicides must not touch the sensitive bare rhizomes, so hand weeding is imperative.
DECIDUOUS RHIZOMES   75-150 CM (30-60 IN)
FULL SUN   ZONES 7-9
I. pallida dalmatica has grey-green leaves, which keep shape and colour through most of the year, and pale blue fragrant flowers in early summer (see The blues), making a useful contrast to lavender and artemisia shapes, the soft colourings blending happily.
EVERGREEN RHIZOME   75 CM (30 IN)
FULL SUN   ZONES 7-9

LAVANDULA LAVENDER

English lavender, evocative of cottage gardens and the formal rose beds of grander estates, expresses the spirit of a mature garden, gnarled stems and grey-green leaves falling over paving or brick. The pale flower-spikes, from which the colour name derives, can now vary towards darker purplish shades as well as pale pink and a tinted white, the two latter smaller and tender. Lavender bushes vary in size, making neat hedges or attractive mounds of grey in sunny borders.

L. angustifolia (syn. *L. spica*) is the true, so-called English lavender, actually a native of Mediterranean lands, where fields of cultivated plants are grown to make scent. It is taller at 1.2 m (4 ft) than the cultivars *L.a.* 'Hidcote' and 'Munstead', which make denser, more

Eryngium giganteum

compact shapes, with darker flower-heads. The pale pink 'Loddon Pink' has thinner pale leaves, and 'Nana Alba' has white flowers; at 45 cm (18 in), both are small in stature.
SMALL TO MEDIUM EVERGREEN SHRUBS
FULL SUN   ZONES 7-10
See also The blues: summer.

MELIANTHUS

M. major is a very beautiful foliage sub-shrub, proving hardier than might be expected for a plant from India and South Africa. Its chief requirement for survival in a hard winter is adequate drainage, there being more losses from roots and crown sitting in frozen water than from low temperatures. Among the most ornamental of all foliage plants, the pinnate leaves are large, grey-green, fingered and

deeply serrated. New growth in spring is pale and luminous. It will only flower in mild climates where the foliage survives the winter. The flowers are deep maroon.
SEMI-EVERGREEN SUB-SHRUB
1.5 M (5 FT)   FULL SUN   ZONES 8-10

NEPETA CATMINT

Beloved by cats, these bushy grey small-leaved plants are indispensable for all soft colour schemes. Sprays of lavender flowers arch over and into neighbouring plants, and if flower-stems are removed, a repeat performance comes in late summer. Lovely with roses, as edgings to paths, less stiff and formal than shaped santolina or lavender. Spaces can be left between clumps of catmint for spring- or autumn-flowering bulbs. Pale daffodils give

Santolina chamaecyparissus

Senecio 'Sunshine'

leaves make a soft picture in summer (see Pinks and mauves).
MEDIUM EVERGREEN SHRUBS
FULL SUN   ZONES 7-9

PYRUS PEAR
P. salicifolia 'Pendula' is deservedly the most popular of weeping grey-leaved trees. Of medium height, it has dark stems and narrow silver leaves, drooping rather than weeping symmetrically. It can be pruned, but looks nicer allowed to grow as it will. It is equally lovely against a dark background or mixed in a bed with many different groups of colour.
MEDIUM DECIDUOUS TREE
FULL SUN   ZONES 5-8

ROSA ROSE
Grey-leaved roses make mounds of pale colour in mixed borders. They need full sun to keep the leaves grey.
   R. × alba has delightful grey-green leaves and white or pale pink clustered flower-heads. Among its cultivars are *R. × a.* 'Maxima', a double white, and 'Celestial', a shell-pink, both flowering once only, in early summer.
   R. glauca (syn. *R. rubrifolia*) has grey-purple leaves and reddish stems with few prickles. Its flowers are clear pink and its fruits bright red. Think of it as an ornamental foliage and fruit shrub rather than a flowering rose.
   R. villosa 'Duplex', Wolley Dod's rose, has bluish-grey downy leaves, deliciously fragrant when crushed, pink-red semi-double flowers and large apple-shaped bristle-clad fruits.
MEDIUM DECIDUOUS SHRUBS
FULL SUN   ZONES 5-9

SALIX WILLOW
Willows range in size between large noble lowland trees and creeping alpine shrubs with twiggy outlines.
   S. alba 'Sericea' is a small silver-leaved tree suitable for a small garden and a useful alternative to the grey-leaved weeping pear, *Pyrus salicifolia* 'Pendula'.
SMALL DECIDUOUS TREE
FULL SUN   ZONES 5-9
S. hastata 'Wehrhahnii' has silvery catkins in spring when the leaves emerge pale green. Later the foliage becomes grey.
MEDIUM DECIDUOUS SHRUB
FULL SUN   ZONES 4-8
S. lanata, the woolly willow from northern Europe, has rounded silvery-grey hairy leaves with stout erect yellowish hairy catkins in spring. It is most attractive by water, but survives in quite dry soil.
SMALL DECIDUOUS SHRUB
FULL SUN   ZONES 2-8

height as the pale grey leaves emerge, and white galtonias will push their flowering stems through the leaves at the end of the season.
   N. 'Six Hills Giant' has pale lavender-blue flower-spikes. It makes a charming large-scale edging plant next to stone or gravel, and the long stems fall gracefully in contrast to masonry.
DECIDUOUS PERENNIAL   90 CM (36 IN)
FULL SUN OR HALF SHADE   ZONES 6-9
See also The blues: early summer.

OLEARIA DAISY BUSH
Olearias are evergreen shrubs with beautiful green, grey and golden leaves. Some have small leaves, grey and simple; others have holly-like undulating edges, with olive-green or grey top surfaces and white or buff undersides. Yet others are hard, linear and almost broom-like with a golden-green surface. Not easy to grow successfully, few are reliably hardy; they like sun but may die in a heat wave. Not fussy about soil type, they need good drainage but plenty of moisture. The fragrant flowers in single sprays or branched clusters are usually white, or may be mauve, pink and pale blue (see appropriate chapters).
   O. × mollis has silvery-white leaves, slightly wavy-edged, and toothed. Almost hardy, it does not tolerate drought conditions or prolonged hot sun, but flowers freely, with large corymbs of white daisies.
SMALL EVERGREEN SHRUB
FULL SUN OR HALF SHADE   ZONES 7-9
O. phlogopappa and the hybrid *O. × scilloniensis* have pale grey-greenish leaves, flowers crowding the stems in dense heads in early summer. White flowering forms seem to be tougher than those with colours.
MEDIUM EVERGREEN SHRUB
FULL SUN   ZONES 7-9

O. macrodonta has undulating leaves, the silvery-white undersurface fully revealed. Flowering freely in summer, this is a wonderful bush, the textured leaves and dense habit making a valuable contribution to the foliage garden. Reasonably hardy.
LARGE EVERGREEN SHRUB
FULL SUN   ZONES 7-9
O. × oleifolia 'Waikariensis' is a hardy hybrid, with silvery lanceolate leaves, gleaming white beneath. White flowers in summer.
SMALL EVERGREEN SHRUB
FULL SUN OR HALF SHADE   ZONES 6-9
See also The whites: early summer.

ONOPORDON
O. acanthium, the Scotch thistle, and *O. arabicum* are giant grey-leaved thistles, usually biennial and monocarpic. Tall, stately and ghostly in evening light, the winged stems and painfully spined leaves are silvery-white, the flowers purple-red and reliably producing seed. These plants' ethereal quality makes them the backbone and middleman of silver gardens, linking white flowers and dark foliage.
DECIDUOUS PERENNIAL   2.4 M (8 FT)
FULL SUN   ZONES 7-9

PHLOMIS
There are herbaceous and shrubby phlomis, including the popular Jerusalem sage, *P. fruticosa*. Grown in gardens, not all are reliably hardy, but they usually survive being cut to the ground annually in cold climates. The best for attractive silvery hairy leaves include *P. chrysophylla*, which makes a rounded bush with grey leaves of distinctly greeny-yellow tint, and *P. anatolica*, with very large leaves. Flowers are golden-yellow in summer. *P. italica*, too, has stems and leaves intensely hairy and white, its lilac-pink flowers and pale

SANTOLINA

Santolinas with grey and green finely divided aromatic leaves are useful plants for making low hedges or for grouping in colour arrangements. They need vigorous pruning each spring, or rapidly become woody and unshapely; the normally harsh-yellow button-flowers are discouraged, too.

S. chamaecyparissus, lavender cotton, makes a dense well-rounded bush, greenish in spring, but later stems and leaves coated with wool become silvery.

S. neapolitiana of gardens (*S. pinnata* subsp. *neapolitiana*) is very similar but the individual leaves are longer and more feathery, the whole effect grey rather than silvery. A cultivar, *S.p.n.* 'Sulphurea', has pale yellow flowers.

SMALL EVERGREEN SHRUBS
FULL SUN   ZONES 7-10

SENECIO

Among the garden senecios are annuals, perennials and shrubby bushes. None of the latter are reliably hardy, but all are very useful making soft grey and silver shapes. These may be dense and flattering, enhancing pale flower colour, or dissected and airy, standing out against more sober leaves.

S. compactus is similar to a miniature of the better-known *S.* 'Sunshine' (see below), the grey hairy leaves outlined in white, with flower-stems even whiter. Buds should be removed, or leaves lose their gloss. In very small gardens it is ideal for low hedging flopping gracefully over stone or gravel.

DWARF EVERGREEN SHRUB
FULL SUN   ZONES 8-10

S. leucostachys is very beautiful, with silver delicately cut foliage. Less a bush than a wall shrub, the lax brittle growth needs firm tying in; poor well-drained soil and a sun-baked corner with wind protection are essential. Well grown, this is one of the best 'silvers', enhanced by clusters of creamy flowers in summer. Cuttings are easy to root and should be taken in summer.

MEDIUM EVERGREEN SHRUB
FULL SUN   ZONES 8-10

S. 'Sunshine' (commonly called *S. greyii* or *S. laxifolius*, but in fact a Dunedin hybrid cultivar) is a perfect hedging plant for seaside or sheltered gardens, and is quite reliable if properly placed and looked after, pruned only in spring, and kept rather dry. Stems and flower-buds are white and woolly, but need removal in midsummer; then the bush renews its pristine appearance and keeps its glow through long winter months.

MEDIUM EVERGREEN SHRUB
FULL SUN   ZONES 8-10

STACHYS

S. olympica (syn. *S. lanata*, *S. byzantina*), lamb's lugs or ears, is a silvery plant, traditional edging in formal rose gardens, interplanted with lavender bushes to carpet the ground under the ugly winter stems of bush roses to a depth of 45 cm (18 in). The non-flowering form, *S.o.* 'Silver Carpet', is smaller at 20 cm (8 in) and keeps its glowing leaves to the end of the summer. It needs good drainage and frequent tidying of withering leaves.

SEMI-EVERGREEN PERENNIAL
FULL SUN   ZONES 7-9

TAMARIX TAMARISK

Excellent wind-resistant shrubs, tamarisks thrive on any soil except shallow chalk. Slender branches bear plume-like foliage and delicate pink flowers. *T. ramosissima* (syn. *T. pentandra*) has grey-green leaves and reddish-brown branches in winter. In bloom, the whole bush becomes a light feathery mass, pink flowers mixing with the pale foliage. A lovely foil to underplanting of grey iris leaves, *Rosa chinensis* 'Mutabilis' and *Lavatera olbia* 'Rosea'.

LARGE DECIDUOUS SHRUB
FULL SUN   ZONES 7-9

TANACETUM

T. haradjanii (syn. *T. densum amanum*) is a superb carpeter; silver leaves individually shaped like tiny ostrich feathers creep and form dense mats. It needs replacing every few years, or it gets ragged and woody.

EVERGREEN PERENNIAL   15 CM (6 IN)
FULL SUN   ZONES 6-9

TEUCRIUM GERMANDER

T. fruticans, tree germander, has small simple leaves of grey-silver, and thrives in dry soil against a warm wall. If happy, it will produce pale lavender flowers throughout the year, and the form *T.f.* 'Azureum', although perhaps not so hardy, has flowers of intense deep blue (see The blues: summer).

MEDIUM EVERGREEN SHRUB
FULL SUN   ZONES 7-9

THYMUS THYME

Creeping thymes abound for border edges, paving cracks and for making lawns or seats. Choose one for the combined role of attractive foliage and fragrance when crushed. They like good drainage, a drystone wall giving a perfect foothold.

T. lanuginosus is a grey carpeter with pretty pink flowers. A selected clone, *T.l.* 'Hall's Variety', has purple buds and flowers freely.

DWARF EVERGREEN SUB-SHRUB
FULL SUN   ZONES 6-9

YUCCA

Yuccas love poor, sandy soil and dislike moisture. Most garden yuccas are hardy, the attractive grey-green strap-like leaves, often recurving and lax, making them useful statuesque plants, perfect for corners or for framing gateways. Some have sharp spines on the leaf-tips, dangerous to children and animals. Creamy, bell-shaped flowers appear on thick stems above the leaves most summers.

Y. filamentosa has soft leaves of glaucous green, easily recognized by the dangling filaments. *Y. recurvifolia* has forward-arching long lax foliage rising from a huge rosette, and flowers on tall stems when at least three years old.

MEDIUM EVERGREEN SHRUBS
FULL SUN   ZONES 8-10

Stachys olympica

Tanacetum haradjanii

COLOURED BARK

Bark colours are seldom bright; they depend for their impact on texture, having a tactile quality and solidity quite different from the surface of leaves or flowers. Smooth or furrowed, polished or peeling, bark will vary greatly with the age of a tree or shrub and becomes an important aid to identification. The silvery trunks of birch or the brown-purple trunks of conifer in dark woodland are most effective in strong clumps seen from a distance, but the sun shining through the papery peeling bark of prunus, maple or birch merits close appreciation. Here we mention a few of the most useful for all the year round effects in an average garden.

ACER MAPLE
The trunks of many maples have handsome striated 'snakebark', marbled bark or peeling old bark which flakes off to reveal paler colours beneath. Since the foliage is not heavy, the bark is usually visible even in summer, contributing to the trees' overall beauty.

A. davidii, with shining green leaves which also colour richly in autumn, has green and white striated bark. Another of the snakebark group is *A. forrestii*, which is further enhanced by gracefully formed green leaves with conspicuous red petioles. *A. grosseri* and its variety *A.g. hersii* have beautiful striped bark.

A. griseum, from the trifoliate group, has peeling bark hanging in shreds or flakes revealing orange-coloured new bark below. Try to plant the tree where it may be seen with the sun behind the trunk. This is a most beautiful tree, easy to grow and valuable in all seasons, leaves colouring well in autumn.

A. palmatum 'Senkaki', coral-bark maple, has young stems of coral-red, most evident in a young tree.

A. pensylvanicum has young wood which is green at first, becomes reddish-brown, and finally is striped with white jagged lines. *A.p.*

Acer griseum

'Erythrocladum', has young shoots which turn bright crimson as the leaves fall in autumn. Difficult to obtain, it is usually grafted on to a strong plant of *A. pensylvanicum*. Its shining winter beauty makes it most desirable.
MEDIUM DECIDUOUS TREES
HALF SHADE   ZONES 6-9

ARBUTUS STRAWBERRY TREE
A. andrachne, with peeling reddish-brown bark on its trunk and older branches, is seldom seen in gardens. More usual is the hybrid *A. × andrachnoides* (with *A. unedo*) with vivid reddish bark, spectacular when lit up by the evening sun. It is lime-tolerant, but perhaps succeeds best in peaty or loamy soil. Evergreen leaves, an attractive habit, conspicuous pitcher-shaped flowers and subtle bark colouring make this a tree for all seasons and all gardens.
SMALL TO MEDIUM EVERGREEN TREE
FULL SUN OR HALF SHADE   ZONES 7-9
See also Foliage framework: green.

Arbutus × andrachnoides

Betula jacquemontii

BETULA BIRCH
Perhaps birch are chiefly valued in gardens for the graceful delicate tracery of their branches and for their creamy-white, pinkish, mahogany or cinnamon-coloured bark. In summer the main trunk is clearly visible, displaying its often gleaming colour below a canopy of fresh green; in winter the orange-brown shades of the young wood, bare of foliage, contrast with the main trunk below. The bark of a birch is merely a thin skin, peeling near the surface, and constantly renewed. To get the best garden effects, rub the bark annually.

The European *B. pendula*, silver birch or 'the lady of the woods', is as beautiful as any. A chalk-white trunk gleams below an elegant fountaining head, each branch with a pendulous tip, and in winter a lacy fretwork of twigs. More spectacular and eye-catching are some of the American and Asian birches. *B. papyrifera*, paper birch, has a natural habitat from Labrador to Nebraska, and its bark is traditionally used by the Indian to make canoes; it is also used for roofing. Unlike the European birch, its bark remains white as the tree ages and matures. *B. ermanii*, the Russian rock birch from Asia, has pinky-white bark and orange-brown branches. *B. jacquemontii*, a variety of *B. utilis*, the Himalayan birch, is variable in colour, generally gleaming and white, perhaps the most spectacular of all birches, and making a beautiful group or a striking specimen. *B. albo-sinensis septentrionalis* from China is the most subtle, the bark silky in texture and changing through shades of coppery-orange, grey and pink. If there is space for only one birch in a garden, this would be my choice.
MEDIUM DECIDUOUS TREES
FULL SUN OR HALF SHADE   ZONES 3-8

CORNUS DOGWOOD
So many dogwoods contribute in beauty of form, flower and foliage in a garden that the glowing colours of winter bark of some species, especially in young wood, seems to be an extra bonus in an already outstandingly desirable genus. For the best effects, plant in isolated masses in a lawn or beside water and be prepared to 'stool' each spring to encourage plenty of young growth to give a thicket of colour the following winter.

C. alba, a wide-spreading suckering shrub, has shoots which by late autumn are a rich red. A cultivar, *C.a.* 'Sibirica', has young wood of bright red which darkens to crimson as spring approaches. Less vigorous than the type, it is ideal in a small garden, but some of the cultivars with attractively variegated silver and gold leaves have young stems almost as glowing in colour and, of course, contribute their own leaf variation to a particular scheme all through the summer.

C. stolonifera suckers freely to make thickets, and the young growth is dark, almost purplish-red. More spectacular in a winter landscape is *C.s.* 'Flaviramea', the bark of the young shoots greenish-yellow. Plant a group of the latter next to *C. alba* 'Sibirica' to make a colour picture almost as vivid as one of autumn-foliage sunset hues.

MEDIUM DECIDUOUS SHRUBS
FULL SUN OR SHADE   ZONES 3-8

EUCALYPTUS GUM TREE

The bark of many eucalypts is as deciduous as the leaves of many trees, changing and peeling annually, making patterns of tattered strips which are as visually desirable as the grey leaves, with their distinctly different juvenile and adult shapes, and deliciously fragrant oil. Choose a hardy eucalyptus to suit your garden.

EVERGREEN SHRUBS AND TREES
FULL SUN   ZONES 8-10
See also The blues: foliage.

MYRTUS MYRTLE

M. luma (syn. *M. apiculata*), growing as a medium-sized bush or in favourable circumstances to small-tree size, has flaking cinnamon-coloured bark, which glows richly below the glossy evergreen leaves. Grown in woodland, the plant seeks light and the trunk becomes most noticeable at eye-level, while a specimen in an open situation tends to make bushy growth obscuring the mottled effect of the creamy surface revealed as the outer cinnamon bark peels. Just lime-tolerant, this bush thrives in a deep rich soil in mild areas.

LARGE EVERGREEN SHRUB OR SMALL TREE
HALF SHADE OR SHADE   ZONES 8-10

PLATANUS PLANE

P. acerifolia (syn. *P. × hispanica*), the London plane, makes London squares and parks beautiful in all seasons. The handsome lobed leaves flutter in the wind, and make rustling carpets in the streets as they fall. The bark of the smooth erect trunks peels off in large flakes, giving an unforgettable mottled and marbled effect. In countries with hotter summers these planes are often lopped or pleached, becoming a feature in street planting. Individual specimens grow quickly in most situations and where there is space for perhaps one large tree in a garden, the beauty of bark of these London planes makes them a possible choice.

LARGE DECIDUOUS TREE
FULL SUN   ZONES 6-9

PRUNUS

Most flowering cherries are grown for their beauty of blossom, but two species from Asia have bark in the first rank for beauty.

P. maackii, Manchurian cherry, has smooth peeling bark like that of birch trees. Brownish-yellow in hue, the trunk glows warm and golden. Plant it where yellow aconites can spread as a carpet below, their gleaming colour highlit by the honey tones of the cherry.

P. serrula, with fine-toothed narrow leaves resembling those of many willows, has glistening polished red-brown peeling bark. No other small tree except perhaps *Acer griseum* can boast of a similar effect.

SMALL DECIDUOUS TREES
FULL SUN OR HALF SHADE   ZONES 5-9

RUBUS BRAMBLE

Among the bramble section of the genus, *R. cockburnianus* and *R. thibetanus* annually throw up stiff thorny stems covered with a waxy whitish bloom. In both the arching stems are purplish-brown. In *R. thibetanus* the colours are more extreme and the elegant ferny pinnate leaves are greyish, silky on the upper surface, white or grey-felted below. In *R. cockburnianus* only the undersurface has this greyness. Ideal for a woodland garden, their thornlike angularity makes them difficult in restricted space, despite their undisputed beauty.

MEDIUM DECIDUOUS SHRUBS
FULL SUN OR HALF SHADE   ZONES 5-9

STUARTIA

Acid-loving shrubs thriving in woodland, stuartias have beautiful summer flowers, excellent leaf tints in autumn and most species have attractive bark. *S. pseudocamellia* (syn. *Stewartia pseudocamellia*), a Japanese species which will attain tree size, has flaking greyish bark, most conspicuous as the tree matures.

LARGE DECIDUOUS SHRUB OR SMALL TREE
HALF SHADE   ZONES 7-9

Stuartia pseudocamellia

Myrtus luma

Prunus serrula

Prunus maackii

AUTUMN COLOUR

The most vivid blazing foliage colours occur on soil tending towards acidity, and climates with hot summers followed by sharp early night frosts help the leaf surface to 'turn' before decay sets in. Even in a temperate zone, a summer significantly hotter than the average will ensure brighter and longer-lasting autumn hues. The woodland garden of trees and shrubs, often on quite a large scale, can have whole glades and drifts designed like oriental carpets, green leaves first turning to deep low-toned crimson, moving to dark reds and brightening io translucent scarlets, followed through to dull or glistening gold hues, then pale and gleaming soft

Cercidiphyllum japonicum

Cornus kousa chinensis behind *Fothergilla monticola*

yellow. Sometimes all these colours develop slowly on one plant over a few weeks. Some bushes, on the other hand, assume such a distinctive and predictable individual leaf colour that solid blocks and drifts need careful composing to make balanced pictures where the pigments are from a restricted palette of crimson, reds, orange and yellow, with little of the quiet greens which from a distance blend and calm even the brightest hues in summer months.

ACER MAPLE

Almost all maples, from shrub size to large forest trees, contribute vivid colours in autumn. Indeed few other genera are more consistent in displaying elegantly shaped (often palmate but not always so) leaves all summer, which assume hues of crimson, scarlet and clear yellow as cold nights allow sugars to accumulate in the leaf surface. The American sugar maple, *Acer saccharum*, even scents the air with sweetness as its leaves begin to turn.

A. capillipes, one of the small Japanese maples with handsome striated bark, is very variable in autumn hue: any single specimen may have leaves of yellow, orange, scarlet or crimson. Thriving with its trunk partly shaded, the broad crown colours best in full exposure.
SMALL DECIDUOUS TREE
FULL SUN OR HALF SHADE   ZONES 6-8
A. ginnala, growing as a shrub, branching from the base, has strong red autumn colour, the leaves turning early, but not hanging on for long. Superficially in habit rather like the fan-shaped parrotia, but much less large, it is useful at the back of a border in quite a modest garden.
LARGE DECIDUOUS SHRUB
FULL SUN OR HALF SHADE   ZONES 6-9
A. griseum, from China, with trifoliate leaves and peeling orange-coloured bark, assumes strong tints of red and orange. One of the most beautiful of trees, it should be in every garden.
SMALL DECIDUOUS TREE
FULL SUN   ZONES 6-9
A. japonicum, a large shrub and after many years a small tree, is not lime-tolerant, but in suitable woodland planting produces glorious colour in autumn, the leaves in varying shades of rich crimson. Few can forget the acer glades at Westonbirt Arboretum, where whole vistas, framed by distant background planting of tall dark conifers, glow with rich colour in autumn.
LARGE DECIDUOUS SHRUB OR SMALL TREE
HALF SHADE   ZONES 6-9
A. palmatum from Japan has cultivars which produce the most consistent and vivid of all autumn leaf colours. *A.p.* 'Heptalobum Osakisuki' has brilliant scarlet leaves. This wide bush-like tree is at its most striking when grown against a dark green background of yew

or other conifers. 'Senkaki', the coralbark maple, is often grown for the coral-red of its young stems which glow in winter. Light green leaves turn a soft pale yellow in autumn.
SMALL DECIDUOUS TREES
FULL SUN   ZONES 7-9
A. platanoides, Norway maple, is a large tree, its hardiness making it useful as a windbreak on a garden perimeter; its plane-like leaves become attractive when they assume autumnal tints of red, brown and clear yellow. Many of its numerous cultivars are smaller specimen trees, but have good colour.
LARGE DECIDUOUS TREE
FULL SUN OR HALF SHADE   ZONES 4-8
A. rubrum, the North American red maple, has lobed leaves turning shades of scarlet and deep yellow, particularly after hot summers. In temperate climates the red becomes a more muted brown shade.
LARGE DECIDUOUS TREE
FULL SUN   ZONES 4-8
A. saccharum, the sugar maple, colours best where extremes of temperature exist, in north-east America, its native habitat. The leaves die off in brilliant shades of orange, gold, scarlet and crimson, each specimen retaining its own particular colour year after year.
LARGE DECIDUOUS TREE
FULL SUN   ZONES 4-8

AMELANCHIER SNOWY MESPILUS

A. laevis, a shrub-like branching tree, has bronzy-pink young foliage in spring, unfurling at the same time as the profusely borne white fragrant flowers (see The whites) are at their best. In autumn its leaves assume rich purplish shades. It is often confused with
A. canadensis.
SMALL DECIDUOUS TREE OR LARGE SHRUB
FULL SUN   ZONES 5-9

CERCIDIPHYLLUM

C. japonicum has leaves very similar in shape to those of *Cercis siliquastra*, the Judas tree, but smaller and opposite; it assumes pale yellow or smoky-pink autumnal colour. In spite of its Japanese origin, it will thrive in any reasonable alkaline or acid soil. With its neat, almost regular, pyramidal outline, it is a valuable tree in a small garden.
SMALL TO MEDIUM DECIDUOUS TREE
FULL SUN   ZONES 4-9

CLADASTRIS

C. lutea, yellow wood, has pinnate leaves which are a luxuriant rich green all summer and turn a clear buttercup-yellow before falling.
MEDIUM DECIDUOUS TREE
FULL SUN   ZONES 6-9

CORNUS DOGWOOD

C. florida, flowering dogwood, can in time become a small tree, but is more usually an elegant wide-spreading shrub. Slightly tender, it is susceptible to spring frosts unless the previous summer season has been hot enough to ripen the wood. Similarly, after a hot summer its foliage colours brilliantly.

C. kousa and its variety *C.k. chinensis*, after blooming in summer when there are comparatively few shrubby flowerers, starts to tint early, by late summer becoming increasingly brilliant, and the leaves hanging on for at least a month. At first the turning colours are low-toned, with streaks and gradations of purple; later the hues become purer, almost translucent and bright.

C. nuttallii is the only one of the tree dogwoods which colour well in autumn. One of the noblest of its genus, from western North America, it lights up a dark forest by the vivid glowing yellows and scarlets of its decaying leaves. Its showy bracts borne in early summer are creamy, flushed with pink. Not reliably hardy, it needs a rich acid soil, and thrives in coastal woodland gardens.

LARGE DECIDUOUS SHRUBS OR SMALL TREES
FULL SUN OR HALF SHADE   ZONES 6-9

COTINUS SMOKE TREE

C. coggygria, the Venetian sumach or smoke bush, and *C. obovatus* (syn. *C. americanus*) both have subtle autumn colouring, the leaves turning successively claret, scarlet and orange. The latter species, although less spectacular in flower, has distinctive young shoots and leaves of purplish-pink. Give these shrubs a position where sunlight can make the autumn foliage translucent.

LARGE DECIDUOUS SHRUBS
FULL SUN   ZONES 4-9

COTONEASTER

C. bullatus not only bears richly coloured red berries early in the autumn, but at the same time its blistered corrugated leaves colour to subtle shades.

C. horizontalis is most effective in late summer, as its handsome herring-bone branches are clothed in red berries for a short period; then the small leaves become an intense rich crimson, lasting for many weeks, especially after a hot summer and early frosts. Grow it in sun to get maximum colour. *C.h.* 'Variegatus', usually smaller and with smaller cream-splashed leaves which assume delicate pink tinges in early autumn, can be grown in an open border.

SMALL TO LARGE DECIDUOUS SHRUBS
FULL SUN   ZONES 6-10

CRYPTOMERIA

C. japonica 'Elegans', a small-growing cultivar of the large specimen tree, has soft feathery foliage which remains through its life in the juvenile state. In autumn it becomes a misty red-bronze, soft and warm and subtle in tone. Use it at the back of a border, where its year-round foliage gives a smoky effect.

SMALL EVERGREEN CONIFER
FULL SUN OR HALF SHADE   ZONES 6-9

DISANTHUS

D. cercidifolius is acid-loving, resembling witch hazel in habit, and perhaps colours more brightly than any other shrub. The leaves, shaped like those of *Cercis siliquastra*, the Judas tree, blaze with crimson lights and become more intensely bright before falling. The small purple flowers are carried in autumn as the leaves are at their most colourful.

MEDIUM DECIDUOUS SHRUB
FULL SUN OR HALF SHADE   ZONES 7-9

ENKIANTHUS

Requiring lime-free soil, these Asian shrubs have attractive urn-shaped flowers in early summer, and the leaves turn every possible shade of yellow and red. *E. campanulatus* has sulphur- to bronze-coloured flowers and the leaves, held on erect regular branches, turn brilliant shades in late summer.

MEDIUM DECIDUOUS SHRUB
HALF SHADE   ZONES 6-9

EUONYMUS SPINDLE TREE

E. alatus develops corky wings in its angled branches, making it easily recognizable. The decaying leaves turn a rich rosy scarlet. Easy to grow, plant in groups in a large garden, or use a single specimen in a modest-sized border of mixed planting.

E. oxyphyllus carries carmine fruit capsules, splitting to reveal scarlet-coated seeds, among the dusky purple-tinted autumn foliage.

MEDIUM OR LARGE DECIDUOUS SHRUBS
FULL SUN   ZONES 5-8

FAGUS BEECH

F. sylvatica, common beech, consistently gives a glowing golden-copper appearance for a long autumn period. Beech make ornamental hedging plants, holding their buff dead leaves all winter.

LARGE DECIDUOUS TREE OR TALL HEDGE
FULL SUN OR HALF SHADE   ZONES 4-8
See also Foliage framework: green.

FOTHERGILLA

Acid-loving shrubs with bottle-brush flower-spikes in spring, fothergilla species all colour splendidly in autumn. Both *F. major* and *F. monticola* have white flower-spikes, the latter now thought to be a form hardly distinct from the former; both have leaves that colour orange and red.

MEDIUM DECIDUOUS SHRUBS
HALF SHADE   ZONES 6-8

Cotinus coggygria

GINKGO

G. biloba, the maidenhair tree, has strange fan-shaped undivided leaves which turn a clear yellow before falling. Often making a symmetrical conical or, in *G.b.* 'Fastigiata', an upright vertical shape, it is tolerant of urban pollution, and grows in any soil. Sometimes grown in city avenues, it is magnificent when the leaves are in their unblemished colour for many weeks in autumn.

MEDIUM DECIDUOUS CONIFER

FULL SUN   ZONES 6-9

HAMAMELIS WITCH HAZEL

Grown mainly for the frost-resistant spider-like yellow or red flowers carried in midwinter on leafless branches, these shrubs generally also colour attractively in autumn.

H. japonica 'Arborea' and the Chinese witch hazel, *H. mollis* (see Clear yellows: winter), have leaves which turn gentle yellow, blending with bronze and buff shades of less spectacular dying leaves of many herbaceous plants to make softer pictures than the blazing reds and orange hues of other woodlanders.

LARGE DECIDUOUS SHRUBS

HALF SHADE   ZONES 6-9

Liquidambar styraciflua

Parrotia persica

HYDRANGEA

H. quercifolia has very large oak-shaped leaves, spectacular as foliage even when green (see Foliage framework, above), but turning a glowing orange-red in early autumn. Thriving in shade and flowering freely without direct sun, the best autumn foliage effects are seen if bushes are in the open.

MEDIUM DECIDUOUS SHRUB

FULL SUN   ZONES 4-9

LIQUIDAMBAR

L. styraciflua, sweet gum, at its best has leaves of fiery crimson in autumn. Maple-like in shape, but easily identifiable by being alternate rather than opposite, the leaves of some specimens do not give much colour. Generally, this seems unrelated to either soil or climate. If a young tree fails to colour, throw it out and try another; do not give it another chance.

LARGE DECIDUOUS TREE

FULL SUN OR HALF SHADE   ZONES 6-9

MALUS FLOWERING CRAB

M. tschonoskii, which will thrive in any soil, is a compact tree with yellowish-green, tinged-purple fruit, and autumn colour of yellow, orange, purple and scarlet, one tree often showing a progression of these rainbow hues in individual leaves. Lacking the more exotic aura of many other Japanese trees, this should be planted frequently, fitting appropriately into all types of garden.

SMALL DECIDUOUS TREE

FULL SUN   ZONES 5-9

See also Pinks and mauves: early summer.

NYSSA

N. sinensis is sometimes a large bushy shrub rather than a tree. It has young red growth through the summer season and leaves of variable deep red and crimson in autumn. It is more lime-tolerant than the more frequently grown tupelo, *N. sylvatica*, which requires moist lime-free soil and woodland conditions. The latter makes a handsome columnar tree, glossy green in summer, rich scarlet, orange and yellow in autumn.

SMALL TO MEDIUM DECIDUOUS TREES

FULL SUN OR HALF SHADE   ZONES 6-9

PARROTIA

P. persica has a branching shrub-like habit, its dense foliage concealing handsome patchwork branches, mottled like the trunk of a London plane tree. The leaves start turning purple, then crimson and gold in early autumn, the colour held over a long period.

SMALL DECIDUOUS TREE

FULL SUN OR HALF SHADE   ZONES 6-9

PARTHENOCISSUS

P. henryana, thriving in shade, has unusual leaves of dark velvety-green, variegated with white and pink along the mid-rib and veins. In autumn the green turns fiery red, combining with the pink and silvery tints to give an exciting effect.

DECIDUOUS CLIMBER   SHADE   ZONES 7-9

P. quinquefolia, Virginia creeper (from the French *vigne-vierge*, not the state of Virginia), is equipped with small adhesive pads and climbs vigorously to cover vertical walls. The five-leaflet leaves turn a brilliant crimson in autumn. It is ideal for disguising ugly architecture, but equally valuable making a rich wall backcloth to autumn borders.

P. tricuspidata 'Veitchii', Boston ivy, from China and Japan, is more vigorous, and is often wrongly called Virginia creeper. More common than the latter, it clothes many tall buildings. Its variably shaped leaves get coarse as the plant matures, but the rich crimson tints of autumn amply compensate for any of its disadvantages.

DECIDUOUS CLIMBERS

FULL SUN OR HALF SHADE   ZONES 4-9

PRUNUS

Small flowering trees, already described in their appropriate chapters for leaf and flower colours, prunus also have species which contribute strong glowing autumnal shades.

P. sargentii, with bronze-red spring foliage, becomes a dense mass of orange and crimson in early autumn.

SMALL DECIDUOUS TREE

FULL SUN OR HALF SHADE   ZONES 6-9

QUERCUS OAK

Q. coccinea, scarlet oak, from eastern North America, has glossy dark green leaves which each turn a brilliant scarlet in autumn, making the whole tree a consistently vivid colour. It and the similar but smaller-leaved *Q. palustris* need deep acid soil. *Q. rubra*, similarly requiring lime-free soil, has dull green leaves which before falling can turn shades of brownish-purple, ruby-red, or mixed yellow and russet, sometimes all these colours at once.

LARGE DECIDUOUS TREES

FULL SUN OR HALF SHADE   ZONES 4-8

RHODODENDRON

The deciduous azaleas, especially the well-tried favourite, *R. luteum* (see Clear yellows: early summer), have leaves which turn blending tints of yellow and orange. Grow a group in a dark corner to make an impact.

MEDIUM DECIDUOUS SHRUBS

SHADE   ZONES 6-9

ROSA ROSE

Roses grown as shrub species often have attractive autumnal leaf colouring which combines with clusters of hips. All the *R. rugosa* cultivars have leaves which turn a clear yellow, while the suckering American *R. virginiana* becomes purple, then orange-red, crimson and finally yellow, combining with glistening red fruits to make a garden feature at the end of a season.

MEDIUM DECIDUOUS SHRUBS
FULL SUN OR HALF SHADE   ZONES 4-9

SORBUS

S. aucuparia, the rowan or mountain ash, with pinnate ferny leaves, has many cultivars of different-coloured fruit and leaf form. Others of the Aucuparia section, such as *S. commixta* 'Embley', with glistening orange fruits, has warm glowing red leaves in autumn; the colouring starts rather late, but leaves hang long on the tree. In *S. hupehensis* the glorious red autumnal colour is enhanced by clusters of white, sometimes pink-tinged fruits which the birds usually leave. *S. scalaris* is rare, and its glossy frond-like pinnate leaves, brownish-crimson when unfurling in spring, colour to deeper-toned rich reds and purple. The fruit is bright red, held in clusters.

SMALL TO MEDIUM DECIDUOUS TREES
FULL SUN OR HALF SHADE   ZONES 4-8

STEPHANANDRA

In gardens two species of stephanandra are grown for their attractive incised green foliage and rich brown stems. Both assume attractive autumn tints and thrive in any sort of soil.

S. incisa has zigzagging brown stems and the leaves take muted red tints in late summer. *S. tanakea* is larger, with arching reddish-brown stems, and colours with distinctly more orange shades. Neither is spectacular in autumn, but they fit easily into all colour schemes since they are more nearly akin to the low tones of a winter landscape than the blazing scarlets and oranges of autumn.

SMALL TO MEDIUM SHRUBS
HALF SHADE OR SHADE   ZONES 6-9

TAXODIUM

T. distichum superficially but not botanically resembles the metasequoia, except that its leaves are arranged alternately. This swamp cypress has a glowing rich green colour in summer which turns to bronze-yellow for many weeks in autumn. Grow it with its roots in water, as in its native American swamps, but not in areas of chalk soil.

LARGE DECIDUOUS CONIFER
FULL SUN   ZONES 6-10

Parthenocissus tricuspidata 'Veitchii'

VACCINIUM

These ericaceous shrubs need an acid soil and a woodland site. Grown mainly for their berries and for their autumn colour they look attractive all summer, and groups planted in moist shade make thickets.

V. corymbosum, swamp blueberry, has long leaves which turn vivid scarlet and bronze, the pale pink urn-shaped flowers borne in early summer being followed by large black berries with a blue bloom.

MEDIUM DECIDUOUS SHRUB
HALF SHADE   ZONES 4-9

VIBURNUM

Many of the viburnum species have rich tones of autumn colour, often glowing most brightly when combined with coloured fruits (see Hot colours: fruits and berries).

LARGE DECIDUOUS SHRUBS
FULL SUN OR HALF SHADE   ZONES 4-8

VITIS GRAPEVINE

Grapevines climb with twining tendrils over pergolas or trellis, or though tall trees. Those from the Far East have the best autumn colour.

V. coignetiae has perhaps the largest leaves among vines; they colour in riotous shades of crimson and scarlet before falling. The size of leaf and the plant's vigour make it difficult for a small garden, but its beauty is indisputable.

V. davidii, less well known, with heart-shaped slender pointed leaves, dark green above but greyish beneath, is handsome, and generally colours to brilliant red in autumn.

V. riparia 'Brandt', a cultivar of the American riverbank grape, has leaves which turn a deep toned bronzy-red in autumn, the veins remaining green. A mysterious colour, reminiscent of a subtle wine, it is quite different from fiery scarlet hues.

V. vinifera 'Purpurea', claret vine, a cultivar of the common grapevine, has purple leaves all summer, which darken to a richer tone in autumn. Its small grapes are dark purple as well, but with a different juicy texture.

DECIDUOUS CLIMBERS   FULL SUN   ZONES 6-9
See also Foliage framework: green.

Vitis coignetiae

COLOUR IN PLANTS

The intrinsic colour of a plant depends on the chemical composition of the pigments and the molecular structure of the surface texture. Each light wave when striking the surface of any part of a plant will be either absorbed or reflected in varying amounts, giving the surface an identifiable colour. Pigments, the coloured molecules containing electrons which determine this reflection or absorption, belong to complex groups and are themselves influenced by the chemical interactions of substances in the cell sap, substances which are part of the necessary proteins, acids, tannins and sugar which ensure plant growth and health. Nitrates, sulphates and phosphates particularly affect the quality and condition of flowers, fruit and leaves; gardeners learn to observe how colour indicates health, and how discoloration points to deficiencies. Every gardener knows how plant colour will vary in the seasonal cycle, and how the colour of a flower can change in a single day or hour. Few practical gardeners need to study all the complexities of pigment behaviour, but an awareness of the scientific implications behind the colours nature provides and a knowledge of their function in ensuring growth and survival will add interest to both practical gardening and colour planning.

Basically, plant pigments are divided into two classes, those which dissolve in cell sap and those which are found in bodies called plastids in the inner lining of a cell's wall. The latter are soluble only in oils. The distribution of different pigments, and sometimes their chemical combination, leads to the amazing gradations of colour and marking in flower petals.

The main soluble pigments are anthocyanins and anthoxanthins. Purple, blue and most red colours are caused by anthocyanins, which as well as affecting flower colour influence leaf and stem colours, giving reddish tints to new shoots and leaves. Three important anthocyanins are pelargonidin, which makes flowers such as the bedding pelargoniums scarlet; cyanidin, giving red and magenta tones to flowers such as roses; and delphinidin, giving mauve, purple and blue to, for example, the delphinium genus, with its wide range of flower colours. Being soluble in water, anthocyanins can react to changes of acidity in soil. On the whole, flowers tend to become redder in acid soil and bluer in alkaline (try putting the stalk of a bluebell in an ant heap – the formic acid produced by angry ants will colour the flower red). A notable exception which is an indication of the complex nature of the plant colour process is the behaviour of *Hydrangea macrophylla*. Its flower is blue when in a soil with high acidity and high iron concentrates; when it is grown in an alkaline soil

Euonymus grandiflorus

the flowers become conspicuously pinker.

Anthoxanthins produce a range of colours from pale ivory to deep yellow. The colour of white petals, although sometimes caused by white pigment, is more often the result of air spaces within the plant tissue. As with ice crystals in snow or bubbles in foam, these air spaces cause light to be refracted and reflected and make the surface appear white. The whiteness of aspen or birch trunks is similarly caused by air spaces in the outer bark.

Anthocyanins and anthoxanthins may occur together in a flower petal and contribute jointly to the colour, giving reddish and brownish shades. Sometimes the anthoxanthins which produce ivory tints combine chemically with anthocyanins and the perceived colour is distinctly bluer.

Most of the plastids found in plant cells belong to the group known as chloroplasts. The best known of the plastid pigments is the green chlorophyll, which is found principally in leaves and stems, but often also tinges flower petals and sepals green. Others are orange carotene and yellow xanthophyll, which influence flower colour, and which make carrots orange and tomatoes red.

Most plant colour seems to be functional.

Flower colour, like scent, is used to lure appropriate pollinators to the pollen store, ensuring fertilization and the production of seed. Coloured fruits and seed capsules attract birds and ensure dispersal. The chlorophyll in leaves, by the process of photosynthesis, enables plants to use solar energy to convert water and carbon dioxide to sugars and oxygen.

The development of complicated coloured floral parts has taken millions of years and is now part of a highly complex pattern. Some plants are totally dependent for pollination on a particular bird or insect, and in a few cases, such as that of yucca and a particular night-flying moth (*Pronuba yuccasella*), plant and pollinator are mutually dependent for survival. Beetles, flies with short or long tongues, bees, wasps and birds all have slightly different vision; flower colour, structure and guide marks for the visiting pollinator have developed to suit. Birds have excellent colour awareness but no sense of smell. Beetles have poor vision but can locate large white flowers with strong scent. Bees have a visible spectrum slightly different from that of humans. They can perceive short waves in the ultraviolet range which are invisible to humans, but cannot distinguish the longer reds, although they do have a limited perception of orange.

Ultraviolet rays absorbed by many white flowers, for example, make the flowers appear blue-green to bees; flowers that reflect ultraviolet and appear blue, purple or red to man will appear violet or black to a bee.

Chlorophyll, the green of the leaf, is arranged so that it functions efficiently for photosynthesis. Its precise organization is adapted according to conditions, and affects leaf structure and appearance in various ways. During daylight, carbon dioxide is taken in through small perforations in the leaf surface. The chloroplasts, which contain the chlorophyll and use all light wavelengths except green (which is reflected), are found inside the cells of the leaf. Water and various minerals for plant growth spread in the sap through the 'nerves' and 'veins' of the leaf surface, where the captured solar energy splits the water into hydrogen and oxygen. Hydrogen combines with carbon dioxide to make sugars, which are then distributed through the plant system, while the oxygen is dispersed into the atmosphere.

Most plants hold their leaves in such a way that a maximum number can face the light, which they need for photosynthesis. Plants therefore tend to spread their leaf surfaces out horizontally, making a mosaic pattern when viewed from below, easiest to appreciate when looking at the leaf pattern of a tree's canopy against the sky, but true of even the humblest low-growing plant.

Although chlorophyll is the most important pigment for photosynthesis, other plastid pigments, as well as pigments soluble in the cell sap, are also present in leaf cells. As chlorophyll breaks down in autumn, droplets of carotenoid pigments are produced, turning leaves pale yellow. Then as nights get colder, the sugar normally dispersed throughout the plant tissues builds up in the leaf tissue and produces active anthocyanin and anthoxanthin pigments in the sap – turning the leaves red and golden. Just as flower colour becomes 'redder' in acid conditions and 'bluer' in alkaline so also the intensity of autumn foliage colour varies with soil. Areas of high acidity produce vivid scarlet and red leaf hues, while in chalky soils of high alkalinity colours are more muted, purplish and low-toned rather than fiery reds. In spring, too, young leaves are often reddish and pinkish, the anthocyanins protecting the sensitive glaucous growth from the strong ultraviolet light rays.

In the leaves of some plants these soluble pigments are present all the time and partly or completely mask the green, giving a bronze or purple effect. In deciduous plants these colours last a whole season, although as summer proceeds they are often less noticeable, the colour becoming more greenish and generally darker. In evergreen plants it is usually only the young foliage which has reddish shades, mature leaves becoming distinctly greener or at least more purplish. However, the partial masking which leads to variegated and marbled effects is not always caused by anthocyanins and anthoxanthins but is sometimes the result of imperfect chloroplasts in the inner or outer layers of leaf cells. When a leaf is edged with white or yellow, the inner layer of green pigment is working normally, but the outer layer lacks chloroplasts or contains only the forerunner of chlorophyll in proto chlorophyll (which makes the colour appear yellowish). In a leaf which appears white or yellow with a green edge it is the inner layer which is defective. In this latter case the chlorophyll often resumes its function and the leaf becomes normally green again. Both holly (*Ilex*) and elaeagnus have coloured leaf forms with central splashes of white or yellow, where whole branches may 'revert' to green – good for the plant's vigour, but unsatisfactory for the gardener seeking special colour effects. Plants with pale-edged leaves (again including forms of holly and elaeagnus) do not, as a rule, revert in this way.

In plants such as grasses, sedges and members of the lily family, including hostas, hemerocallis, lily of the valley, Solomon's seal and phormium, the imperfect chloroplasts produce longitudinal stripes of cream or yellow contrasting with the normal leaf green.

Normally, plants with such variegated leaves, where areas of the vital chlorophyll are masked, are at a disadvantage. Nearly all need more care and protection in cultivation, and yellow-leaved or variegated-leaved forms or cultivars are noticeably slower in growing, and perhaps never achieve the same height and breadth as the green-leaved 'type'.

Variations in texture can have a marked effect on the appearance of a colour. The actual colour in the leaves or flowers of two plants may be identical in terms of systems for measuring colour, and yet observers can have totally different impressions of colour quality, because the textures are different. A petal may have a greasy surface, caused by highly reflective starch grains acting like a mirror under the outer cell skin, where pigment is composed of large oily drops; such a petal will have a bright, intense colour and a glossy sheen, and be quite different in appearance from a petal of a similar colour but with an absorbent surface. The petal surfaces of plants such as gloxinia and pansy, and the black falls of hermodactylus, have small regular projections, all equal in length and pointing the same way, giving the effect of a velvet pile. Other flower petals have projections parallel to the midrib of the petal, so that each line or ridge becomes a focus reflecting light and producing the appearance of shot silk. A papery surface gives a translucent appearance, light shining through the petal, particularly glowing and beautiful as the sun goes down and its horizontal rays suffuse leaf or petal at eye level.

Subtle grey, silvery or bluish shades are produced when the outer surfaces of leaves are hairy, or are covered by wax, which modifies the appearance of the green. Such plants usually come from hot climates, where hairs and wax protect the leaves from excessive sunlight, by reflecting and deflecting the strong light. Hairy and wax-coated surfaces also reduce water loss in conditions of drought and in the opposite situation, in areas of high rainfall, hairs prevent leaves from becoming coated with water. These grey, silvery and glaucous effects are immensely variable, even through one season. As the need of a plant to protect itself varies so leaf colour responds. So-called 'silvers' and 'greys' become distinctly greener when grown in shade, and often greener at flowering time when the plant has ensured its survival. In a hot, dry season some plants can develop a protective waxy bloom to give the leaves a glaucous blue-green appearance. After a particularly hot summer even the leaves of brassica in a kitchen garden become conspicuously blue-green and glowing.

Most leaves have a short six months of life, but evergreen leaves (usually shed annually, although some conifers hold their leaves for seven or eight years) are adapted to survive the winter. They have a thicker skin and often a coating of wax, which slows down transpiration – essential in winter when shortage of water is acute. (Conifers with their thin leaves have reduced the area for possible transpiration to a minimum.) Evergreen shrubs such as camellias, escallonias, fatsia, holly, myrtle and osmanthus all have waxy, thick leaves. Other evergreens – some viburnums, loquat (*Eriobotrya*), and some rhododendrons – have leathery ridged leaves and leaf colours often vary between upper and lower surfaces, with small hairs, wool and felt on the under-surface giving brown or grey tones. Deeply impressed veins give the leaves of *Rhododendron falconeri* a ribbed effect on the upper surface, and it has a dark rust-coloured tomentum or felt underneath. *Magnolia grandiflora* 'Goliath' has glossy-surfaced curved leaves with buff undersides. Some trees have the leaves attached to the stems with long stalks which allow them to flutter and turn over in the wind, exposing their undersides. The silver maple *Acer saccharinum* and the weeping lime *Tilia petiolaris* expose their grey under-surfaces in this way, giving a light, airy effect of greys and tender greens.

CLIMATE AND GROWING CONDITIONS

Each of the plants in the colour catalogues has been allocated figures referring to the range of climatic zones in which it will happily grow. A zone number gives an indication of plant hardiness in relation to the expected minimum lowest temperature of a region. No map, however detailed, can adequately depict all the geographical complexities which represent not only the broad bands of latitude but pockets where altitude makes an area conspicuously colder or warmer than the surrounding terrain.

Within any one zone, particular regions may be endowed with more or less favourable conditions just as on a smaller scale in any one garden plants can be positioned in individual situations that suit their needs to a greater or lesser extent. Useful as zoning data are to the gardener as a starting point, other influences on plant growth also have to be considered. Among these are actual frost occurrence and its timing, seasonal rainfall distribution, humidity and dryness, soil characteristics, and the intensity and duration of sunlight, as well as planting positions in sun or shade.

Microclimate pockets within broader zones can be further influenced by horticultural techniques. In a fairly protected garden it is normally worth while at least making an attempt at growing plants from a zoned region higher (i.e. warmer) than the one you live in: zones overlap, and the garden (with or without any special characteristics) may be on the borderline of the more favoured neighbour. But don't experiment with plants of marginal hardiness if they are to be part of the permanent structure – specimen trees for example, or shrubs positioned for design balance, for screening or for hedging purposes. You can be adventurous instead with the 'infillers', those plants which can be quickly replaced without putting major effects at risk. On the other hand, an increase of altitude or an exceptionally exposed or windy aspect will prevent growth of some of the plants recommended as 'safe' for the average site in a zone.

All plant growth stops when temperatures fall to 6°C (45°F); in summer growth is inhibited if the ground temperature reaches 32°C (90°F). These limiting factors affect the length of the growing season in any given garden, just as the expected timing of the last spring frost affects the date at which you can plan to bed out more tender plants. The gardener can both take advantage of favourable aspect and also improve conditions in certain ways. Slopes which catch maximum warmth from the sun's rays increase the length of the summer growing season, as well as ensuring frost drainage. Plants can be protected from dehydrating winds and sun (in some cold regions, all evergreen shrubs are wrapped up like parcels to prevent transpiration during the coldest months). Protective mulches retain moisture during the summer and if applied at the end of the hot season keep the heat in. Walls and paths of stone and brick reflect heat to ripen and harden wood, helping plants to survive low winter temperatures later; hot dry beds under south-facing walls provide a perfect site for those bulbs which need to be baked when dormant. Shelter is best provided by fences and by hedges, which filter winds and control gusts and incidence on the lee side.

A thick covering of snow acts as an insulator giving a blanket covering to the roots and crowns of perennials. Plants which endure hard winters in their native habitat by remaining dormant for a long period often dislike more temperate climates where unpredictable warm spells induce premature growth and are then followed by a return to severe cold; in these circumstances plants – especially young ones which have few reserves – often weaken and die.

The relatively more efficient drainage of raised beds provides the right conditions for alpines and for Mediterranean-type plants which are often tolerant of low winter temperatures, but which cannot survive water freezing round the crown of the root.

Plants are at their most vulnerable when newly planted, so when in doubt about potential hardiness, try to ensure that the six months following planting will give them a good chance of becoming successfully established before they are subjected to cold.

PLANT HARDINESS ZONES

Hardiness zones depict a 10°F geographical progression of bands from colder to warmer latitudes, which are derived from data on average minimum winter temperatures. This chart defines the temperature range of each zone.

Plants described in this book are allocated a range of zones in which they are most likely to survive and thrive, but aspect, site and seasonal fluctuations also influence performance.

Maps delineating plant hardiness zones on a continental scale can give the gardener only the broadest indication of what plants to attempt to grow: local conditions can favour an individual garden so that it is effectively a zone or more higher (i.e. warmer) than the surrounding countryside, and conversely an exposed site can be equivalent to placing the garden in a lower, more northerly and therefore colder zone where Europe and North America are concerned.

Zone	Centigrade	Fahrenheit
1	below −46°	below −50°
2	−46° to −40°	−50° to −40°
3	−40° to −34°	−40° to −30°
4	−34° to −28°	−30° to −20°
5	−28° to −22°	−20° to −10°
6	−22° to −16°	−10° to 0°
7	−16° to −12°	0° to 10°
8	−12° to −6°	10° to 20°
9	−6° to −1°	20° to 30°
10	−1° to 4°	30° to 40°

Broadly speaking, Zone 9 includes western and Mediterranean France, Portugal and the western coastal areas of the British Isles and Eire which are influenced by the Gulf Stream. Zone 8 includes most of inland and eastern Britain, mid and eastern France, Holland and the extreme north-west of Germany. Zone 7 includes the eastern Scottish Highlands, eastern France and Massif Central, most of western and north-eastern Germany and the southernmost tip of Sweden.

The north-south progression of the zones from cold to warm (which originated in the USA) is reversed in the southern hemisphere, but since most Australians and New Zealanders live in the more temperate areas, most of the non-native trees, shrubs and perennials can be grown fairly easily. However, here other considerations apply: as important as a plant's tolerance of cold are its need for regular watering and its ability to withstand heat.

BIBLIOGRAPHY AND SOURCES

GENERAL: DESIGN AND GARDENING

Crowe, Sylvia
Garden Design Country Life, London, 1958

Hicks, David
Garden Design
Routledge & Kegan Paul, London, 1982

Hobhouse, Penelope
The Smaller Garden Collins, London, 1981

Johnson, Hugh
The Principles of Gardening Mitchell Beazley,
London, 1979; Bookthrift, New York, 1982

Page, Russell
The Education of a Gardener Collins, London, 1962

Robinson, Florence
Planting Design
McGraw Hill, London & New York, 1940

COLOUR THEORY

Birren, Faber
Creative Color Reinhold Publishing Co.,
New York, 1961
Principles of Color Reinhold Publishing Co.,
New York, 1970

Boigey, M. J.
The Science of Colour and the Art of the Painter
J. Bale & Sons, London, 1925

Chevreul, M. E.
*The Principles of Harmony and Contrast of Colours and
their Application to the Arts*
George Bell & Sons, London (3rd ed), 1890
The Principles of Harmony and Contrast of Colours . . .
(with introduction and notes by Faber Birren)
Van Nostrand Reinhold, New York, 1981

Goethe, Johann Wolfgang
Theory of Colours (trans. Charles Lock Eastlake) John
Murray, London, 1840; Frank Cass, London, 1967

Guillard, Jacqueline et Maurice
Claude Monet at the Time of Giverny
Centre Culturel du Marais, Paris, 1983

Hobhouse, Penelope
Gertrude Jekyll on Gardening Collins, London, 1983;
David R. Godine, Boston, 1984

Jekyll, Gertrude
*Wood and Garden: notes and thoughts, practical and
critical, of a working amateur* Longmans, London,
1899; Salem House, Salem, 1983
Colour in the Flower Garden Country Life Library,
George Newnes, London, 1908

Leonardo Da Vinci
Notebooks (selection, edited with commentary by
Irma A. Richter) OUP, London, 1982

Lindsay, Jack
Turner: His Life and Work Granada (Panther),
London, 1973

Rood, Ogden Nicholas
*Modern Chromatics, with Applications to Art and
Industry* C. Kegan Paul & Co., London, 1879
Modern Chromatics . . . (with preface, introduction
and commentary notes by Faber Birren)
Van Nostrand Reinhold, New York, 1974
NOTE: This edition omits Rood's text on garden
colour, but is valuable for Faber Birren's comments.

Van der Kemp, Gerald
A Visit to Giverny Editions d'Art Lys, Versailles, 1980

Verity, Enid
Colour Leslie Frewin, London, 1967
Colour Observed Macmillan, London, 1980;
Van Nostrand Reinhold, New York, 1980

Wilcox, Michael
Colour Theory for Watercolours (ed J. A. Swain)
Colour Mixing, London, 1982

Wilson, José and Leaman, Arthur
Colour in Decoration Studio Vista, London, 1971;
Van Nostrand Reinhold, New York, 1971

PLANT REFERENCE

Bean, W. G.
Trees and Shrubs Hardy in the British Isles
John Murray, London (8th ed), 1970 to 1980

Chatto, Beth
The Dry Garden Dent, London, 1978
The Damp Garden Dent, London, 1982

Gibson, Michael
The Book of the Rose
Macdonald and Jane, London, 1980

Grounds, Roger
*The Multi-Coloured Garden: a new approach to
gardening with coloured foliage*
Pelham Books, London, 1982
NOTE: Consult for excellent plant catalogue and
descriptions rather than for design criteria.

Hillier's Manual of Trees and Shrubs David & Charles,
Newton Abbot (4th ed) 1977, (5th ed) 1981

Ingwersen, Will
Ingwersen's Manual of Alpine Plants W. Ingwersen
and Dunnsprint Ltd, Eastbourne, 1979

Lloyd, Christopher
Clematis Collins, London, 1977

Mathew, Brian
Dwarf Bulbs Batsford, London, 1973

Encyclopaedia of Garden Plants and Flowers
Reader's Digest Association London (2nd ed), 1978

Dictionary of Gardening Royal Horticultural Society,
Clarendon Press, Oxford (2nd ed), 1956

Smith, A. W.
A Gardener's Dictionary of Plant Names
Cassell, London, 1972

Stearn, William
*Botanical Latin. History, grammar, syntax, terminology
and vocabulary* Nelson, London, 1966; (reissued
1967)
Botanical Latin . . . (annotated and revised for 2nd
ed) David & Charles, Newton Abbot, 1973

Thomas, Graham Stuart
Plants for Ground-Cover Dent, London, 1970;
(revised 1977)
Perennial Garden Plants Dent, London, 1976; 2nd
revised ed 1982 (for The Royal Horticultural Society)

Underwood, Mrs Desmond
Grey and Silver Plants Collins, London, 1971

PLANT COLOUR

Becket, Gillian
The Secret Life of Plants (based on an original text by
Jaroslav Pazourek; trans. by Eva Pavlatova)
Octopus, London, 1982

Bristow, Alec
The Sex Life of Plants: a study of the secrets of reproduction
Barrie & Jenkins, London, 1979

Jaeger, Paul
The Wonderful Life of Flowers (trans. J. P. M. Brenan)
Harrap, London, 1961

Proctor, J. and S.
Nature's Use of Colour in Plants and Their Flowers
Peter Lowe, 1978

Proctor, Michael and Yeo, Peter
The Pollination of Flowers Collins, London, 1973

INDEX

Figures in italics refer to illustrations.

Editor

Penny David

Art Editors

Roger Walton and Caroline Hill

Other editorial contributors

Josephine Christian Miren Lopategui
Don Evemy Douglas Matthews (index)
Fred Gill Tom Wellsted

Illustrator

Sally Launder

Photography

The publishers wish to thank Liz Strauli for her assistance with picture research and Martyn Rixand Brian Arbon for help in identifying plants. They also gratefully acknowledge permission to reproduce photographs granted by The Royal Botanic Gardens, Kew, The Royal Horticultural Society's Garden, Wisley, The National Trust, and by Clare College and Emmanuel College, Cambridge. They especially thank the innumerable owners of private gardens for their kind co-operation.

B = bottom; C = centre; L = left; R = right; T = top

Pam/Michael Boys: 67L

Karl Dietrich Bühler: 89, 109

Linda Burgess: 5, 11, 13, 14, 49, 50, 53(Sissinghurst), 69L, 71B, 83B, 86, 101, 102, 107, 121T, 122L, 126B, 139, 165, 185B, 186B, 191, 221T

Mike Burgess: 116R

Robert César: 9(La Mormaire), 29(Kerdalo), 31(Kerdalo), 37(Giverny), 131(Kerdalo), 156 (Kerdalo), 195(Les Moutiers), 230

Geoff Dann: 6, 20, 21, 24, 27(The Priory, Kemerton), 38(Tintinhull), 39(Tintinhull), 47(Wisley), 51, 61T, 61B, 62T, 62B, 63, 65L, 66T, 66B, 67R, 68T, 68B, 69R, 70B, 73, 75T, 75B, 76, 77L, 77R, 78, 79T, 79B, 80, 81T, 82T, 82B, 85, 88L, 92BR, 93L, 93R, 94T, 94BL, 95T, 95B, 96TR, 96BL, 98T, 98B, 99, 100BL, 100BR, 103T, 104T, 105, 114B, 115T, 115B, 121B, 122R, 124, 126TL, 128T, 128B, 129T, 129B, 132(Tintinhull), 133(Wisley), 138T, 143T, 144B, 146T, 149B, 150T, 151, 161TL, 161TR, 163B, 164R, 164L, 170T, 171T, 176, 178(The Priory, Kemerton), 182B, 187TL, 187TR, 187B, 189B, 205T, 205B, 213T, 215C, 216B, 217, 219, 220L, 220R, 224B, 225, 226T, 226B, 228, 240

John Glover: 64L, 64R, 70T, 92BL, 96TL, 100T, 104B, 208

Jerry Harpur: 46, 55(Brook Cottage, Alkerton), 87(Clare College), 132T('Hermitage', Priors Marston), 132B (Brook Cottage), 197('Hermitage')

Peter Healing: 10 (The Priory, Kemerton)

Neil Holmes: 138BR, 144T, 168, 193T, 222T, 227T

Pat Hunt: 19 (Barnsley House), 25(Barnsley House), 28(Barnsley House), 48(Parham), 135

Jacqui Hurst: 7, 175, 216T, 218B

Kunsthistorisches Museum, Vienna: 17(*Le jardin de Giverny*, Claude Monet)

John Malins: 198(Tintinhull)

Tania Midgley: 1(*Cornus konsa chinensis*), 15(Mill Court), 43, 47B, 54(Cranbourne), 56(Cranbourne), 57(Goulden Manor), 60, 65R, 74L, 74R, 81B, 108R(Cranbourne), 110, 111(Savile Gardens), 114TL, 116L, 117R, 118, 119T, 119BL, 120, 140, 141T, 142L, 147B, 154(Snowshill Manor), 155(Willow Hill), 163T, 164L, 173, 182T, 199(Great Dixter), 201TL(Barnsley House), 201BR(Cloudsley Road), 202(Great Dixter), 203(Westend House), 206B, 207T, 211, 212, 213B, 214B, 215B

Gary Rogers: 23(Pusey), 88R

Daan Smit: 114TR, 150B, 177, 186T, 190T, 204

Harry Smith: 71T, 72, 83T, 92TR, 97, 103B, 104C, 117L, 119BR, 123, 125L, 125R, 126TR, 127, 129C, 138BL, 141B, 142R, 143B, 145, 146B, 147T, 148, 149T, 160L, 160R, 161B, 162, 166R, 167, 169T, 169B, 171B, 172T, 172C, 172B, 183, 185T, 188, 189T, 190B, 192T, 192B, 193B, 206T, 207C, 207B, 209TL, 209TR, 209B, 210T, 210B, 214T, 215T, 218T, 221B, 222BL, 222BR, 223TL, 223TR, 223BL, 223BR, 224T, 227B

Pamla Toler: 3(Bampton Manor), 48, 94BR, 108L(Dalgarin), 153(The Priory, Kemerton), 157 (The Priory, Kemerton), 170B, 179(East Lambrook Manor), 184